Crime and Punishment in England

Crime and Punishment in England

A sourcebook

Andrew Barrett
Christopher Harrison
Keele University

UCL PRESS
UCL PRESS
Taylor & Francis Group

Published in the UK in 1999 by UCL Press

UCL Press Limited
Taylor & Francis Group
1 Gunpowder Square
London EC4A 3DE

and

325 Chestnut Street, 8th Floor
Philadelphia
PA 19106
USA

The name of University College London (UCL) is a registered
trade mark used by UCL Press with the consent of the owner.

ISBNs: 1-85728-871-8HB
1-85728-872-6PB

British Cataloguing-in-Publication Data
A catalogue record for this book is available from the British Library.

Every effort has been made to contact copyright holders for their
permission to reprint material in this book. The publisher would be
grateful to hear from any copyright holder who is not here
acknowledged and will undertake to rectify any errors or omissions in
future editions of this book.

Printed and bound by T.J. International, Padstow, UK

Contents

CONTENTS

Introduction

The Documents

In the first chapter legal records predominate, largely because they are the principal surviving records. They may appear obscure and difficult at first but, read with care, they are a fruitful source of enquiry; that at least has been the experience of our student readers. From the sixteenth century we start to find commentaries on crime and punishment such as Harman's *Caveat for Common Cursitors* (1566). From the seventeenth century we find broadsheet accounts of trials, and from the late seventeenth century newspaper accounts of crimes and trials, which enrich our understanding of criminals and reactions to them. By the eighteenth century writers such as Fielding and Howard provide detailed description and critical analysis.

While London must always figure large in any account of crime and punishment in England, we have also selected provincial cases from across the country, from Yorkshire to Sussex, from East Anglia to Somerset. Again, although we have selected some well-known cases, such as that of the murder of customs officials in 1748, we have deliberately brought in obscure and little-known material, some of which appears in print for the first time, in order to challenge any stereotyping of crime which might ensue from concentrating on a few well-known cases.

In compiling the documents for the nineteenth century, we have endeavoured to include material not readily accessible. Although some of the authors, such as Charles Dickens, will be widely recognized, there are also extracts from lesser-known authors and a large amount of previously unpublished archive material. The documents are taken from a wide variety of sources: private commentaries; journals; parliamentary papers; newspapers; official police, court and prison records; autobiographies; novels; and statutes. In keeping with the first half of the book, they also cover both London and the provinces. Although organized into chapters on crime, policing, criminal justice and punishment, one will find material relevant to these four subject areas in all of the chapters. For example, there is no direct reference to drunkenness or prostitution in the chapter on crime, but those crimes are found in the chapters on policing and criminal justice.

Reading documents

What do historians mean by a "primary source"? A simplistic definition would be something produced at or soon after the event being investigated. But what then of an autobiography, such as the Chief Constable's *Life* (see p. 247), which might contain descriptions of events which took place years prior to the date of writing? Again, primary sources can take many forms: maps, pictures, photographs, film, even television can be primary sources, but generally speaking we think of them as something written.

Reading primary documentary source material can be daunting. A few tips may help the student reader. There are some fairly standard questions which apply to most documentary sources.

Who wrote it?
When was it written?
What was the context within which it was written?
Why was it written? Which leads to two further questions:
  – What did the writer intend to reveal?
  – What does the writer inadvertently reveal?

Supplementary questions include:

Is this document unique or one of group or series?
Is the document personal, narrative, administrative, parliamentary or legal
  in origin?
What other evidence relates to this record?

One could add to this list, and not every question is relevant in every case, but some sort of checklist is useful.

That still does not answer all the problems students encounter. One is basic understanding of the text. Some find it best to read through a source quite quickly the first time to get the general drift of the document and then later to return to it, reading more carefully.

A major challenge for many is the language; not whether it is in a foreign language, for all Latin and French documents have been translated, but rather the English in which they are rendered. Many find the archaisms of a past age difficult to grasp. One way around this difficulty is to read the document out loud, as this often allows an apparently difficult passage to become clear.

The language used in nineteenth-century documents is more familiar than that of previous centuries yet this does not obviate the need for careful reading. Even familiar words can change meaning over time. For example, the word "police" had a much broader meaning in the early nineteenth century than today, less associated with a single professional body than with the general maintenance of order.

Thoughtful and informed reading is the key to true understanding. To grasp meaning, to spot significance, to enter into the world of a past age, one must give the exercise time and thought. A source only becomes meaningful when we give it significance. There should, then, be a dialogue between the source and its reader. Above all, listen carefully to what the writer has to say. The true historian is like an eavesdropper on the past. Think of each document as a fragment of the past, as a moment frozen in time. Our job is to thaw out that fragment, to revivify it, to make it real once more. It is at this point you move from being a student of history to being an historian.

Acknowledgements

Grateful acknowledgements are given to the following for permission to reproduce material from their archives and publications:

Cambridgeshire Archives Service for material from the County Records Office, Huntingdon; Staffordshire Record Office; Chester Archives.
Records in the Cheshire Record Office are reproduced with the permission of Cheshire County Council and the owner/depositor to whom copyright is reserved.
Crown copyright material in the Public Record Office, (HO 6/4; SP12/147; JUST 1/142) is reproduced by permission of the Controller of Her Majesty's Stationary Office.

Thanks are due to the following learned societies for permission to reproduce from their publications: Oxfordshire Record Society, Royal Historical Society, Selden Society, Southampton Record Society, Somerset Record Society, Staffordshire Record Society, Sussex Record Society.

The articles from *The Times* are reproduced by permission of News International and must not be photocopied.

In some cases we have been unable to track down the owner of copyright of published material but would wish, if informed, to acknowledge it in any future edition.

Chapter 1

Crime and Punishment in Medieval England

This chapter illustrates some of the basic concepts and practices of English medieval law, in particular the "criminal" law in the counties.

1   The origins of the English criminal legal system

"The origin of the criminal law [was] the assumption by the state of the responsibility for avenging personal injuries."[1] *What, in the case of England, did this mean in practice? The Anglo-Saxon system of criminal justice was mainly concerned to prevent feuds provoked by violent or serious crime. The system was designed to force the victim or, if he was dead or incapacitated, his family to accept compensation rather than turn to violence. The levels of compensation were established by the kings in consultation with their secular and ecclesiastical counsellors. This initiated some of England's earliest criminal legislation, as illustrated by these early seventh-century laws of Aethelbert.*

1.1   Anglo-Saxon Laws

The Laws of Aethelbert[2]

10.   If a man lies with a maiden belonging to the king, he shall pay 50 shillings compensation.

14.   If a man lies with a nobleman's serving maid, he shall pay 12 shillings compensation.

16.   If a man lies with a commoner's serving maid, he shall pay 6 shillings compensation.

21.   If one man slays another, the ordinary wergeld to be paid as compensation shall be 100 shillings.[3]

---

[1] A. Harding, *Inaugural lecture*, p. 1.

[2] F. L. Attenborough (ed.), *The laws of the earliest English kings* (1922), pp. 4–17.

[3] Wergeld, or wergild, was the fixed sum with which a man's death had to be atoned for to his kindred, i.e. what you had to pay if you killed a man. The sum varied according to status; thus an earl's wergeld was larger than a coerl's.

22. If one man slays another, he shall pay 20 shillings before the grave is closed, and the whole of the wergeld within 40 days.
23. If a homicide departs from the country, his relatives shall pay half the wergeld.

40. If an ear is struck off, 12 shillings compensation shall be paid.
41. If an ear is pierced, 3 shillings compensation shall be paid.
42. If an ear is lacerated, 6 shillings compensaton shall be paid.
43. If an eye is knocked out, 50 shillings shall be paid as compensation.

Ine's Laws[4]

In general, financial compensation seems to have been preferred to corporal punishment, as this late seventh-century law of Ine's illustrates.

12. If a thief is taken [i.e. caught in the act], he shall die the death, *or* his life shall be redeemed by the payment of his wergeld.

In the above case, the offender's wergeld determines the level of compensation. Only if the criminal was a notorious evil-doer and a danger to the whole community was corporal punishment insisted upon.

37. If a commoner has *often* been accused of theft and is at last proved guilty . . . his hand or foot shall be struck off.

1.2   Trials

Compurgation

One of the two basic methods of proof in Anglo-Saxon England was trial by compurgation. Under this system law-worthy men, the compurgators, were summoned to swear to the truth of the submission of the defendant or complainant, NB not on the basis of evidence presented in the court but on their knowledge of the disputants and the alleged offence. It was, says Warren, a form of arbitration with a tendency towards compromise.

Trials by ordeal

But what happened if one could not get one's neighbours to swear on one's behalf or if the crime was so serious that such methods were deemed insufficient? In those cases trial was by ordeal. In these trials it was God who was pronouncing judgment. The Latin for an ordeal was judicium dei, *i.e. the judgment of God.*

---

[4] Attenborough, *The laws of the earliest English kings*, pp. 37–61.

There were four basic forms of trial by ordeal: by hot iron, by hot water, by consecrated bread (the corsnæd), and by cold water.

Below is an Anglo-Saxon decree laying down the rules by which hot iron and hot water ordeals were to be conducted. Note the vital function of the church in this process.

Decree concerning hot iron and hot water ordeals[5]

And with regard to the ordeal, by the commands of God and of the archbishop and all the bishops, we enjoin that no one shall enter the church after the fire with which the iron or water for the ordeal is to be heated has been brought in, except the mass-priest and him who has to go to trial. And from the stake to the mark, nine feet shall be measured by the feet of him who goes to the trial.[6]

1. And if the trial is by water, it shall be heated until it becomes so hot as to boil, whether the vessel (containing it) be made of iron or brass, lead or clay.
2. And if the accusation is "single", the hand shall be plunged in up to the wrist in order to reach the stone; if it is "threefold", up to the elbow.
3. And when the ordeal is ready two men shall go in from either party, and they shall be agreed that it is as hot as we have declared.
4. And [then] an equal number of men from each party shall enter, and stand along the church on both sides of the ordeal, and all these shall be fasting and shall have abstained from their wives during the night; and the mass-priest shall sprinkle holy water over them all, and each of them shall taste the holy water. And [the mass-priest] shall give them all the book[7] and the symbol of Christ's cross to kiss. And no one shall continue to make up the fire after the consecration has begun, but the iron shall lie upon the embers until the last collect. Then it shall be laid upon the post, and no other words shall be spoken in the church, except that God be earnestly prayed to make clear the whole truth.[8]
5. And the accused shall go to the ordeal, and his hand shall be sealed up; and after three days[9] it shall be inspected [in order] to ascertain whether it has become discoloured or remained clean within the sealed wrappings.

---

[5] Attenborough, *The laws of the earliest English kings*, pp. 171–2.
[6] The heated iron had to be carried from the post (stake) to the measured mark.
[7] Probably the gospels.
[8] The key phrase: it is God who is to reveal the truth of the matter.
[9] The theologically significant period, viz. the time between Christ's crucifixion and resurrection.

6. And if anyone breaks these rules, the ordeal shall in his case be invalidated, and he shall pay a fine of 120 shillings to the king.

Of incendiaries and those who secretly compass death[10]

This decree illustrates one of the special circumstances in which ordeal was used.

With regard to incendiaries and those who secretly compass death, we have declared that the oath shall be augmented threefold and the weight of the iron used in the ordeal shall be increased until it weighs three pounds. And the man who is accused shall go to the ordeal, and the accuser shall choose either the ordeal by water or the ordeal by iron whichever he prefer. If he [the accused] cannot produce the oath and is proved guilty, the chief men of the borough shall decide whether his life shall be spared or not.

Trial by Corsnæd

Trial by corsnæd *was where the defendant had to swallow a morsel of barley bread or cheese (usually blessed). If he failed so to do, he was deemed guilty as this prayer, invoked at the time of such an ordeal, reveals.*[11]

O Lord Jesus Christ . . . grant, we pray thee, by thy Holy name, that he who is guilty of this crime in thought or deed, when this creature of sanctified bread is presented to him for proving of the truth, let his throat be narrowed, and in thy name let it be rejected rather than devoured . . .

Ordeal by cold water

In this ordeal the defendant was lowered into a vessel of water. If he floated, he was guilty; if he sank, innocent. This ordeal was considered particularly undignified and was reserved for serfs. The introduction of it to all cases brought under the Assize of Clarendon in 1166 hastened the decline of its use.

Let the hands of the accused be bound together under the bent knees after the manner of a man who is playing the game of *champ-estroit*. Then he shall be bound around the loins with a rope strong enough to hold him; and in the rope will be made a knot at the distance of the length of his hair; and so he shall be let down gently into the water so as not to make a splash. If he sinks down to the knot, he shall be drawn up and saved; otherwise let him be adjudged a guilty man by the spectators.[12]

---

[10] Attenborough, *The laws of the earliest English kings*, p. 171.
[11] A. Harding, *The law courts of medieval England* (1973), p. 27.
[12] W. L. Warren, *Henry II* (1973), p. 283, n. 1.

4

Trial by ordeal was less used after 1066 and was banned by the Fourth Lateran Council in 1215. In England trial by battle seems to have replaced trial by ordeal in many cases.

Trial by Battle

Trial by battle was introduced into England by the Normans. There is no English account that has survived, so here is a contemporary chronicle account of a trial by battle following the murder, by his vassals, of the Count of Flanders in 1127. One of the conspirators, Guy of Steenvoorde, was challenged to trial by battle by Herman the Iron. This is the story of that encounter.

Herman the Iron[13]

Both sides fought bitterly. Guy had unhorsed his adversary and kept him down with his lance just as he liked whenever Herman tried to get up. Then his adversary, coming closer, disembowelled Guy's horse, running it through with his sword. Guy, having slipped from his horse, rushed at his adversary with his sword drawn. Now there was a continuous and bitter struggle, with alternating thrusts of swords, until both, exhausted by the weight and burden of arms, threw away their shields and hastened to gain victory in the fight by resorting to wrestling. Herman the Iron fell prostrate on the ground, and Guy was lying on top of him, smashing the knight's face and eyes with his iron gauntlets. But Herman, prostrate, little by little regained his strength from the coolness of the earth . . . , and by cleverly lying quiet made Guy believe he was certain of victory. Meanwhile, gently moving his hand down to the lower edge of the cuirass where Guy was not protected, Herman seized him by the testicles and, summoning all his strength for the brief space of one moment, he hurled Guy from him; by this tearing motion all the lower parts of the body were broken so that Guy, now prostrate, gave up, crying out that he was conquered and dying.

The [new] count . . . ordered Guy to be hanged next to the dead provost [another of the conspirators] on the same gallows.

The monks of Bury St Edmunds opt for Trial by Battle, 1287[14]

Trial by battle in civil cases was limited by the Assize of Clarendon, and by the late thirteenth century was very rare, but it did happen as this famous account from Bury St Edmunds illustrates.

---

[13] J. B. Ross (ed.), *The murder of Charles the Good, Count of Flanders by Galbert of Bruges* (2nd edn, 1967), pp. 212–13.

[14] Antonia Gransden (ed. & tr.), *The chronicle of Bury St Edmunds* (1964), pp. 88–9 cited in Harding, *The law courts of medieval England*, p. 157.

On the morrow of St Hilary's day [14 January] the aforementioned Justices in Eyre sat at Cattishall. In this eyre John de Creyk, Godfrey de Beaumont and Ralph de Berners sued us for our manors of Semer and Groton.

When the case had been investigated, we at length declared that we would defend our right by judicial combat, as we suspected that the surrounding district supported and was in league with our opponents.[15] Accordingly a day one month after Easter was assigned for the parties to appear before the King's Bench and the case was adjourned until then.[16]

The abbot paid a certain champion called Roger Clerk, who came from the district of Lincoln, 20 marks in advance from his own money. After the duel Roger was to receive 30 marks more from him. The champion during the whole time of waiting stayed with us, accompanied by his trainer, although under challenge . . .

On St Calixtus's day [14 October] our enemies were victorious and our champion slain in judicial combat in London. And so our manors of Semer and Groton were lost without any hope of recovery.

Trial by battle remained fairly common in criminal cases until much later, particularly in the case of Approvers (see below).

Trial by jury

Trial juries in criminal cases emerged out of the use of juries to try civil cases re disputed land using a new writ, the writ of novel disseisin. Out of these develop-ments came the grand juries and trial juries of the later Middle Ages.

Juries of presentment, local juries reporting on local crimes to the Justices in Eyre, became a regular feature of the system of justice from the mid-twelfth century onwards. Coroners, formally established in 1194, used juries which in a sense were special juries of presentment.

1.3 Writs

A writ was a written instruction to commence an action at law. In the Middle Ages most such actions concerned land. The "Writ of Right", normally used in cases of disputed land tenure, generated a long and cumbersome process. The writ was issued to the lord demanding that he "do right" to the complainant and threatening that if he did not, the king's officer, the sheriff, would intervene.

---

[15] That is to say, the monks did not trust a local jury.

[16] The case, begun in Suffolk, was now to be moved to the King's Bench, a permanent court at Westminster, which heard pleas of the Crown (what we would now call criminal cases).

Writ of Right[17]

The king to N., greeting. I command you to do full right without delay to R. in respect of one hundred shillings of rent in such and such a vill which he claims to hold of you by free service, etc. If you do not do it, the sheriff will, that I may hear no further complaint for default of right in this matter. Witness, etc.

The Writ of Novel Disseisin[18]

After the anarchy of Stephen's reign (1135–54), there were many land actions outstanding. The writ of novel disseisin, probably introduced at the Assize of Clarendon in 1166, was designed to speed up the process of resolving disputes over land. The writ had a number of unique characteristics:

1. *The writ only applied to novel (i.e. recent) disseisin (i.e. dispossession) and only to free tenements.*
2. *The writ was issued automatically upon receipt of the complaint.*
3. *The writ was sent to the sheriff and if the complainant gave a security to bring the action then the sheriff had to:*
   (a) restore the complainant to the tenement and to the chattels of the tenement until a specified date;
   (b) summon a jury at once; require the jury to view the land in dispute; endorse their names on the back of the writ; return the writ to the Justices when they came; require the jury to attend before those visiting justices.
   (c) summon the disseisor or, if he disappeared, his bailiff.
4. *Action only lay in the royal courts, i.e. local franchises did not protect the disseisor. There was no option for trial by battle.*

A disseisor who lost the action was to be treated as a criminal and imprisoned. By 1198 the successful complainant could claim damages.

The king to the sheriff, greeting. N. has complained to me that R. unjusticely and without a judgment has disseised him of his free tenement [*de libero tenemento suo*] in such-and-such a vill since my last voyage to Normandy [i.e. recently]. Therefore I command you [the sheriff] that, if N. gives you security for prosecuting his claim, you are to see that his chattels which were taken from the tenement are to be restored to it, and that the tenement and chattels remain in peace [*esse in pace*] until the

---

[17] Taken from G. D. G. Hall (ed. & tr.), *Glanvill* (1965 edn), p. 138. This treatise was written by an unknown justice sometime between 1187 and 1189.
[18] Hall, *Glanvill* (1965 edn), pp. 167–8.

Sunday after Easter. And meanwhile you are to see that the tenement is viewed by twelve free and lawful men of the neighbourhood, and their names endorsed on this writ. And summon them by good summoners to be before me or my justices on the Sunday after Easter to make the recognition [i.e. to give their verdict]. And summon R. [the defendant], or his bailiff if he himself cannot be found, on the security of gage and reliable surities to be there then to hear the recognition. And have there the summoners, and this writ and the names of the sureties. Witness, etc.

The Writ of Mort d'Ancestor[19]

This writ was initiated at the Assize of Northampton, 1174. It was devised to provide a simple way of establishing the proper descent of land but only in simple cases involving inheritance from father, mother, brother, sister, uncle or aunt. There were three questions:
> *(a) Did O. die seised of such-and-such land?*
> *(b) Did he die recently?*
> *(c) Is G. the next heir of O?*
In other respects the writ followed that of novel disseisin.

The king to the sheriff, greeting. If G. son of O. gives you security for prosecuting his claim, then summon by good summoners twelve free and lawful men of the neighbourhood of such and such a vill to be before me or my justices on a certain day, ready to declare on oath whether O. the father of the aforesaid G. was seised in his demesne as of fee of one virgate of land of that vill on the day that he died, whether he died after my first coronation, and whether the said G. is his next heir. And meanwhile let them view the land; and you are to see their names are endorsed on this writ. And summon by good summoners R., who holds that land [i.e. the person who is keeping G. out of his inheritance], to be there to hear the recognition. And have there the summoners and this writ. Witness, etc.

Many other writs were introduced by the end of the twelfth century. And with them came an elaboration of the law requiring the knowledge of skilled professional lawyers to deal with the variety of options now opened up to the litigant.

2   The medieval criminal justice system

Royal Justices perambulating the shires hearing pleas of the Crown was Henry II's brilliant innovation of 1166 when it was decreed that twelve freemen from

---

[19] Hall, *Glanvill*, p. 150.

each hundred[20] and four from each vill should present (i.e. name) those sus-
pected of murder, theft, robbery, and also name those who protected them and
prevented them being brought to trial before the itinerant Justices. By the thir-
teenth century these general eyres had become the main instrument of royal
justice in the shires.

2.1   Extracts from the Shropshire Eyre Roll of 1256[21]

The court met at Shrewsbury from Friday 14 January to Wednesday 16 Febru-
ary 1256, a lengthy period reflecting the weight of business being conducted at
the court, 482 civil cases and 428 Crown pleas (i.e. criminal cases). There were
four Justices, an abbot (who should not have been sitting as a judge) and three
others, all experienced in the administration and/or the judiciary.

Civil Pleas[22]

Plea of Novel Disseisin[23]

An assize comes to give a verdict as to whether William de la Grene, chaplain, and his brother, Nicholas, unjustly disseised William of Hampton of his free tenement in Alveley since the king's first crossing of the sea into Brittany.

William of Hampton complains that they disseised him of four acres of arable.

William [de la Grene, chaplain] and the others say that William of Hampton complains unjustly, because he showed only three acres to the view.

Further, William the chaplain says that a certain Henry son of William of Alveley gave him a good and peaceful seisin of those three acres, and William of Hampton never had seisin.

William of Hampton admits that Henry son of William once made a charter of feoffment to William de la Grene for the land, but says that William never had seisin through the charter. For Henry son of William had demised [i.e. leased] the land to a certain Henry of Perry for the term of twenty years, a long time before the charter was made: he made the

---

[20] Each shire was divided into hundreds, the number of which depended upon the population, density and wealth of each county.

[21] Taken from Harding, *The law courts of medieval England*, pp. 147–51. An edition and translation of the whole roll by Alan Harding is to be found in "Selden Soc.", xcvi (1981).

[22] These are what we would now call civil cases.

[23] On the writ of novel disseisin, see above.

charter to William within that term and without conveying seisin. Afterwards, Henry of Perry died before the end of the twenty years and in his last will he left the remainder of the term [to his wife].[24] And a certain Henry of Morfe later married her and had seisin of the land.[25] In the course of time came William of Hampton and prevailed upon Henry son of William of Alveley to enfeoff him with the land and make him a charter according to which he should pay rent to Henry of Morfe for the remainder of Henry's term. And William of Hampton prevailed upon Henry of Morfe to remit to him the remainder of his term, so that both through Henry son of William as feoffor and through Henry of Morfe as farmer William of Hampton had good and peaceful seisin of the land till William de la Grene and the others disseised him. As to the truth of this he appeals to the assize.

The jurors swear that it is true. So William of Hampton shall recover seisin by view of the recognitors, and William de la Grene and the others are in mercy. Damages, half a mark.[26]

Failed plea of Novel Disseisin

Did Roger son of William of Myddle, Hugh son of Alice, William Provost, John son of John, Roger Forester, Reginald Costard . . . and William Pynot [23 names altogether] disseise Reginald of Sleap of common pasture pertaining to his free tenement in Bomere? He complains that they have disseised him of common in heathland about two hundred acres in extent, where he used to common his beasts of every sort all the year round.

Roger and the others have not come, but their bailiff, William of Prees, answers for them and says that they are all the men of John l'Estrange and claim nothing in Reginald's alleged tenement and common except at the will of the said John: William calls the assize to witness to this.

One of the recognitors, William of Bicton, has not come and is in mercy.[27]

Verdict: Roger and the others have no claim except at the will of John l'Estrange. So they are quit, and Reginald takes nothing and is in mercy.[28]

---

[24] Note that leases of land but not freehold property could be devised by will, i.e. left by will.

[25] In marrying the widow, he gained access to her property.

[26] Note the use of a jury to decide the truth of the claim. When it says that William recovered seisin, it means that he recovered tenure of the property. Note the care with which that land was to be identified. A mark was 13s 4d, so half a mark was 6s 8d, a month's wages.

[27] When the sheriff returned the writ, he listed on the back of it the jurors or recognitors who should appear. As we can see here, failure to attend made that person liable to penalty.

[28] An example of what happened if one lost a plea of novel disseisin.

Plea of Mort D'Ancestor[29]

An assize comes to give a verdict as to whether Coleman of Ludlow, uncle of Coleman of Ludlow, was seised of a messuage and 44 acres of land in Sheet and half a virgate in Whettleton and a messuage and two acres in Stokesay on the day he died, etc. and whether Coleman is his next heir.

Adam of Stokesay holds a messuage and two acres of the land, William Coterel five acres . . . Gillian, who was Coleman's wife, seven acres . . . the Master of the Hospital of St John at Ludlow ten acres and a half . . . [The land is now split into eleven parcels.]

Gillian who was Coleman's wife says that Coleman [the nephew and plaintiff, called "le Blund" as well as of Ludlow] has brought the assize against her unjustly, for she holds the land in dower, as that assigned to her by Coleman, uncle of Coleman le Blund, who would be bound to warrant her if someone else sued her for it. Coleman le Blund cannot deny this, so Gillian is quit, and Coleman takes nothing by the assize and is in mercy.

William and all the others say that Coleman has brought the assize unjustly, for Coleman his uncle did not die seised of their tenements: a long time before his death he granted them to William and the others. They put themselves on the assize.

Verdict: Coleman the uncle did die seised, and Coleman le Blund is the next heir, so he recovers seisin, and William and the others are in mercy.[30]

Attorneys

As we can see here, there was no requirement at this stage, or indeed until very much later, for an attorney to be a trained lawyer.

The Abbot of Croxden appoints brother John, one of his monks, and brother John, one of his lay-brothers, as his attorneys in a plea concerning pasture-rights against John de Beleg and his wife Joan.[31]

A nuisance

The same assize, with the same jurors, comes to give a verdict as to whether Odo of Hodnet made a ditch in Hopton to the nuisance of the same Robert's tenement in Hopton. Robert complains that whereas he used to have a drove-way for his cattle and right of way for the carting of

---

[29] An example of the use of a writ of mort d'ancestor to establish who is the legal heir of a property.

[30] That is to say, he recovers the property.

[31] Note that these attornies are not lawyers but simply individuals nominated to act on behalf of a litigant.

his corn, the ditch deprives him of these rights. Odo says nothing to stop the assize.

Verdict: no nuisance, because Robert was never accustomed to cart corn there, and no right of way is threatened by reason of the ditch. So Odo is quit, and Robert in mercy.

Foreign Pleas[32]

Force of Arms

Geoffrey Falconer put in an appearance on the fourth day to answer Walter brother of William of Hyde, Robert son of Robert Short, Walter Mewy and Walter of Woodmanton as to why he and William of Hyde came with force and arms to Geoffrey's land in Beoley and carried off his plough without permission to William's home and beat and maltreated him against the peace, etc.

And the defendants have not come, and they defaulted on previous occasions so that the sheriff was ordered to distrain them through all their lands, etc . . . and have their persons on this day.[33]

The sheriff returned that they are all staying in Herefordshire and have no land nor tenement in Gloucestershire by which they can be distrained. So the sheriff of Herefordshire is ordered to distrain them etc.[34] and to have their bodies at Westminster one month from Easter. [In the margin against this case is a note that the case was adjourned to Shrewsbury from the Gloucestershire session of the eyre.]

Crown Pleas[35]

Unjust imprisonment

Presentment that Roger of Welhope, a serjeant of Thomas Corbet, and his fellows took Richard of Norbury and imprisoned him at Cause; and Richard could not get free until he gave them 12 pence. So judgment on Roger.

Murder

Eynun of The Haye killed Walter Pinchun and fled and is suspected. So let him be exacted and outlawed. He had no chattels.[36] The first finder is

---

[32] These were cases beyond the county, i.e. outside the jurisdiction of the court.

[33] To distrain was to seize goods and/or animals in order to force the defendants to come to court to plead.

[34] Hence this appears under "foreign pleas", that is to say, involving persons or property outside of the county.

[35] These were what we would now call criminal cases.

[36] If he had so, they would have been seized.

present and is not suspected.[37] And the villages of Mawley and Cleobury did not pursue [the killer] and are in mercy.[38]

Sanctuary for a Murderer

A stranger and his wife were lodging at the house of Isolda of Cleobury and there killed Philip son of Isolda and fled and placed themselves in the church of Neen, admitted the deed and abjured the realm before the coroners. His chattels, 3 pence.[39]

Neen Savage, Neen Sollars and Hopton Wafers did not make pursuit and are in mercy.[40]

The twelve jurors did not present the finder and are in mercy.[41]

Sheriff's misdemeanour

Hamund of Birches was arrested and imprisoned in the prison of Bridgnorth when R. of Grendon was sheriff, and obtained the king's writ of replevin for his release on bail, but he gave half a mark to R. the sheriff before he could obtain release.[42] So judgment on the sheriff.

Hamund puts himself on the country for good or ill.[43]

Verdict: not guilty of any misdeed. So he is quit.

Murder

A stranger whose name is unknown was found dead in a field by the village of Clive. The first finder has come and is not suspected. It is not known who killed him.

Deodand

William son of Herbert was crushed by a wagon and died three days later. Judgment: misadventure.

---

[37] The first finder of a body was required to report his or her find and attend the eyre.

[38] That is to say, the villagers failed to raise the hue and cry.

[39] The Crown seized the chattels of a convicted felon or outlaw; the seigneurial lord, his land.

[40] Note, three villages named. Because they did not raise the hue and cry, they were deemed culpable.

[41] These were the jurors of presentment, i.e. the local people required to present offences in their village. As we can see here, failure to do so, or to report the first finder of a body, rendered the jurors liable to punishment.

[42] That is to say, despite the fact that he had a writ ordering his release, he still had to bribe the sheriff before he could get out of gaol.

[43] That is to say, he elected for trial by jury for the unspecified offence for which he was originally imprisoned.

Value of the cart and oxen, 24 shillings and 6 pence.[44] On this there was testimony that Hugh the chaplain of Momeresfeud took an ox from the deodand as heriot[45] for the Abbot of Shrewsbury, because William made a will and enjoyed church law, leaving the ox to the church of Momeresfeud of which the Abbot of Shrewsbury is rector. Judgment on William.

Trespass

William Blethin appeals Reginald son of Andrew of Holdgate that when he was in the king's peace in a certain wood belonging to Walter de Clifford called Bernstre on the Tuesday after the Assumption in the thirty-fourth year [of King Henry] Reginald came and assaulted, wounded and maltreated him against the peace, etc. Reginald asks that it be awarded to him that when Walter appealed him before, he said that this was done in the thirty-fifth year and now he says the thirty-fourth. Since this is proved by the coroners' rolls, the appeal is considered null, and William shall be imprisoned.[46]

But for the sake of the king's peace let there be inquiry of the country as to the truth of the matter. The jurors say that the said Reginald is guilty of the said trespass. So he shall be imprisoned.

Afterwards the said William Blethin came and made fine by half a mark by the pledge of Richard Tyrel.[47] The said Reginald is poor.

Murder

Unknown malefactors came to the house of Stephen of Boscobel and killed Stephen and tied up his whole family. They fled and it is not known who they were. Claverley, where this happened, did not make pursuit.

Hundredal bailiff's misdemeanours[48]

Presentment that Walter son of Ivo of Petton and Walter son of William of Petton gave Robert of Preen, bailiff of the hundred of Munslow, a measure of wheat so that they should not be arrested . . . [The jurors list sums taken from six other people for the same reason.] . . . So judgment on Robert.

---

[44] The instrument which caused death was called the deodand and, in general, was seized by the Crown.

[45] Death payment due from a peasant to a manorial lord.

[46] Because he has failed to prove his case.

[47] That is to say, he paid 3s 4d to get out of gaol.

[48] The bailiff of a hundred was a sheriff's officer. They were notorious for their corruption.

False accusation

Brun of Norton [and 23 others] . . . suspected of thieving and receiving thieves, have come and put themselves upon the country for good or ill. And the jurors say on their oath that they are not guilty of any misdeed. So they are quit.

Afterwards it was found that William of Calverhall indicted Richard the smith of Calverhall and his brothers Thomas and William out of hatred and spite. So he is in mercy.

Wounding

Simon of Preen appeals William son of Robert Bedell of Preen that when he was in the peace of the lord king on the twelfth day of Christmas in the thirty-ninth year [of King Henry] in the village of Plaish, William came there and assaulted him with a sword of Cologne and gave him a wound in the back and another in the head and a third in the stomach with a lance. And that he did this wickedly and feloniously he offers, etc. ["to prove on his body": i.e. by battle]. Simon also appeals William's brothers, Adam and Hugh, of beating him – that they wickedly beat and maltreated him with a stick.

William comes and says that he is a clerk and ought not to answer here. At this, there comes the official of the Bishop of Hereford who claims him as a clerk.[49] But that it may be known in what condition he is handed over, let there be inquiry of the country. And the jurors say that he is guilty of that deed, and as such he is handed over to the bishop.

Adam and Hugh come and ask that it be awarded to them that Simon has been inconsistent in his appeal, and since this is confirmed by the coroners' rolls the appeal is adjudged null. And let the truth be inquired of the country.

The jurors say that the said Adam and Hugh were aiders and abettors when the felony was done. So they are committed to gaol. Afterwards come Hugh and Adam and make fine with the king by half a mark by the pledge of Richard of Acton and Henry the carpenter of Preen.[50]

Afterwards it was found that Simon possesses nothing, and on the order of S. of Walton he is to be delivered to Sir James of Audley.

---

[49] Clerics were not liable to answer for their offences in the secular courts but had to be handed over to the church courts.

[50] That is to say, they paid a fine to get out of prison.

2.2   Bills to the Justices in Eyre[51]

Examples of the way an individual could initiate an action before the king's Justices in Eyre.

Assault and false imprisonment

William Piers of Brompton complaineth to the Justices of our lord the king[52] that whereas he was going in the peace of God and in the peace of the king in the town of Ludlow on the Sunday next before the Feast of St Michael in the eighteenth year of the reign of King Edward that now is, whom God preserve, Roger Clayband, Reynold of Posenhall, Hugh Bruton, Adam of Cayton, William the son of John of Boreford, William the dyer, Harry of Chabenore, William the son of William the Galis, together with all the commonalty of the town of Ludlow, whose names are unknown save that of Lawrence of Ludlow, came and suddenly attacked him with swords, axes, knives and other sharp-edged arms, and wounded him in the head and stripped off his hose, whereby he lost consciousness; and they maimed his left arm and a finger of his right hand and left him for dead; and they dragged him to prison and there they kept him for two days and two nights in prison and put him in shackles, wrongfully and against the peace, to the damage of this William of a hundred pounds; whereof he prayeth remedy for God's sake. Pledges for prosecution: Adam Wall of Brompton; Roger the summoner of Brompton.[53]

Unlawful detention of chattels[54]

In this case, we can see the importance of charters as evidence of right to property.

Avice the wife of John of Coleshill prayeth the Justices of our lord the king and craveth of you for the sake of the queen's soul that you will have pity upon her and show favour unto her against Harry of Thickness; for the aforesaid Avice, in the sight of the good folk of Newcastle, deposited with the aforesaid Harry the charters of all her land that he might take care of them, and this Harry now wrongfully detaineth the aforesaid charters; and the aforesaid Avice is now ejected from her land because she hath not these charters. Therefore the aforesaid Avice prayeth for the love of

---

[51] From Harding, *The law courts of medieval England*, p. 154, a translation from the French by W. C. Bolland in *Select bills in eyre* ("Selden Society", 1914), pp. 20–21, 41.

[52] The king's Justices in Eyre.

[53] It was common in medieval law for a complainant to need pledges to guarantee that he would prosecute his case.

[54] In this case, charters.

God and for the queen's soul's sake that the truth may be inquired of. [Endorsement:] Failed to prosecute.

2.3 Description of pleading in criminal cases[55]

If a man be impleaded for felony he may find here the crown laws, by means of which he may defend himself; and if he be convicted, what judgment he will suffer; and how one may abate an appeal and by what exceptions; and how he will be impleaded and what delays he will be able to cause before having to reply. And be it known that a man will never be hanged so long as he does not admit his guilt by his own mouth.

Tricking a thief into opting for trial by jury

A thief was once indicted by the country and brought before Laurence de Brok, then sitting as Justice in such a place. And the Justice said:

"My good friend, you are indicted by the country of such a thing: how do you wish to acquit yourself of such a theft?"

And the other replied to him . . . that he would defend himself by his body.[56] And the Justice spoke in the same way as the former Justice, and the thief stuck to battle; and the Justice wondered how he could bring the thief to give another reply, and asked him: "Are you a good and honest man?"

"Yes, indeed," said he who had been answering as above, "and I am ready to defend myself by my body against this accusation."

And the Justice continued: "I say are you good and honest?" and the thief said: "Yes, sir, I am," and the Justice said: "How do you wish to prove it?" and the thief said: "By the country, to be sure."

And the country came, and said he was a thief and had committed such a theft, for which he had been indicted, and several others: so he was hanged; and in such a way he was tricked.[57]

A man taken for a killing done in self-defence

"Sheriff, why has this man been taken?"

"Sir, for the death of a man whom he is supposed to have killed in self-defence, as he says."

---

[55] Harding, *The law courts of medieval England,* pp. 155–6, from J. M. Kaye (ed. & tr.), *Placita corone* ("Selden Society", 1966), pp. 19–20, 22–4.

[56] That is to say, by trial by battle.

[57] Stung by the judge's innuendo, the defendant inadvertently put himself "on the country", i.e. offered to be tried by his peers, thus forgoing his right to trial by battle.

"What is your name?"

"Sir, Thomas de N."

"Thomas, what was the name of the man whom you killed in premeditated attack, feloniously as a felon?"

"Sir, if you please, I have never been a felon and never did mischief to living man, in premeditated attack; and so I have done nothing wrong against the man whose name you ask: who, feloniously as a felon and in premeditated attack tried to kill me on such a day, at such an hour, in such a year in my own house in such a township, for no fault on my part and solely on account of his own malice."

"Tell us the circumstances."

"Sir, I was unwilling to lend or hire to him a horse for the purpose of riding about his business in the district: for I feared that I should be deprived of my horse, or of any other thing which I might have lent or hired to him, for he was an unprincipled man, full of fraud and subtle tricks, untrustworthy and of ill fame. And because I refused him the loan of my horse he ran at me in my own house with a Welsh knife, horn handled, in his right hand and inflicted several wounds on my head, shoulders, feet, and elsewhere on my body wherever he could reach. I did not at first return his blows; but when I realized that he was set on killing me I started to defend myself: that is to say I wounded him in the right arm with a little pointed knife which I carried, making no further onslaught and acting in this way only to save my own life."

"Did he die of such a wound?"

"In truth, sir, I do not know: but had he not received this wound he would have killed me, feloniously as a felon and in premeditated attack."

"Who put you in this prison?"

"Sir, my neighbours: for they were afraid of being involved in this affair and suffering loss thereby."[58]

"What happened to the other?"

"Sir, he at once fled out of their grasp."

"Thomas, you have greatly embroidered your tale and coloured your defence: for you are telling us only what you think will be to your advantage, and suppressing whatever you think may damage you, and I do not believe you have told the whole truth."

"Sir, I have told the whole truth, and related the affair from the beginning to the end in every detail: and of this I trust myself to God and the country for both good and evil."

And so let an inquest be held. And the jury said the same as Thomas had related.[59] So the Justice then says:

---

[58] A community which failed to report a felony and/or failed to imprison the alleged felon was liable itself to punishment.

[59] That is to say, the case was put to the trial jury who found the defendant not guilty.

"Thomas, these good people testify by their oaths to the truth of what you have said. So our judgment is that what you did to him, you did in self-defence. But we cannot release you from this prison without the king's special order. However we will send a report of your case to the king's court and ensure that you receive his special grace."

"Sir, I thank you."

2.4 Sanctuary[60]

A suspected criminal who reached the sanctuary of a church could not be seized for forty days.

Thomas Wayland, the king's Chief Justice, was indicted before a lower royal court, on a charge of having harboured some of his own men who had murdered a man, and was convicted by a jury. He feared to put himself at the king's mercy and fled to the house of the Friars Minor at Bury St Edmunds.[61] There by the king's order he was besieged for several days by men of the neighbourhood; when there was little hope left he assumed the friar's habit.[62] On hearing this the king sent a knight from his familiar circle to make the guard even more secure in collaboration with the officials of the country. At length, after two months' siege and when nearly all the friars had dispersed in various directions, Thomas took off his friar's habit, put on secular clothes and came out, and was taken to the king and imprisoned in the Tower of London . . .

2.5 A murder plea before the Trailbaston Commissioners at Lancaster, 1306[63]

The jurors present that Robert Clark of Liverpool killed William Walker of Liverpool on the Monday next before the feast of Saint Andrew the Apostle in the twenty-seventh year of the reign of the present king. Robert was arrested for it, and now appears. Asked how he wishes to acquit himself of the said death and felony, he denies them and puts himself on his country for good or ill.[64]

---

[60] Gransden, *The chronicle of Bury St Edmunds*, pp. 92–3.

[61] That is to say, he took sanctuary in the Franciscan Priory.

[62] By so doing he claimed to be a friar and hence placed himself under ecclesiastical jurisdiction and, therefore, protection.

[63] Public Record Office. Just. 1/422, m. 1 (Latin). Translation by Alan Harding.

[64] That is to say, he pleads not guilty and opts for trial by jury.

The jurors say on their oath that this Robert Clark was coming from Chester with a certain William Brown, and this Robert demanded that an account be rendered to him by the aforesaid William, who received money, goods and chattels from him to trade with for their common profit. The same William refused to account to him and answered insolently, whereupon a quarrel broke out.

The quarrelling went on till they arrived at the town of Liverpool, where they were heard by William Walker, the said William Brown's cousin, who was staying in the town, and he protested vehemently to the said Robert Clark about the dispute which had been going on between this Robert and the said William Brown his cousin. He took William Brown's side entirely and joined with him in insulting the same Robert with rude words, and at length he drew a long knife and tried to stab Robert, who was expecting this and fled down a blind alley between two houses to avoid being killed. The same William Brown and William Walker, with the dagger in his hand, pursued Robert furiously into the alley to kill him, and unable to find a way out of the alley to escape them Robert drew his sword and held it up to defend himself. The said William ran at Robert in his determination to kill him and made to stab him through the body with the said dagger, and did thrust it through his cloak. And so he ran on to Robert's sword, disembowelled himself and died. They say therefore that this did not happen by the felony or malice aforethought of this Robert but by the said William's running on to the sword which Robert had drawn to defend himself.

Therefore the said Robert is returned to prison to await the king's grace, etc., but his chattels are forfeit because he fled.

Afterwards the lord king ordered by his writ that the record and process should be sent to him, and they are sent along with the writ.[65]

2.6   An Approver, 1249[66]

An approver was a convicted felon who, to escape death, had to bring ten successful cases before the courts, i.e. he had to turn king's evidence in ten cases. If, as in this case, he was successful, he escaped punishment but was forced to abjure the realm, i.e. he had to go into exile.

Walter Bloweberme, an approver, comes and appeals Walter Small of Winchester of larceny, saying that Walter was with him at Salisbury at

---

[65] Presumably with a view to issuing a pardon.

[66] From M. T. Clanchy (ed.), "Highway robbery and trial by battle in the Hampshire eyre of 1249" in R. F. Hunnisett & J. B. Post (eds), *Medieval legal records: edited in memory of C. A. F. Meekings* (1978), p. 51.

Whitsun and there together they stole clothes, shoes and many other things, and he offers to prove that this is true as above.

Walter comes and denies everything and for good or ill puts himself on the verdict of the country . . .

The same Walter comes and appeals Hamo Stare of Winchester by the same words, namely that they were at the house of Edeline Cross at Winchester and there stole clothes and other goods, whereof Hamo had as his share two coats, namely one of Irish cloth and one partly of Abingdon cloth and partly of London burel, and that Hamo was a party with him in committing the said larceny he offers to prove by his body[67] as the court shall adjudge. Hamo comes and denies everything and says that he is willing to defend himself by his body. So it is adjudged that there be battle between them. The battle between them is struck and Hamo has given in. So to judgment on him. He had no chattels.

Because Walter has made proof against 10 appellees, as he agreed, namely on six at Guildford . . . who became approvers, and he has appealed another four – and one defended himself by his body and was convicted, and three have fled – it is therefore adjudged that Walter may abjure the realm.

2.7   Harbouring outlaws[68]

William Pope of Alton, accused of the harbouring of outlaws from the pass of Alton, comes and denies everything and for good or ill puts himself on the verdict of 3 hundreds, namely Alton, Selborne and Odiham.

The jurors say that he is guilty, because they say that John de Bendinges, John Barkham and Richard Bennet robbed certain merchants in the pass of Alton and the aforesaid persons went out from William's house to intercept those merchants in that pass, and he was a party with them.

2.8   Coroners

The office of coroner (keeper of the Crown's pleas) was inaugurated in 1194. In each county four gentlemen were elected at the county court to hold the office. Some boroughs secured the right to have their own coroners. The coroner's function was to report to the visiting Justices in Eyre any cases arising under pleas of the Crown, in particular pleas relating to murder, manslaughter and sanctuary. The coroner sat with a jury of local men. Their verdicts were reported to the visiting Justices and the coroner's rolls consist of the record of those

---

[67] That is to say, he opts for trial by battle.
[68] Clanchy, "Highway robbery and trial by battle".

judgments. Note the care with which the value of the instrument of death, the deodand, was recorded. This was because the Crown was entitled to take the deodand or its equivalent value.

2.9 Rolls of the Staffordshire Coroners[69]

Election

James of Bogay was elected to the office of coroner at Stafford in full county court in the month of March in the ninth year of King Richard the Second.[70]

A Murder in Newcastle, 1386

Twelve jurors [named] of the burgage of the town of Newcastle-under-Lyme, . . . present, and say on their oaths that at the hour of vespers on Easter Sunday in the aforesaid year [22 April 1386] a dispute arose at Newcastle, in the iron-market opposite William Brieryhurst's house, between William, son of John Small of Newcastle, and John, son of Henry Hobson of Cheadle, so that the said John feloniously struck the said William in the right side with a certain knife, and thus he came to his death.[71]

He died forthwith after receiving the rites of the church. His mother Geva was near him when he died, and she raised the hue. [The men] of the said burgage came and sent for James of Bogay, the coroner, on whose view the deceased was buried on the following day.

The felon fled forthwith, and he had no chattels. The knife was worth a penny.

Accidental Death, 1387

Twelve jurors of the townships of Balterley, Betley, and Audley present, and say on their oaths that, at the hour of prime on Tuesday the feast of St Barnabas the Apostle in the tenth year of the said King Richard, [6 a.m. on 11 June 1387] Richard of Stoke, collier,[72] cut down a branch of an oak in the park of Heighley, and by mischance it fell upon his head and crushed him, and he died forthwith.

Alice his wife first found him, and she raised the hue; the said townships came, and sent for James of Bogay, the coroner, on whose view the deceased was buried on the following day.

---

[69] C. Gross (ed.), *Select cases from the coroners' rolls*, "Selden Soc." ix (1896), 99–101.

[70] Evidence that the coroners were elected at the county court.

[71] There is still a street in Newcastle called the Iron Market, and it is still a place where young townsmen fight.

[72] A charcoal maker.

Pledges for the said Alice's appearance before the itinerant justices: William Jane, Richard Booth. The branch was of no value.[73]

Murder, 1389

Twelve jurors of the townships of Madeley and Onneley present, and say on their oaths that at the hour of cock-crow on Thursday next before the feast of St Nicholas the Bishop in the thirteenth year of King Richard the Second [2 December 1389], Ralph, son of Hugh of Stoke of Adlington in Cheshire, went to the house of Richard Underwood at Wrineford in Staffordshire, and there, by reason of an ancient grudge, premeditating the said Richard's death, struck him upon the left leg with a sword, and thus caused his death; but he lived a week, and had the rites of the church, and then died at daybreak.

The said townships came and sent for James of Bogay, the coroner, on whose view the deceased was buried on the following day. The felon fled forthwith, and he had nothing outside of Cheshire.[74]

Dispute leading to death, 1390

Twelve jurors of the townships of Leek, Cheddleton, Grindon, and Endon present, and say on their oaths that on the night of Monday in Whit week in the thirteenth year of King Richard the Second [23 May 1390] a dispute arose at Leek between William Hunt and Henry Maycock (both of Leek) opposite the cross in High Street, and the said William feloniously struck the said Henry with a dagger in the left side to the heart, whereby he came to his death, and died forthwith.

The said Henry's wife Cecily was near him when he died, and she raised the hue. The aforesaid townships came and sent for James of Bogay, the coroner, on whose view the deceased was buried on the following day.

The felon was arrested, and was sent to the king's gaol at Stafford. He had chattels worth twenty shillings, which were delivered to the said townships. The dagger was worth three pence.

Robbery leading to manslaughter, 1397

Inquest was taken at Marston [?] on Tuesday next after the Holy Trinity in the twentieth year of King Richard the Second [19 June 1397] before Robert of Lockwood, one of the king's coroners in Staffordshire, on view of the body of John Swale, by the oath of [twelve] jurors of four neighbouring

---

[73] We can see here that even in the case of an accidental death, the firstfinder had to repeat his or her evidence before the Justices in Eyre.

[74] As a felon the murderer's goods were liable to seizure but, because he lived in another county, the coroner could not directly order the seizure of those goods.

townships. They say on their oaths that on Monday next after the said feast in the said year and place Nicholas of Cheddleton was going along the king's highway with linen and woollen cloths and other goods, when he was met by certain thieves who tried to kill and rob him. And the said Nicholas in self-defence struck one of the robbers, named John Swale, right over the head with a staff worth a penny, of which blow he died forthwith, but he had the rites of the church and was buried [on view of the coroner].

And immediately after the said felony the said Nicholas fled with all his goods and chattels, etc.

Murder, 1410

Inquest was taken at Weston before Thomas of Wollaston, one of the king's coroners in Staffordshire, on Wednesday next after the feast of the Apostles Peter and Paul in the eleventh year of King Henry the Fourth, [2 July 1410] on view of the body of John Taylor of Weston, by four neighbouring townships, to wit, Weston, Walton, Norbury, and Meer, by the oath of [twelve men]. They say on their oath that [Richard Barber entered John Taylor's house and killed him with a sword].

And the said Richard fled after having thus committed the felony. And [they say] that he had no goods or chattels. The sword was worth two shillings, for which the township of Weston will account.

Self-Defence leading to death, 1413

Inquest was taken at Penkridge before the said Thomas of Wollaston, one of the king's coroners in the said county, on Friday next before Lady Day in the fourteenth year of the said reign, [24 March 1413?] on view of the body of Ranulf Felton, by four neighbouring townships, to wit, Penkridge, Dunston, Peletvale, and Levedale, by the oath of [twelve men]. They say [that Ranulf tried to kill William Johnson, who in self-defence then hit Ranulf with a bill and caused his death].

And the said William Johnson fled after having thus committed the said felony. The bill was worth four pence, for which the township of Penkridge will account.

2.10 Rolls of the Northamptonshire Coroners[75]

A convicted outlaw beheaded for leaving the King's highway, 1322

A convicted outlaw who had abjured the realm was only subject to the king's protection on the king's highway.

---

[75] Gross, *Select cases from the coroners' rolls.*

One of the said robbers,[76] called John of Ditchford, fled to the church of Wootton and took refuge there,[77] by reason of the said felony, and on the said Wednesday [24 March 1322] he confessed before Richard Lovel, the coroner, and before the said four townships that he was guilty of the said felony; and he there abjured the realm of England, the port of Dover being assigned to him. His chattels, a sword, a knife, and a courtepy,[78] were appraised at eighteen pence, for which the township of Wootton will account.

On the following Friday, the said John of Ditchford was found beheaded in the fields of Collingtree. Inquest was taken before Richard Lovel, the coroner, by the oath of twelve [men] and four townships, to wit, Collingtree with Middleton, Courteenhall, Wootton, and Rothersthorpe. They say that on the preceding Wednesday the said John abjured the realm of England before the coroner at Wootton, and on the same day he abandoned the king's highway and the warrant of Holy Church, to wit, the cross, and fled over the fields of Collingtree toward the woods. Hue was raised against him, and he was pursued by the township of Wootton and others, until he was beheaded while still fleeing. His head was carried by the four townships to the king's castle at Northampton by order of the said coroner.

Murder, 1321

Thomas Jordan of Marston was found slain in his house at Thenford on Sunday next after the feast of the Assumption of Blessed Mary in the fifteenth year of King Edward, son of King Edward, [16 August 1321] and he had a wound on the crown of his head, which seemingly was made with a stick.

Inquest was taken before Richard Lovel, by the oath of twelve [men] and four townships. They say that on the preceding Sunday a quarrel arose in the king's highway at Thenford between the said Thomas Jordan and John of Cornwall, the then hayward of Chacombe, and John struck Thomas upon the crown of the head with a stick called a Kentish staff, while [Thomas] was fleeing, inflicting a wound [which extended] to the brain, and of which he died on the following Friday, after having confessed and partaken of the communion.

And they say that John fled forthwith, whither they know not. They also say that he had no chattels. They were asked concerning the force, precept, aid, and harbouring of the said felon, and they say that they know no

---

[76] They had killed and robbed a man.
[77] That is to say, he sought sanctuary.
[78] A short cloak of coarse cloth.

one guilty thereof. Also they were asked if any [other] persons were present, and [they say that] there were none.

Humphrey of Bassingbourne, the then sheriff of Northampton, has been ordered [to arrest the felon].

Four townships, Marston, Thorpe Mandeville, Farthinghoe, and Warkworth, say and present the same.

2.11   Court of a fair, 1262/3[79]

Fairs presented particular problems. People came from far and wide. If justice was to be done, it had to be done quickly. These fair courts were known colloquially as Piepowder (O.fr. piedpoudreux = dusty feet) Courts.

Trade debt

Adam Waderove complains of Geoffrey of Oxford, for that he unjustly detains and deforces him of 3s 1d and therefore unjustly, because whereas the said Geoffrey came on Monday last in the Fair of St Ives opposite the house of Roger Alexander's son and bought of the said Adam 5 fleeces of wool for 3s 2d the said Geoffrey only paid him 1d and thus has gone off with the said 3s 1d and with the said 5 fleeces and still detains them and is in seisin of them to his [Adam's] damage and dishonour 6s 8d; and he produces suit.

The said Geoffrey was present and defended the words of court and the damage and dishonour of Adam [to the amount of] 6s 8d but made a certain confession, namely he said that he could not deny that he bought the said wool for 3s 2d and was in seisin of it as Adam alleged against him, but he said that Adam sold him the wool by weight as being 8½ lb of wool and he [Geoffrey] found in it a deficiency of 1 lb, and that he, Geoffrey, was always ready and willing to pay the said Adam the said money provided that Adam would allow him out of it the value of the 1 lb of wool which was deficient from the said weight of 8½ lb; he offered to prove [this] sufficiently, if the court should award [him the proof]. A day is given him to make his proof to-morrow three-handed.

[*The Court of the Fair continued on the next day*]

Geoffrey of Oxford came and sufficiently proved three-handed that . . . [the facts were as he had stated them]. Therefore by judgment of the court the said Geoffrey may deduct from the said 3s 1d the value of 1 lb of wool, and shall pay to the said Adam the whole of the residue, to wit 2s 8½d . . . And let the said Adam be in mercy for his false claim; fine 6d . . .

---

[79] Of St Ives which belonged to the Abbot of Ramsey. 46 Henry III. From Harding, *The law courts of medieval England*, p. 146.

2.12   The manor court rolls of Tooting Beck (Surrey, 1403)[80]

There is no such thing as a typical manor court roll. This record is given simply to remind the reader that most justice for most people was conducted in manor courts. Much of the criminal business, now heard in magistrates' courts, and civil business, now heard in the county court, was dealt with in these pre-Conquest institutions which were active until the later seventeenth century and survived until the 1920s.

The first Court of Dom Michael of Kymptone, Prior of Mertone,[81] held there with view of frank pledge on the 18th day of the month of October in the beginning of the fifth year of the reign of King Henry the Fourth after the Conquest [18 October 1403], John Schaldebourne being Cellarer.

Customary tenants

John Atte Grene	Thomas Hauldone
William Sleford	Agnes Arcour
Richard Tubbynge	John Holdegryme
John Pykestone	John Yuery
Johanna Crafte	William Crafte
Nicholas Cook	John Atte Hethe
William Symond	William Brygth
Richard Bradwatere	William Colbrond
John Morgone	Nicholas Cork
Richard Tylere	Sara Brodwatere

All these did fealty.[82]

Further, a precept is made that William Otys be distrained to answer to the lord, before the next Court, for trespass done in the lord's grove by breaking the hedges.

Further, the homage have day to bring back William Day Cartere, the lord's bondman, before next Court, on pain of 40s.[83]

Richard Bradwatere (2d) surrenders for leave to make agreement with John Yuery in a plea of covenant. Therefore he is in mercy.[84]

---

[80] G. L. Gomme (ed.), *Court rolls of Tooting Beck manor* (vol. 1, 1909), pp. 69–77.

[81] The manor belonged to the Augustinian Priory of Merton, just along the road from Tooting.

[82] That a new manorial lord, Michael, had just been elected prior, meant that the tenants had to do fealty for their holdings. Note the presence of women in the list.

[83] The man had left the manor without permission and it is here the duty of the jury (*homage*) to get him to appear before the court to answer for his offence.

[84] That is to say, he owes an amercement, in this case 2d, to make his agreement.

Richard Bradwatere (2d) surrenders for leave to make agreement with the aforesaid John in a plea of trespass. Therefore he is in mercy.

Richard Bradwatere (2d) surrenders for leave to make agreement with the aforesaid John in a plea of trespass. Therefore he is in mercy.[85]

Richard Bradwatere (6s 8d) surrenders for trespass done with his beasts in the lord's meadow. Therefore he is in mercy.[86]

The same Richard (6d) surrenders for trespass done with his horses in the lord's oats. Therefore he is in mercy.

John Morgone (2d) surrenders for trespass done with his beasts in the lord's grove. Therefore he is in mercy.

A precept is made that Nicholas Cook be distrained to show the lord, before the next Court, how and in what manner he holds one piece of ground called Scutteshaghes.[87]

John Pykestone complains against Richard Bradwatere in a plea of trespass.[88] And he complains that with his pigs he made havoc in the grass within his close of the value of 3s 4d, his damages amounting to 3s 4d. And the said Richard, being present in Court, acknowledged in part. And he seeks that the damages may be assessed by the homage. And the homage assess the said damages at 3s. And therefore it is adjudged by the steward that the said John shall recover the said 3s. And the said Richard (2d) is in mercy. And a precept is made to levy the said 3s from the goods and chattels of the said Richard before the next Court.

Richard Bradwatere complains against John Pykestone in a plea of trespass. And he complains that with his beasts he made havoc in one parcel of barley of the value of 12s, his damages amounting to 3s 4d. And the said John, being present in Court, is to make his law with three compurgators[89] that he did no trespass against him as, etc., the sureties for his law being Nicholas Cook and William Crafte.[90]

The same Richard Bradwatere complains against John Pykestone in a plea of trespass. And he complains that he has taken away from him one bolt worth 10d, his damages amounting to 6d. And the said John, being present in Court, is to make his law with three compurgators that he did

---

[85] Presumably this is a different trespass.

[86] In the margin is the note "Attachment" which means that the bailiff had to attach, i.e. seize goods or animals to the value of the large amercement to ensure payment.

[87] Distraint was a little bit like attachment except that it was a threat rather than an instruction to seize goods or chattels.

[88] This long series of pleas and counter-pleas illustrates the way local people used the court for their own ends.

[89] That is to say, he is to produce three neighbours who will swear that Pykestone's animals did not cause the damage alleged. We can see here the use of a pre-Conquest system of justice, i.e. compurgation.

[90] These men guarantee that Pykestone will produce his compurgators.

no trespass against him, etc., the sureties for his law being Nicholas Cook and William Crafte.

The same Richard complains against the same John in a plea of trespass. And he complains that with his beasts he made havoc in one parcel of oats of the value of 8s, his damages amounting to 3s 4d. And the said John, being present in Court, acknowledged in part. And he seeks that the damages may be assessed by the homage.[91] And the homage assess the said damages at 2½d recover the said 2½d. And the said John is in mercy. And a precept is made to levy the said 2½d from the goods and chattels of the said John, for the use of the aforesaid Richard, before the next Court.

The same Richard complains against John Pykestone in a plea of trespass. And he complains that he killed two of his little pigs worth 5s, his damages amounting to 2s. And the said John, being present in Court, is to make his law with three compurgators, before the next Court, that he did no trespass against him, etc., the sureties for his law being Nicholas Cook and William Crafte.

The same Richard complains against John Pykestone in a plea of trespass. And he complains that he killed a lamb of his worth 16d, his damages amounting to 4d. And the said John is to make his law with three compurgators, before the next Court, that he did no trespass against him, etc., the sureties for his law being as above.

The same Richard complains against the same John in a plea of trespass. And he complains that with his beasts he made havoc in one acre sown with wheat, of the value of 10s, his damages amounting to 3s 4d. And the said John, being present in Court, is to make his law with three compurgators, before the next Court, that he did no trespass against him, etc., the sureties for his law being as above.

The same Richard Bradwatere complains against John Pykestone in a plea of trespass. And he complains that he killed two of his ducks worth 12d, his damages amounting to 12d. And the said John, being present in Court, is to make his law with three compurgators that he did no trespass against him as, etc., the sureties for his law being as above.

John Pykeston (3s 4d) because he says that the said Richard has falsely impleaded him in full Court. Therefore he is in mercy.[92]

Nicholas Cook complains against John Holdegryme in a plea of trespass. And he complains that his grass has been destroyed owing to a defect in the said John's enclosure, the damages of the said Nicholas

---

[91] In some manors a special jury of *taxatores* was sworn in to decide such questions.

[92] That is to say, the court did not accept Pykestone's plea that Bradwater had brought all these cases illegitimately. There can however be little doubt that the two men were in dispute with each other. Such a long list of pleas and counter-pleas is unusual.

amounting to 3s 4d. And they have day by request of the parties. And afterwards he did not prosecute his suit. Therefore he is in mercy.

The homage present[93] the default of William Symond (2d). Therefore he is in mercy.[94]

Also they present that the tenement of Nicholas Cook (2d) is out of repair and ruinous. Therefore he is, etc. And a precept is made that he repair the said tenement before the next Court, on pain of 6s 8d. And because the homage (2d) have concealed this, therefore they are in mercy.[95]

Also they present that Nicholas Cook has withdrawn one autumnal day-work, and one day-work of meadow mowing, for the space of two years.[96] And the said Nicholas (2d), being present in Court, acknowledged it, and places himself in the lord's grace. Therefore he is in mercy.

View of frank pledge held there the day and year as above[97]

William Sleford, tithing man[98] there [Streteham] with his tithing, presents on this day, as head tax, 3d Borgh silver,[99] the chief pledge being exempted.

Also he presents the default of John Atte Grene (2d), and William Colbrond (2d). Therefore they are in mercy.[100]

Also he presents that Richard Tubbynge (2d) is a tranter of ale. Therefore he is in mercy.

Also he presents that John Atte Grene (2d) is a common brewer, and has broken the assize. Therefore he is in mercy.

Further, a precept is made that John Burgeys be distrained to place himself in tithing before the next Court.[101]

William Crafte, tithing man there [Beek] with his tithing, presents on this day, as head tax, 11d Borgh silver, the chief pledge being exempted.

Also he presents that the king's highway called the Crosweye is flooded for lack of the scouring of Nicholas Cook's ditch. (Remitted.) Therefore he is in mercy. And a precept is made that he scour the said way before the next Court, on pain of 6s 8d.[102]

---

[93] The jury now makes its presentments.

[94] That is to say, William failed to appear.

[95] We can see here how a manorial jury could be held responsible for suppressing information.

[96] This is a very late date for labour services to be demanded and illustrates why the church as landlord was so unpopular.

[97] The court now moves into its public, criminal jurisdiction.

[98] Each manor was divided into tithings, groups of neighbours require to report on each others' misdemeanours. One of the tithing was elected each year to act as tithing man.

[99] Perhaps a pre-Conquest tax. These local poll taxes were not uncommon.

[100] The men had failed to appear at the court, an offence.

[101] It was an offence not to be in a tithing.

[102] That is to say, if he fails to scour the ditch by the next meeting of the court, he will be fined the above sum.

Also he presents that Simon Webbe (6s 8d) has encroached on the lord's demesne to the extent of one swath of meadow. Therefore he is, etc.

Nicholas Cook, ale-taster[103] there, presents that John Pykestone once (2d), Robert Crafte once (2d), John Morgone commonly (12d), and Nicholas Cook commonly (12d), have brewed and broken the assize. Therefore they are in mercy.

Nicholas Cook was removed from the office of ale-taster, and in his place John Atte Hethe was elected and sworn.

Affeerers
William Crafte   Richard Tylere[104]

Amount of this Court with view . . .[105]

---

[103] Whereas in Streteham the tithing man presented offences under the assize of ale, in [Tooting] Bec proper, there was a special (elected) officer of the court, the ale-taster.

[104] Affeerers assessed the level of amercements to be imposed on those found guilty by the homage jury.

[105] The amount was not filled in.

Chapter 2

Crime and Punishment
in the Sixteenth Century

1 The contemporary view on crime in Tudor England
(Extracts from the cony-catching pamphlets)

1.1 Extracts from Thomas Harman's Caveat for Common Cursitors (1566)[1]

Thomas Harman, a Kent JP, lived at Crayford near Dartford, close to London. For health reasons he was forced to live at home. There he interviewed many travellers passing his house. It was out of those enquiries that he wrote one of the earliest and most authoritative of the so-called cony-catching pamphlets. (A "cony" in common parlance was a rabbit, but in canting language, i.e. criminal argot, a victim.) The Caveat consists of a Preface and Epistle to the Reader followed by 23 descriptions of various categories of vagabond. To this is attached a list of vagabonds known to him, a glossary of canting language, and a fictional dialogue in the canting language. Spelling, punctuation and paragraphing have been modernized.

How Harman came by his material[2]

I have of late years gathered a great suspicion that all should not be well, and, as the proverb saith: "Something lurk and lay hid that did not plainly appear." For I, having more occasion, through sickness, to tarry and remain at home than I have been accustomed, do, by my there abiding, talk and confer daily with many of these wily wanderers of both sorts, as well men and women, as boys and girls, by whom I have gathered and understand their deep dissimulation and detestable dealing, being marvellous subtle and crafty in their kind, for not one amongst twenty will discover, either declare their scelerous secrets.[3] Yet with fair flattering words, money,

---

[1] The most accessible edition is in A. V. Judges (ed.), *The Elizabethan underworld* (London, 1930); there are long extracts in R. H. Tawney & Eileen Power (eds), *Tudor economic documents*, iii (1924).

[2] These sub-headings are the editor's and not in Harman's original.

[3] i.e. "will reveal or declare their wicked secrets".

and good cheer, I have attained to the type by such as the meanest of them hath wandered these thirteen years, and most sixteen and some twenty and upward, and not without faithful promise made unto them never to discover their names or anything they showed me. For they would all say, if the upright-men[4] should understand thereof, they should not be only grievously beaten, but put in danger of their lives, by the said upright-men.

There was a few years since a small briefs[5] set forth of some zealous man to his country, of whom I know not, that made a little show of their names and usage, and gave a glimpsing light, not sufficient to persuade, of their peevish, pelting, and picking practices, but well worthy of praise. But, ... with no less travail than good will, I have repaired and rigged the ship of knowledge, and have hoist up the sails of good fortune, that she may safely pass about and through all parts of this noble realm, and there make port sale of her wished wares, to the confusion of their drowsy demeanour and unlawful language, pilfering picking, wily wandering, and liking lechery of all these rabblement of rascals that ranges about all the coasts of the same, so that their undecent, doleful dealing and execrable exercises may appear to all, as it were in a glass. That thereby the Justices and shrieves [i.e. sheriffs] may in their circuits be more vigilant to punish these malefactors, and the constables, bailiffs and borseholders,[6] setting aside all fear, sloth, and pity, may be more circumspect in executing the charge given them by the aforesaid Justices.

Harman's list of the dangers to society from vagabondage

Then will no more this rascal rabblement range about the country; then greater relief may be showed to the poverty of each parish; then shall we keep our horses in our pastures unstolen; then our linen clothes shall and may lie safely on our hedges untouched; then shall we not have our clothes and linen hooked out at our windows as well by day as by night;[7] then shall we not have our houses broken up in the night, as of late one of my neighbours had, and two great bucks of clothes stolen out, and most of the same fine linen; then shall we safely keep our pigs and poultry from pilfering; then shall we surely pass by the highways leading to markets and fairs unharmed; then shall our shops and booths be unpicked and spoiled; then shall these uncomely companies be dispersed and set to labour for their living, or hastily hang for their demerits.

---

[4] Modern equivalent would be gang-leaders.
[5] Book.
[6] "Borseholder" was a Kent term for a tithingman; they were locally elected peace-keepers.
[7] See the Angler, below.

33

The advantages of getting rid of rogues

Then shall it encourage a great number of gentlemen and others, seeing this security, to set up houses and keep hospitality in the country, to the comfort of their neighbours, relief of the poor, and to the amendment of the commonwealth; then shall not sin and wickedness so much abound among us; then will God's wrath be much the more pacified towards us; then shall we not taste of so many and sundry plagues, as now daily reigneth over us; and then shall this famous empire be in more wealth and better flourish, to the inestimable joy and comfort of the Queen's most excellent Majesty, whom God of His infinite goodness, to His great glory, long and many years make most prosperously to reign over us, to the great felicity of all the peers and nobles, and to the unspeakable joy, relief, and quietness of mind of all her faithful commons and subjects. Now, methinketh, I see how these peevish, perverse, and pestilent people begin to fret, fume, swear, and stare at this my book, their life being laid open and apparently painted out, that their confusion and end draweth on apace. Whereas indeed, if it be well weighed, it is set forth for their singular profit and commodity, for the sure safeguard of their lives here in this world, that they shorten not the same before their time, and that by their true labour and good life, in the world to come they may save their souls, that Christ, the second Person in [the] Trinity, hath so dearly bought with His most precious blood. So that hereby I shall do them more good than they could have devised for themselves. For behold, their life being so manifest wicked and so apparently known, the honourable will abhor them, the worshipful will reject them, the yeomen will sharply taunt them, the husbandmen utterly defy them, the labouring men bluntly chide them, the women with a loud exclamation wonder at them, and all children with clapping hands cry out at them.

A Hooker, or Angler, according to Harman

These hookers, or anglers, be perilous and most wicked knaves, and be derived or proceed forth from the upright-men. They commonly go in frieze jerkins and gallyslops, pointed beneath the knee. These, when they practise their pilfering, it is all by night; for, as they walk a day-times from house to house to demand charity, they vigilantly mark where or in what place they may attain to their prey, casting their eyes up to every window, well noting what they see there, whether apparel or linen, hanging near unto the said windows, and that will they be sure to have the next night following. For they customably carry with them a staff of five or six foot long, in which, within one inch of the top thereof, is a little hole bored through, in which hole they put an iron hook, and with the same they will pluck unto them quickly anything that they may reach therewith, which hook in the day-time they covertly carry about them, and is never seen or taken out till they come to the place where they work their feat.[8]

Such have I seen at my house, and have oft talkest with them and have handled their staves, not then understanding to what use or intent they served, although I had and perceived by their talk and behaviour great likelihood of evil suspicion in them. They will either lean upon their staff, to hide the hole thereof, when they talk with you, or hold their hand upon the hole. And what stuff, either woollen or linen, they thus hook out, they never carry the same forthwith to their stalling kens, but hides the same a three days in some secret corner, and after conveys the same to their houses abovesaid, where their host or hostess giveth them money for the same, but half the value that it is worth, or else their doxies[9] shall afar off sell the same at the like houses.

I was credibly informed that a hooker came to a farmer's house in the dead of the night, and putting back a draw window of a low chamber, the bed standing hard by the said window, in which lay three persons (a man and two big boys), this hooker with his staff plucked off their garments which lay upon them to keep them warm, with the coverlet and sheet, and left them lying asleep naked saving their shirts, and had away all clean, and never could understand where it became. I verily suppose that when they were well waked with cold, they surely thought that Robin Goodfellow, according to the old saying, had been with them that night.

A Counterfeit-Crank according to Harman[10]

These that do counterfeit the crank be young knaves and young harlots, that deeply dissemble the falling sickness. For the crank in their language is the falling evil. I have seen some of these with fair writings testimonial, with the names and seals of some men of worship in Shropshire and in other shires far off, that I have well known, and have taken the same from them. Many of these do go without writings,[11] and will go half naked, and look most piteously.[12] And if any clothes be given them, they immediately

---

[8] The method described here is still in use, as revealed in 1996 video-recording which showed two crooks, working at night, poking a pole with a hook on the end of it through the letter box of a clothing store and yanking out garments from a display unit.

[9] Women-folk.

[10] One who pretends to be epileptic.

[11] i.e. without licences to beg.

[12] Shakespeare provides a graphic picture of such beggars when Edgar, the wronged son of the earl of Gloucester, is forced to disguise himself as a madman.

> While I may 'scape
> I will preserve myself; and am bethought
> To take the basest and most poorest shape
> That ever penury, in contempt of man,
> Brought near to beast; my face I'll grime with filth,

sell the same, for wear it they will not, because they would be the more pitied, and wear filthy cloths on their heads, and never go without a piece of white soap about them, which, if they see cause or present gain, they will privily convey the same into their mouth, and so work the same there, that they will foam as it were a boar, and marvellously for a time torment themselves. And thus deceive they the common people, and gain much. These have commonly their harlots as the other.

1.2   The case of Nicholas Jennings, London, 1566

This very detailed account, also taken from Harman's Caveat, is the best we have of such criminals. It illustrates the skill and success of such counterfeit-cranks as also the ramshackle law-enforcement of Tudor London.

Upon All-Hallows Day in the morning last, Anno Domini 1566,[13] or [ere = before] my book was half printed, I mean the first impression, there came early in the morning a counterfeit-crank under my lodging at the Whitefriars, within the cloister in a little yard or court, whereabouts lay two or three great ladies, being without the liberties of London, whereby he hoped for the greater gain.[14]

This crank there lamentably lamenting and pitifully crying to be relieved, declared to divers there his painful and miserable disease. I being risen and not half ready, heard his doleful words and rueful moanings; hearing him name the falling sickness, thought assuredly to myself that he was a deep dissembler. So, coming out at a sudden, and beholding his ugly and irksome attire, his loathsome and horrible countenance, it made me in a marvellous perplexity what to think of him, whether it were feigned or truth. For after this manner went he: he was naked from the waist upward, saving he had a old jerkin of leather patched, and that was loose about him, that all his body lay out bare. A filthy foul cloth he wear

---

Blanket my loins, elf all my hair in knots,
And with presented nakedness outface
The winds and persecutions of the sky.
The country gives me proof and precedent
Of Bedlam beggars, who with roaring voices,
Strike in their numb'd and mortified bare arms
Pins, wooden pricks, nails, sprigs of rosemary;
And with this horrible object, from low farms
Poor pelting villages, sheep-cotes, and mills,
Sometime with lunatic bans, sometime with prayers,
Enforce their charity. Poor Turleygood! poor Tom!
King Lear, Act 2, sc. 3. See also Act 3, sc. 4 and 6.

[13] 1 November 1566.
[14] He selected a place outside of the City's jurisdiction.

on his head, being cut for the purpose, having a narrow place to put out his face, with a bauer made to truss up his beard, and a string that tied the same down close about his neck; with an old felt hat which he still carried in his hand to receive the charity and devotion of the people for that would he hold out from him; having his face from the eyes downward, all smeared with fresh blood, as though he had new fallen, and been tormented with his painful pangs, his jerkin being all berayed with dirt and mire, and his hat and hosen also, as though he had wallowed in the mire. Surely the sight was monstrous and terrible.

I called him unto me, and demanded of him what he ailed.

"Ah, good master," quoth he, "I have the grievous and painful disease called the falling sickness."

"Why," quoth I, "how cometh thy jerkin, hose and hat so berayed with dirt and mire, and thy skin also?"

"Ah, good master, I fell down on the back-side here in the foul lane hard by the waterside; and there I lay almost all night, and have bled almost all the blood out in my body."

It rained that morning very fast; and, while I was thus talking with him, a honest poor woman that dwelt thereby brought him a fair linen cloth, and bid him wipe his face therewith, and there being a tub standing full of rain-water, offered to give him some in a dish that he might make himself clean. He refuseth the same.

"Why dost thou so?" quoth I.

"Ah, sir," saith he, "if I should wash myself, I should fall to bleeding afresh again, and then I should not stop myself."

These words made me the more to suspect him. Then I asked of him where he was born, what his name was, how long he had this disease, and what time he had been here about London, and in what place.

"Sir," saith he, "I was born at Leicester. My name is Nicholas Jennings; and I have had this falling sickness eight years, and I can get no remedy for the same; for I have it by kind. My father had it, and my friends before me; and I have been these two years here about London, and a year and a half in Bethlem."[15]

"Why? Wast thou out of thy wits?" quoth I.

"Yea, sir, that I was."

"What is the keeper's name of the house?"

"His name is," quoth he, "John Smith."

"Then," quoth I, "he must understand of thy disease. If thou hadst the same for the time thou wast there, he knoweth it well."

"Yea, not only he, but all the house beside," quoth this crank, "for I came thence but within this fortnight."

---

[15] Bedlam, the London hospital for the insane, was located just outside the precincts of the City at Bishop's Gate.

I had stand so long reasoning the matter with him that I was a-cold, and went into my chamber and made me ready. And [I] commanded my servant to repair to Bethlem, and bring me true word from the keeper there whether any such man hath been with him as a prisoner having the disease aforesaid, and gave him a note of his name and the keeper's also. My servant, returning to my lodging, did assure me that neither was there ever any such man there, neither yet any keeper of any such name. But he that was there keeper, he sent me his name in writing, affirming that he letteth no man depart from him unless he be fet [i.e. fetched] away by his friends, and that none that came from him beggeth about the City.

Then I sent for the printer of this book, and showed him of this dissembling crank, and how I had sent to Bethlem to understand the truth, and what answer I received again, requiring him that I might have some servant of his to watch him faithfully that day, that I might understand trustily to what place he would repair at night unto; and thither I promised to go myself to see their order, and that I would have him to associate me thither.

He gladly granted to my request, and sent two boys, that both diligently and vigilantly accomplished the charge given them, and found the same crank about the Temple, whereabout the most part of the day he begged, unless it were about twelve of the clock he went on the backside of Clement's Inn without Temple Bar. There is a lane that goeth into the fields. There he renewed his face again with fresh blood, which he carried about him in a bladder, and daubed on fresh dirt upon his jerkin, hat and hosen, and so came back again unto the Temple, and sometime to the waterside, and begged of all that passed by. The boys beheld how some gave groats,[16] some sixpence, some gave more. For he looked so ugly and irksomely, that every one pitied his miserable case that beheld him. To be short, there he passed all the day till night approached.

And when it began to be somewhat dark, he went to the waterside, and took a sculler, and was set over the water into St George's Fields, contrary to my expectation, for I had thought he would have gone into Holborn, or to St Giles in the Field.[17] But these boys, with Argus' and lynxes' eyes, set sure watch upon him, and the one took a boat and followed him, and the other went back to tell his master.

The boy that so followed him by water, had no money to pay for his boat hire, but laid his penner and his inkhorn to gage for a penny. And by that time the boy was set over, his master, with all celerity, had taken a boat and followed him apace. Now had they still a sight of the crank, which crossed over the fields towards Newington.[18] And thither he went,

---

[16] A silver coin worth four pence. Six pence would be a good day's wages for a labourer.
[17] They were across the river to the west of Southwark.
[18] Newington was a village to the south of Southwark.

and by that time they came thither it was very dark. The printer had there no acquaintance, neither any kind of weapon about him; neither knew he how far the crank would go, because he then suspected that they dogged him of purpose. He there stayed him [i.e. the printer arrested the crank], and called for the Constable, which came forth diligently to inquire what the matter was. This zealous printer charged this officer with him as a malefactor and a dissembling vagabond. The Constable would have laid him all night in the cage that stood in the street.[19]

"Nay," saith this pitiful printer, "I pray you have him into your house. For this is like to be a cold night, and he is naked. You keep a victualling house. Let him be well cherished this night, for he is well able to pay for the same. I know well his gains hath been great to-day and your house is a sufficient prison for the time, and we will there search him."

The Constable agreed thereunto. They had him in, and caused him to wash himself. That done, they demanded what money he had about him.

Saith this crank, "So God help me, I have but twelve pence," and plucked out the same of a little purse.

"Why, have you no more?" quoth they.

"No," saith this crank, "as God shall save my soul at the day of judgment."

"We must see more," quoth they, and began to strip him. Then he plucked out another purse, wherein was forty pence. "Tush," saith this printer, "I must see more."

Saith this crank, "I pray God I be damned both body and soul if I have any more."

"No," saith this printer, "Thou false knave; here is my boy that did watch thee all this day, and saw when such men gave thee pieces of six-pence, groats, and other money. And yet thou hast showed us none but small money."

When this crank heard this, and the boy vowing it to his face, he relented, and plucked out another purse, wherein was eight shillings and odd money. So had they in the whole that he had begged that day 13s 3½d. Then they stripped him stark naked, and as many as saw him said they never saw a handsomer man, with a yellow flaxen beard, and fair-skinned, without any spot or grief. Then the good wife of the house fet her goodman's old cloak, and caused the same to be cast about him, because the sight should not abash her shame fast maidens, neither loath her squeamish sight.

Thus he set him down at the chimney's end, and called for a pot of beer, and drank off a quart at a draft, and called for another, and so the third, that one had been sufficient for any reasonable man, the drink was so strong. I myself the next morning tasted thereof.

---

[19] The cage was a primitive open-air lock-up.

But let the reader judge what and how much he would have drunk and he had been out of fear! Then when they had thus wrung water out of a flint in spoiling him of his evil-gotten goods his passing pence, and fleeting trash, the printer with this officer were in jolly jealousy, and devised to search a barn for some rogues and upright-men, a quarter of a mile from the house, that stood alone in the fields, and went out about their business, leaving this crank alone with his wife and maidens. This crafty crank, espying all gone, requested the good wife that he might go out on the back-side to make water, and to exonerate his paunch. She bade him draw the latch of the door and go out, neither thinking or mistrusting he would have gone away naked. But, to conclude, when he was out, he cast away the cloak, and, as naked as ever he was born, he ran away over the fields to his own house, as he afterwards said.

Now the next morning betimes, I went unto Newington, to understand what was done, because I had word or it was day that there my printer was. And at my coming thither I heard the whole circumstance, as I above have written. And I, seeing the matter so fall out, took order with the chief of the parish that this 13s 3½d might the next day be equally distributed by their good discretions to the poverty [i.e. the poor] of the same parish, whereof this crafty crank had part himself, for he had both house and wife in the same parish, as after you shall hear.

But this lewd loiterer could not lay his bones to labour, having got once the taste of this lewd lazy life, for all this fair admonition, but devised other subtle sleights to maintain his idle living, and so craftily clothed himself in mariners' apparel, and associated himself with another of his companions. They, having both mariners' apparel, went abroad to ask charity of the people, feigning they had lost their ship with all their goods by casualty on the seas, wherewith they gained much. This crafty crank, fearing to be mistrusted, fell to another kind of begging, as bad or worse, and apparelled himself very well with a fair black frieze coat, a new pair of white hose, a fine felt hat on his head, a shirt of Flanders work esteemed to be worth sixteen shillings, and upon New Year's Day came again into the Whitefriars to beg.

The printer, having occasion to go that ways, not thinking of this crank, by chance met with him, who asked his charity for God's sake. The printer, viewing him well, did mistrust him to be the counterfeit-crank which deceived him upon All-Hallows Day at night, demanded of whence he was, and what was his name.

"Forsooth," saith he, "my name is Nicholas Jennings, and I came from Leicester to seek work, and I am a hat-maker by my occupation, and all my money is spent; and if I could get money to pay for my lodging this night, I would seek work to-morrow amongst the hatters."

The printer, perceiving his deep dissimulation, putting his hand into his purse, seeming to give him some money, and with fair allusions brought him into the street, where he charged the Constable with him, affirming him to be the counterfeit-crank that ran away upon All-Hallows Day last. The Constable being very loath to meddle with him, but the printer knowing him and his deep deceit, desired he might be brought before the Deputy of the Ward,[20] which straight was accomplished, which when he came before the Deputy, he demanded of him whence he was, and what was his name. He answered as before he did unto the printer. The Deputy asked the printer what he would lay unto his charge. He answered and alleged him to be a vagabond and deep deceiver of the people, and the counterfeit-crank that ran away upon All-Hallows Day last from the Constable of Newington and him, and requested him earnestly to send him to ward [i.e. prison]. The Deputy, thinking him to be deceived, but nevertheless laid his commandment upon him, so that the printer should bear his charges if he could not justify it. He agreed thereunto. And so he and the Constable went to carry him to the Counter.[21] And as they were going under Ludgate, this crafty crank took his heels and ran down the hill as fast as he could drive, the Constable and the printer after him as fast as they could. But the printer of the twain being lighter of foot, overtook him at Fleet Bridge, and with strong hand carried him to the Counter, and safely delivered him.

In the morrow, the printer sent his boy that stripped him upon All-Hallows Day at night to view him, because he would be sure, which boy knew him very well. This crank confessed unto the Deputy that he had hosted the night before in Kent Street in Southwark, at the sign of The Cock, which thing to be true, the printer sent to know, and found him a liar; but further enquiring, at length found out his habitation, dwelling in Master Hill's rents,[22] having a pretty house, well stuffed, with a fair joint-table, and a fair cupboard garnished with pewter, having an old ancient woman to his wife. The printer being sure thereof, repaired unto the Counter, and rebuked him for his beastly behaviour, and told him of his false feigning, willed him to confess it, and ask forgiveness. He perceived him to know his deep dissimulation, relented, and confessed all his deceit.

And so remaining in the Counter three days, [he] was removed to Bridewell,[23] where he was stripped stark naked, and his ugly attire put upon him before the masters thereof, who wondered greatly at his dissimulation. For which offence he stood upon the pillory in Cheapside, both in his ugly and handsome attire.[24] And after that went in the mill while his ugly picture was a drawing.[25] And then [he] was whipped at a

---

[20] A local peace-keeping officer in the City of London.
[21] A London prison.
[22] In property owned by Master Hill.
[23] The London prison dealing with vagabonds.
[24] Good example of a shaming punishment.
[25] The "mill" was probably a treadmill.

cart's tail through London, and his displayed banner carried before him unto his own door and so back to Bridewell again, and there remained for a time, and at length let at liberty, on that condition he would prove an honest man, and labour truly to get his living. And his picture remaineth in Bridewell for a monument.

1.3   Robert Greene on crime in Elizabethan London

Robert Greene was one of a number of London writers who wrote about "professional" criminals. These extracts from his A Notable discovery of Coosenage now daily practised by sundry lewd persons *published in 1592 gives a good idea of the complexity and alleged specialism of London criminals. It also demonstrates the way "crime" had already become "entertainment". Spelling and punctuation have been modernized.*

Greene's categorization of crime in London[26]

A table of the words of art used in the effecting these base villainies wherein is discovered the nature of every term, being proper to none but to the professors thereof.

High law	robbing by the highway side
Sacking law	lechery
Cheating law	play at false dice
Cross-biting law	cozenage by whores
Cony-catching law	cozenage by cards
Versing law	cozenage by false gold
Figging law	cutting of purses, & picking of pockets
Barnard's law	a drunken cozenage by cards

These are the eight laws of villainy, leading the high way to infamy.

In High Law

The thief is called a *high lawyer*. He that setteth the watch, a *scrippet*. He that standeth to watch, an *oake*. He that is robbed, the *martin*. When he yeeldeth, *stooping*.

---

[26] His object is to demonstrate that these professional London criminals had their own specialized language, called elsewhere "canting".

In Sacking Law

The bawd if it be a woman, a *pander*; the bawd, if a man, an *apple squire*; the whore, a *commodity*; the whore house, a *trugging place*.

In Cross-Biting Law

The whore, the *traffic*; the man that is brought in, the *simpler*; the villainies that take them, the *cross-biters*.

In Cony-Catching Law

The party that taketh up the connie, the *setter*. He that plaieth the game, the *verser*; he that is coosned, the *connie*; he that comes in to them, the *barnackle*; the money that is won, *purchase*.

In Versing Law

He that bringeth him in, the *verser*; the poor country man, the *cousin*; and the drunkard that comes in, the *suffier*.

In Figging Law

The cutpurse, a *nip*; he that is half with him, the *snap*; the knife, the *cuttle boung*; the pick pocket, a *foin*; he that faceth the man, the *stale*; taking the purse, *drawing*; spying of him, *smoking*; the purse, the *bong*; the money, the *shells*;[27] the act doing, *striking*.

In Barnard's Law

He that fetcheth the man, the *taker*; he that is taken in, the *cousin*; the landed man, the *verser*; the drunken man, the *barnard*; and he that makes the fray, the *rutter*.

These quaint terms do these base arts use to shadow their villainy withal: for, *multa latent quae non patent*, obscuring their filthy crafts with these faire colours, that the ignorant may not espy what their subtilty is. But their end will be like their beginning, hatched with Cain, and consumed with Jadas [? Judas]. And so bidding them adieu to the devil, and you farewell to God, I end.

---

[27] We still talk about "shelling out for meal", meaning to pay for a meal.

Greene on cony-catching

Introduction to cony-catching[28]

Thus are the poor conies robbed by these base minded caterpillars. Thus are serving men oft enticed to play, and lose all. Thus are apprentices induced to be Conies, and so are cozened of their masters' money, yea young gentlemen, merchants, and others, are fetched in by these damnable rakehels, a plague as ill as hell, which is, present loss of money, & ensuing misery. A lamentable case in England, when such vipers are suffered to breed and are not cut off with the sword of justice.

This enormity is not only in London, but now generally dispersed through all England, in every shire, city, and town of any receipt, and many complaints are heard of their egregious cozenage.

The poor farmer simply going about his business, or unto his attorney's chamber, is catcht [i.e. caught] up & cozened of all. The serving-man sent with his Lord's treasure, loseth oft times most part to these worms of the commonwealth, the apprentice having his master's money in charge, is spoiled by them, and from an honest servant either driven to run away, or to live in discredit for ever. The gentleman loseth his land, the merchant his stock, and all to these abominable cony-catchers, whose means is as ill as their living, for they are all either wedded to whores, or so addicted to whores, that what they get from honest men, they spend in bawdy houses among harlots, and consume it as vainly as they get it villainously. Their ears are of adamant, as pitiless as they are trecherous, for be the man never so poor, they will not return him one penny of his loss.

The tale of the Suffolk shoemaker

Near to Bury St Edmunds in Suffolk, there dwelt an honest man a shoemaker, that having some twenty marks[29] in his purse, long a-gathering, and nearly kept, came to the market to buy a dicker of hides,[30] and by chance fell among cony-catchers, whose names I omit, because I hope of their amendment. This plain countryman drawn in by these former devises was made a cony, and so straight stripped of all his 20 marks, to his utter undoing. The knaves escaped, and he went home a sorrowful man.

Shortly after, one of these cony-catchers was taken for a suspected person, and laid in Bury gaol, the sessions coming, and he produced to the bar.[31] It was the fortune of this poor shoemaker to be there, who

---

[28] The cony is the victim.

[29] 20 marks had the same value as £13 13s 4d, the equivalent of three times a wage-labourer's annual wage.

[30] A dicker of hides was ten hides.

[31] The Quarter Sessions came and he was called to the bar, i.e. brought to trial.

spying this rogue to be arraigned, was glad, and said nothing unto him, but looked what would be the issue of his appearance. At the last he was brought before the Justices, where he was examined of his life, and being demanded what occupation he was, said none.

"What profession then are you of, how live you?"

"Marry," quoth he, "I am a gentleman, and live of my friends."

"Nay that is a lie," quoth the poor shoemaker, "under correction of the worshipful of the bench, you have a trade, and are by your art a cony-catcher."

"A cony-catcher," said one of the Justices, and smiled, "what is he, a warriner, fellow? Whose warren keepeth he, canst thou tell?"

"Nay, sir, your worship mistaketh me," quod the shoemaker, "he is not a wariner, but a conycatcher."

The bench, that never heard this name before, smiled, attributing the name to the man's simplicity, thought he meant a warriner, which the shoemaker spying, answered, that some conies this fellow caught, were worth twenty mark a peece, and for proof quoth he, I am one of them. And so discoursed the whole order of the art, and the baseness of the cosening.

Whereupon the Justices looking into his life, appointed him to be whipped, and the shoemaker desired that he might give him his payment, which was granted. When he came to his punishment, the shoemaker laughed, saying, tis a mad world when poor conies are able to beat their catchers, but he lent him so friendly lashes, that almost he made him pay an ounce of blood for every pound of silver.

1.4 *Greene on the art of cross-biting*

Introduction to cross-biting

The cross-biting law is a public profession of shameless cozenage, mixt with incestuous whoredomes, as ill as was practised in Gomorha or Sodom, though not after the same unnatural manner. For the method of their mischievous art (with blushing cheeks & trembling heart let it be spoken) is, that these villainous vipers, unworthy the name of men, base rogues (yet why do I term them so well) being outcasts from God, vipers of the world, and an excremental reversion of sin, doth consent, nay constrain their wives to yield the use of their bodies to other men, that taking them together, he may cross-bite the party of all the crowns he can presently make, and that the world may see their monstrous practises, I will briefly set down the manner.

They have sundry preys that they call *simplers*, which are men fondly and wantonly given, whom for a penalty of their lust, they fleece of all that ever they have. Some merchants, apprentices, servingmen, gentlemen, yeomen, farmers, and all degrees, and this is their form. There are resident in London & the suburbs, certain men attired like gentlemen, brave fellows, but basely minded, who living in want, as their last refuge, fall unto this cross-biting law and to maintain themselves, either marry with some stale whore, or else forsooth keep one as their friend. And these persons be commonly men of the eight laws before rehearsed: either *high lawyers, versers, nips, cony-catchers*, or such of the like fraternity.

These when their other trades fail, as the *cheater*, when he has no cousin to grime with his stop dice, or the *high lawyer*, when he hath no set match to ride about, and the *nip* when there is no term, [i.e. law term], fair,[32] nor time of great assembly, then to maintain the main chance, they use the benefit of their wives or friends, to the cross-biting of such as lust after their filthy enormities.

Some simple men are drawn on by subtle means, which never intended such a bad matter. In summer evenings, and in the winter nights, these *traffics*, these common truls I mean, walk abroad either in the fields or streets that are commonly haunted, as stales to draw men into hell, and afar of, as attending *apple squires*. Certain *cross-biters* stand aloof, as if they knew them not; now so many men so many affections. Some unruly mates that place their content in lust, letting slip the liberty of their eyes on their painted faces, feed upon their unchaste beauties, till their hearts be set on fire. Then come they to these minions, and court them with many sweet words.

Alas their loves needs no long suits, for they are forthwith entertained, and either they go to the tavern to seal up the match with a pottle of Ipocras,[33] or straight she carries him to some bad place, and there picks his pocket, or else the *cross-biters* comes swearing in, & so out-face the dismayed companion, that rather then he would be brought in question, he would disburse all that he hath present. But this is but an easy cosnage. . . .

Now sir comes by a country farmer, walking from his inn to perform some business, and seeing such a gorgeous damsel, he wondering at such a brave wench, stands staring her on the face, or perhaps doth but cast a glance, and bid her good speed, as plain simple swains have their lusty humours as well as others. The trull straight beginning her exordium with a smile, saith, "How now, my friend, what want you? Would you speak with any body here?" If the fellow have any bold spirit, perhaps he will offer the wine, & then he is caught, tis enough.

In he goes, and they are chambered. Then sends she for her husband, or her friend, and there either the farmer's pocket is stripped, or else the

---

[32] Notorious places then as now for petty crime.
[33] Hippocras: a spiced wine.

46

cross-biters fall upon him, and threaten him with Bridewell[34] and the law. Then for fear he gives them all in his purse, and makes them some bill to pay a sum of money at a certain day.[35]

2   Crime & punishment in Tudor London

2.1   Cases from the London chronicles

Crime was a continuing fascination for London's chroniclers.

Poisonings

And this year [1518/19] was a man sodden in a cautherne [i.e. boiled in a caldron] in Smithfield, and let up and down divers times til he was dead, for because he would have poisoned divers persons.

And this year [1533/4] was a cook boiled in a caldron in Smithfield for he would have poisoned the bishop of Rochester, Fisher with divers of his servants, and he was locked in a chain and pulled up and down with a gibbet at divers times til he was dead.

And the 10 day of March [1543] was a maid boiled in Smithfield for poisoning of divers persons.[36]

Vagabondage

The 13 January [1552] was whipped seven women at the carts' arse, four at one and three at another, for vagabonds that would not labour, but play the unthrift.[37]

Deception

The 9 December [1552] there was one Anthony Fowlkes, a gentleman, set in the pillory in Cheap [London], and had his ear nailed to the pillory, for deceiving certain citizens . . . And for his deceipt he was judged by my Lord Mayor and Alderman at a court at the Guild Hall . . . to have this penance. And when he had stood on the pillory til the clock was past 12, he would not rent his ear [off] but one of the beadles slit it upwards with a penknife to loosen it, and so he was had to prison again for two days after.[38]

---

[34] A London prison.
[35] Gives an I. O. U.
[36] J. G. Nicholas, *Grey Friars chronicle of London* (1851), pp. 30, 35, 45.
[37] *Ibid*, p. 73.
[38] W. D. Hamilton, *Wriothesley's chronicle*, ii, 80 (spelling modernized).

False marriage

And at that time [1538] was drawn from the Tower the lady Margaret Bowmer wife unto Sir John Bowmer, and he made her his wife, but she was the wife of one Cheyny, for he [i.e. Cheyny] sold her unto Sir Bowmer. And she was drawn when she came to Newgate into Smithfield [i.e. she was drawn on a hurdle from the one place to the other], and there burned the same fore-noon.[39]

Rape

This 12 of December [1552] at the Sessions of Gaol Delivery held at Newgate, Nicholas Ballard, gentleman, which in August last past was punished for an adulterer with one Myddlton's wife, and after sent to Newgate [a London prison] for a rape, . . . was this day araigned for the said rape, . . . and by a jury this day found guilty of the rape . . . And after verdict given against him he asked the benefit of his book [i.e. he claimed benefit of clergy], and read, and so was burnt in the hand and had to the bishop's convict prison.[40]

Incest

Item the last day of July and the first of August [1551] rode in a cart a tailor of Fleet Street and his sister rode on a cart about London, and both [had] their heads shaven for avoutry [normally means "adultery" but in this case "incest"], that he had two children by her. And the third day was banished [from] the city both; but he would have given much to be excused, but it would not be taken.[41]

Fornication

The first day of June [1553] was set up at the Standard in Cheap a "pillar" new made of a good length from the ground, and two young servants tied unto it with a chain that they might go about it [i.e. might be secured to the pillar], and [the] two beaten with rods sore on their backs for because they had two wenches in to their master's house; and on the morrow after, which was the Sunday, and then was [*sic* were] two other in the same case beaten at the same pillar, and so as many as pleased the Mayor after-wards, etc.[42]

---

[39] A harsh punishment by any standard. Her "husband" Sir John was hanged and then beheaded. *Grey Friars chronicle of London*, pp. 40–41.
[40] *Wriotheseley's chronicle*, ii, pp. 64–5 (spelling modernized).
[41] *Grey Friars chronicle of London*, p. 70.
[42] *Grey Friars chronicle of London*, p. 78.

Prostitution

The 6 July 1548 there was a single woman called Founsinge Besse which was a whore of the stews, and, after the putting down of them,[43] was taken and banished out of divers wards of this city. And now taken in a garden by Finsbury Court with one of the King's trumpeters. Which for her vicious living not yet amended was had to the Counter[44] in Bread Street, and from thence was led with basons "tynged" afore her into Cheap afore the Standard. And there [she was] set on the pillory, her hair cut off by the ears and a paper [i.e. a notice] set on her breast declaring her viscious living. And so [she] stood from ten of the clock til eleven, which punishment hath been an old and ancient law in this city [i.e. London] of long time and now put in use again.[45]

Offences committed in the Royal Court[46]

Offences committed in the Royal Court were subject to direct royal justice. When Henry VIII's favourite archer slew a servant within the Palace of Westminster, he was hanged there and then on specially constructed gallows. And as we can see from the case below, when Sir Thomas Knevett struck a Master Cleere within the court, he was ordered to have his own hand amputated.

The King's master cook [was] ready with his knife to have done the execution, and the serjeant of the scullery with his mallet, the irons laid in the fire to have seared him, and the King's Master Surgeon with the searing clothe ready. And when the execution should have been done the King sent Mr Long to stay it till after dinner, and then the officers of household sate again, and then the King pardoned him.[47]

2.2   *London cases from Machyn's* Diary[48]

Machyn was a London Merchant Tailor. He was probably a funeral furnisher, and most of his diary consists of descriptions of funerals. But he does interleave these descriptions with notes inter alia on crime and punishment, a selection of which are given below. The headings are the editor's.

The printed transcript gives the original, often idiosyncratic spelling of the author. This I have modernized to assist intelligibility. Roman numerals have

---

[43] The Southwark brothels were closed down in the 1540s.
[44] A London prison.
[45] *Wriotheseley's chronicle*, ii, p. 4.
[46] A. H. Thomas & I. D. Thornley, *The great chronicle of London* (1938), p. 379.
[47] *Wriothesely's chronicle*, i, p. 125. There is no doubting direct royal authority here.
[48] J. G. Nicholas (ed.), *The diary of Henry Machyn*, "Camden Soc.", xlii (1848).

*been rendered into Arabic numerals or English words as appropriate. The word
"care" is used frequently and I have rendered it as "cart".*

Shaming punishments

*Shaming punishments seem to have been an important part of the London penal
system until the third quarter of the sixteenth century. The "ridings" – sitting on
a horse the wrong way round – echoes later reports of "skimmingtons", where
neighbours mocked a cuckolded husband by treating him in the same way. Note
too the use of beating of "basins", so-called "rough music".*

For cruelty to a maid servant (1552)

The 16th day of April rode through London in a cart, a woman with a
banner painted with a young damsel and a woman, with a card in the
woman's hand carding her maid naked painted, the which she left but
little skin of her; and about her mistress's neck a card hanging down for
this punishment her mistress had of her. And she was carted unto her own
door in a cart, and there was proclamation [made] of her shameful deed-
doing, of the which the damsel is like to die (p. 17).
(A "card" was a shaped wooden instrument with many pins inset into it,
used to straighten or "card" wool.)

Deception (1552)

The 17th of June there were set in the pillory [a man and] a woman. The
woman bought a piece of mutton [and when she] had it, she took a piece
of a tile and thrust it into the midst of the mutton, and she said that she
had it off the butcher and would have him punished. For it was hanged
over the pillory and so there were they set both (p. 21).

City officer for committing bawdry (1552/3)

The 3rd day of March rode in a cart one of the Beadles of the Beggars,
for bawdry, dwelling in Saint Bartholomew Lane beside my Lord Mayor
(p. 32).

A riding (1553/4)

The 7th day of March rode a butcher round about London, his face
towards the horse tail, with half a lamb before and another behind, and
veal and a calf borne before him on a pole, raw (p. 57).

Riding a whore (1557)

The 7th day of December there was a woman rode in a cart for whoredom and bawdry (p. 160).

Riding a horse (1557)

The 10th day of December there rode a man through London, his face towards the horse's tail (p. 161).

Whipping and shaming of a whore (1557)

The 17th day of December did ride in a cart a young man and a woman, the wife of John a badoo the bawd. And she was the bawd and she was whipped at the cart's arse, and the harlot did beat her, and an old harlot of three score [i.e. 60] and more led the horse, like an old whore (p. 161).

Procuring a child (1559/60)

The 22nd of March did ride in a cart, with a basin tingling afore, two that rode about London that came out of Southwark, for the woman was bawd to a girl of eleven year old, and brought her to a stranger (p. 228).

Brother/sister incest (1560)

The 12th day of June did ride in a cart about London two men and three women: one man was for he was the bawd, and to bring women unto strangers; and one woman was the wife of [the landlord of] the Bell in Gratious Street, and another the wife of [the landlord of] the Bull's Head beside London Stone, and both were bawds and whores; and the other man and woman were brother and sister, and were taken naked together (p. 238).

Bawd to daughter and maid (1560)

The 28th day of June did ride in a cart about London Mistress Warner, sometime the wife of Master Warner sometime Serjeant of the Admiralty, for bawdry to her daughter and [her] maid, and both the daughter and maid [were] with child, and she a whore (p. 239).

The 10th day of August was buried within the Tower . . . my Lady Warner the wife of Sir Edward Warner (p. 241).

A riding (1560/61)

The 29th day of January did ride about London, his face towards the horse-tail, . . . and selling of measly bacon (p. 248).

The 31st day of January the same man was set on the pillory and two great pieces of measly bacon hanging over his head, and a writing [put] up that a two year ago he was punished for [the] same offence for the like thing (p. 248).

Three in a bed (1563)

The 16th day of June did ride in a cart to the Guild Hall Doctor Langton the physician in a gown of damask line with velvet . . . and a cap of velvet, and he had pinned a blue hood on his cap, and so came through Cheapside on the market day, and so about London, for he was taken with two young wenches ["wenches young" in orig.] at once (p. 309).

Suicides

Suicide was a felony. Are these accounts here because suicide was so rare at that time, or are they here simply because they are the more remarkable cases? We don't know. Note the number of young male suicides.

1556

The 16th day of April, early in the morning did Vyntoner, servant at the Sign of the Swan, . . . did hang himself in a gutter on high (p. 103).

1561

The same day [1 May] at afternoon did Master Godderyke's son, the gold smith go up to his father's guilding-house, took a bow-string and hanged himself at the Sign of the Unicorn in Cheapside (p. 258).

1562

The same day [25 May] was a young man did hang himself at the Polles Head, the inn in Carter Lane (p. 283).

Miscellaneous cases

It is the matter-of-fact reporting of these cases and punishments which is so remarkable to modern ears. Nowhere does Machyn give any hint that he thinks the punishments too harsh.

James Ellis (1552)

The same day [30 April] was Sessions at Newgate for thieves and a cut-purse especially was for one James [Ellis], the great pickpurse and cutpurse that ever was arraigned, for there was never a prison and the Tower but he had been in them (p. 18).

The 9th day of July was hanged one James Ellis, the great pickpurse that ever was and cutpurse, and seven more for theft, at Tyburn (p. 22).

Fraud (1552)

The first day of July there was a man and a woman on the pillory in Cheapside. The man sold pots of strawberries, the which the pot was not half-full, but filled with fern (p. 21).

Breaking rope saves felon (1552/3)

The 3rd day of January was carted from the Marshelsea unto Saint Thomas of Watering a tall man, and went thither with the rope about his neck. And so he hanged a while and the rope burst, and a while after and then they went for another rope, and so likewise he burst it [and fell] to the ground. And so he escaped with his life (p. 30).

Woman poisoner (1552/3)

The 13th day of January was put upon the pillory a woman for she would have poisoned her husband dwelling within the Paul's bakehouse, and the 14th day she was whipped at a cart-arse, and naked upward, and the 18th day following she was again upon the pillory for slandering (pp. 29–30).

Collared and chained (1553)

The 30th day of June was set a post hard by the Standard in Cheap, and a young fellow tied to the post [with a collar] of iron about his neck and another to the post with [a chain; and] two men with two whips whipping him about the post [for pretended] visions and for opprobrious and seditious words (p. 34).

Conspiracy to murder (1555/6)

The Friday the 7th day of March was hanged in chains[49] beside Huntingdon one Conears, and Spenser afterward, for the killing of a gentleman; and

---

[49] The body being left exposed as a further punishment.

53

there beside where they hang, the which one Benett Smith did promised and hired them, and promised them £10 to do that deed (p. 102).

The 9th day of March was hanged at Brickhill, Benett Smith, in Buckinghamshire, for the death of Master Rufford gentleman, the which Conears and Spenser slew (p. 102).

The 27th day of March was hanged beyond Huntingdon, in chains, one Spenser, for the death of Master Rufford of Buckinghamshire, by [i.e. besides] his fellow Conears hangs (p. 103).

Deception (1556)

The 17th day of April was one on the pillory for falsely deceiving of the Queen's subjects selling of rings for gold, and was neither silver nor gold but copper, the which he has deceived money [? many]. This was done in Cheap (p. 103).

Hangman hanged (1556)

The 2nd day of July was rode in a cart five unto Tyburn [i.e. the place of execution]. One was the hangman with the stump-leg – for theft. The which he had hanged many a man and quartered many, and had many a noble man and other (p. 109).

Instant mutilation for attacking a witness (1556)

The 16th day of December was the Sessions at Newgate. And there was one John Boneard and one Gregory a Spaniard, smith arraigned for a robbery that they would have done to Alexander, the Keeper of Newgate. And there was one that gave evidence against them that Gregory had a knife, and he did thrust into the man before the judges. And after he was cast [i.e. condemned]. And continent [i.e. forthwith] there was a gibbet set up at the Sessions's gate, and there his right hand stricken off and nailed upon the gibbet, and continent he was hanged up. And Boneard was burned in the hand [i.e. branded] And Gregory hanged all night naked (pp. 121–2).

Female poisoner (1560)

The 22nd day of May was a maid set on the pillory for giving her Mistress and her household poison, and her ear cut, and [she was] burned in the brow (p. 235).

The 23rd day of May the same maid was set on the pillory . . . and after had her other ear cut for the same offence (p. 235).

The 28th day of May there was a maid set on the pillory for the same offence [of poisoning], and burned in the brow (p. 236).

Burglars and cutpurses (1560/61)

The same day was arraigned in Westminster Hall five men, three was for burglary and two were cutpurses, and cast [i.e. condemned] to be hanged at Saint Thomas of Watering; one was a gentleman (p. 251).

Newgate Sessions (1560/61)

The same day [21 Feb.] Sessions at Newgate, and [there] was cast 17 men and two women to [be hanged] (p. 251).

The 22nd day of February came the summons for to have their judgment and so [blank] burned in their hand at the place of judgment (p. 251).

The 24th day of February went to hang 18 men and two women, and certain were brought to be buried in certain parishes in London; the Barber-Surgeons had one of them to be anatomy at their hall (pp. 251–2).

Counterfeiting documents (1560/61)

The 4th day of March was a tall man whipped about Westminster and through London and over London Bridge and [into] Southwark for counterfeiting the Master of the Queen's Horse's hand (p. 252).

Blasphemy of the mad (1561)

The 10th day of April was whipped one that came out of Bedlem for he said he was Christ, and one Peter that came out of the Marshelsea, both whipped, for he said that he was the same Peter that did follow Christ (p. 255).

Gentleman rapist (1561)

The 18th day of April was arraigned at Newgate Master Putnam gentleman for a rape, and cast [i.e. condemned], and divers others (p. 256).

Murder (1561)

The 19th day of April were cast three, two men and a woman for killing of a man beside Saint James, and other (p. 256).

Hangings (1561)

The 21st of April were hanged nine, at Hyde Park Corner three, and six at Tyburn (p. 256).

Attempting to help prisoner escape (1561)

The 18th day of June was a woman set in the stocks at Newgate Market for certain files and other instruments, the which she brought to her husband for to file the irons off his legs, and other things (p. 260).

Execution by drowning; Pardons (1562)

The 25th day of April were hanged at Wapping, at the low water mark, five for robbery on the sea; and there was one that had his halter about his neck and yet a pardon came betime (p. 281).

2.3   The case of Lord Sturton

This case, also taken from Machyn's *Diary, illustrates the punishment of the higher orders following a fall from grace 1556/7.*

The 28th day of January was had to the Tower my Lord Sturton for murder of two gentlemen, the father and the son and heir, Master Argyll [*sic* Hartgill] and his son, the which was shamefully murdered in his own place (p. 125).

The 17th day of February was my lord Sturton come from the Tower and one of his men unto Westminster before the Council [viz. Privy Council] and judges, and there the evidence was declared before his own face that he could not deny it (p. 126).

The 18th day of February came from the Tower unto my Lord Privy Seal before certain of the Privy Council four of my lord Sturton's servants, and there they were examined of the death of Master Argyll and his son. And after they were carried back again by four of the guard unto the [Tower] (p. 126).

The 26th day of February was arraigned at Westminster Hall my lord Sturton, and before the judges and divers of the Council as my lord Broke the Lord Steward, and my Lord Treasurer, and divers other lords and knights. And long it were ere he would answer, and so at last my Lord Justice stood up and declared to my lord [that if] he would not answer to the articles that was [*sic* were] laid against him [i.e. he refused to plead] that he should be pressed to death by the law of the realm. And after he did answer, and so he was cast [i.e. condemned] by his own words to be hanged, and his four men, and so to be carried to the Tower again til they have further commandment from the Council (pp. 126–7).

The 2nd day of March rode from the Tower my lord Sturton with Sir Robert Oxinbridge the lieutenant, and four of my lord's servants, and with certain of the guard, through London and so to Hownslow. And there they lay all night at the Sign of the Angel, and the morrow after to Staines and so to Basingstoke, and so to Sturton, to suffer death, and his four men. And two more men for robbing of a rich farmer in that country to be hanged, for there was laid by the same farmer before the Council that a knight and his men did rob him, and the knight was laid in the Fleet til it pleased God that the thief was taken. The knight his name is called Sir [blank] Wrothun knight (p. 128).

The same day was hanged at Salisbury in the market place the lord Sturton for the death of old Master Argyll and young Argyll his son, the which they were shamefully murdered by the lord and divers of his servants, the which he made great lamentation at his death for that wilful deed that was done . . . (p. 128).

2.4 A school for pickpockets, London, 1585[50]

This account comes from an official report from William Fleetwood, Recorder of London to William Cecil, Lord Burghley, a member of the Privy Council. We can see from this report of the London judge that there was some evidence of "organized crime" to support the cony-catching pamphlet writer's allegations. Note that the London lawyer uses similar terms to those used by the London writer Greene.

One Wotton, a gentleman born, and sometime a merchant of good credit, who falling by time into decay, kept an alehouse at Smart's Key near Billingsgate. And after, for some misdemeanour being put down, he reared up a new trade of life, and in the same house, he procurred all the cutpurses about this city to repair [i.e. come] to his house. There was a school house set up to learn young boys to cut purses.[51] There were hung up two devices, the one was a pocket the other a purse. The pocket had in it certain counters, and was hung about with hawk's bells, and over the top did hang a little sacring bell.[52]

And he that could take out a counter without any noise was allowed to be *a public foister*; and he that could take a piece of silver out of the purse without the noise of any bells was adjudged *a judiciall nipper*.

Nota that *a foister* is a pick-pocket, and *a nipper* is termed a pickpurse, or a cutpurse.

In Wotton's house at Smart's key are written on a table [i.e. tablet] divers poysies [i.e. poems], and among the rest one is this:

---

[50] Tawney & Power, *Tudor economic documents*, I (1924), pp. 337–9 (spelling modernized).
[51] Note this now incorrect use of the verb "to learn", meaning "to teach".
[52] Hawks were hung with bells so the hunter could locate them if they flew off. A "sacring bell" was one originally used to ring at Mass at the time of consecration of the host.

Si spie sporte, si non spie, tunc steale[53]

Another is thus:

Si spie, si non spie, foist, nip, lift, shave and spare not

Note that *foist* is to cut a pocket, *nip* is to cut a purse, *lift* is to rob a shop or a gentleman's chamber [i.e. room], *shave* is to filch a cloke, a sword, a silver spoon, or such like, that is negligently looked unto.

3   Crime & punishment outside London

3.1   An Italian view of English crime, c. 1500[54]

This comes from a Venetian ambassadorial report. It is hardly a very flattering view of the English and their criminals. Elsewhere, the writer criticizes the English practice on sanctuary and benefit of clergy.

When a chief magistrate of the place has received notice of any such malefactor, he causes him immediately to be thrown into prison, and then twelve men of that place are elected, who must decide according to their consciences, whether the prisoner has or has not committed the crime of which he is accused.[55] And if the greater number vote that he has, he is considered to be guilty.[56] He is not, however, punished at that time; but it is necessary that twelve other men be chosen who must hear the cause over again.[57] And if their verdict should agree with the former one, the days of the delinquent are brought to a close. . . .

Such severe measures against criminals ought to keep the English in check, but, for all this, there is no country in the world where there are so many thieves and robbers as in England in so much that few venture to go alone in the country, except in the middle of the day, and fewer still in the towns at night, and least of all in London.

---

[53] I would translate this as "If anyone is watching, play; if not, then steal." Note the mixture of dog Latin and criminal argot.

[54] C. A. Sneyd (tr.), "A relation . . . of the island of England", *Camden Soc.* o.s. xxxvii (1847), pp. 33–4.

[55] This is the grand jury.

[56] Technically what the grand jury did was establish whether or not there was a case to answer, i.e. whether or not to return a true bill. Note that here it is claimed they operated on a majority verdict.

[57] This is the trial jury.

3.2   Harrison on punishments and offenders under Elizabeth[58]

William Harrison was a Puritan minister with a living in Essex. His Description of England *is an attempt to describe every aspect of the society of his day.*

Introduction

In cases of felony, manslaughter, robbery, murder, rape, piracy, and such capital crimes as are not reputed for treason or hurt of the estate, our sentence pronounced upon the offender is, to hang till he be dead. For of other punishments used in other countries we have no knowledge or use; and yet so few grievous crimes committed with us as elsewhere in the world. To use torment also or question by pain and torture in these common cases with us is greatly abhorred, since we are found always to be such as despise death, and yet abhor to be tormented, choosing rather frankly to open our minds than to yield our bodies unto such servile haulings and tearings as are used in other countries. And this is one cause wherefore our condemned persons do go so cheerfully to their deaths; for our nation is free, stout, haughty, prodigal of life and blood, . . . , and therefore cannot in any wise digest to be used as villains and slaves, in suffering continually beating, servitude, and servile torments. No, our gaolers are guilty of felony, by an old law of the land, if they torment any prisoner committed to their custody for the revealing of his accomplices.[59]

Treason

The greatest and most grievous punishment used in England for such as offend against the State is drawing from the prison to the place of execution upon an hurdle or sled, where they are hanged till they be half dead, and then taken down, and quartered alive; after that, their members and bowels are cut from their bodies, and thrown into a fire, provided near hand and within their own sight, even for the same purpose. Sometimes, if the trespass be not the more heinous, they are suffered to hang till they be quite dead. And whensoever any of the nobility are convicted of high treason by their peers, that is to say, equals (for an inquest of yeomen passeth not upon them, but only of the lords of parliament), this manner of their death is converted into the loss of their heads only notwithstanding that the sentence do run after the former order.[60]

---

[58] Taken from William Harrison, *Description of England* (London, 1577; 2nd edn, 1587). Spelling and punctuation have been modernized.

[59] English xenophobia has a long history!

[60] One perhaps surprising advantage of nobility.

Trial

In trial of cases concerning treason, felony, or an other grievous crime not confessed, the party accused do yield, if he be a noble man, to be tried by an inquest (as I have said) and his peers; if a gentleman, by gentlemen; and a inferior, by God and by the country, to wit, the yeomanry (for combat or battle is not greatly in use), and, being condemned of felony, manslaughter, etc., he is ertsoons hanged by the neck till he be dead, and then cut down and buried. But if he be convicted of wilful murder, done either upon pretended malice or in any notable robbery, he is either hanged alive in chains near the place where the fact was committed (or else upon compassion taken, first strangled with a rope), and so continueth till his bones consume to nothing.

We have use neither of the wheel nor of the bar, as in other countries; but, when wilful manslaughter is perpetrated, beside hanging, the offender hath his right hand commonly stricken off before or near unto the place where the act was done, after which he is led forth to the place of execution, and there put to death according to the law.

Varieties of crime and punishment

In like sort in the word felony are many grievous crimes contained, as breach of prison (1 Edward II), disfigurers of the prince's liege people (5 Henry IV), hunting by night with painted faces and visors (1 Henry VII), rape, or stealing of women and maidens (3 Henry VIII), conspiracies against the person of the prince (3 Henry VII), embezzling of goods committed by the master to the servant above the value of forty shillings (17 Henry VIII), carrying of horses or mares into Scotland (23 Henry VIII), sodomy and buggery (25 Henry VIII), conjuring, forgery, witchcraft, and digging up of crosses (33 Henry VIII), prophesying upon arms, cognizances, names, and badges (33 Henry VIII), casting of slanderous bills (37 Henry VIII), wilful killing by poison (1 Edward VI), departure of a soldier from the field (2 Edward VI), diminution of coin, all offences within case of praemunire, embezzling of records, goods taken from dead men by their servants, stealing of whatsoever cattle, robbing by the high way, upon the sea, or of dwelling houses, letting out of ponds, cutting of purses, stealing of deer by night, counterfeits of coin, evidences charters, and writings, and divers other needless to be remembered.

If a woman poison her husband, she is burned alive; if the servant kill his master, he is to be executed for petty treason; he that poisoneth a man is to be boiled to death in water or lead, although the party die not of the practice; in cases of murder, all the accessories are to suffer pains of death accordingly.

Perjury is punished by the pillory, burning in the forehead with the letter P, the rewalting [i.e. cutting down] of the trees growing upon the grounds of the offenders, and loss of all his movables. Many trespasses also are punished by the cutting off of one or both ears from the head of the offender, as the utterance of seditious words against the magistrates, fraymakers, petty robbers, etc. Rogues are burned through the ears; carriers of sheep out of the land, by the loss of their hands; such as kill by poison are either boiled or scalded to death in lead or seething water.

Heretics are burned quick; harlots and their mates, by carting, ducking, and doing of open penance in sheets in churches and market steeds, are often put to rebuke. Howbeit, as this is counted with some either as no punishment at all to speak of, or but little regarded of the offenders, so I would with adultery and fornication to have some sharper law, for what great smart is it to be turned out of hot sheet into a cold, or after a little washing in the water to be let loose again unto their former trades? Howbeit the dragging of some of them over the Thames between Lambeth and Westminster at the tail of a boat is a punishment that most terrifieth them which are condemned thereto; but this is inflicted upon them by none other than the Knight Marshall, and that within the compass of his jurisdiction and limits only.

. . . As in theft therefore, so in adultery and whoredom, I would wish the parties trespassing to be made bond or slaves unto those that received the injury, to sell and give where they listed, or to be condemned to the galleys, for that punishment would prove more bitter to them than half-an-hour's hanging, or than standing in a sheet, though the weather be never so cold.

Manslaughter in time past was punished by the purse, wherein the quantity or quality of the punishment was rated after the state and calling of the party killed: so that one was valued sometime at 1200, another at 600, or 200 shillings. . . .

Such as kill themselves are buried in the field with a stake driven through their bodies. Witches are hanged, or sometimes burned; but thieves are hanged (as I said before) generally on the gibbet or gallows, saving in Halifax, where they are beheaded after a strange manner, and whereof I find this report.

There is and has been of ancient time a law, or rather a custom, at Halifax, that whosoever does commit any felony, and is taken with the same, or confesses the fact upon examination, if it be valued by four constables to amount to the sum of thirteenpence-halfpenny, he is forthwith beheaded upon one of the next market days (which fall usually upon the Tuesdays, Thursdays, and Saturdays), or else upon the same day that he is so convicted, if market be then holden. The engine wherewith the execution is done is a square block of wood of the length of four feet and a half, which does ride up and down in a slot, rabbet, or regall, between two pieces of timber, that are framed and set upright, of five yards in height. In the nether end of the sliding block is an axe, keyed or fastened with an iron into the wood, which being drawn up to the top of the frame is there fastened by a wooden pin (with a notch made into the same, after the manner of a Samson's post), unto the midst of which pin also there is a long rope fastened that cometh down among the people, so that, when the offender hath made his confession and hath laid his neck over the nethermost block, every man there present doth either take hold of the rope (or putteth forth his arm so near to the same as he can get, in token that he is willing to see true justice executed), and, pulling out the pin in this manner, the head-block wherein the axe is fastened doth fall down with such a violence that, if the neck of the transgressor were as big as that of a bull, it should be cut in sunder at a stroke and roll from the body by a huge distance. If it be so that the offender be apprehended for an ox, oxen, sheep, kine, horse, or any such cattle, the self beast or other of the same kind shall have the end of the rope tied somewhere unto them, so that they, being driven, do draw out the pin, whereby the offender is executed. . . .

Rogues and vagabonds are often stocked and whipped; scolds are ducked upon cucking-stools in the water. Such felons as stand mute, and speak not at their arraignment, are pressed to death by huge weights laid upon a board, that lieth over their breast, and a sharp stone under their backs; and these commonly held their peace, thereby to save their goods unto their wives and children, which, if they were condemned, should be confiscated to the prince.

Thieves that are saved by their books and clergy, for the first offence, if they have stolen nothing else but oxen, sheep, money, or such like, which be no open robberies, as by the highway side, or assailing of any man's house in the night, without putting him in fear of his life, or breaking up his walls or doors, are burned in the left hand, upon the brawn of the thumb, with a hot iron, so that, if they be apprehended again, that mark betrayeth them to have been arraigned of felony before, whereby they are sure at that time to have no mercy. . . .

Pirates and robbers by sea are condemned in the Court of the Admiralty, and hanged on the shore at low-water mark, where they are left till three tides have overwashed them. Finally, such as having walls and banks near unto the sea, and do suffer the same to decay (after convenient admonition), whereby the water entereth and drowneth up the country, are by a certain ancient custom apprehended, condemned, and staked in the breach, where they remain for ever as parcel of the foundation of the new wall that is to be made upon them, as I have heard reported.

And thus much in part of the administration of justice used in our country, wherein, notwithstanding that we do not often hear of horrible, merciless, and wilful murders (such I mean as are not seldom seen in the countries of the main), yet now and then some manslaughter and bloody robberies are perpetrated and committed, contrary to the laws, which be severely punished, and in such wise as I have before reported.

Annoyers of the Commonwealth

Certes there is no greater mischief done in England than by robberies, the first by young shifting gentlemen, which oftentimes do bear more port than they are able to maintain.

Secondly by serving-men, whose wages cannot suffice so much as to find them breeches; wherefore they are now and then constrained either to keep highways, and break into the wealthy men's houses with the first sort, or else to will up and down in gentlemen's and rich farmer's pastures, there to see and view which horses feed best, whereby they many times get something, although with hard adventure. It hath been known by their confession at the gallows that some one such chapman hath had forty, fifty, or sixty stolen horses at pasture here and there abroad in the country at a time, which they have sold at fairs and markets far off, they themselves in the mean season being taken about home for honest yeomen, and very wealthy drovers, till their dealings have been betrayed.

Our third annoyers of the commonwealth are rogues, which do very great mischief in all places where they become. For, whereas the rich only suffer injury by the first two, these spare neither rich nor poor; but, whether it be great gain or small, all is fish that cometh to net with them. And yet, I say, both they and the rest are trussed up apace. For there is not one year commonly wherein three hundred or four hundred of them are not devoured and eaten up by the gallows in one place and other. It appeareth . . . [that] Henry the Eighth, executing his laws very severely against such idle persons, I mean great thieves, petty thieves, and rogues, did hang up threescore and twelve thousand of them in his time. He seemed for a while greatly to have terrified the rest. But since his death the number of them is so increased, yea, although we have had no wars, which are a great occasion of their breed (for it is the custom of the more idle sort, having once served, or but seen the other side of the sea under colour of service, to shake hand with labour for ever, thinking it a disgrace for himself to return unto his former trade), that, except some better order be taken, or the laws already made be better executed, such as dwell in uplandish towns and little villages shall live but in small safety and rest.

Proposed reforms

For the better apprehension also of thieves and man-killers, there is an old law in England very well provided whereby it is ordered that, if he that is robbed (or any man) complain and give warning of slaughter or murder

63

committed, the constable of the village whereunto he cometh and crieth for succour is to raise the parish about him, and to search woods, groves, and all suspected houses and places, where the trespasser may be, or is supposed to lurk; and not finding him there, he is to give warning unto the next constable, and so one constable, after search made, to advertise another from parish to parish, till they come to the same where the offender is harboured and found.[61] It is also provided that, if any parish in this business do not her duty, but suffereth the thief (for the avoiding of trouble sake) in carrying him to the gaol, if he should be apprehended, or other letting of their work to escape, the same parish is not only to make fine to the king, but also the same, with the whole hundred wherein it standeth, to repay the party robbed his damages, and leave his estate harmless.

Certainly this is a good law; howbeit I have known by my own experience felons being taken to have escaped out of the stocks, being rescued by other for want of watch and guard, that thieves have been let pass, because the covetous and greedy parishioners would neither take the pains nor be at the charge, to carry them to prison, if it were far off; that when hue and cry have been made even to the faces of some constables, they have said: "God restore your loss! I have other business at this time." And by such means the meaning of many a good law is left unexecuted, malefactors emboldened, and many a poor man turned out of that which he hath sweat and taken great pains toward the maintenance of himself and his poor children and family.

3.3 Miscellaneous cases outside London

Oxford Sessions (1556)[62]

The 3rd day of October was the Sessions at Oxford, and there were condemned 60 to die.

Petty theft (Southampton, 1557)[63]

The 4th September 1557 John Stowell, sawyer, was in the gaol for 14 days and the fifteenth day for divers "pekres" of small timber planks and other small things by him taken at times was by one assent [i.e. by the assent of all] commanded to the pillory with a paper written of his offence and there stood all the market time. The which was for the first time of his fault [i.e.

---

[61] A reference to the hue and cry.
[62] Nicholas (1848), p. 115.
[63] A. L. Merson, *The third book of the rembrance of Southampton, 1514–1602*, vol. 2 (Southampton, 1955), p. 59.

it was his first offence]. And if he do the like fault again then to lose his ear standing in the pillory & so to be banished this town [Southampton] for ever.

Cutpurse in Devizes (1560)[64]

June 20 – Master Mayor [et al.] called before him one John Davys which confesseth he was born in Exeter, which Davys was taken a cutting a purse. Wherefore he was put in Ward [i.e. prison] and had his ear nailed to the pillory for the same offence.

Prostitution (Southampton, 1570)[65]

The 7 November 1570 . . . by full consent of Master Mayor and his bretheren . . . it was agreed that Julian Davis, wife to John Davis, of the town of Southampton, mariner, for that she was found in the house of Collet Comes, widow, with a French man suspiciously locked in to the house alone by the said Collet Comes, that she [i.e. Julian] should be carted about the town with a paper on her head declaring her offence and the said Collet to ride with her in the cart with a paper on her head declaring her to be a bawd, and from thence forth to be banished the town and no more to remain therein.

A case of mercy in Shrewsbury in 1580[66]

This case demonstrates the informal but crucial intervention of the Church in a criminal case. Note the large number of convictions but relatively small number taken for execution.

This year 2 November the Quarter Sessions were kept in Shrewsbury. . . . there were 25 persons condemned of the which there were five that went to the place of execution and the rest were saved by their book and women supposed to be with child.[67] It is to be noted as concerning the five persons which came to the place of execution, four of them were put to death, and the fifth, being a maid and for a small triful being condemned who being [of] such patience and godly behaviour in her journey towards her death and how she was mortified to die in persuading also the stubborness of her fellows at the place of execution, was stayed by one

---

[64] B. H. Cunnington (ed.), *Some annals of the Borough of Devizes* (Devizes, 1925), Part 1, p. 40.

[65] *The third book of the rembrance of Southampton, 1514–1602*, vol. 2, pp. 121–2.

[66] W. A. Leighton (ed.), "Early chronicles of Shrewsbury, 1372–1603", pp. 284–5.

[67] Those who escaped execution did so either by claiming benefit of clergy by reading the "hanging" verses, or by claiming to be pregnant.

Mr Doctor Bouckley, a learned preacher of God's word,[68] which did well view the conversation of the said maid, upon great pity, brought her home for a time, promising to beg her life, and so did, which maid liveth in the fear of God and doth very well.[69]

Lewd slanders (Devizes, 1583)[70]

On this day [7 August] Elizabeth Webb, wife of John Webb, made a complaint against Edith Marten, wife of William Marten, that she the said Edith had in very lewd speeches and slanderous terms said that the said Elizabeth Webb was a whore and a false forsworn woman, in that with others had been before Master Mayor and had taken a false oath and such as did depose the same there was no honesty in them, which words were verified by the testimony of John Cady [and others]. For which misdemeanours the said Edith was committed to ward and to ride in the cucking stool from the Guild Hall unto the dwelling house of the said Marten and the cucking stool to stand at her door.[71]

The case of Preacher Davye, 1581[72]

This information on a drunken ecclesiastical "flasher" and wife-beater was reported to the Privy Council in January 1581. We do not know the outcome.

About five years past, he, misusing his wife, drove her for safeguard of herself into the street. At which time, there came by two women, being neighbours, to whom she moaned herself. Where upon they went up to him to persuade him, to which women he showed sundry evil behaviours, amongst others using sundry oaths asked whether they as being taken with love of him to see his fair skin came to him, and with that showed himself all naked before. Where upon the said women, taking a chamber pot or urinal full of urine standing there, cast it in his bosom, and with much ado got away.

About six years past, at a gold smith's house in Cheapside, being bidden to supper, and his wife, [he] kept such disordered rule and being drunk they could not get him out of the house until midnight, and then

---

[68] Edmund Bulkeley was Prebendary of Chester and Minister of St Mary's and the town's public preacher. Such intervention was not unique; it does indicate the potential authority of a preacher at that time.

[69] This means he appealed to the Crown for a Royal Pardon for the maid and, by implication, got it.

[70] B. H. Cunnington (ed.), *Some annals of the Borough of Devizes* (Devizes, 1925), Part 2, p. 2.

[71] Good example of a shaming punishment.

[72] Public Record Office, SP12/147, fo. 100 [no. 35].

were forced to have the constable and watch to have him forth where he was like to have broken the constable's neck down a pair of stairs if he had not by great hap saved himself, where upon he was carried to the Counter.[73]

About three years past, [he] preaching at St Anne's church by Aldersgate, was bidden to dinner to the alderman deputy to whom he was a stranger and to the rest of the company, where he used himself to sundry honest women in such sort as the whole company was ashamed.

Shaming punishments (Devizes, 1584)[74]

1 May – Dorothy Browne of this Borough and Thomas Cooke of South Wraxall were for their lewd behaviours together adjudged by John Willys – Deputy to Matthew Spencer, Mayor – and other his brethren – to be led about the town with basons.

Passing on a vagrant (Devizes: 1603)[75]

That James Bee, a sturdy vagrant beggar and Dorothy his wife together with one child were taken the 14th March at the said Borough of Devizes, having with him a counterfeit passport pretending losses by fire, where the day and year aforesaid, the said James was openly whipped for a wandering rogue according to the law and is assigned to pass forthwith from parish to parish by the officers thereof, the next straight way to Culgarthe in the county of Cumberland where as he confesseth he dwelt last. And he is limited to be at Culgarthe within six weeks now next ensuing the date hereof at his peril.

3.4   Quarter Sessions cases (Staffordshire)

Theft of oxen: jury presentment, 1583[76]

The jurors for the Queen present that Robert Griffith late of Buttington (Montgomery), husbandman, on 27 July 1583 was committed to Stafford gaol by Robert Staunford, esquire, a justice of the peace, into the custody of William Bull keeper of the same gaol for suspicion of felony, to wit for the theft of four oxen of the goods of a certain man unknown, and to stay there until by due form of law he should be delivered from the gaol.[77]

---

[73] The Counter was a London prison.

[74] Cunnington, *Some annals of the Borough of Devizes*, Part 2, p. 3.

[75] Cunnington, *Some annals of the Borough of Devizes*, Part 2, p. 41.

[76] Collections for a History of Staffordshire, 1927, p. 178, known as Staffordshire Historical Collections hereafter S.H.C.

[77] Delivered in this sense means brought to trial.

Whether the aforesaid Robert on 11 September in the said year violently broke out of the said gaol and escaped and went voluntarily at large against the form of the statute and the peace of the Queen, etc.
Endorsed
  True bill

Allegation of an assault, 1586[78]

Let it be enquired of for the Queen if John Norris late of Forbridge (Staffs), yeoman on 26 May 1586 with force of arms at Forbridge, unlawfully and violently assembled himself and assaulted a certain Thomas Woodall late of Forbridge aforesaid, yeoman, being then and there in the peace of God and of the said Queen, and made an affray, and the same Thomas Woodall then and there struck, wounded and ill-treated, so that his life is despaired of, and committed other enormities to the great damage of the said Thomas Woodall, and as a bad example of divers lieges of the Queen and against the form of the statute in such like case provided, and against the Queen's peace, etc.[79]

Another assault, 1586[80]

Let it be enquired of if Thomas Jones late of Willenhall (Staffs), labourer on 2 August 1586 with force of arms at Nechills, assaulted a certain Elizabeth Hynton widow, being in the peace of God and of the Queen, and wounded her so that her life is despaired of, against the Queen's peace, etc.

Attempted arrest of an offender by the sheriff's bailiff, 1586[81]

Let it be enquired of for the Queen, that whereas Philip Okeover esquire, sheriff of the county of Stafford by virtue of the Queen's writ directed to him, made his certain warrant to a certain Thomas Ripton his bailiff that he should attach Nicholas Redgford of Barton under Needwood, Staffs., labourer, and should cause him to come before the said sheriff, according to the form of the said warrant.[82] Which said Thomas Ripton on 20 April

---

[78] S.H.C. 1927, p. 137.
[79] The violence alleged in the indictment is common form; the case may not have been as extreme as here alleged.
[80] S.H.C. 1927, p. 180.
[81] S.H.C. 1927, p. 137.
[82] Clear evidence of the procedure by which an arrest was authorized by a sheriff and then implemented, albeit unsuccessfully in this case, by one of his officers.

1586 took and arrested Nicholas Redgford at Barton under Needwood and wished to bring him before the sheriff, whether the aforesaid Nicholas Redgford on that day with force of arms, to wit with sticks, swords and knives, assaulted the said Thomas Ripton in the execution of the warrant . . . and then and there rescued himself from his custody and escaped at large, against the Queen's peace, etc.

Endorsed

True bill on the testimony of Thomas Ripton[83]

Highway robbery, 1586[84]

Let it be enquired of for the Queen, if Edward Stevenson otherwise called Little Ned, late of Stoke [Notts.], yeoman, and Henry Mayfelde late of the town of Nottingham . . . yeoman, on 27 April 1586 at Shenston (Staffs.), a certain William Cumberford,[85] gentleman, being in the peace of God and the Queen, and being then and there on the highway, together with other persons unknown, with force of arms namely with sticks, swords, shields, knives, and "dagges", assaulted and put him in great bodily fear, and £72[86] in ready money, one gold ring worth £5, and a sword worth 20 shillings of the goods and chattels of the same William feloniously stole from his person, against the peace of the Queen, etc.

Judgment

Endorsed

True bill on the testimony of William Cumberford
Convicted

Horse-theft, 1586[87]

Let it be enquired of for the Queen if Edward Hargreave late of Hatherton, (Staffs), tailor on 24 April 1586 with force of arms at Bromwich (Staffs.) broke and entered the close of a certain Humfrey Hopkins and stole a white freckled mare worth 33s 4d against the peace of the Queen, etc.

Endorsed

True bill by the testimony of Humfrey Hopkins

---

[83] That is to say, the grand jury found that there was a case to answer based on the sheriff's bailiff's testimony.

[84] In this case the men went to trial and were convicted. S.H.C. 1927, p. 139.

[85] Cumberford was a recusant, i.e. a Catholic dissenter; nevertheless, the courts provide him with the protection of the law.

[86] This is a huge sum of money, three times the annual income of a yeoman farmer.

[87] S.H.C. 1927, p. 178.

A common nuisance and rogue, *c.* 1595/6[88]

An example of the way villagers could bring a troublesome neighbour before the Justices.

Articles against William Walker of Oscotte

1. Inprimus, the said Walker is a common drunkard, a great disturber and disquieter of his neighbours, slandering and reviling them with most unseemly terms and speeches not fit to be used.
2. Item the said Walker in his drunkeness hath assaulted certain persons upon the high way, and did beat a woman very sore meeting her upon the way.
3. Item he hath killed divers sheep and geese of his neighbours and hath cut up the gates and fences of their grounds and laid them open.
4. Item since Michaelmas last he came into the pasture of Richard Spurrier of Oscotte and threw an axe at a bullock or steer of his being there. Where with he had almost [houshewewed] the said bullock and cut him so sore he could scarcely be saved alive and yet halteth and much the worse for the same hurt . . .

The Justices ordered Walker to be of good behaviour.

Refusal to do military service (*c.* 1594)

An appeal from Thomas Meyre to the JPs c. 1594

I, Thomas Meyre, being constable of Fenton and Longton, did . . . charge and command John Bolton the younger and Robert Bolton his brother to be at a General Muster at Stafford. . . . They did give me very evil speeches and would not obey the commandment nor appear . . . Craving at your worships hands for that I have been greatly abused at their hands that I may have some redress at their hands that others may take example.[89]

4   Manor courts

4.1   The officers of a manor court

Summary of the officials attending the joint court leet of Cannock & Rugeley (Staffs.) in the later sixteenth century.

---

[88] S.H.C. 1932, p. 136 (English modernized).
[89] S.H.C. 1932, p. 130 (English modernized).

Steward

Usually a member of the Lord's Council, sometimes the Receiver-General. He brought with him at least one clerk and the records of the manor: rentals and court rolls. He was assisted by an under-steward who was resident in the manor and paid directly from the profits of the manor.

Reve-bailiff

Elected from amongst the copyholders and freeholders by the jury but appointed by the steward on behalf of the lord. Responsible for the collection of the "old rents" and for "appraising", i.e. valuing with the help of a jury, strays plus goods and animals seized in lieu of amercements, i.e. the fines levied by the court.

Bailiff

A salaried official appointed by the lord, responsible for collecting all other rents and the "profits of justice" and for summoning juries.

Jury

Elected from amongst the freeholders and copyholders, they were responsible for promulgating by-laws, checking the presentments of all the minor officials, making their own presentments, and checking all surrenders and admissions.

The lesser officials

Tithingmen – elected by the jury; responsible for presenting communal and individual criminal offences.

Ale-Tasters – elected by the jury; responsible for presenting offences against statute and the by-laws governing brewing and baking.

Foresters – appointed by the Lord; responsible for all offences, real and technical, on Cannock Chase.

Pinder & Keeper of the Fields – elected by the jury; oversaw the common fields and impounded strays.

Constables – appointed in court by the Steward; responsible with the Tithingmen for keeping the peace within the manor; responsible for the hue and cry, for stocking offenders, and for whipping vagabonds. They were also officers of the Hundred Court and the Quarter Sessions.

4.2 A selection of "criminal" cases brought before the court leet of Cannock & Rugeley (Staffs.)[90]

In each court there were regular presentments for brewing and baking offences, in effect licences to brew and bake, and for offences relating to the open fields and the misuse of Cannock Chase for pasturing beasts, etc. There were also many presentments each court for affrays. The following are a selection of the more unusual cases.

April 1574
William Harryman amerced [i.e. fined] 4d for an affray on Richard Attye.

October 1574
Alice Russheton, widow, amerced 4d for keeping a common house and selling high-priced food. [In effect a licence to sell food.]

John Wolsley, gent., amerced 1s 8d for making an affray with an unknown man on Richard Birde and drawing blood against the Queen's peace.

April 1575
Humphrey Bardell amerced 1s for keeping a tinker and his wife at his house against the by-laws.

Francis Hydegge, labourer, fined £10 for carrying a handgun and shooting a dove at Rugeley against the statute (33 Hen. VIII, c. 6).

William Harryman, constable of Rugeley, amerced 1s for saying opprobrious words against the jury for amercing him at the last court [it was the previous April leet].

William Harrison amerced 3s 4d for an affray on William Oldeacres.

William Assheton amerced 6s 8d for permitting several unknown persons to play illegal games in his house against the recently made statute.

William Nevoe is amerced 20s for keeping a certain woman of ill fame in his house until she had a baby boy, against the ordinances of the court and that Margaret Turner is in the lord's mercy for keeping in her house two women of ill fame, one called Great Jane and the other called Mother Margaret.

---

[90] Staffs. Rec. Off., D(W)1734/2/1/184 & 186.

Elizabeth Hyde, widow, amerced 3s 4d for washing sheep skins in the river at Brereton [thus polluting the water].

October 1575
Nicholas Adey (cleric) and John Pannell convicted of an affray on each other with fists; each was amerced 1s 10d.

April 1576
John Olyver amerced 6s 8d for keeping two unlicensed lodgers in his house.

John Pannell fined 2s for hunting hares with a greyhound he being a man worth less than 40s. His two sons also fined for the same offence.

Richard Mason amerced 1s for keeping Mary Patricke in his house knowing her to be whore. William Arnold & William Assheton, constables of Rugeley, amerced 2s & 3s 4d respectively for having the same Mary many times in their houses.

William Arnold amerced 6s 8d for allowing his house to be used for playing dice and "shovell aboarde" [i.e. shove-happeny]; William Assheton was amerced 6s 8d for the same offence.

October 1576
William Arnold amerced 13s 4d for permitting dice-playing for profit in his house; William Assheton 10s for a similar offence.

Henry Chapman amerced 8d for not scouring his ditch and 1s for saying rude words about the steward of the court [i.e. the judge].

Nicholas Adey, vicar of Rugeley & Richard Baker are amerced 10s & 6s 8d respectively for permitting dice-playing for profit in their houses.

Elizabeth Fyssher is a common scold for which her husband John is amerced 6s 8d.

October 1578
Richard Byrde and seven others amerced 8d each for letting their cattle graze in the seasonal open field.

Five men fined 20s each for soaking hemp in the common stream [causing pollution of the stream].

Richard Lees amerced 1s 8d for enclosing part of one of the common fields [thus restricting the grazing of his neighbours].

The two Cannock constables amerced 1s each for failing to raise the hue and cry following a felony in Cannock by unknown persons.

When the reeve of Cannock, on the orders of the steward, took one cow as an attachment from Thomas Tromwyn, the latter resisted and took his cow back. Tromwyn was amerced 1s 8d.

May 1579
Robert Blake, constable of Cannock, presented eleven men, not having lands to the value of 20 marks, for wearing a cap on Sunday, against statute law. Each was fined 3s 4d.

Francis Dallycote and his wife Agnes amerced for breaking the hedge surrounding the common field.

October 1579
John Barre was amerced 6s 8d for putting his sign on a stray sheep [i.e. for rustling one of his neighbour's sheep].

Ellen Evans has quarrelled with William Oliver many times and is a common scold for which her husband is amerced 1s.

April 1580
John Tomkyns is amerced 6s 8d for keeping strangers believed to be thieves in his house.

October 1580
Thomas Annesley is amerced for an affray on Agnes wife of Jacob Clarke; Agnes Clarke is amerced 1s for an affray on Margaret Annesley.

April 1582
Four men amerced 1s each for entering the lord's warren and taking rabbits.

April 1585
John Morris and John Aston, common brewers in Hednesford are amerced 4d each.

Elizabeth, servant of John Morris stole the hedge wood from Thomas Bostocke and took it to John Morris's house, so Morris is amerced 1s.

Henry Aberley amerced 1s for keeping 2 bitches at his house in Cannock Wood which so barked and howled that the tenants of Cannock were too frightened to graze their cattle and sheep there.

October 1586

Ralfe Webbe amerced 1s for leaving the court during the process of swearing in officers and jurors to the contempt of the court and the steward.

October 1592

Three men from Great Wyrley amerced 1s each for refusing the order of the Surveyors of the Way to come and help repair the common ways [i.e. roads].

Joan and Jane Gotyer, daughters of Thomas Gotyer, are amerced 1s each for fishing in Rysom Brook in Rugeley during divine service on a Sunday.

October 1593

Edward Blurton amerced 6d for emptying his privy in the Queen's highway; Thomas Chetwyn, gent., amerced 6d for a similar offence.

October 1594

Thomas Oldeacres was amerced 1s 8d for an affray on one of the tithingmen in the execution of his duties.

William Pereson amerced 1s 8d for refusing to keep watch when requested so to do by the constables.

5   Church courts

The Church operated as an instrument of social and sexual as well as religious control and through its courts enforced its own laws. Perhaps the most extensively used punishment by the Church was public penance. Although not strictly speaking a church service, penance was directed to be and was performed at time of public service. This was a form of public shaming.

More convicted persons failed to perform their penance than any other punishment. The reason is not hard to find when one reads Archbishop Grindal's "Direction" on how such penances should be conducted by the minister.

5.1   Archibishop Grindal's direction for penance[91]

First, I wish at every public penance a sermon, if it be possible, be had.

Secondly, in the same sermon the grievousness of the offence is to be opened; the party to be exhorted to unfeigned repentance, with assurance

---

[91] W. Nicholson (ed.), *The remains of Edmund Grindal* ("Parker Soc.", 1843), pp. 455–7.

of God's mercy, if they so do; and doubling of their damnation, if they remain either obstinate, or feign repentance where none is, and so lying to the Holy Ghost.

Thirdly, where no sermon is, there let a homily[92] be read, meet for the purpose.

Fourthly, let the offender be set directly over against the pulpit during the sermon or homily, and there stand bareheaded with the sheet, or other accustomed note of difference; and that upon some board raised a foot and a half, at least, above the church floor; that they may be *in loco editiore, et eminentiores omni populo* [in a higher place, and above all the people].

Fifthly, item, it is very requisite that the preacher, in some place of his sermon, or the curate after the end of the homily, remaining still in the pulpit, should publicly interrogate the offenders, whether they do confess their fault, and whether they do truly repent; and that the said offenders or penitents should answer directly every one after another (if they be many), much like to this short form following, *mutatis mutandis*.

PREACHER	Dost thou not here before God, and this congregation assembled in his name, confess that thou didst commit such an offence, viz. fornication, adultery, incest, &c.?
PENITENT	I do confess it before God and this congregation.
PREACHER	Dost thou not also confess, that in so doing thou hast not only grievously offended against the majesty of God, in breaking his commandment, and so deserved lasting damnation, but also hast offended the church of God by thy wicked example?
PENITENT	All this I confess unfeignedly.
PREACHER	Art thou truly and heartily sorrowful for this thine offence?
PENITENT	I am from the bottom of my heart.
PREACHER	Dost thou ask God and this congregation heartily forgiveness for thy sin and offence; and dost thou faithfully promise from henceforth to live a godly and christian life, and never to commit the like offence again?
PENITENT	I do ask God and this congregation heartily forgiveness for my sin and offence; and do faithfully promise from henceforth to live a godly and Christian life, and never to commit the like offence again.

This done, the preacher or minister may briefly speak what they think meet for the time, place, and person desiring in the end the congregation

---

[92] Homilies were printed sermons to be used where no preacher was available.

present to pray to God for the penitent, &c. and the rather, if they see any good signs of repentance in the said penitent.

Provided always, that order be given by the ordinaries,[93] when they assign penances, that if the penitents do shew themselves irreverent or impenitent at their penances, that then their punishments be reiterated; and be removed fron the church to the market-place: that though themselves may thereby seem incorrigible, yet their public shame may be a terror to others.[94]

If the ordinary see cause to commute the wearing of the sheet only (for other commutation I wish none), then appoint a good portion of money to be delivered, immediately after the penance done in form aforesaid, by the penitent himself to the collectors for the poor.[95] With this proviso, that if he shew not good signs of repentance, he is to be put again to his penance with the sheet and then no money at no time to be taken of him.

5.2 Cases brought before the early modern church courts of Essex

This selection from the Elizabethan and early Jacobean Essex archidiaconal courts, taken from W. Hale (ed.), A series of precedents and proceedings in criminal causes 1475 to 1640 *(1847), illustrates the range of criminal cases heard by the lower church courts. It does not reflect either the number or the proportion of cases heard by such courts. In particular, the proportion of sexual offences was much higher than that revealed in this selection. The headings and sub-headings are supplied by the editors.*

Clerics: ecclesiastical offences

Rector failing to serve parish (19 December 1575)

Mark Simpson, rector of Pitsey.[96] Reported that he is insufficient to serve the cure in that they [i.e the parishioners] are not edified by him.

The court examined him. The case was continued 17 January 1575/6 and judgment given . . . that he shall procure four sermons in the year, as also four communions, by some learned preacher or preachers, licensed. And for every Sunday or holyday that his parishioners miss service by

---

[93] An ordinary was the cleric with jurisdiction in an area or place. Usually it was the bishop or his nominee, the archdeacon.

[94] Here the aim changes from the desire to bring the sinner to repentance to the desire to inflict exemplary punishment in order to encourage others to live morally.

[95] Here we see how the richer parishioner could avoid at least the most extreme element of public shaming.

[96] See below, where he is accused of usury.

himself or some curate of him, he shall give 3s 4d to the poor men's box. And also he shall instruct the children with the Catechism, according to the Injunctions, under pain of the law.

Suspected papist and unlicensed preacher (18 July 1577)

The court alleged that Thomas Brayne, curate of Cranham, is suspected of Papistry, and that he allowed the pictures of certain saints, and also that he doth preach, being unlicensed and also of small learning.

The said Brayne confessed that sometime he doth expound upon the Gospels and Epistles. And he denies the other saving that he did see certain images and pictures, but otherwise he did not regard them.

The court accepted his confession. And it ordered him in future that he shall not expound any part of the Scriptures, either Gospels or Epistles, or otherwise preach without licence, under pain of the law.

Putting sheep in the church (3 June 1579)

John Goldring, clerk, rector of Langdon Hilles was charged that his servant, by his consent or procurement, did put his sheep into Langdon church.

The day and place aforesaid the said John Goldringe came and confessed that a little after Candlemas last [2 February], his servants endeavouring and procuring to have his sheep saved from the covering of the great snow which at that time did so greatly fall both by night and day, and his servants not being able to bring them into any house, and having a care to have them saved, they having the key of the church door at Langdon Hilles near which church his sheep were then pastured, they then locked the same sheep into the church, where they were two days, first and last, being working days.[97] And then by great labour and pains, his servants, when the fall of the snow was ended, they put them into another place, and made clean the church. All of which was done for great and extreme necessity sake and not in any contempt; all of which was done by his consent.

Whence the lord archdeacon accepted his confession and ordered the same John Goldring this penance . . . and he shall distribute amongst the poor of the parish 6s 8d.

Preacher's licence (6 May 1591)

Amos Lewis, curate of Granham confessed that he hath expounded [i.e. preached] and is not yet licensed thereto, but would that Master Archdeacon

---

[97] The point being made here, I think, is that, these being "working days", the church was not being used for services.

would appoint some time that he might preach before his worship, and if he should accept of him he would request his worship to be means unto my Lord of London that he may be licensed to preach.[98]

A day appointed for the same.

Failure to visit the sick, etc. (13 July 1591)

Master Clipsam, rector of Stanford le Hope. Reported that he visiteth not the sick. When he is absent he seldom leaveth any to serve the cure in his absence. He and his wife very often depart the church in sermon time. Wherefore they are suspected to favour the popish religion.

Burial service irregularity (6 June 1593)

Master Bainbrigg, minister of Norton Mansfeld. Reported for burying the dead corpse of one father Cooke not saying service in manner & form as it is in the Book of Common Prayer prescribed.

He confessed that he did not go to the grave according to the Book of Common Prayer, by reason of a great wind, & he not being well durst not go into the danger of taking cold in the air, but he saith that he read the whole service, according to the Book of Common Prayer.

Whence my lord ordered him that on Sunday next he shall acknowledge that he hath omitted his duty in not burying the dead according to the order prescribed.

Recalcitrant unbeneficed cleric (3 September 1599)

William Farrington, clerk of Chipin Ongar. We certify you that one William Farrington, clerk, as he saith, liveth idly in our town without serving any cure, contrary to the articles & laws ecclesiastical.

Item, we present him for not receiving the sacrament in our church for three quarters of this year, of purpose going out of the town every communion to avoid it.

Item, we present him to be a malicious, contentious & uncharitable person, & a railer of our minister & of most of the inhabitants that profess religion, calling them all heretics, hypocrites such as he hath ever & in every place detested, clowns, etc.

Item, we present him for his open absence from prayers on the Sabbath days, in contempt of our minister, & for his usual departure out of the church, at such time as he cometh before the people be dismissed, contrary to the articles.

---

[98] Only a minority of clerics were licensed to preach. Lewis is here seeking such a licence from the Bishop of London ("my Lord of London").

Puritan cleric (19 July 1603)

Master George Watson, preacher at Billarykey. He has that day and place to certify that he hath administered the sacraments of the Lord's Supper and of baptism, in decent sort, according to the Book of Common Prayer, with the surplice, in the church of Billaryckcy: and that he doth use the sign of the cross in baptism.

He swears and alleges that he is not bound to observe these things, which were enjoined him, and that he is only to attend his office of preaching.

Because he has refused to observe the form of the Book of Common Prayer, the judge suspended him from entering the church, and forbad him to exercise his office and ministry.

Failure to keep parish register (23 May 1604)

Robert Boothe, rector of Ramsden Bellowes. Presented for not registering the weddings, christenings and buryings. He was cited.

Clerics: secular offences

Usury (9 April 1578)

Mark Simpson, clerk, rector of Pitsey.[99] The court presented that he is suspected to be a usurer.

The said Simpson confessed that he lent out a little money, and had but 2s of the pound, after the rate of ten in a hundred [i.e. 10 per cent]. But he did not urge the same, but only the parties themselves, whom he lent the money to, did of their own good will, give him after the same rate, but not by compulsion he did urge the same.

The court accepted the confession and ordered him to do penance the next Sunday in Pitsey church, in the time of divine service, and he shall openly in service time read the fifteenth psalm and acknowledge his fault, and hand over to the collectors [of the poor] 5s.

Rector as lord of misrule (14 January 1596/7)

Master John Fabian, rector of the parish church of Whirl Magna. It is noted by public fame that on Sunday at night the second of January last he did to the scandal of his calling and offence of good Christians behave himself very dissolutely and wantonly in the parish of Kelvedon, etc. in

---

[99] The same man as cited above, see p. 77.

taking upon him to be a lord of misrule or Christmas lord, etc. amongst certain yongelinges, etc. He was suspended.

Theft of documents from parish chest (15 May 1600/1)

Master Newman, vicar de Canwedon. Reported that he was consenting & privy unto the picking the lock of our parish chest, wherein we keep our evidences and writings: out of which chest, there was certain evidences taken away at the same time.

Further, we say our said vicar is very slack & negligent in going the perambulation for these two years past.

Clerics: sexual offences

Bigamy charge against rector (25 May 1593)

Robert Hunter, rector of Easthorndon. Reported that there is a common fame that Master Hunter our parson hath two wives alive.

The said Master Hunter came in person and objected by my lord to the article and confessed that in the time of Queen Mary's reign, before he was made minister, he was married to one Margaret Wattes. And that she died as he hath heard about 12 years agone last past. And that within three or four years after her departure from him he was married to Elizabeth Turner, of Southweld, in the parish church there, with whom he lived 28 years. And that he married with the said Elizabeth Turner, the said Margaret Wattes his first wife then living, for that he saith that the said Margaret Wattes, was then the lawful married wife of Richard Mingsden of Maidstone, in the county of Kent.

To appear further.

Further alleged that he giveth ill example of life by unquiet living, beating & chaining of his wife to a post, and is a slanderer of his neighbours.

To bring the Lord Bishop Grindal's order for the allowance of his second marriage.

Sexual offences of curate (12 April 1599)

Master James Wallinger, curate of Laindon Hilles. We do present one Master James Wallinger our curate, for that there is a common fame and report with and amongst honest & credible persons, that the said James liveth incontinently with one Suzan Hales, single woman of the parish of Graies Thorock; and that there is a vehement suspicion of incontinency of him, in that behalf; for that (as it is reported) he was taken in bed with her.

He confessed that there is such a fame & report within the said parish of Laindon Hilles & that he was taken in bed with the said Susan in his own house in Laindon Hilles aforesaid about the second day of March last past between ten & twelve of the clock in the night time by the conspiracy of others.

Also we do present the said James Wallinger to be a common swearer & a blasphemer of the name of God, and to be a man whose tongue is full of ribaldry & filthy speeches; to the great discredit of his coat & calling & to the evil ensample [i.e. example] of others.

Item, we present the same James Wallinger for a common brawler & a debate maker, & a sower of sedition, between neighbour & neighbour. He was suspended.

Offences by or against church officers

Plays in church during Lent (22 April 1577)

Vincent Harcotts & William Rookes, lately churchwardens of Westham. They had been excommunicated for not appearing. They [now] came and did their faith, and the court absolved and restored them. And then the court objected to them that whilst they were there churchwardens, they suffered and caused in Lent last past two sundry holydays, there was two plays kept in the church, by common players ... And the people were suffered to stand upon the Communion Table, divers of them.

The same Vincent Hancottes and William Rookes confessed the same to be true, adding that the same plays were suffered for that they had a poor man in decay, and some relief off the same players to the use of the same poor man. The court accepted their confessions.

The same William Rookes affirmed that he coming into the church perceived that the players went about to play, he speaking to them declared that he would not give his consent [and] that they should not play there, and he would not be blamed for them. But he tarried and heard the play, and therein he consented to the play.

The court ordered them that upon the Sunday next, in service time, they shall confess that they are sorry that they did suffer the church to be profaned, and in their negligence therein, he, the same Vincent to give 5s, and William Rookes to give 2s 6d.

Bribing a court official (16 December 1590)

Edward Eve, of All Saints parish, Malden confessed that he gave 10s to Gilbert the apparitor to the end that he might not be called into this court.

Paying the church assessment (18 January 1591)

John Miles, of Raleighe. It is reported that he did unorderly, against the churchwardens' will, let forth the people forth of the church, the core being about the gathering of a cessement towards the repairing of the glass windows.

He denied that he did any way interrupt or trouble the said church-wardens in the gathering of their cessement.

Then the judge dismissed him, with the admonition to be of good behaviour towards the churchwardens.

Theft of parish endowment (14 June 1599)

James Warly, of Billirica. It is reported by the churchwardens of Graies Thorock, that whereas of long time, long before the memory of any man living, there were belonging to our parish church 40 mother sheep, the benefit whereof should yearly redound to the relief of the poor, in beer, bread & cheese; yet one James Warly of Billirica, confederating with one Robert Attridg of Kent, hath made away the said sheep, contrary to the will of the dead, whereby the poor are robbed of their due.

False presentment by churchwardens (9 March 1603)

Thomam Blackmore, William Heynes, churchwardens of Southbemflitt. The judge asked them on oath whether they do know, that the wife of Robert Lewgare, will not permit or suffer water to be sprinkled or poured upon a child, when it is baptized, neither the child to be signed with the sign of the cross?

They responded on oath that they neither know, nor have heard, that the said Lewgar's wife is any such person, as is mentioned in the present-ment; nor do believe her to be so.

Then the judge asked whether the presentment exhibited under their names & hands be true, yea or no?

They answer it is not true: and the said Blackmore affirmed on oath that he was sick and did not subscribe the presentment.

Then the judge dismissed the said Blackmore, and ordered the said Heynes, to ask the said Lewgar's wife's forgiveness, for presenting of her without a cause, in the presenting Lewgar.

At his petition the judge dismissed the said Heyenes without ordering a penance.

Laity: ecclesiastical offences

False claiming of witchcraft (30 October 1575)

Joan Allen of Leghe. Reported that she came to Widow Jackson, a witch, for counsel, as the talk goeth.

She came and confessed that she did make a lie that she was with a cunning woman.

The court ordered her that upon All-Hallows Day next she shall confess her fault.

Fighting and tale-bearing (16 June 1591)

John Woolbere & Ameas Gardiner, of Blackmore. Reported with these words, viz. for that they fall out and fight in the street; and go from house to house, with tales to make discord between neighbours.

Failure to receive communion (12 July 1591)

John Burr, gent., of Barking. He replied that he hath received according to his conscience. And further he confesseth that his conscience will not permit him to receive, according to the Book of Common Prayer: but he allegeth, that he cometh to his parish church of Barking, to hear divine service.

The court ordered that he shall receive the communion in his parish church of Barking, according to the Book of Common Prayer, before Christmas next.

Cost of purgation (18 December 1591)

Lodovic Billinges, of Barking. It is reported that he hath failed in his purgation.[100]

He alleged that he is a very poor man and not able to procure his neighbours to come to the court and bear their charges.[101]

Ordered to acknowledge his fault.

Penance case (30 July 1600)

Bowers Gifforde. I certify by these presents that Joan Mildberde of the parish aforesaid did all the time of divine service & of the sermon stand in a white sheet, but would not confess her fault, although I persuaded her earnestly so to do.

Attack on parson and sexton (18 November 1592)

Zachary Some, of Sandon. Reported by the churchwardens that he hath uncharitably abused their parson, for that the said Zacharye called him

---

[100] In purgation one brought law-worthy persons to the court to swear to one's good behaviour.

[101] The implication is that Billinges would have to pay the expenses of his compurgators.

prattling fool, for preaching against drunkenness; saying moreover, that he could, if he had authority within a fortnight space, make as good a sermon as he.

Also that he & William Reynold of Westhanfield did unreverently behave themselves in the church of Sandon, upon a Saturday at night, being the 27th day of May, by throwing of pesokes [i.e. hassocks] at the head of the sexton & thereby brake his head.

Refusing to say the Ten Commandments (19 January 1593)

Richard Brett, of Friering. Reported by the churchwardens that he refused to say the Ten Commandments, etc.

He confessed & was ordered to acknowledge his fault.

Public attack on public penance (28 April 1595)

Richard Thornton, of Westham. We present Richard Thornton, for that upon Sunday being the first day of December last, he did publicly encourage an adulteress (who was then doing penance) to go forward & to return again to her former folly, the morrow after, as fresh as ever she did. Who being reproved by one of the sidemen, for giving such lewd counsel and encouragement to sin, hath very uncharitably abused the said sideman with reproachful speeches.

Excommunicated. Later absolved.

Assault on minister (29 April 1595)

Joan Madyson, of Buttesbury. Reported that she unreverently abused Master Simons our minister in striking him upon his head in such sort that she brake the same & made the blood run down.

The court decreed the said Margaret to be excommunicated.

Secreting of communion bread (15 July 1595)

Joan Wheeler, of Dengie. For brawling in the church on Whitsunday last before the communion, & for that she did not eat the bread of the communion, but put it in her pocket at Easter last was twelvemonth.

Reserved.

Pew dispute (10 February 1595/6)

Matthew Everedd, of Rettingden. Reported that there is a pew made by Matthew Everedd & it did breed contention.

He saith that there is no contention now for it.

Dancing on a Sunday (11 January 1597/8)

William Haynes, of Sowthbemflete. Detected for that upon Sunday before Michaelmas in the time of afternoon service he was dancing with minstrels on a green by Thomas Harris his howse.

Fighting during sermon time (26 April 1598)

Thomas Browne, of Lees magna. It is reported that the 5th day of March being the Lord's day, being both of them in the church, in the time of the sermon, [they] went forth into a meadow & there did fight: for many in the church did hear them & went forth, which was a great disquieting to the parish.

To acknowledge his fault.

Football during the Sunday service (26 April 1598)

Hugo Bailye, of Badowe magna. Reported that in the time of Evening Prayer he was in the churchyard with a football under his arm, by means whereof the youths of other parishes there was so much noise amongst them, that the minister could not be heard, to the profaning of the Sabbath day.

He saith that he went out & took the ball from the youths & was coming into the church.

The court admonished and dismissed him.

Refusal to pay for ringing of funeral knell (2 July 1599)

Robert Hanger, of Waltham Stowe. Reported for that he cometh very seldom to church, & is indebted to the parish, for ringing of a knell, at the death of his son 16d, which he obstinately refuseth to pay, contrary to order & custom.

The court ordered him to pay.

Mock funeral (26 September 1600)

Richard Prentyce of Easterlye. We upon the report of the sexton with other do present Richard Prentyce [and three others] for carrying William Goodmin upon the old hearse into the church yard & John Jobson for aiding in ringing the bells.

Living and giving birth in the parish church (20 October 1600)

William Wallis and wife of Stanford Rivers reported for that they have made their habitation in the south porch of the parish church, & therewithal he doth not otherwise provide, but hath suffereth his wife to travail in childbirth therein & to continue there her whole month.

Eucharistic heresy (19 July 1603)

Alice Harvey of Sowthamingfield. Presented for that she holdeth an unreverend opinion of the sacrament of the Lord's Supper, to wit, that there is no difference between the action of receiving bread and wine there than eating and drinking in a common alehouse, and that she hath no need of any such means, to put her in remembrance of the passion of Christ.

Excessive fees for administration of wills (20 December 1604)

Francis Willson of Westham cited to respond to certain articles for that he receiveth fees of diverse poor people and large sums of money to procure administrations, &c., and doth not dispatch their business; and namely he took 30s of Widow Coates.

The court dismissed him with the admonition that he behave properly in these matters.

Troublesome parishioner (2 September 1605)

Andrew Walmesley of Duddinghurst reported for a very seditious and contentious fellow troublesome both in the church, and also otherwise in the parish. And such a one as did the 9 day of June 1605 in time of divine service in the forenoon molest the minister and the whole parish there present in answering him contemptuously, when he was demanded for a certificate of his absolution, saying that he would not depart when he was admonished so to do, so that the minister was urged [*recte* urged him] thereby to go out of his pew, and out of the church from divine service, until that afterwards other honest men did persuade him, when he said he would not, by the admonition of the said minister, with other words and speeches, not decent for him then to use.

Non-attendance at church

Recusancy fines (12 July 1591)

Master Gage and wife, of Laighton. His servant allegeth that his master is indicted to pay unto her Majesty as a recusant, viz. £20 every month: and for proof whereof, he exhibiteth a tally for the payment thereof out of the Exchequer, and also an acquittance for the payment of one half now past.

The court accepted and ordered action to be suspended until the next court.

Recusant refuses to attend church (12 July 1591)

Master Thomas More and his wife, of Laighton. The said Master More appeared in his own person and confessed that truth it is that he hath not received the communion, and hath not come to church, to hear divine service of long time. And allegeth that he hath ben imprisoned in divers places, for that his conscience would not permit him to come to church & receive the communion. And he doth now remain her Majesty's prisoner, and goeth abroad being bound to answer, when the Council shall call for him. And therefore ought not to be further any ways molested, as appeareth by a warrant under the hand of the Right Honourable Master Anthony Astley, one of the clerks of the Council. And that he is also indicted to her Majesty & his goods and lands is seised to her Majesty; and therefore requireth to be dismissed.

To appear and prove the other process to be.

Warrant to excuse church attendance (12 July 1591)

Lady Margery Throgmorton of the parish of Westham. Similarly. On that day came Master Richard Swarton and in the name of the said Lady Throgmorton confessed that the presentment is true; but allegeth that the said lady his mistress, hath a sufficient warrant, to dispense both for herself and for her whole household servants that they, nor either of them, shall not be troubled by the ordinary[102] of the place, or any other whatsoever; but only to be at the council's commandment, whensoever they shalbe called, as appeareth by a warrant from the said council.

Playing musical instruments on a Sunday (9 August 1598)

Edward Pharowe, of Hoklye Alleged reported very negligent in coming to church, who upon the first Sunday in Lent in the afternoon had company at his house dancing; he playing upon his musical instruments. So both he & they were absent from evening prayer, passing away that afternoon, he in playing & others in dancing: but who they were, we know not for certain.

Recusancy of William Birde (the composer) (11 May 1605)

William Bird & Helen his wife of Stondon Massie. Presented for popish recusants. He is a gentleman of the King's Majesty's Chapel, and as the minister and churchwardens do hear, the said William Birde, with the

---

[102] The "ordinary" was the person having ecclesiastical authority over a person or place. It was usually the bishop or his archdeacons.

assistance of one Gabriel Colford, who is now at Antwerp, hath been the chief and principal seducer of John Wright, and an heir of John Wright of Kelvedon, in Essex, gent. and of Anne Wright the daughter of the said John Wright the elder.

And the said William [in fact, Helen] Bird as it is reported and as her servants have confessed, have appointed business on the Sabbath Day for her servants, of the purpose to keep them from church, and hath also done her best endeavour to seduce Thoda Pigbone her now maid servant, to draw her to popery, as the maid hath confessed. And besides hath drawn her maid servants from time to time these seven years, from coming to church. And the said Ellen refuseth conference.

And the minister and churchwardens have not as yet spoke with the said William Birde, because he is from home, &c. And they have been excommunicate these seven years.

Laity: secular offences

Seeking the aid of a witch (26 April 1585)

John Shonnke senior of Romford. Reported that he went to Father Parfoothe for help for his wife, which Parfoothe is suspected to be a witch.

The said Shonnke came and confessed to the accusation and saith that for the help of his wife he went to him. And if it were again, he would the like to help his wife, which Parfoothe is counted to be a witch, and is allowed for a good witch.

The court accepted his confession and ordered him to purge himself by public penance at the time of divine service in the chapel of Haveringe, confessing himself heartily sorry for seeking men's help and refusing the help of God.

Wife-beating (3 June 1592)

William Hylls, of Sandon. Reported to be a very lewd and uncharitable man with his wife, and hath used her most ungodly, not only by refusing her company, but also by beating her most cruelly, without any pity or compassion.

Hylls came on that day and confessed that he upon occasion that his wife had beated and misused his sister and some fatherless children, whom he keepeth in his house, he gave her eight strokes with a wand: for the which he is sorry for now, and promiseth never to use himself in like sort hereafter.

To acknowledge his fault.

Disorderly living (20 February 1593)

Charles Payne, of Buttesburye. Reported that he liveth very disorderly, neither frequenting his parish church, neither in any order amongst his neighbours; but will most unreverently blaspheme the name of God by cursing, swearing, even at his own mother.

He confessed the same, and was admonished to acknowledge his fault, and ask his mother's forgiveness.

Vandalism (11 March 1595/6)

John Southend, of Warley magna. We present one John Sowthen butcher, for that he beastly & lewdly did defile a stile leading to the church on New Year's day at night.

Drunken mother (29 April 1597)

Jane wife of John Minors, of Barking. We present Jane the wife of John Minors for keeping her child unbaptized a whole month.

Also detected for that she very unwomanlike, came to be churched at the end of the said month, together with her child to be baptized, and feasted at a tavern 4 or 5 hours in the forenoon: and in the afternoon came to the church, rather to be seen, then upon any devotion, as it seemed; for whilst the minister was burying a corpse, she went out of the church, unchurched, unto the tavern again. And when she was spoken unto by the clerk to return to church again & to give God thanks after her delivery, she answered it was a ceremony. The which abuses of the said Jane, seeing they are so public & notorious, & the example unpunished, may prove dangerous, we pray that your worship would enjoin, that her satisfaction may be also public; to the content of many of good worth.

Dominus commisit vices suas Magistro Wignall et aliis per eum convocandis ad audiendum et terminandum, etc.

Slanderous rhyme (12 July 1597)

Thomas Ellis of Boreham. Detected he hath reported a rhyme upon names of sundry men & women in our parish but will not beknowledge who made it nor of whom he had it.

He confessed that he had a rhyme of the girl of the sideman, etc.

The court admonished and dismissed him.

Throwing stones at the church (13 July 1597)

John Stud, of Saint Peter's in Mawldon. Detected that he did upon the 6th day of June being Sunday, did stand in the street & throw stones, which fell upon the church & brake the tiles of the church.
Cited.

Sorcery (12 April 1599)

Thomas Ward, of Purleigh. We present Thomas Ward, as by report, to seek help at sorcerer's hands.

He confessed that he having lost certain cattle & suspecting that they were bewitched, he went to one Tailer in Thaxted, a wizard to know whether they were bewitched or not, and to have his help.

To acknowledge that he is heartily sorry for the same.

Drunkards (2 May 1599)

Nicolas Marden, of Curringham. Reported that he & one John Smith of the parish of Curringham & one Richard Cottes of Orsett & George Landishe of Barkinge, after great abuse in drinking, did at their parting, take with them into the field, at the town's end where they meant to part, four or six pots of beer; & there setting them down, did themselves upon their bare knees humbly kneel down, & kissing the pots & drinking one to the other, & prayed for the health of all true & faithful drunkards; & especially for Master Andrew Browghton, as they said the maintainer & upholder of all true & faithful drunkards. And having done they kissed each other [and] for a memory of their worthy act did every man make his mark or name, upon an ashen tree, that stood there by them.

To acknowledge their fault.

Vandalism (16 May 1600)

William Thresher, of Alveley. Reported for cutting out the names of William Hurt & Thomas Collines churchwardens, out of the post whereunto the church stile was joined, most maliciously defacing the same, there joined by an order from Romforde to be set up by us, to the great dislike of many in the same parish & scandal to the church of God; & made his vaunts & common jests of it after he had done it.

91

Morris dancing (26 September 1603)

Henry Page of Sowthwelde. Presented for making preparation with others for to dance the morrice in the sermon while; and that they met with the bridegroom and came dancing the morrice home with them.

Females fighting (25 October 1603)

The wife of John Woodde of Prittlewell. Presented for a troublesome and a contentious person with widow Browne and her daughter in fighting together and calling one another in undecent terms as whore, bitch and such like.

Sexual offences of the laity

Penance for adultery (20 March 1575/6)

Margaret Orton, convicted of adultery with Anthony Bennell of Barkinge.

Memorandum that Margaret Orton according to her appointment hath done her penance in the parish church of Barkinge in Essex before the second lesson at morning prayer upon Sunday 18th day of March, 1575/6. And there was read the first part of the Homily against Whoredom & Adultery, the people there present exhorted to refrain from such wickedness, whereby they might incur the displeasure of Almighty God for violating his holy law, and she penitent, etc. for her offences, etc.

The court pronounced her to be sufficiently punished.

Rape (1 July 1590)

Joan Somers of Downham. The court denounced her for fornication and she replied that upon a certain working day happening about Christmas last, this respondent being in a plough field serving her dame's cattle, the said Ryce Evans came unto her and told her that she might now cry her heart out before anybody could hear her cry, and so indeed as she saith, he did violently abuse her body and committed fornication with her.

A widow's sexual incontinence (26 October 1591)

Joan Fryday alias Wright, of Cumngham. Reported that in the time of her widowhood she defiled her body, by common fame.

Christopher Fryday, husband of the said Joan and in the name of his said wife came and denied the allegation. And otherwise he claimed that she was called before the Lord Commissary of Essex, and he showed a written instrument under the hand of Thomas More, the Commissary's actuary, as there assigned to purge herself of that crime.

The court decreed the said Joan Fryday to be excommunicated.
[Case was continued 25 November 1591]
The lord judge absolved her.

She saith that she was presented only by evil report of one Gabriell Holt, late of the same parish, who was a suitor unto her in the way of marriage. And in that she liked not of him, he very maliciously did slander this respondent, and said that he did defile this respondent's body. And he himself bid one of the sidesmen present this respondent therefore.

Ordered that she is to provide a certificate as to her honest conversation.[103]

Churching of a mother (2 May 1592)

The wife of Robert Aylet, of the parish of Hornchurch. It is reported that she never gave thanks after the delivery of two children. And after the delivery of the third she came to give thanks, without any other woman with her, to the offence of her neighbours.

Bigamy, etc. (5 May 1592)

John Tytman, of Woodham Mortimer reported for that he confesseth himself to have two wives living, and for not receiving the communion at Easter last, for not coming orderly to church, and for a brawler and scolder with his neighbours.

Penance following sexual incontinence (2 May 1592)

William Peacocke, of Leighton.

The said William Peacocke shall prepare himself to receive the holy communion with the whole congregation, or with so many of them as then shall happen to receive.

And when the whole company of communicants are gathered together in the choir, and before the communion be administered, he the said William Peacocke shall publicly after the minister (in part of his punishment for his said offence) confess that he hath grievously offended the majesty of Almighty God, and deserved his wrath and heavy judgment, for his lewd offence, by him wickedly committed with the foresaid Alice Stane. For the which he shall confess himself heartily sorry; desiring Almighty God in mercy to accept of his penitency and contrition, and to pardon his said offence and vouchsafe in mercy to receive him into the number of his elect, promising that by the help of God he will never commit the like offence again.

---

[103] Euphemism for "good behaviour".

Also he shall desire all good people, then there present, or wheresoever else, whom he by his evil example hath offended, to pardon and forgive him.

And lastly he shall entreat the people all to pray unto Almighty God for and with him, and shall after the minister say the Lord's prayer Our Father, &c.

Marriage mask (20 March 1593)

Jasper Dormer, gent., of Stanford le Hope reported for marrying his wife in their parish church in her mask and for having of two wives alive at once & that he was never divorced from her.

Incest with daughter (13 January 1595/6)

William Foster, of Barking. We present William Foster of our town, upon the suspicion of a most shameful matter of incest, with his own daughter. The ground of which suspicion we build not only upon common report, but upon the assertion of honest women, who have had the examination of the young wench.

Ordered to purge himself.

Woman dressed as a man (15 May 1596)

Joan Towler, of Downham. Reported for that she came into our church in man's apparel upon the Sabbath day in the service time.

Brothel (15 May 1596)

John Manister and wife of Woodhamferris. Reported for that they keep an open house of bawdry.

Breach of promise (23 May 1598)

William Walford, of Sowthfambridge. He confessed that he was asked in the church and had purposed to have married the said Joan Packman, but for secret causes & specially for that the said Joan is not sound in body, nor hath any hair on her head, he will not proceed any furder, etc.

Marriage under a bush (16 October 1599)

David Harbert, and wife of Eastham. Reported that he & Elizabeth his wife, for that a common fame hath been raised by Katherine Gawen, of Eastham aforesaide widow, that the said David Harbert & Elizabeth his wife were married under a bush; the said Elizabeth answering to the same, "Did my husband tell you that?"

Sleeping with own mother (13 January 1600/1)

Edward Saunders, of Stambridge magna. Reported that he hath often lain with his own mother an old woman to the great offence of many.

Unseemly churching of woman (12 May 1602)

Wife Collins, of Sowthebemflete. It is reported that she coming to the church to be churched, or to give God thanks for her delivery upon the Sabbath day, came very undecently & contrary to order, unto the church, without kercher, midwife, or wives; & placed herself in her own stall, not in the stall appointed: by the which she showed herself derisiouse, in coming so like a light & common woman, so that she returned not churched according to the book: which she best liked, and saith that in places from whence she came, the use is such, neither did she at any time otherwise.

Marriage jest (25 October 1602)

William Gylchrist, of Westham. It is reported that upon Sunday, being the 27th of June last, when there was a marriage to be solemnized, he the said Gilchrist in derision of holy matrimony, got a bough hanged with ropes ends & beset with nettles & other weeds, & carried the same in the street & churchyard before the bride, to the great offence of the congregation.

Cuckoldry and marriage (3 July 1605)

Edward Row of Thorocke parva. Presented for that he at the marriage of Thomas Brock and Rebecca Foster, did fasten a pair of horns, upon the church-yard gate, of the parish of Grayes Thorocke; and being rebuked for the same, afterwards did avow that he did it, and if it were to do again, he would do it.

Chapter 3
Crime and Punishment in the Seventeenth Century

1 The criminal process in the seventeenth century

1.1 Assize Court's concern to secure able constables, tithingmen and other officers (Taunton Assizes, August 1657)[1]

Constables, etc.

Whereas it appeareth to this court upon the presentment of the grand inquest of this county that many constables of hundreds now chosen are persons inconsiderable both for estates and qualifications, not knowing what is to be done in their offices, and that in many places in this county the office of tythingmanship by custom goeth from house to house so that the office is many times supplied by hired persons and the execution of justice very often neglected.[2] This court doth therefore order and desire the Justices of the Peace of this county at their sessions and the stewards of hundreds at their court leets to take special care for the future that none be elected constables but such as are of abilities, knowledge, and known integrity, and that for the future there be no more deputy tithingmen suffered to serve in that office but such as shalbe allowed of under the hands of two of the Justices of the Peace of this county. And the undersheriff of this county is hereby required to send copies of this order to the several Justices of the Peace of this county, who are hereby desired to see the same put in execution.

Water bailiffs, etc.

Whereas it appeareth to this court on the presentment of the grand inquest of this county that there are several men that go up and down fourteen hundreds of the eastern side of this county under the notion of water bailiffs, eyslaying fines and receiving monies from several poor

---

[1] J. S. Cockburn (ed.), *Somerset assize orders, 1640–59* ("Somerset Rec. Soc.", lxxi (1971)), nos. 143 and 144.
[2] That is to say, the nominated tithingmen were putting inadequate deputies in their place.

people there, and that the statute for destroying crows and rooks is not put in execution.

This court doth therefore desire four of the Justices of the Peace of this county, or any two of them, to call the said water bailiffs before them, or any two of them, and see their commission and examine by what authority they do the same, and if they see cause, to bind them over to the next assizes to be holden for this county, there to answer the same.

And this court doth further order that the constables, churchwardens, and overseers of the poor of every parish within this county do take care that the statute for the destroying of crows, rooks, and other vermin be put in execution; and that cuckingstooles[3] be likewise set up in their several parishes where anciently they have been and now are not any.

And the sheriff of this county is hereby required to send copies of this order to the several constables of the hundreds within this county to the intent that it may be put in execution.

1.2 Oxfordshire JP's licence to keep a tippling house (1617)[4]

The terms of the licence clearly indicate the degree of control the licensing magistrates intended to exercise over ale-house keepers.

Oxon. Memorandum. We His Majesty's Justices of the Peace . . . undernamed have licensed Justin Egerley of Brittington, husbandman, to sell ale and beer, and to use the trade of victualling, within the said place, for the space of one whole year next ensuing. And [we] have taken recognizance of him with two sufficient sureties[5] according to the law and form of the statute in that case provided, not only to observe and keep the Articles hereunder written, but also all other his Majesty's laws and statutes in these cases provided. In witness whereof we have hereunto set our hand and seals [22 April 1617]

1. *Imprimis* that he shall suffer no neighbours' children or servants or any other dwelling in the same parish to tipple in his house.
2. *Item* that none be suffered to tipple in his said house on the Sabbath or festival days, at the service or sermon time, nor any other day above one hour, nor at any time after 9 of the clock at night.

---

[3] Ducking-stools.

[4] Extracted from M. S. Gretton (ed.), *Oxfordshire justices of the peace in the seventeenth century* (Oxfordshire Rec. Soc., xvi (1934)), p. xxxi.

[5] What usually happened was that the prospective ale-house keeper had to enter into a bond of £10 to obey the terms of his licence, and that his two sureties had to indemnify the court to the tune of £5 each if he broke those terms.

3. That he suffer no dicing, carding, playing at tables,[6] or any other unlawful game to be used in his house.
4. That he suffer no drunkards, drunkenness, or any other evil rule to be in his house. If any happen to be, he shall presently[7] acquaint the constable, or other officer with it, that such offenders may be punished and such abuses reformed.
5. That if any vagabonds or any other suspicious persons come to his house and do there offer any goods to be sold,[8] he shall presently acquaint the constable, or other officer withal, that such persons may be apprehended and brought before some Justice of the Peace to be examined if there be cause.
6. That he brew his drink that he may sell the best at 6s the barrel, and the small [beer] at 3s.
7. That he draw out his drink and sell it at the ale-quart and ale-pint, and not by cups and jugs, and sell the best at 3d the ale-gallon and the small at 2d[9] the ale-gallon.

1.3   Control of alehouse licensing (Taunton Assizes, March 1652)[10]

Here we see the assize court judges attempting to influence the application of the law in a particular county.

Forasmuch as it appeareth to this court upon the presentment of the grand inquest of this county of the great multiplicity of ale-houses in this county, by reason whereof many disorders are daily committed and the Lord's Day much profaned to the great dishonour of Almighty God. This court doth therefore desire the Justices at their next quarter sessions to divide themselves into divisions and to agree how many of them shall meet together in each division and to observe and keep their monthly meetings and to license none but there only, or in open Quarter Sessions, and such as shalbe sufficient people and bring with them good certificates from the chiefest parishioners where they dwell, and be bound with very good sureties to keep the assize of beer and ale according to the statute in that behalf made.

---

[6] Shove-happeny.
[7] i.e. immediately.
[8] The ale-house was seen as a principal place for "fencing" stolen goods. It still is!
[9] Small beer was weaker and hence cheaper.
[10] As we can see, this is a recurring theme. Cockburn, *Somerset assize orders*, no. 120.

1.4 Seventeen Articles put to Constables by the Oxfordshire JPs, 1687[11]

These are the replies of the Petty Constable of Chipping Norton at the Trinity Sessions of the Oxfordshire Quarter Sessions of 1687. They indicate the range of cases a local constable was expected to deal with and report on.

1. We have not apprehended any rogues, vagrants or sturdy beggars since the last sessions.
2. We have not received any such by pass.[12]
3. Our officers have not been charged with any convey.[13]
4. We know of none that did receive such persons as did not apprehend them or did suffer any such persons to lodge in their out-houses.
5. We have duly kept our watch and ward and privy searches and have found no suspicious persons.
6. We have no unlicensed ale-house within our liberty[14] not any that suffer tippling or drinking or unlawful gaming in their houses.
7. We know of none that have continued tippling or drinking in any tavern, inn, or ale-house contrary to the laws.
8. We have no brewer that hath served any unlicensed ale-house with ale or beer.
9. We know of none that hath been drunk within our liberty.
10. We know of no profane swearers or cursers within our liberty.
11. We know of no butcher that hath put any meat to sale on the Lord's Day.[15]
12. We know of none that hath travelled or done any worldly labour or exposed any goods or wares [for sale] or used any exercise or pastime on the Lord's Day.
13. We have had no inmates[16] admitted since the last Sessions.
14. We have had no unlawful destroyer of game nor any that do carry such game to sell.
15. We have no forestallers, regrators, or badgers in our Liberty.[17]

---

[11] *Oxfordshire Rec. Soc.*, xvi (1934), p. lxvi.

[12] i.e. those licensed by a justice to move about.

[13] A vagrant being sent back to his or her home parish was the responsibility of the constable through whose parish they passed.

[14] i.e. jurisdiction.

[15] i.e. Sunday.

[16] Incomer.

[17] Forestaller was a trader who bought produce (normally grain) before it got to the market, later to sell it at a high price. A badger was an itinerant trader in corn. A broker was a middleman in trade.

16. Our high ways are now repairing and our bridges are in good repair; we have none that neglect or refuse to do their service for the repairing of the same.
17. We know of no travelling wagon, cart or carriage that go on the common high ways drawn with more than five horse beast at length contrary to the statute or greater weight than the statute allows.

1.5 Rules to be observed by the clerk at Quarter Sessions[18]

These are based on the mid-century notebook of Richard Bragge, a former deputy clerk to the justices in the Western Division of the Sussex Quarter Sessions. (Sussex was divided into two divisions because of its length.) It gives as good account as any of the elaborate bureaucratic procedure followed in Quarter Sessions in the seventeenth century, however, at the point of trial the proceedings were swift, with the trial jury hearing many cases and returning their verdicts in short order. These "rules" do not cover the extensive administrative business undertaken at Quarter Sessions.

Oyes

The Cryer is commanded to make three Oyes, which made the Cryer saith after him thus:

Attendance

"All manner of persons that have anything to do with the general Quarter Sessions to be holden here for this day . . . draw near and give your attendance."

Sheriff

"Sheriff of Sussex return the precepts to thee directed and delivered and give thine attendance."

Bailiffs

"All Bailiffs of Hundreds and Liberties answer to your names, every man as he is called."

Then call them as in the calendar returned by the sheriff.

---

[18] A summary of the Rules as published in B. C. Redwood (ed.), *Quarter sessions order book, 1642–49* (Lewes & Chichester, 1954), pp. 210–14 (*Sussex Record Society*, Record Publication, no. 3).

[The same was done for constables, justices, coroners, and stewards, and then the jurymen. The names of those defaulting attendance were summoned once more, presumably to establish an accurate list.]

Oath to the Grand Jury[19]

This done, call one of the constables whom you will make foreman and give him this oath:

> You shall well and truly enquire and true presentment make of all such points and articles as shall be given to you in charge or belongeth to your charge touching this present sessions: the King's majesty's counsel, your fellows and your own you shall well and truly keep. You shall not present anything for hatred or malice neither shall you conceal any matter through favour or affection. But justly and uprightly according to your evidence and your own knowledge, you shall make a true presentment and no concealment, so help you God and the contents in the Book.[20]

[Similar oaths were given to the other Grand Jurymen, in this county all constables.]

When you have sworn the full jury as 13, 15, 17, or more according to your number of those which appear, then bid the Cryer "Countes". And when the Cryer has counted them all over, he must say . . . "Thirteen good men and true stand together and hear your charge."[21] *[The same procedure was followed with the other juries of enquiry.]*

Charge

When all the juries are empanelled and sworn, cause the Cryer to make one Oyes, which done, let him say after you thus: "The King's Majesty's Justices command all manner of persons to keep silence while the Charge is in giving."

[The clerk then read the relevant statutes, etc. to the juries. The court then did its administrative business which could be considerable.]

---

[19] The grand jury decided whether or not there was a case to answer.

[20] The book, of course, was the Bible, on which jurors and witnesses swore their oath.

[21] In this county, at least, the grand jury was made up of an odd number which suggests that they could bring in majority verdicts as to whether or not there was a case to answer.

Bills of indictment & prosecutors

[*Those bringing bills of indictment and those bound to prosecute were then ordered to appear. If they did not, the relevant prisoner was discharged. The bills of indictment were then written into the record of the court.*]

Witnesses' Oath

[*Those presenting the bills of indictment, i.e. those making the accusations, were then sworn in.*]

"The evidence that you two or either of you shall give to the Grand Jury upon this bill of indictment against A.B. shall be the truth, the whole truth, and nothing but the truth, so help you God."

The bill with the witnesses is then sent by a bailiff to the Grand Jury.[22]

Adjournment of the court

"All manner of persons that have any more to do at this general quarter sessions may depart for this time, and must keep your hour here again at one of the clock in the afternoon."[23]

Calling the court upon adjournment

"You good men that were adjourned to this hour draw near and give your attendance."

Grand Jury Verdicts

[*The grand jury then returned and said whether or not there was a case to answer in each instance. Only then were the prisoners brought into the court.*]

Arraignment of the prisoners

First bid him hold up his hand and then say, "Thou art indicted . . . etc." (as in the indictment). "Art thou guilty of this felony and burglary, or not guilty?"

---

[22] Is the implication of this that the grand jury heard this initial evidence in private during the adjournment?

[23] This is clear evidence that it took a full morning to go through these procedures.

If he say not guilty then ask say, "How wilt thou be tried?" If he say by God and the country, then say "cul. prit"[24] and write over his name "ponit se".[25]

If the prisoner answer "guilty", then write over his name "cogn".[26] [*This was then done with each prisoner.*]

Trial of the prisoners

Call the [trial] jury . . . saying, "You good men empanelled between our sovereign lord the king and the prisoners at the bar, answer to your names."

Then call the prisoners severally again to the bar and say unto them, "These men whom you shall hear called and do personally appear are to pass upon the trial of your lives. If you will challenge them or any of them, you must challenge them as they come to the book to be sworn, before they be sworn."

Then bid the foreman of the jury look upon the prisoners and give him his oath.

Oath to the [trial] jury

"You shall well and truly try and true deliverance make between our sovereign lord the king and the prisoners at the bar whom you shall have in charge, you shall true verdict give according to your evidence, so help you God."

[*The same oath was then given to each juryman in turn.*]

Countes

When you have sworn them all, bid the Cryer, "Countes". And when he hath counted them all after your naming them, he must say, "Twelve good men and true stand together and hear your charge."

Then call the first prisoner again to the bar and, bidding him hold up his hand, say to the jury:

> Look upon him you that are sworn, he hath been indicted . . . (according to the whole indictment through, and then saying to the jury) he hath been arraigned of this felony and burglary and hath pleaded not guilty. And for his trial hath put himself upon

---

[24] This stood for the Anglo-French *culpable prist* meaning "guilty; ready" which was short for *culpable: prest d'averrer nostre bille* meaning "guilty: [and I am] ready to aver our indictment". Thus, the word "culprit" meant originally someone arraigned on an indictment for a felony and only later came to mean someone who is guilty of a crime.

[25] *Ponet se [super patriam]*, meaning "He put himself [upon the country]."

[26] *Cognovit*, meaning he has admitted [the indictment].

God and the country, which country are you. Your charge is to inquire whether he be guilty of this felony and burglary in manner and form contained in this indictment . . .

Witnesses

Then call the evidence of witnesses upon the bill against the prisoners and give them this oath: "The evidence that you and every of you shall give . . . against [the] prisoner at the bar shalbe the truth, the whole truth, and nothing but the truth, so help you God."
[*This procedure was then repeated for each prisoner in turn.*]

Accessory

If there be an accessory arraigned with the principal, then you must say to the jury in the end of the oath aforesaid, "If you quit the principal, you shall not need to inquire of the accessory."

Oath of the bailiff sent with the jury of life and death to keep them

"You shall well and truly keep this jury from meat, drink, fire and candle-light until they are agreed of their verdict. You shall suffer no man to speak with them, neither shall you yourself speak unto them unless it be to ask them whether they be agreed in their verdict or not, so help you God."[27]
[*Then the jury retired to consider its verdict.*]

Verdict

When the jury comes in with their verdict after you have called them over say to them, "Are you agreed of your verdict?" And they answering, "Aye," say again to them, "Who shall speak for you?" and they will answer their foreman.

Then call the first prisoner, and bidding him hold up his hand,[28] say to the foreman "Look upon the prisoners, how say you, is he guilty of the felony and burglary whereupon he stands indicted and arraigned? or not guilty?"

The like passage is to be observed with every other prisoner.

---

[27] The oath indicates the stringent conditions under which the trial juries worked. Clearly, long debate was not encouraged.

[28] Remembering that prisoners were tried in batches, it was necessary to make absolutely certain that the jury knew which individual they were giving verdict on, hence the raised hand.

When the court proceeds to give judgment, call the prisoners severally and bid them severally hold up their hands and ask them severally thus:
"What canst thou say for thyself being convicted of this felony why thou shouldst not receive judgment to die?"[29]

Traverse jury

[*A similar procedure was then applied to trial of misdemeanours by the traverse jury.*]

Adjournment

"The King's Majesty's justices give all men leave to depart for this time."

2   Crime in the seventeenth century

2.1   The trial of Mervin Touchet, Lord Audley, Earl of Castlehaven, for a rape and sodomy, 1631[30]

Mervin Touchet was Baron Audley of Heighley Castle (Staffs.) and Earl of Castlehaven (Ireland). He bought Fonthill Gifford (Wilts.) from his mother's family in 1620. He married first Elizabeth Barnham, heiress of a London alderman. Their eldest son and heir, James, was born c. 1610. After Elizabeth died, Mervin married Anne, daughter of the Earl of Derby and widow of Grey Brydges, Baron Chandos in July 1624.

When 13 or 14, James was married to Elizabeth Brydges (referred to in the following depositions as the young Lady Audley) who was then aged twelve. Elizabeth was Mervin's second wife's child by her first marriage. Thus, the young Elizabeth was both Mervin Touchet's step-daughter and daughter-in-law.

As a result of the events described in the following depositions and examinations, James denounced his father to the king in November 1630 and on 1 December 1630 Castlehaven was imprisoned in the Tower. His trial followed.

On 6 April 1631 a Wiltshire grand jury found three indictments against Castlehaven: one as accessory to a rape upon his own wife, the other two for buggery with his menservants. Because he was a peer, he was tried by his peers in the House of Lords by whom he was found guilty and executed on 14 May 1641.

This case raises many questions both of fact and interpretation. Was the Countess of Castlehaven the innocent victim of a dastardly rape by Brodway

---

[29] This was not a mere formality as many convicted prisoners were reprieved and subsequently pardoned.
[30] W. Cobbett (ed.), *Cobbett's complete collection of state trials*, iii (1809), cols. 402–18.

or did she embroider a sexual encounter to bring about the destruction of her licentious, bisexual husband?

Why was the sexual abuse of the twelve-year-old young Lady Audley not an issue in the prosecutions?

Why did the court take such an extreme view of the allegations of sodomy? Do we hear in the evidence the authentic voice of a gay past?

Given the number of individuals active in what one can only describe as the sexual circus at Fonthills, why did it take so long for complaint to be made? Was such irregular behaviour common in noble households of the time?

Last but not least, how typical were the proceedings as described at Tyburn, where one has what might be described as the theatre of execution revealed?

The pre-trial action

The Friday before the trial the judges met to discuss ten points of law raised by the case. What follows are the questions and answers.

1. *Whether a peer of the realm might waive his trial by peers, and plead he will be tried by God and his country?*
    Answer He might not, for his trial by peers was no privilege, but the law declared by Magna Charta. . . .
2. *Might a peer challenge his peers?*
    Answer He might not . . . because they were not on their oath, but upon their honour. . . .
3. *Could a peer have a counsel?*
    Answer If matter of law appeared, he might, not for matter of fact.
4. *Could a wife be a witness against her husband?*
    Answer She might, for she was the party wronged. In like manner a villain (vassal) might be a witness against his lord in such cases.
5. *Whether, if he stood mute, could he demand his clergy?*
    Answer If he stood mute in case of rape or buggery, he might have his clergy in either.[31]
6. *Whether in a rape there must be penetration?*
    The **answer** was in the affirmative.[32]

Arraignment

Lord Coventry, lord keeper of the great seal, was appointed Lord High Steward for the trial, i.e. he was placed in charge.

---

[31] The judges met on this point again and decided that clergy was available in case of rape, but not in cases of buggery.

[32] The judges revised their opinion at a later date, ruling that ejaculation without penetration did constitute a rape.

The lords took their seats at eight in the morning and the case opened at nine. The lords sat on benches either side of a large table covered with a green cloth. Below them sat the judges and court officials.

The 27 named peers were called individually. The indictments were then received. Only then was the prisoner brought to the bar and asked to plead. Audley asked if he could have counsel; this was refused.

The indictments were then read. Audley was asked how he pleaded. He said not guilty and asked to be tried by God and his peers.

The Lord High Steward then asked the peers to try the case on the evidence.

Sir Robert Heath, attorney-general, then outlined the cases against Audley. On the alleged rape, he pointed out that rape was possible on an unchaste woman as much as a chaste woman. On the charges of sodomy, he argued that Audley had rejected God and given himself over to lust. He then called on the proofs to be read.

The deposition of Walter Bigg

Walter Bigg deposed that Amptil was page to Sir H. Smith, and had no more means when he came to my Lord Audley but the mare he rode on. He [i.e. Castlehaven] entertained him as his page eight years, and afterwards let him keep horses in my lord's grounds, by which I think he enriched himself by £2000, but he never sat at table with my lord til he had married his daughter, and then he gave him to the value of £7000.

That Skipworth was sent from Ireland to be my lady's page, and that his father and mother were very poor folks there. He spent of my lord's purse £500 and he gave him at one time £1000, and hath made divers deeds of land unto him.

My lord was first a Protestant, but after buying Fonthill,[33] he turned his religion.

Lord Audley's examination[34]

That Henry Skipworth had no means when he came to him [i.e. Castlehaven], and that he had given him £1000, and that Skipworth lay with him when he was straitened in rooms; and that he gave a farm of £700 to Amptil that married his daughter, and at other times to the value of £7000. And that there was one Blandina in his house 14 days, and bestowed an ill disease there, and therefore he sent her away.

---

[33] Audley's house in Wiltshire; the original family seat was Heighley castle in Staffordshire.
[34] This was taken prior to the trial.

The examination of the Countess of Castlehaven
[i.e. Mervin Touchet's wife]

Shortly after the earl married her, viz. the first or second night,[35] Amptil[36] came to the bed's side, while she and her husband were in bed, and the Lord Audley spake lasciviously to her, and told her, "that now her body was his, and that if she loved him, she must love Amptil; and that if she lay with any other man with his consent, it was not her fault but his; and that if it was his will to have it so, she must obey and do it."

That he attempted to draw her to lie with his servant Skipworth; and that Skipworth made him believe he did it, but he did not. That he would make Skipworth come naked into his chamber, and delighted calling up his servants to shew their privities; and would make her look on, and [he] commended those with the largest.

That one night being a-bed with her at Founthill, he called for his man Brodway, and commanded him to lie at his bed's feet. And about midnight (she being asleep) called him to light a pipe of tobacco. Brodway rose in his shirt, and my lord pulled him into bed to him and her and made him lie next to her. And Brodway lay with her and knew her carnally, whilst she made resistance, and the lord held both her hands and one of her legs the while. And as soon as she was free, she would have killed herself with a knife, but that Brodway forcibly took the knife from her and broke it. And before the act of Brodway, she had never done it.[37]

That he delighted to see the act done; and made Amptil to come into bed with them, and lie with her whilst he might see it; and she cried out to have saved herself.

The examination of Lawrence Fitz-Patrick, confirmed under oath

That the earl had committed sodomy twice upon his person. That Henry Skipworth was the special favourite of my Lord Audley and made him lie with his own lady. And that he saw Skipworth in his sight do it, my lord being present. And that he lay with Blandina[38] in his sight, and four more of the servants, and afterwards the earl himself lay with her in their sights.

The second examination under oath of Fitz-Patrick

That the lord Audley [i.e. Castlehaven] made him lie with him at Founthill and Salisbury, and once in the bed, and emitted between his thighs, but did not penetrate his body, and that he heard he did so with others.

---

[35] They married 22 July 1624.
[36] One of Audley's menservants and married to one of his daughters by his first marriage.
[37] Not clear what she means. Is she claiming that she had not had sex with an Audley servant until this time?
[38] Blandina was a whore.

That Skipworth lay with the young lady often and that the earl knew it, and encouraged him in it, and wished to have a boy by him, and the young lady.[39]

That Blandina lived half a year in my lord's house, and was a common whore.

The examination of Henry Skipworth, confirmed under oath

That the earl often solicited him to lie with the young lady, and persuaded her to love him. And [the earl] persuaded her that his son loved her not. And that in the end he usually lay with the young lady, and that there was love between them both before. And that his lord said he would rather have a boy of his [i.e. Skipworth's] begetting than any other. And that she was but twelve years of age when he first lay with her, and that he could not enter her body without art. . . .

And that my lord made him lie with his own lady, but he knew her not, but told his lord he did.

That he spent £500 per annum of the lord's purse, and for the most part, he lay with the said earl. That the earl gave him his house at Salisbury, and a manor of £600.

That Blandina lay in the earl's house half a year, and was a common whore.

Then was read the examination of the young Lady Audley[40]

That she was married to her husband by a Romish priest in the morning, and at night by a prebend at Kilkenny.

That she was first tempted to lie with Skipworth by the earl's allurement; and that she had no means but what she had from Skipworth; but she would not lie with Pawlet. He also solicited her to lie with one Green. That the earl himself saw her with Skipworth lie together divers times; and nine servants of the house had also seen it.

When the earl solicited her first, he said that upon his knowledge, her husband loved her not, and threatened that he would turn her out of doors if she did not lie with Skipworth; and that if she did not, he would tell her husband that she did. That she being very young, he [i.e. Skipworth] used oil to enter her body first. And afterwards he usually lay with her, and it was with the earl's privity and consent.

Brodway's examination who confesseth

That he lay at the earl's bed's feet, and one night the earl called to him for tobacco. And as he brought it him in his shirt, he caught hold of him and

---

[39] The young Lady Audley, the earl's step-daughter who was married to his son, James.
[40] The implication appears to be that she was not present.

bid him come to bed. Which he refused, but to satisfy my lord, at last he consented and came into bed on my lord's side. Then my lord turned upon his wife and bid him lie with her, which he did. And the earl held one of her legs and both her hands, and at the last (notwithstanding her resistance) he lay with her. Then the earl used his body as the body of a woman, but never pierced it, only emitted between his thighs.

He hath seen Skipworth lie with the young lady in bed together. And when he [Skipworth] had got upon her, the earl stood by and encouraged him to get her with child.

And that he hath made him the said Brodway kiss his own lady, and often solicited him to live with her, telling him that he himself should not live long, and that it might be his making. And that he hath said the like to Skipworth.

The Earl's defence

After various technical challenges, all rejected by the judges, the earl concluded his defence, claiming that there had been a conspiracy against him.

1. Woe to that man whose wife should be a witness against him.
2. Woe to that man whose son should prosecute him, and conspire his death.
3. Woe to that man whose servants should be allowed witnesses to take away his life.

And he willed that the lords take this into their consideration, for it might be some of their cases, or the case of any man of worth, that keeps a footman or other, whose wife is weary of her husband, or his son arrived to full age, that would draw his servants to conspire his father's death.

He said further that his wife had been naught [i.e. naughty] in his absence, and had had a child, which he concealed to save her honour.

That his son was now become 21 years old, and he himself old and decayed; and the one would have his lands and the other a young husband. And therefore, by the testimony of them and their servants added to their own, they had plotted and conspired his destruction and death.

Verdict

The peers withdrew and took two hours to reach their verdicts, which were given individually. On the rape charge 26 out of the 27 found the earl guilty. On the sodomy charge, 15 found him guilty and 12 not guilty.

The sentence

The verdict having been given, the prisoner was brought back before the bar of the House. The Lord Steward (the presiding judge) then gave the verdict.

Forasmuch as thou Mervin, Lord Audley, Earl of Castlehaven have been indicted for divers felonies by three several indictments: one for a rape, the other two for sodomy, and hast pleaded not guilty to them all, and for thy trial hast put thyself upon God and thy peers, which trial thou hast had, and they found thee guilty of them all, what canst thou say for thyself, why the sentence of death should not be pronounced against thee?

Whereupon he answered he could say no more, but referred himself to God and the king's mercy. Then the lord Steward said, "My heart grieveth for that which my tongue must utter, but justice is the way to cut off wickedness, therefore hear thy sentence."

"Thou must go from hence to the prison from whence thou camest, and from thence to the place of execution, there to be hanged by the neck till thou be dead, and the Lord have mercy on thy soul."

Execution

He was executed at Tower Hill on Saturday 14 May 1631 before a notable company. He admitted having been "a vicious liver" but continued to deny the charges against him.

He made a long protestation as to his religious orthodoxy and thanked the king for permitting beheading to be substituted for the original sentence of hanging. He was then executed with a single axe-blow.

2.2 The trial of Lawrence Fitz-Patrick and Giles Brodway at King's Bench for a rape and sodomy[41]

Following Audley's trial, two of his servants who had given evidence against him were brought to trial despite earlier promises of immunity from prosecution. Their testimonies especially at their execution add important additional evidence to that recorded at the original trial.

On Monday the 27th of June 1631, the marshal of the King's Bench brought Fitz-Patrick and Brodway to the bar where a jury of sufficient and able Wiltshire men impanelled to go upon and try them.[42]

---

[41] Cobbett, *Cobbett's collection of state trials*, iii, cols. 419–26.
[42] It was common practice that the trial jury was made up of men from one's own county.

Broday

The countess of Castlehaven herself was in court to give evidence against Brodway; and she came in upon the instant, when the Lord Chief Justice (Sir Nicholas Hyde) demanded of her whether the evidence she had formerly given at her lord's arraignment was true, and was the full matter of charge she had then to deliver against the prisoner?

Whereupon she answered, "It was."

My Lord said, "Madam, you have sworn that Brodway, prisoner at the bar, hath lain with you by force, which may be, and yet no act committed. Did he enter your body?"

She said that in her former oath taken when she testified he lay with her by force, her meaning was that he had known her carnally and that he did enter her body.

Then she was wished to look on the prisoner unto which motion and commandment she made a short reply. That although she could not look on him but with a kind of indignation and with shame in regard of that which had been offered unto her and she suffered by him, yet she had so much charity in her and such respect to God and his truth, that she had delivered nothing for malice and therefore hoped that her oath and evidence thereupon should be credited. And so [she] desired to be believed and dismissed. Which being granted, she departed with as much privacy as might be into her coach.

Fitz-Patrick

Fitz-Patrick being asked concerning his guiltiness or innocency, demanded who were his accusers. The Lord Chief Justice answered, "You have accused yourself sufficiently." Fitz-Patrick replied that he thought neither the laws of the kingdom required, nor was he bound to be destruction of himself; what evidence he had formerly given was for the king against the earl, and no further.

The Lord Chief Justice replied it was true the law did not oblige any man to be his own accuser, yet where his testimony served to take away any one's life and made himself guilty of the same crime, therein it should serve to cut him off also.

Then the jury demanded of the court satisfaction concerning the words of the statute which run "To charge him alone to be and accounted a felon in law that committed buggery with man or beast" of which fact the earl was found guilty and had suffered.

The Lord Chief Justice replied that forasmuch as every accessory to a felon is a felon in law, so, he being a voluntary prostitute, when he was not only of understanding and years to know the heinousness of the sin, but also of the strength to have withstood his lord, he was so far forth guilty.

Verdict and Sentence

Whereupon the jury found the bill, and the sentence of death was passed on them both.

Aftermath

On the king's instruction, the prisoners were not sent straight to execution. The judges wrote urging execution and no pardon.

Brodway, who was arraigned for the rape very impudently denied his own confession taken before the lords, the peers in the trial of my lord Audley. He pretended that was amazed and knew not what he subscribed, and professed himself guiltless with great execrations. He would not be satisfied unless the lady was produced, face to face, which she was. Who by her oath, *viva voce*, satisfied the auditors both concerning the truth of the fact and his own impudence.

Fitz-Patrick, who was arraigned for the buggery, confessed his examination to be true, but like one very ignorant, or rather senseless, would have them true against the lord Audley and not against himself, which was impossible. He pretended he was promised security from danger if he would testify against the lord Audley and so sought to raise a suspicion, as if he had wrought upon, to be a witness to bring the lord Audley to his end.

They were both found guilty, to the full satisfaction of all that were present. And we for our parts thought it to stand with the honour of common justice, that seeing their testimony had been taken to bring a peer of the realm to his death for an offence as much theirs as his, that they should as well suffer for it as he did, lest any jealousy should arise about the truth of the fact and the justness of the proceedings. . . .

The king by this means being truly informed how things stood, signified his pleasure that they should be executed, but to have a week's time for repentance.

Execution

On Wednesday 16 July 1631 the two convicted prisoners were taken to Tyburn to be hanged. Before the executions each of them made a speech, extracts of which are recorded below. They add significant detail both as to fact and the psychology of the offenders.

Fitz-Patrick's statement

After proclaiming his allegiance to the church of Rome, he went on to details of the case.

Then he proceeded to shew he had been examined by my Lord Chief Justice touching the corruptness of my lord of Castlehaven's life, wherein he said he confessed nothing to prejudice the said earl.

That being within three days after sent for by the lords of the council,[43] my lord Dorset had entrapped and ensnared him to his destruction for saying upon his honour and speaking it in the plural number (as the mouth of the whole board) that whatsoever he delivered should no ways prejudice himself, he thereby got him to declare the earl guilty of buggery. Wherein [he] himself being a party, was the only cause he came to suffer death. . . .

Then he demanded of the company if the earl denied the sin at his death, and wished my lord had not (if he did) for it was true; his lordship had both buggered him and he his lordship.

That it was true (for some private discontentment) he bore a little malice to the earl and Skipworth, for which he asked God forgiveness.

That for Brodway, if he had done anything to the countess, he did it not out of his own ill corrupt nature, but was provoked and persuaded to it by the earl.

He cleared the young lord[44] as never being any occasion or means of his father's death, in hiring or persuading him to give evidence as he had done.

He confessed that he had lived an ill life in that he had delighted in drinking, whoring, and all manner of uncleaness, but now he was heartily sorry.

[*He blamed this on his failure to go to confession. He then offered the standard prayer for the king and the state, and turned to prayer.*]

Brodway's statement

His time being come to stand and have the halter put about his neck, and so declare himself, he willingly suffered the one, and proceeded to the other.

First asking Fitz-Patrick if he had done, he pulled a sheet of paper out of his pocket, which being writ broadways, he could not spread it to read. Therefore [he] desired to have his hands untied, which was done. And he read it distinctly to the assembly. The effect whereof was to declare himself guilty, in the sight of almighty God, of death and damnation, for that he had broke all the commandments in thought, word and deed, and sinned in pride of life, lust of the eye, conceit of his own beauty, matchless strength, and other natural gifts, in desire of revenge, not pitying the poor, unlawful riches, not repairing to sermons, not observing the sabbath, &c.

[*He proclaimed his belief in the pardon of his saviour Jesus Christ, read three prayers from a little book entitled* Learn to Die, *then handed the book to his*]

---

[43] That is to say, the Privy Council.
[44] That is to say, the son James.

kinsman who accompanied the cart on horseback. He read another prayer, commended himself to the sheriff, and threw away his posy of flowers. He then made a further statement.]

Gentlemen, though true it is what I formerly have delivered touching my guiltiness and desert of death, my meaning was and is only in respect of my sins towards God, and no further as for breach of the laws of the kingdom than only once lying with the lady Castlehaven, through persuasion of the earl, who was then in bed with her. And using some small force for the purpose, I did emit but not penetrate her body.

I came not to my lord with the desire or intent to serve him, but was rather inclined for the sea. Only Mr Skipworth had drawn me there for society-sake. And not hearing from my friends concerning my intended voyage, and being more kindly respected by the earl than I looked for, I stayed from week to week, and from month to month, contrary to my intention.

Then my lord, making me his bed-fellow, did one day when Skipworth was with him in the garden (but walking some way apart), break out in speeches to me to this purpose. "Brodway, thou art young, lusty, and well-favoured, and therefore canst not but prevail with any woman thou attemptest. Wherefore, for that I am old and cannot live long, my wife wholly delighting in lust, which I am neither able or willing to satisfy, thou mayest do well to lie with her, and so pleasing her, after my death marry her, and thereby raise thy fortune."

Fitz-Patrick knows my lord had solicited me again and again, hearing him use this language when we were in bed together and he lying at the bed's feet.

Which to clear, he charged Fitz-Patrick to speak his knowledge, who replied, "It was true".

Then he was asked by one of the lords, "Whether when my lord solicited him, my lady desired to have him know her carnally?" To whom he said, "No, he would not wrong her, though she hated him infinitely. But," said he, "I know well if I were minded and able to proffer, she would not say nay, for Mr Skipworth and Amptil lay with her commonly."

He added that Skipworth confessed to him he had often known her, and gotten a child on her, which she, like a wicked woman, had made away. Which was the sole and only occasion he the said Skipworth now hated her, and therefore had turned to the young lady Audely. All which he presumed Skipworth would confess upon his oath. That the countess was the wickedest woman in the world, and had more to answer for than any woman that, as he thought.

115

[*Asked if he spoke from malice, he denied it, then went on as follows.*]

My lord would have had him done it long before. For one night coming to him at his bedside, he caught him and bid him come to bed to him and his wife. That thereupon he made to him as if he would, but being got from him, departed the chamber, never intending to do so foul a deed. And that for the reasons aforesaid, he hated her of all men living. Howbeit, that one time, satisfying my lord's desire, he came to bed to them, where (being gratified) nature provoked him to a kind of desire, and he emitted but did not enter her body, as he hoped for salvation. That he never knew any woman carnally whilst he lived in my lord's house.

That it was not his intention to bring to light either my lord's or my lady's shame, but that when he was on his oath, he could not but speak the truth, his nature never being prone to lying. . . .

[*His speech concluded, he took out a lace handkerchief and asked the executioner to place it on his head. A minister then read the 143rd Psalm. Brodway then confessed his adherence to the Church of England, asked the executioner to rebind his hands, and then requested that he be buried in his own country, which request was granted by the sheriffs.*]

Then lifting up his hands to heaven, he said, "Lord Jesus receive my spirit", and the cart was drawn away.

Fitz-Patrick, lifting up his hands and commending himself to God, was executed in like manner.

2.3   Calendar of the Sussex Quarter Sessions, Michaelmas, 1642[45]

This calendar and the one following indicate the range of cases being dealt with in Quarter Sessions in the mid-seventeenth century.

Justices

Five justices sat over three days. (The normal length of a sessions was two days.)

Orders

The following orders were made:

---

[45] Redwood, *Quarter sessions order book* (1954), pp. 23–5 (*Sussex Record Society*, Record Publication, no. 3).

(a)   A wage dispute was referred to an arbitrator.
(b)   The annual pension of an elderly maimed soldier was raised from £3 to £4.
(c)   The widowed mother of a man accused of fathering a bastard child and who refused to pay for its upkeep was ordered to appear before the next sessions.
(d)   Repair costs to a foot-bridge were ordered to be paid by the relevant parish.
(e)   The constable of a hundred who had failed to pay another peace-keeping officer 28s 2d outstanding fees, was ordered to appear before the next sessions.
(f)   Provision was taken to ensure that the home parish support a poor man and his family and not pass the charge on to a neighbouring parish.

Discharges

(a)   A defendant, having cleaned his part of the river, is discharged.
(b)   William Susan, having repaired his part of the highway, is discharged.
(c)   Edmund Calverley was found not guilty by a jury of 12 of blocking a footpath and was discharged.

Bound over to next meeting of the sessions

(a)   Roger Woodborne, currier, and Mary his wife bound over in £20 to answer charge of being accessory to a felony.
(b)   Robert Woodyer, yeoman, bound in £10 to prosecute the above two.
(c)   John Page, yeoman, bound in £20, with two sureties for good behaviour of £10 each, to appear at the next sessions.
(d)   Nicholas Allen, tailor, bound in £20 to appear and answer to charge of bastardy; two sureties of £10.
(e)   William Morris, husbundman, bound in £20 to appear next sessions and meanwhile to keep the peace towards William Susan; one surety of £10.
(f)   William Susan, yeoman, bound in £20 to appear next sessions and meanwhile to keep the peace towards William Morris; one surety of £10.

Appointment

Thomas Luxford, gent., appointed Overseer of the Poor for the parish of Wivelsfield.

Outcome of trials (all misdemeanours)

Not guilty

(a) Robert Smyth, collier (i.e. charcoal-maker), not guilty of stealing a wether worth 10d.
(b) Edward Chauntler, husbandman, not guilty of stealing two shirts worth 4d, breeches, 4d and doublet, 3d.

Guilty

(a) Robert Styephen and three others guilty of not keeping watch and ward. Fined 2s each.
(b) William Tompkins, yeoman, and Richard Gosden, husbundman, for assault and taking a horse. Fined 6d each.
(c) John Tester, mason, and Anne, his wife, for an assault. Fine 12d.
(d) Edward Greene, tailor, for an assault. Fine 12d.
(e) Thomas Frend, husbundman, for an assault. Fine 2s 6d.
(f) William Holmwood, chandler, for an assault. Fine 12d.
(g) Elizabeth Carnall, widow, now married to Drew Harman, for an assault. Fine 12d.
(h) Richard Sares, husbundman, for an assault. Fine 6d.
(i) Richard Neale, husbundman, for an assault. Fine 6d.
(j) Robert Ollow, collier, for an assault. Fine 6d.

2.4 Calendar of the Sussex Quarter Sessions, Easter 1643[46]

Justices

Eleven justices sat for two days.

Appointments

(a) Treasurer for maimed soldiers appointed.
(b) Treasurer for charitable uses appointed.
(c) Richard Browne of Shiplake discharged from the office of constable and Thomas Willard appointed in his place.

Orders

The following orders were made:

---

[46] Redwood, *Quarter sessions order book*, pp. 50–4 (*Sussex Record Society*, Record Publication, no. 3).

(a) Churchwardens and overseers of the poor ordered to pay disputed rent.
(b) Dispute over support of orphan child to be resolved by parishes involved.
(c) Financial support for a poor boy determined.
(d) Father of a bastard child ordered to provide support.
(e) Abandoned mother and children returning to her poor mother's parish, the mother being on parish relief, the daughter and grandchildren are ordered back to their original parish to be supported there.
(f) Constable ordered to pay over 20s collected on a fine of an alehouse-keeper to the overseers of the poor.
(g) Banned alehouse-keeper has set up another ale-house which is to be closed.
(h) Appointed overseer of the poor refused permission to put in a substitute.
(i) Jane Cobb, apprentice, accused of a felony, "shalbe discharged out of the service of the service of her said master and her apprentice-ship, the indentures in that behalf notwithstanding."
(j) John Hodley ordered to pay 12d a week for the support of his grandmother.
(k) A maimed soldier given an annual pension of £4.

Discharges

(a) A defendant, having trimmed his trees and hedges, is discharged.
(b) A defendant, having repaired his part of the highway, is discharged.
(c) Edmund Calverley was found not guilty by a jury of 12 of blocking a footpath and was discharged.

Bound over to next meeting of the sessions

(a) Eight men plead not guilty to a forcible entry of 20 acres and are bound over in £20 to the next sessions.
(b) John Chatfield pleads not guilty to the charge of being a common drunkard and is bound over in £20 to the next sessions.
(c) Henry Borne, tanner, pleads not guilty to an assault and is bound over in £20 to the next sessions.
(d) Thomas Thunder, yeoman, is bound over to next sessions in £20 to answer an indictment.
(e) Richard Browne, yeoman, is bound over in £40 to the next sessions and to fulfil an order to maintain a bastard; two sureties of £20 each.
(f) Edward Pankhurst, shearman, is bound over in £20 to the next sessions to fulfil an order to maintain a bastard; one surety of £20.

Outcome of trials

Not guilty

(a) John Robbins, husbundman, not guilty of stealing 40 hoops worth 40d. Released on payment of fee of 6s.
(b) Richard Norman, husbundman, not guilty of stealing 40 hoops worth 40d. Released on payment of fee of 7s 4d.

Guilty

(a) John Morris, labourer, pleaded guilty to stealing a wether worth 10d. Punishment: to be whipped.
(b) Anthony Holford, yeoman, for an assault on John Bowyer. Fine 10s.
(c) John Bowyer, gent., with William Bowyer, gent.,[47] for an assault on Anthony Holford. Fine 6s 8d.
(d) Simo Ren for taking doves. Fine 10s.
(e) Edward Drew, yeoman, with Langridge, for an assault. Fine 15s.
(f) William Langridge with Drew above, for an assault. Fine 12s 6d.
(g) John Atree. Fine 10s.
(h) John Nicholson, husbundman, for being a single-man and living at his own hand. Fine 6d.

2.5 Calendar of prisoners in Oxford county gaol, April 1687[48]

This and the following calendars gives an idea of the range of cases being dealt with in Quarter Sessions by the later seventeenth century.

Oxon. A Calendar of the prisoners in the castle of Oxford for felony and other misdemeanours. 5 April 1687

Thomas Carter senior
    Charged with felony & burglary for breaking open the house of Henry Cross in the night time as an accessory before the fact, etc.
    Committed [to gaol] by Edmund Goodere, Esq.
John Carter senior
    Who did feloniously break open the dwelling house of the said Cross, etc.
    Committed Edmund Goodere, Esq.

---

[47] Note the status of these defendants.
[48] *Oxfordshire Rec. Soc.*, xvi (1934), pp. 18–19.

Richard Noun

Charged also for breaking open of the said Cross's house in the night time who did desperately wound him in twenty several places and taking from him divers of his goods.

Committed by Sir Littleton Osbaldeston, Knight.

Tabitha Smith

Charged for speaking treasonable and seditious words against his Majesty and the government.

Committed by Dr John Venn, Vice-Chancellor of Oxford.

Peter Beer

Upon suspicion of breaking open the house of Richard Perkins in the night time and feloniously taking thence a basket full of table linen.

Committed by George Chamberlayne and Humfrey Wykham, Esquires.

Thomas West

Who is suspected to be guilty of the murder of a bastard child by him begotten, etc.

Committed by Robert Waterfall, Warden of Henley.

William White

To be transported, etc.

Nathaniel Wood

Charged with the felonious stealing and carrying away of certain leaning [probably linen] and other things of Tobias Peade which he hath confessed.

Committed by Sir Timothy Tyrell.

John Lloyd

For not paying a fine of ten marks.

2.6 Calendar of prisoners in Oxford county gaol, May 1687[49]

Cases in italics are carried forward from the previous calendar. One can see that there are only two new cases.

Thomas Carter senior

Charged with felony & burglary for breaking open the house of Henry Cross in the night time as an accessory before the fact, etc.

Committed by Edmund Goodere, Esq.

John Carter senior

Who did feloniously break open the dwelling house of the said Cross, etc.

Committed Edmund Goodere, Esq.

---

[49] *Oxfordshire Rec. Soc.*, xvi (1934), p. 29.

Richard Noun

Charged also for breaking open of the said Cross's house in the night time who did desperately wound him in twenty several places and taking from him divers of his goods.

Committed by Sir Littleton Osbaldeston, Knight.

He admitted the indictment: to be whipped, imprisoned in the house of correction for one month, and then to be sent to Abbot's Bramley (Kent).

John Poole & Charles Norcott

For endeavouring to break open the dwelling house of Joan Carter & taken away a horse & beast, etc.

Tabitha Smith

Charged for speaking treasonable and seditious words against his Majesty and the government.

Committed by Dr John Venn, Vice-Chancellor of Oxford.

Peter Beer

Upon suspicion of breaking open the house of Richard Perkins in the night time and feloniously taking thence a basket full of table linen.

Committed by George Chamberlayne and Humfrey Wykham, Esquires.

Thomas West

Who is suspected to be guilty of the murder of a bastard child by him begotten, etc.

Committed by Robert Waterfall, Warden of Henley.

William White

To be transported, etc.

Margaret Saunderson

Charged with the felonious picking of the pocket of Jane Busby & taking thence some money which she hath confessed, etc.

Committed by Edmund Johnson mayor, Sir Littleton Osbaldeston, [and] Richard Hinton, Esq.

John Lloyd

For not paying a fine of ten marks.

2.7 Calendar of prisoners in Oxford gaol October 1687[50]

John Harris

Charged upon suspicion of stealing several horses from Weston on the Green, etc.

Committed by Sir Timothy Tyrrell.

William White

Upon suspicion of stealing a roan gelding.

Committed by John Stone, Esq.

---

[50] *Oxfordshire Rec. Soc.*, xvi (1934), pp. 44–5.

Edward Davis
  Charged with stealing linen which he hath confessed.
  Committed by Sir Robert Dashwood.
Eadeth, wife of Henry Saunders
  Hath assaulted and beaten Elizabeth, the wife of Edward Stiles that she
  is in a very dangerous condition.
  Committed by Sir John Doyly.
  Discharged.
John Carter
  Judgment respited until further order.
Margaret Saunderson
  Reprieved after judgment, to remain still.
Peter Beer
  Reprieved after judgment.
Thomas Carter
  Reprieved after judgment.
John Floyd
  Remains in gaol for a fine to the king.
William White
  To remain until Justice Hollaway order otherwise.
Tabitha Smith
  Indicted for seditious words, to remain until she be delivered by due
  course of law.
William Howse
  Servant to Thomas Ringe, committed by Sir John Doyly for refusing his
  master's service.
  *Impetrat futurum exoneratum super solucionem iijs to his Master Finis vjs
  viijd et imprisonandus domo correctionis pro negligenica.*

2.8   A case of "wrecking", 1677[51]

Here "wrecking" means plundering an already shipwrecked vessel.

Deposition made July 30, 1678, at Elswick, before Ralph Jenison, Esq.

William Berry and Thomas Bowman, say, that, on Saturday, the 10th of
November last past, betwixt two and three of the clock in the morning,
the good ship or bark, called the *Margett of Leath*, whereof John Finley
was then master, came on shore at Seaton seas, at the port of Blyth's

---

[51] *Depositions from the castle of York relating to offences committed in the northern counties in the
seventeenth century* ("Surtees Soc.", xl (1861), no. ccxi).

Nuke. And they being in danger to be lost, and the ship in danger to be sunk or broke, the passengers being afraid of their lives, being a dozen or sixteen in number, would not stay aboard the said ship, but were set ashore. And before the ship's company could return again to their ship, one William Cresswell of Cresswell, gent., and John Boult and William Curry, both of Bedlington, came aboard the said ship, and broke open the doors and hatches and went down into the hold, and did likewise break open several trunks and boxes, and took away several goods, which these deponents do conceive to be worth at least £200.

2.9   Two cases of piracy, 1649[52]

Deposition made March 12, 1650/1 before John Harrison and John Burton bailiffs of Scarbrough.

Piracy on the high seas

Wm. Batty of Scarbrough, mariner, sayth that betwixt Michaelmass and Martinmass[53] in 1649, one John Denton, captain of a ketch, with one piece of ordonnance, and about 30 men, did take the good ship called the *Amity of Scarbrough*, whereof one Robert Rogers was master, from the said Robert Rogers, betwixt Scarbrough Road and Fyley Bay. And, after the said Denton had boarded, entered his men, and taken the said ship, he did put aboard about 7 or 8 of his men to carry the ship away, who carried it as far as near to Flambrough Head, and kept the said Rogers, this informant and some other mariners, prisoners aboard the said ketch, until the said Rogers, being unwilling to lose his ship, being at that time but 2 year old, did agree with Denton to pay him a certain sum of money for to have his ship again, which was done, and all the prisoners were set at liberty.

Piracy of a grounded vessel

Leonard Greene of Whitby, saith, that in the year 1649, about Christmas, or three weeks before, being a servant in a ship being in Tees water, and laden with alum and butter, one Capt. John Denton, with his men, came into the said ship, when she was on dry ground, and broke open a chest and took out a bag of money, and several suits of apparel, and took near two hundred firkins of butter.

---

[52] *Depositions from the castle of York*, no. xxxiii.
[53] 29 September and 11 November.

Being this day with Capt. Denton in York Castle, and having some speech about the surprising of the ship that belonged to Mr Wiggoner and his partners, but was hindered by some cobblemen belonging to Burlington. In revenge whereof the said Capt. Denton said, that if it had not been for the company that was with him, he would have landed his men and fired Burlington Key.

2.10   Highway Robbery

While highway robbery does occur in the sixteenth century, it is rare. By the later seventeenth century it has become more common. Two points to notice: the value of the goods/money taken and secondly the propensity of highway robbers to operate as a gang.

A case of highway robbery, 1663[54]

This report, given by the victim, illustrates the terror which such attacks generated.

Deposition taken August 15, 1663 before John Tempest, Anthony Byerley, Samuell Davison, and Stephen Thomson, Esqrs.

John Williamson of Rawdon, clothier, saith, that himself, with his servant and daughter, were travelling from his house at Rawdon on the 5th instant towards Rippon about his profession of a clothier, and that, as he was going on Killinghall Moore, they were overtaken by three persons, who did assault them, clapping a pistol to his breast, and bade him deliver his money or he should die for it. Whereupon he was forced to submit to them, and one of them, who, as he now understands, calls himself John Smyth, who likewise clapped the pistol to his breast, did search his pockets, and took out 14s and one penny. Another of the said persons did thereupon cut the wametow[55] and took off the pack cloths which were upon a driven horse, and out of them took £40 which he gave to a person who, as he understands, calls himself by the name of Thomas Lightfoot. The said Thomas Lightfoot did search the informant's daughter Sarah in a very rude and uncivil fashion, and did take out of her pocket a little box, wherein there was 1s and three pence. It was about ten of the clock in the forenoon.

---

[54] *Depositions from the castle of York*, no. cxi.
[55] The strap that went round the packhorse's belly.

A catalogue of highway robberies in the early 1680s[56]

This forms part of a deposition made by Elizabeth Burton who had been a kept woman of a group of highwaymen based at the Talbot in Newark. The ringleader of the group, John Nevison, was eventually executed in May 1684. The deposition suggests that very large sums could be made through highway robbery.

The robberies which this examinate did hear them confess they had committed were as follows:

1. One between Grantham and Stamford done by three of them (viz. Nevison, Everson, and Brommett), where they took about £300 from a shop-keeper of which this examinate had as much as paid for a quarter's table.[57]
2. One near to Maltby in Yorkshire done by three, Nevison, Bracy and Tankerd, where they took about £200 from one Malim of Rotheram, when he was going towards Gainsborough mart . . . , whereof they gave this examinate £2.
3. That of Linconshire where they took a great booty, but which of them committed the same she knoweth not.
4. One in Yorkshire, committed by Nevison, Bracy, Tankerd, and Wilbore, where they took above £300 of which this examinate had 9s to buy her a white petticoat.
5. One between Gainsborough and Newark, committed by Nevison, Everson, and Tankerd, where they took about £200 from a Londoner that had been at the last mart, as well as one "caudle" cup of silver and a tankard and two silver bodkins. All of which she found in the portmanteau, and is now or was lately in their room at the Talbot, marked with the letter T, except the two bodkins which they gave her, one of which she lost, the other she yet hath. As also 25s to buy her a serge petticoat, and a pair of "bodyes".
6. One between Long Billington and Gunnerby, on Whitsun Monday last, committed by Bromett and Bracy, where they took about £30 from a drover, supposed to be a Yorkshireman. Of this they gave this examinate so much as paid for a quarter's table, and bought the waistcoat on her back.
7. One near Edlington in Yorkshire committed by Nevison and Bracy, between Martinmas and Christmas last, where they got about £50.
8. One near Stilton in Huntingtonshire, about May was a twelvemonth, committed by Tankerd and Brommett, where they took but £5 of which they only gave this examinate a new half crown.

---

[56] *Depositions from the castle of York*, no. ccxxxviii.
[57] That is to say, it paid for her board for a quarter of a year.

9. That near Rotheram, from a butcher, on Rotheram Fair day was twelvemonths, committed by Bracy and Nevison, where they took £30 and gave this examinate 16s wherewith she bought four ells of Holland.[58]

10. One near Roistone, between Mayday and Lammas last, committed by all six, where they took £250 of which this examinate had two pieces of gold, as much silver as paid for half a year's table, and 6s 8d more to buy her some shifts.

She further saith that she thinks the master of the Talbot is privy to their carriages, for that she hath often seen them whisper together, as also William Anwood, the ostler there, she having often seen the said parties give him good sums of money and order him to keep their horses close, and never to water them but in the night time.[59]

2.11   Breaking into a deer park, 1654[60]

A true bill[61] against Thomas Johnson of Ripon, John Hudsey of Ripon, gent. Christopher Terry, barber, and William Kettlewell, saddler, for having on July 5, 1654, broken the park of Sir Charles Egerton, Kt., called Markinfield Park, and chased and killed, and wounded the bucks and does.

3   Punishment in the seventeenth century

3.1   Punishments imposed at the mid-seventeenth-century Sussex Quarter Sessions[62]

The majority of punishments recorded were fines. What follows are examples of other rarer punishments.

House of Correction, 1643[63]

Forasmuch as Joan Wickerson, wife of Robert Wickerson of Blatchington, upon complaint made to this court of divers misdemeanours being required to find sureties for her good behaviour, departed without licence of the

---

[58] A linen fabric.
[59] Presumably to avoid having the horses recognized.
[60] *Depositions from the castle of York*, no. lxvii.
[61] That is to say, the grand jury found that there was a case to answer.
[62] Redwood, *Quarter sessions order book*.
[63] *Ibid.*, p. 30.

court or finding any sureties, it is ordered that the said Joan Wickerson shall be sent to the house of correction there to remain for one month and to dealt withal as a lewd and incorrigible person.

Branding of beggars, 1645[64]

Thomas Smyth & Michael Jackson, labourers, guilty of being sturdy beggars, were branded with the letter R on their backs and delivered.

Pressing to death, 1645[65]

Richard Harris, labourer and John Pope, labourer, refused to be tried and are adjudged to be pressed to death.

Benefit of clergy, 1645[66]

Richard Drury, husbundman, Thomas Drury, labourer, & John Rouse, labourer, found guilty of stealing 3 wethers worth 12d each, were convicted of a felony, had their book read [i.e. claimed benefit of clergy], are branded in the hand, and then delivered.

Whippings, 1645[67]

William Finch, gardener, pleaded guilty of stealing a saddle worth 3d, a bridle worth 6d, and a saddlecloth worth 2d; and Anthony Sherlock, husbundman, and William Woodcock, husbundman, pleaded guilty to stealing a ewe worth 8d, were convicted of petty larceny and are to be openly whipped and then delivered.

Imprisonment to await trial at Assizes, 1647[68]

Andrew Briscow to be kept in gaol until the next general gaol delivery to answer to a felony charge.

Imprisonment until fine and fees paid, 1647[69]

Nicholas Powell and William Powell, husbundmen, to be kept in gaol until they pay their fine of 10s and fees of 6s 9d.

---

[64] *Ibid.*, p. 64.
[65] *Ibid.*, p. 74.
[66] *Ibid.*, p. 90.
[67] *Ibid.*, p. 90.
[68] *Ibid.*, p. 118.
[69] *Ibid.*, p. 118.

Imprisonment for failing to obey a bastardy order, 1648[70]

[Thomas Arnold, husbundman, had been paying for his bastard child, but had stopped his payments.]

A warrant shall be made to attach the said Thomas Arnold and to convey him to the common gaol at Horsham, there to remain until he shall pay the arrears . . .

3.2   *A remarkable prison escape (May 1655)*[71]

Following the Penruddock uprising in favour of Charles II, a number of rebels were captured, tried at special Assizes at Chard, and sentenced to death. Most were reprieved, but three, including Thomas Hunt, who was to be beheaded, were not. This is an account of what then ensued. As will be seen, the escape of a political prisoner was a serious matter for the sheriff. This account comes from the sheriff's memorandum book, i.e. his own personal record.

By reason of the difficulty of procuring an axe (which must be eleven inches for such a purpose) and the preparing a scaffold, I was necessitated to put off the execution of Captain Hunt,[72] who having two sisters coming to visit him Wednesday night, the ninth day of May, about ten of the clock at night, shifting clothes with one of them (whilst his two chamber fellows, who lay at his bed's feet, went down to drink), went down with his other sister through the house past two or three doorkeepers and the guard of soldiers without, and so past away; but whether or how it could not be learned.

The sister that stayed behind in the chamber hangs the Captain's cloak and hat and doublet on the chair and goes into his bed. Foote and Pickover (condemned persons), coming into the chamber, thought him asleep and so lay down in the trundle bed. In the morning, calling to the Captain, they perceived that twas his sister that was in the bed and the Captain gone.

That morning, being Thursday the tenth day of May, it was conceived the Captain should have been executed, the scaffold being erected in the market place near the shire-hall in Ilchester. About nine of the clock William Pullen came with the news to me of the escape. I presently [i.e. immediately] dispatched a servant post to London with letters to the Protector, to General Desborough and to Colonel Sydenham, two of the Council, and to Mr Lislebone Longe, then Master of Requests. These

---

[70] *Ibid.*, p. 155.
[71] This comes from the sheriff's memorandum book. Cockburn, *Somerset assize orders.*
[72] The instruction was that Captain Hunt should be beheaded not hanged.

letters brought the first news and by God's blessing kept off what many expected and my friends feared would fall on me, and the rather in respect that the gentleman was of my name.[73] Colonel Sydenham and Mr Longe approved themselves cordial friends, and the Protector upon reading my letter seemed well satisfied at length. [*Non nobis domine, sed tuo nomini detur gloria.*] As soon as my letter to the Protector was read, came in two soldiers with a letter to the Protector to give him an accompt [i.e. account] of the escape of Hunt, but though the letter was stuffed with many notorious untruths put in by a gentleman in the country to do me mischief, yet, it pleased God, it did me no hurt at all. I have spared to name my enemy because I would forget the injury, and would have my relickacions [? relations] also to forget it; but the love of my friends I can not forget. The next day after the escape Mr John Cary and Mr John Barker, the two next Justices, made a strict examination into the business of the escape and upon it finding me altogether clear, sent up the examinations to the Protector and Council, and did me right.

They confined the two sisters to a chamber as prisoners. They were brought to two Assizes but were never tried. After they had remained confined at Ilchester two years, they were at Taunton Assizes bailed by Judge Newdegate with the consent of the whole bench.

3.3   Care for a mentally ill prisoner (Chard Assizes, March 1658)[74]

This remarkable case shows that the assize courts could and did take account of the mental health of a prisoner in determining how he or she should be treated. Note, too, the intervention of the local minister of religion.

Whereas this court is informed that John Rudge of Bicknaller, a prisoner now remaining in the common gaol, is sometimes a distracted person and visited with the falling sickness[75] and is likely there to perish for want of relief. And whereas Mr Bartholomew Safford, the minister of Bicknaller, and Simon Longe, an Overseer of the Poor of that place, have desired this court that the said John Rudge may be released out of the gaol and carefully sent to the House of Correction at Taunton which is nearer unto them to send him relief, and desired that he may remain there in safe custody, and they will be careful to send him necessary relief. All which this court taking into consideration doth order that the said John Rudge be accordingly sent to the said House of Correction, there to be safely

---

[73] The sheriff and the prisoner were both called Hunt.
[74] Cockburn, *Somerset assize orders*, no. 65.
[75] Probably a form of epilepsy.

kept from doing any hurt and set to work as he shalbe able, provided that the parish of Bucknaller allow him what shalbe thought fit by the two next Justices of the Peace for his maintenance weekly more than his work come to and for his necessary supply towards the recovery of his health.

3.4 The state of York Castle prison, mid-seventeenth century[76]

These documents illustrate the vulnerability of prisoners to depradations from their gaolers.

Letter from a York citizen to the Justice of Assize, August 1642

Is this special pleading from a local trader or a genuine complaint?

My Lord,

It had been fitter for me to have waited on you myself, than to have presented my respects to you this way; but, my Lord, I have been so desperately ill these six weeks, I have hardly been able to stir out of my bed.

My humble suit to your Lordship is, in the behalf of a great many poor distressed people that are now prisoners within the Castle of York, that have nothing to subsist withal, but the charity of well disposed persons; and, as the case stands with them, the benefit of what they have is very small, for they are not suffered to buy a bit of bread or a drop of drink, nor so much as a half-penny worth of milk, or a little firing[77] in the winter, but what they are compelled to buy of the keepers of the prison, where they pay 2d or 3d for that which is not sometimes worth a penny. My Lord, my lodging being not far from the Castle Gate, the neighbours have made a great request to me to be a suitor to your Lordship, that at this Assizes your Lordship would be pleased to make an order that these poor people, as formerly they have done, may send into the town for such provision as they are able to compass, where they may have it at the best hand I hope your Lordship will pardon the boldness of your most humble servant,

John Wortham From my lodging this 9th of August, 1642.

A petition from the prisoners in York Castle against their gaolers, 1654

They have hindered divers prisoners from having their meat, and drink at the best hand, and to compel them to come to the high table, and did lye

---

[76] *Depositions from the castle of York*, pp. xxxii–xxxiv.
[77] That is to say, fuel.

some in double irons. That some prisoners sending for their drink within the castle, where they can have more for sixpence than they can have in the cellars for nine pence, the gaolers did abuse the prisoners and took their drink from them and gave it to the low gaol prisoners. The gaolers' servant gets a share of the charities given to the prisoners.

On July 10 last divers prisoners going to the sessions at Malton, the gaolers refused to divide the Cottrell bread til they were gone, and got their share. The gaolers doth refuse to hang up the stablishmnent of fees in a public place, etc.

A further petiton, this time to the foreman of the grand jury
for the county of York

The humble petition of the prisoners in the castle of York, complaining of the several abuses committed and done by Thomas Crore and William Croke, jailors.

Sheweth, that, contrary to a table of several fees and Acts of Parliament, the aforesaid jailors hath demanded and taken several sums of money for chamber-rent, and likewise for our own beds and bedding, and doth compel us to pay for ease of irons (being in execution), although we have paid the sum to the former jailors to we was [sic] committed, lodging felons and debtors together in one room or chamber, taking more fees than one, viz. for every action one fee, although we are discharged from all such actions by the sheriff, taking unjust fees from the prisoners when discharged receiving £16 8s from 6 men committed and indicted for high treason at the last assizes, as fees due to them, beside £6 for ease of irons, they or their servants taking or receiving money at several times from three persons indicted for murder at the Lent assizes last, promising that the jury should acquit and discharge, and allowing weekly out of the county bread a greater share to felons and condemned persons than they do to debtors. Allowing condemned persons not only to dispose of it, but of most of the concerns in the gaol not only to dispose of it, but of the mostly concerns in the gaol. Tolerating persons condemned for high treason, for murder, for felony in execution, excommunication, besides 180 Quakers, at the least, to go into the city and county of York, but to play-houses, taverns, coffee-houses, etc., not lodging in the gaol above the number of 90 Quakers at any one time, from March last to July instant, taking several sums of money besides bond and judgment not only from men committed as misdemeanours, but from all sorts of felons for ease of their irons.

We distressed prisoners humbly crave to take into consideration, moving the judges and Justices of Peace not only that the abuses may be regulated, but that at table of fees may be settled, and we shall be ever bound to pray, etc.

3.5   Petition of Oxford prisoners for relief, 1687[78]

This petition from the Oxford city gaol to the magistrates for help indicates the parlous state that prisoners could get into. The response of the Justices is hardly generous.

The humble petition of the poor distressed prisoners in the castle.

Humbly sheweth that your petitioners are very poor and very many in number whereby they are forced to undergo great want and suffer great calamities.

Wherefore your petitioners humbly beseech your worships to make some order for their relief.

Noted

Allowed 4s a week.

3.6   Care for the victim (Taunton Assizes, August 1652)[79]

A fascinating case where the remand prisoner is promised bail if the victim is helped and recovers from the alleged assault.

Whereas this court is informed that there is one Tabitha Couch of Glaston which is dangerously wounded by one Rebecca Dorvill, wife of Ralph Dorvill of the same place, and that the said Rebecca Dorvill is now committed to prison for the said offence.[80] This court doth therefore order, by and with the consent of the said Ralph Dorvill and Rebecca Dorvill, that the said Ralph Dorvill shall pay unto the said Tabitha Couch the sum of 5s weekly towards her maintenance until she shalbe again recovered, and give satisfaction to the chirurgion[81] for his pains and care taken about her. And when the said Tabitha Couch shalbe recovered, then the said Rebecca Dorvill, upon giving such security for her good behaviour and to appear at the next assizes to be holden for this county as Mr John Carew, one of the Justices of the Peace of this county, shall think fit, shalbe discharged out of prison.

3.7   Institution of a Regular Preacher in the Gaol, 1654[82]

These notes come from the sheriff's memorandum book, i.e. his own personal record. This is an early example of an attempt to provide regular spiritual guidance to prisoners.

---

[78] *Oxfordshire Rec. Soc.*, xvi (1934), p. 45.
[79] Cockburn, *Somerset assize orders*, no. 118.
[80] That is to say, she is in prison awaiting trial.
[81] That is to say, pay the surgeon.
[82] Cockburn, *Somerset assize orders*, nos. 164–7.

Note

I caused my gaoler to set up a pulpit in the prison and procured ministers to preach in the prison every Wednesday, or every other Wednesday at farthest, and caused the keeper to have the minister to dinner. Mr John Powell, the then minister of Ilchester, I desired to begin the lecture on Wednesday 1 January 1655.

Copy of Sheriff Hunt's letter to Preacher Powell, 29 December 1654

Sir, I give you many thanks for your readiness to contribute your assistance to that good work of preaching to the poor prisoners. If you gain but one soul here, you will not loose your reward. I hope ere this the pulpit is ready; if it bee, let me beg this favour from you, that you will begin the lecture there the next Wednesday. It will be a good beginning of the year, and surely, sir, it will never be matter of grief to you to remember your forwardness to begin this Christian work. For the next day I shall desire the assistance of Mr Wyatt, and others afterward to keep it up, and I hope to prevail with the Justices to allow a convenient stipend to the minister of Ilchester or Northover to preach once every Lord's Day in the prison. Well sir, I wish you may happily begin and that God's blessing may accompany your endeavour. There will not be wanting the prayers of, sir, your very loving friend, Robert Hunt, sheriff.

Powell's reply of the same date

Much honoured Sir. The pulpit in the prison is ready, and so is your pulpit man, who will (by God's blessing) in obedience to your commands begin the lecture in the prison the next Wednesday, when, and at any other time, I shall serve you with very much cheerfulness, for I am, sir your very faithful servant, John Powell.

Letter from Sheriff Hunt to the Justices concerning a salary for
a prison chaplain, 5 January 1655

Gentlemen and my honoured friends.

There are now in the gaol near sixty poor prisoners. Tis a usual saying, and I fear too true, that they come in bad and go out worse. In order to the redress of this evil I have caused the keeper to set up a pulpit in the prison and have desired the minister of Ilchester to begin the lecture[83] there, which he did with much willingness on Wednesday last. And I shall procure some neighbour minister to keep up the lecture every Wednesday,

---

[83] In this context, a lecture was an extended sermon.

or every other Wednesday at farthest. But truly, gentlemen, I
the next sheriff should live far off, the lecture thus set up ma
ground. And to prevent it I do (with all submission to your t
ments) conceive twil be the best way, if the bench please, am
pensions to settle a small one upon the minister of Ilchester fc
being, who may constantly preach to the prisoners and instruct t....... upon
all occasions.

Gentlemen, tis my humble request to you that you will doe this charitable work. And if you cast your bread upon these waters, you may by
God's blessing find it the next assizes in the conversion of a poor thief.
And then you will not repent of your charity, nor will it be any grief of
mind to you when you shall pass out of this world to remember that you
were instrumental to the saving of poor souls, nor matter of shame to you
when at the last day it shalbe told you that you sent to visit poor prisoners'
souls. Such a work as this, gentlemen, is beseeming the piety you profess,
and will lodge a worthy esteem of you in the bosoms of all honest men. It
will procure you a reward hereafter from your great master, and at present
many thanks from your very humble servant, Robert Hunt, sheriff.

Sheriff Hunt's note of the outcome of his appeal

The Justices were pleased to allow a pension of £8 *per annum* to be paid
quarterly to the minister that did preach every Sunday to the prisoners,
and it was paid duly all my time.

Chapter 4

Crime and Punishment in the Eighteenth Century

1 The criminal process in the eighteenth century

1.1 Reform Proposals, 1751[1]

In January 1751, Henry Fielding, the Bow Street magistrate and author of Tom Jones, *published his* Enquiry into the causes of the late increase of robbers, *perhaps the most comprehensive survey of London crime in the eighteenth century. In it he proposed a number of reforms, some of which were subsequently enacted. (See below, p. 150.) The* Enquiry *reveals a concern at the continuing growth in crime, and suggests a number of ways in which criminals might be dealt with. Perhaps the most significant part of Fielding's analysis is the way he links this crime-wave to the socio-economic conditions of the poor. For him, the criminal problem is located amongst what he calls the vulgar, i.e. the common people. He also sees crime as an intrusion on hard-won political liberties; crime is, for Fielding, un-English. He is also very critical of the limited public institutions for dealing with crime.*

Introduction

The great increase of robberies within these few years is an evil which to me appears to deserve some attention; and the rather as it seems (tho' already become so flagrant) not yet to have arrived to that height of which it is capable, and which it is likely to attain, for diseases in the political, as in the natural body, seldom fail going on to their crisis, especially when nourished and encouraged by faults in the constitution. In fact, I make no doubt, but that the streets of this town, and the roads leading to it, will shortly be impassable without the utmost hazard; nor are we threatened with seeing less dangerous gangs of rogues among us, than those which the Italians call the Banditi.

Should this ever happen to be the case, we shall have sufficient reason to lament that remissness by which this evil was suffered to grow so great

---

[1] Henry Fielding, *An enquiry into the causes of the late increase of robbers, &c. with some proposals for remedying this growing evil* (London, 1751).

a height. All distempers, if I may once more resume the allusion, the sooner they are opposed, admit of the easier and the safer cure. The great difficulty of extirpating desperate gangs of robbers, when once collected into a body, appears from our own history in former times. . . .

For my own part, I cannot help regarding these depredations in a most serious light: nor can I help wondering that a nation so jealous of her liberties, that from the slightest cause, and often without any cause at all, we are always murmuring at our superiors, should tamely and quietly support the invasion of her properties by a few of the lowest and vilest among us. Doth not this situation in reality level us with the most enslaved countries? If I am to be assaulted and pillaged, and plundered, if I can neither sleep in my own house, nor walk the streets, nor travel in safety, is not my condition almost equally bad whether a licensed or unlicensed rogue, a dragoon or a robber, be the person who assaults and plunders me? The only difference which I can perceive is, that the latter evil appears to be more easy to remove.

If this be, as I clearly think it is, the case, surely there are few matters of more general concern than to put an immediate end to these outrages, which are already become so notorious, and which, as I have observed, do seem to threaten us with such a dangerous increase. What indeed may not the public apprehend when they are informed as an unquestionable fact that there is at this time a great gang of rogues, whose number falls little short of a hundred, who are incorporated in one body, have officers and a treasury, and have reduced theft and robbery into a regular system. There are of this society of men who appear in all disguises, and mix in most companies. Nor are they better versed in every art of cheating, thieving, and robbing, than they are armed with every method of evading the law, if they should ever be discovered and an attempt made to bring them to justice. Here, if they fail in rescuing the prisoner, or (which seldom happens) in bribing or deterring the prosecutor, they have for their last resource some rotten members of the law to forge a defence for them, and a great number of false witnesses ready to support it.[2]

Having seen the most convincing proofs of all this, I cannot help thinking it high time to put some stop to the further progress of such impudent and audacious insults, not only on the properties of the subject, but on the national justice, and on the laws themselves. The means of accomplishing this (the best which suggest themselves to me) I shall submit to the public consideration, after having first enquired into the causes of the present growth of this evil, and whence we have great reason to apprehend its further increase. Some of these I am too well versed in the affairs of this world to expect to see removed; but there are others, which without being

---

[2] Compare this description of criminal gangs with Harman's (p. x).

over sanguine, we may hope to remedy; and thus perhaps one ill consequence, at least, of the more stubborn political diseases, may cease.

Sec. I Of too frequent and expensive diversions among the lower kind of people

Here Fielding blames rising standards of living in London for the crime wave.

First then, I think, that the vast torrent of luxury which of late years hath poured itself into this nation, hath greatly contributed to produce, among many others, the mischief I here complain of. I aim not here to satirize the great, among whom luxury is probably rather a moral than a political evil. But vices no more than diseases will stop with them, for bad habits are as infectious by example, as the plague itself by contact. In free countries, at least, it is a branch of liberty claimed by the people to be as wicked and as profligate as their superiors. Thus while the nobleman will emulate the grandeur of a prince, and the gentleman will aspire to the proper state of the nobleman, the tradesman steps from behind his counter into the vacant place of the gentleman. Nor doth the confusion end here, it reaches the very dregs of the people, who aspiring still to a degree beyond that which belongs to them, and not being able by the fruits of honest labour to support the state which they affect, they disdain the wages to which their industry would entitle them, and abandoning themselves to idleness, the more simple and poor-spirited betake themselves to a state of starving and beggary, while those of more art and courage become thieves, sharpers[3] and robbers.

Could luxury be confined to the palaces of the great, the society would not perhaps be much affected with it; at least, the mischiefs which I am now intending to obviate can never be the consequence. For tho', perhaps, there is not more of real virtue in the higher state, yet the sense of honour is there more general and prevalent. But there is a much stronger reason. The means bear no proportion to the end: for the loss of thousands, or of great estate, is not to be relieved or supplied by any means of common theft or robbery. With regard to such evils therefore the legislature might be justified in leaving the punishment, as well as the pernicious consequence, to end in the misery, distress, and sometimes utter ruin of private family.[4] But when this vice descends downward to the tradesman, the mechanic, and the labourer, it is certain to engender many political mischiefs, and among the rest is most evidently the parent of theft and

---

[3] Card-sharpers, i.e. those who cheat at cards.
[4] Here, as elsewhere, Fielding argues that different rules should apply to different orders (classes) in society.

robbery, to which not only the motive of want but of shame conduces. For there is no greater degree of shame than the tradesman generally feels at the first inability to make his regular payments; nor is there any difficulty which he would not undergo to avoid it. Here then the highway promises and hath, I doubt not, often given relief.[5] Nay I remember very lately a highwayman who confessed several robberies before me, his motive to which, he assured me (and so it appeared) was to pay a bill that was shortly to become due. In this case therefore the public becomes interested, and consequently the legislature is obliged to interpose.

To give a final blow to luxury by any general prohibition, if it would be advisable, is by no means possible. To say the truth, bad habits in the body politic, especially if of any duration, are seldom to be wholly eradicated. Palliatives alone are to be applied; and these, too, in a free constitution must be of the gentlest kind, and as much as possible adapted to the taste and genius of the people.

The gentlest method which I know, and at the same time perhaps one of the most effectual, of stopping the progress of vice, is by removing the temptation. Now the two great motives to luxury, in the mind of man are vanity and voluptuousness. The former of these operates but little in this regard with the lower order of people. . . . Voluptuousness or the love of pleasure is that alone which leads them into luxury. Here then the temptation is with all possible care to be withdrawn from them.

Now what greater temptation can there to voluptuousness than a place where every sense and appetite of which it is compounded and delighted; where the eyes are feasted with show, and the ears with music, and where gluttony and drunkenness are allured by every kind of dainty; where the finest women are exposed to view, and where the meanest person who can dress himself clean, may in some degree mix with his betters, and thus perhaps satisfy his vanity as well as his love of pleasure?

Fielding then goes on to examine the cost of attending "places of pleasure" and "temples of idleness" such as the Haymarket. He is particularly scathing about the cost of masquerades.

Sec. II   Of drunkenness: a second consequence of luxury among the vulgar

But the expense of money and loss of time, with their certain consequences, are not the only evils which attend the luxury of the vulgar. Drunkenness is almost inseparably annexed to the pleasures of such people. A vice by

---

[5] That is to say, the debtor tradesman turns to highway robbery to pay his debts.

no means to be construed as a spiritual offence alone, since so many temporal mischiefs arise from it, amongst which are frequently robbery and murder itself.

After rehearsing various laws governing the drink trade, Fielding goes on to discuss the debilitating effects of drink on the lower orders.

The drunkenness I here intend, is that acquired by the strongest intoxicating liquors, and particularly by that poison called gin which, I have great reason to think, is the principal sustenance (if it may be so called) of more than an hundred thousand people in this metropolis. Many of these wretches there are who swallow pints of this poison within the twenty-four hours, the dreadful effects of which I have the misfortune every day to see, and to smell too. But I have no need to insist on my own credit, or on that of my informers, the great revenue arising from the tax on this liquor (the consumption of which is almost wholly confined to the lowest order of people) will prove the quantity consumed better than any other evidence.

Now, besides the moral ill consequences occasioned by this drunkenness, with which, in this treatise, I profess not to deal; how greatly must this be supposed to contribute to those political mischiefs which this essay proposes to remedy? This will appear from considering, that however cheap this vile potion may be, the poorer sort will not easily be able to supply themselves with the quantities they desire; for the intoxicating draught itself disqualifies them from using any honest means to acquire it, at the same time that it removes all sense of fear and shame, and emboldens them to commit every wicked and desperate enterprise.[6] Many instances of this I see daily. Wretches are often brought before me, charged with theft and robbery, whom I am forced to confine before they are in a condition to be examined. And when they have afterwards become sober, I have plainly perceived, from the state of the case, that the gin alone was the cause of the transgression, and have been sometimes sorry that I was obliged to commit them to prison.

But beyond all this, there is a political ill consequence of this drunkenness, which, though it doth not strictly fall within my present purpose, I shall be excused for mentioning, it being indeed the greatest evil of all, and which must, I think, awaken our legislature to put a final period to so destructive a practice. And this is that dreadful consequence which must attend the poisonous quality of this pernicious liquor to the health, the strength, and the very being of numbers of his majesty's most useful subjects. . . .

---

[6] Substitute drugs for gin and one has the contemporary view of a major cause of contemporary crime.

Sec. III   Of gaming among the vulgar

I come now to the last great evil which arises from the luxury of the vulgar, and this is gaming,[7] a school in which most highwaymen of great eminence have been bred.

Fielding explicitly excludes the gentry and nobility from the restrictions he proposes for the lower orders.

As to gaming in the lower classes of life, so plainly tending to the ruin of tradesmen, the destruction of youth, and to the multiplication of every find of fraud and violence, the legislature hath provided very wholesome laws.

Fielding then surveys the existing laws.

Sec. IV   Of laws that relate to provision for the poor

Fielding rehearses the relevant laws before going on to distinguish between the poor unable to work (who should be supported), the poor looking for work (who also should be helped), and the idle poor. He believes most London poor come into the latter category. He then goes on to talk about Houses of Correction where such persons were often sent.

And with regard to work, the intention of the law is, I apprehend, as totally frustrated, insomuch that they must be very lazy persons indeed who can esteem the labour imposed in any of these houses as a punishment. In some, I am told, there is not any provision made for work. In that of Middlesex in particular, the governor hath confessed to me that he hath had no work to employ his prisoners, and hath urged as a reason, that having generally great numbers of most desperate felons under his charge, who, notwithstanding his utmost care, will sometimes get access to his other prisoners, he dares not trust those who are committed to hard labour with any heavy or sharp instruments of work, lest they should be converted into weapons by the felons.

What good consequence then can arise from sending idle and disorderly persons to a place where they are neither to be corrected nor employed, and where with the conversation of many as bad, and sometimes worse than themselves, they are sure to be improved in the knowledge, and confirmed in the practice of iniquity? Can it be conceived that such persons will not come out of these houses much more idle and disorderly

---

[7] That is to say, gambling.

141

than they went in? The truth of this I have often experienced in the behaviour of the wretched brought before me; the most impudent and flagitious[8] of whom, have always been such as have been before acquainted with the discipline of Bridewell, a commitment to which place, tho' it often causes great horror and lamentation in the novice, is usually treated with ridicule and contempt by those who already have been there.

For these reasons, Fielding believes magistrates prefer to issue a reprimand rather than send offenders to Houses of Correction.

But 'till this plan[9] shall be produced; or (which is more to be expected) 'till some man of greater abilities, as well as of greater authority, shall offer some new regulation for this purpose, something, at least, ought to be done to strengthen the laws already made, and to enforce their execution. The matter is of the highest concern, and imports us not only as we are good men and good Christians, but as we are good Englishmen. Since not only preserving the poor from the highest degrees of wretchedness, but the making them useful subjects, is the thing proposed, a work, says Sir Josiah Child, which would redound some hundreds of thousands *per annum* to the public advantage. Lastly, it is of the utmost importance to that point which is the subject matter of this treatise, for which reason I have thought myself obliged to give it a full consideration. "The want of a due provision" (says Lord Hale) "for education and relief of the poor in a way of industry, is that which fills the goals with malefactors, and fills the kingdom with idle and unprofitable persons that consume the stock of the kingdom without improving it, and that will daily increase, even to a desolation in time. And this error in the first concoction is never remediable but by gibbets and whipping."

In serious truth, if proper care should be taken to provide for the present poor, and to prevent their increase by laying some effectual restraints on the extravagance of the lower sort of people, the remaining part of this treatise would be rendered of little consequence, since few persons, I believe, have made their exit at Tyburn,[10] who have not owed their fate to some of the causes before mentioned. But as I am not too sanguine in my expectations on this head, I shall now proceed to consider of some methods to obviate the frequency of robbers, which if less efficacious, are perhaps much easier than those already proposed. And if we will not remove the temptation, at least we ought to take away all encouragement to robbery.

---

[8] Deeply criminal.
[9] For providing for the poor.
[10] The favoured place of execution in London.

Sec. V   Of the punishment of receivers of stolen goods

Here Fielding tackles the issue of how stolen goods are subsequently marketed.

Now one great encouragement to theft of all kinds is the ease and safety with which stolen goods may be disposed of. It is a very old and vulgar, but a very true saying, "that if there were no receivers, there would be no thieves". Indeed could not the thief find a market for his goods, there would be an absolute end of several kinds of theft, such as shop-lifting, burglary, &c., the objects of which are generally goods and not money. Nay, robberies on the highway would so seldom answer the purpose of the adventurer that very few would think it worth their while to risk so much with such small expectations.

But at present, instead of meeting with any such discouragement, the thief disposes of his goods with almost as much safety as the honestest tradesman. For first, if he hath made a booty of any value, he is almost sure of seeing it advertised within a day or two, directing him to bring the goods to a certain place there he is to receive a reward (sometimes the full value of the booty) and no questions asked. This method of recovering stolen goods by the owner, a very learned Judge formerly declared to have been, in his opinion, a composition of felony. And surely if this be proved to be carried into execution, I think it must amount to a full conviction of that crime. But, indeed, such advertisements are in themselves so very scandalous, and of such pernicious consequence that if men are not ashamed to own they prefer an old watch or a diamond ring to the good of the society, it is pity some effectual law was not contrived to prevent their giving this public countenance to robbery for the future.

But if the person robbed should prove either too honest, or too obstinate, to take this method of recovering his goods, the thief is under no difficulty in turning them into money. Among the great number of brokers and pawnbrokers several are to be found who are always ready to receive a gold watch at an easy rate, and where no questions are asked, or, at least, where no answers are expected but such as the thief can very readily make.

Besides the clandestine dealers this way who satisfy their consciences with telling a ragged fellow or wench, they hope they came honestly by silver or gold and diamonds, there are others who scorn such pitiful subterfuges, who engage openly with the thieves, and who have warehouses filled with stolen goods only.

Fielding argues that the law is ineffective in stopping this evil. He argues that public advertisement for return of stolen property should be forbidden, that receiving should be made an offence, and that pawnbrokers should be regulated.

Sec. VI   Of laws relating to vagabonds

The other great encouragement to robbery, besides the certain means of finding a market for the booty, is the probability of escaping punishment.

This Fielding believes particularly true of London. He also believes the problem comes from lack of control over the wandering poor in the common lodging-houses in London which he then goes on to describe.

The following account I have had from Mr Welch, the high constable of Holborn,[11] and none who know that gentleman, will want any confirmation of the truth of it.

> That in the parish of St Giles's there are great numbers of houses set apart for the reception of idle persons and vagabonds, who have their lodgings there for twopence a night. That in the above parish, and in St George, Bloomsbury, one woman alone occupies seven of these houses, all properly accommodated with miserable beds from the cellar to the garret, for such twopenny lodgers. That in these beds, several of which are in the same room, men and women, often strangers to each other, lie promiscuously, the price of a double bed being no more than threepence, as an encouragement to them to lie together. That as these places are thus adapted to whoredom, so are they no less provided for drunkenness, gin being sold in them all at a penny a quartern,[12] so that the smallest sum of money serves for intoxication. That in the execution of search-warrants, Mr Welch rarely finds less than twenty of these houses open for the receipt of all comers at the latest hours. That in one of these houses, and that not a large one, he hath numbered 58 persons of both sexes, the stench of whom was so intolerable, that it compelled him in a very short time to quit the place.

Nay, I can add, what I myself once saw in the parish of Shoreditch, where two little houses were emptied of near seventy men and women; amongst whom was one of the prettiest girls I had ever seen, who had been carried off by an Irishman, to consummate her marriage on her wedding-night, in a room where several others were in bed at the same time.

If one considers the destruction of all morality, decency and modesty, the swearing, whoredom, and drunkenness, which is eternally carrying on in these houses, on the one hand, and the excessive poverty and misery of

---

[11] See below, p. 166, for more on Saunders Welch.
[12] A pint.

most of the inhabitants on the other, it seems doubtful whether they are more the objects of detestation, or compassion: for such is the poverty of these wretches that, upon searching all the above number, the money found upon all of them (except the bride, who, as I afterwards heard, had robbed her mistress) did not amount to one shilling; and I have been credibly informed, that a single loaf hath supplied a whole family with their provisions for a week. Lastly, if any of these miserable creatures fall sick (and it is almost a miracle that stench, vermin, and want should ever suffer them to be well) they are turned out in the streets by their merciless host or hostess, where, unless some parish officer of extraordinary charity relieves them, they are sure miserably to perish, with the addition of hunger and cold to their disease.

This picture, which is taken from the life, will appear strange to many, for the evil here described, is, I am confident, very little known, especially to those of the better sort. Indeed this is the only excuse, and I believe the only reason, that it hath been so long tolerated: for when we consider the number of these wretches, which, in the out-skirts of the town, amounts to a great many thousands, it is a nuisance which will appear to be big with every moral and political mischief. Of these the excessive misery of the wretches themselves, oppressed with want, and sunk in every species of debauchery, and the loss of so many lives to the public, are obvious and immediate consequences. There are some more remote, which, however, need not be mentioned to the discerning.

Among other mischiefs attending this wretched nuisance, the great increase of thieves must necessarily be one. The wonder in fact is, that we have not a thousand more robbers than we have; indeed, that all these wretches are not thieves, must give us either a very high idea of their honesty, or a very mean one of their capacity and courage.

Where then is the redress? Is it not to hinder the poor from wandering, and this by compelling the parish and peace officers to apprehend such wanderers or vagabonds, and by empowering the magistrate effectually to punish and send them to their habitations? Thus if we cannot discover, or will not encourage any cure for idleness, we shall at least compel the poor to starve or beg at home: for there it will be impossible for them to steal or rob, without being presently hanged or transported out of the way.

Sec. VII   Of apprehending the persons of felons

I come now to the third encouragement which the thief flatters himself with, viz. in his hope of escaping from being apprehended. Nor is this hope without foundation. How long have we known highwaymen reign in this kingdom after they have been publicly known for such? Have not some of these committed robberies in open day-light, in the sight of many people, and have after rode solemnly and triumphantly through the neighbouring towns without any danger or molestation. This happens to every rogue who is become eminent for his audaciousness, and is thought to be desperate. . . . Officers of Justice have owned to me that they have passed by such with warrants in their pockets against them without daring to apprehend them.[13]

Fielding goes on to cite the numerous grounds in law under which an arrest can be made. He then examines (below) the diffulties of imposing the law.

But tho' the law seems to have been sufficiently provident on this head, there is still great difficulty in carrying its purpose into execution, arising from the following causes.

First, with regard to private persons, there is no country, I believe, in the world, where that vulgar maxim so generally prevails, that what is the business of every man is the business of no man; and for this plain reason, that there is no country in which less honour is gained by serving the public. He therefore who commits no crime against the public, is very well satisfied with his own virtue; far from thinking himself obliged to undergo any labour, expend any money, or encounter any danger on such account.

Secondly, the people are not entirely without excuse from their ignorance of the law: for so far is the power of apprehending felons, which I have above set forth, from being universally known, that many of the peace officers themselves do not know that they have any such power, and often from ignorance refuse to arrest a known felon 'till they are authorized by a warrant from a justice of peace. Much less then can the compulsory part to the private persons carry any terror of a penalty of which the generality of mankind are totally ignorant; and of inflicting which they see no example.

Thirdly, so far are men from being animated with the hopes of public praise to apprehend a felon, that they are even discouraged by the fear of shame. The person of the informer is in fact more odious than that of the felon himself; and the thief-catcher is in danger of worse treatment from the populace than the thief.

Fielding concludes by citing the leniency of juries in dealing with burglars.

Sec. VIII   Of the difficulties which attend prosecutions

Fielding lists the reasons why prosecutors were reluctant to prosecute: fear; too delicate to appear in court; too idle; too mean to bear the cost of prosecution; too poor to bear the cost of prosecution; too tender-hearted to prosecute. He argues that in the case of poor prosecutors, the county or the nation should bear the cost.

---

[13] The impunity of the violent and outrageous criminal is a recurring theme in English criminal history.

Sec. IX   Of the trial and conviction of felons

Here Fielding stresses the difficulty of getting good and acceptable evidence before the court.

Sec. X   Of the encouragement given to robbers by frequent pardons

He argues that excessive granting of pardons does harm to the criminal justice system.

Sec. XI   Of the manner of execution

But if every hope which I have mentioned fails the thief, if he should be discovered, apprehended, prosecuted, convicted, and refused a pardon, what is his situation then? Surely most gloomy and dreadful, without any hope, and without any comfort. This is, perhaps, the case with the less practised, less spirited, and less dangerous rogues, but with those of a different constitution it is far otherwise. No hero sees death as the alternative which may attend his undertaking with less terror, nor meets it in the field with more imaginary glory. Pride, which is commonly the uppermost passion in both, is in both treated with equal satisfaction. The day appointed by law for the thief's shame is the day of glory in his own opinion. His procession to Tyburn, and his last moments there, are all triumphant, attended with the compassion of the meek and tender-hearted, and with the applause, admiration, and envy of all the bold and hardened. His behaviour in his present condition, not the crimes, how atrocious soever which brought him to it, are the subject of contemplation. And if he hath sense enough to temper his boldness with any degree of decency, his death is spoke of by many with honour, by most with pity, and by all with approbation.

How far such an example is from being an object of terror, especially to those for whose use it is principally intended, I leave to the consideration of every rational man; whether such examples as I have described are proper to be exhibited must be submitted to our superiors. The great cause of this evil is the frequency of executions: the knowledge of human nature will prove this from reason; and the different effects which executions produce in the minds of the spectators in the country where they are rare, and in London where they are common, will convince us by experience.[14] The thief who is hanged today hath learnt his intrepidity from the example of his hanged predecessors, as others are now taught to despise death, and to bear it hereafter with boldness from what they see today.

---

[14] Yet again, London is seen as unique in its criminality.

One way of preventing the frequency of executions is by removing the evil I am complaining of, for this effect in time becomes a cause, and greatly increases that very evil from which it first arose. The design of those who first appointed executions to be public, was to add the punishment of shame to that of death, in order to make the example an object of greater terror. But experience hath shewn us that the event is directly contrary to this intention. Indeed a competent knowledge of human nature might have foreseen the consequence. To unite the ideas of death and shame is not so easy as may be imagined. All ideas of the latter being absorbed by the former. To prove this, I will appeal to any man who hath seen an execution, or a procession to an execution; let him tell me when he hath beheld a poor wretch, bound in a cart, just on the verge of eternity, all pale and trembling with his approaching fate, whether the idea of shame hath ever intruded on his mind? Much less will the bold daring rogue who glories in his present condition, inspire the beholder with any such sensation.

Fielding then quotes from the poets in defence of his proposition.

To effect this, it seems that the execution should be as soon as possible after the commission and conviction of the crime, for if this be of an atrocious kind, the resentment of mankind being warm, would pursue the criminal to his last end, and all pity for the offender would be lost in detestation of the offence. Whereas, when executions are delayed so long as they sometimes are, the punishment and not the crime is considered, and no good mind can avoid compassionating a set of wretches, who are put to death we know not why, unless, as it almost appears, to make a holiday for, and to entertain the mob.

Secondly, it should be in some degree private. And here the poets will again assist us. Foreigners have found fault with the cruelty of the English drama, in representing frequent murders upon the stage. In fact, this is not only cruel, but highly injudicious: a murder behind the scenes, if the poet knows how to manage it, will affect the audience with greater terror than if it was acted before their eyes. Of this we have an instance in the murder of the king in *Macbeth*, at which, when Garrick acts the part,[15] it is scarce an hyperbole to say, I have seen the hair of the audience stand on end. Terror hath, I believe, been carried higher by this single instance, than by all the blood which hath been spilt on the stage. To the poets I may add the priests, whose politics have never been doubted. Those of Egypt in particular, where the sacred mysteries were first devised, well knew the use of hiding from the eyes of the vulgar, what they intended

---

[15] David Garrick (1717–79), famous actor and theatre director.

148

should inspire them with the greatest awe and dread. The mind of man is so much more capable of magnifying than his eye, that I question whether every object is not lessened by being looked upon; and this more especially when the passions are concerned: for these are ever apt to fancy much more satisfaction in those objects which they affect, and much more of mischief in those which they abhor, than are really to be found in either.

If executions therefore were so contrived, that few could be present at them, they would be much more shocking and terrible to the crowd without doors than at present, as well much more dreadful to the criminals themselves, who would thus die in the presence only of their enemies; and where the boldest of them would find no cordial to keep up his spirits, nor any breath to flatter his ambition.

Thirdly, the execution should be in the highest degree solemn. It is not the essence of the thing itself, but the dress and apparatus of it, which make an impression on the mind, especially on the minds of the multitude to whom beauty in rags is never a desirable, nor deformity in embroidery a disagreeable object.

Now the following method, which I shall venture to prescribe, as it would include all the three particulars of celerity,[16] privacy, and solemnity, so would it, I think, effectually remove all the evils complained of, and which at present attend the manner of inflicting capital punishment.

Suppose then, that the court at the Old Bailey was, at the end of the trials, to be adjourned during four days; that, against the adjournment-day, a gallows was erected in the area before the court; that the criminals were all brought down on that day to receive sentence; and that this was executed the very moment after it was pronounced, in the sight and presence of the judges.

Nothing can, I think, be imagined (not even torture, which I am an enemy to the very thought of admitting) more terrible than such an execution; and I leave it to any man to resolve himself upon reflection, whether such a day at the Old Bailey, or a holiday at Tyburn, would make the strongest impression on the minds of every one.

Conclusions

Thus I have, as well as I am able, finished the task which I proposed, have endeavoured to trace the evil from the very fountain-head, and to shew whence it originally springs, as well as all the supplies it receives, till it becomes a torrent, which at present threatens to bear down all before it.

And here I must again observe, that if the former part of this treatise should raise any attention in the legislature, so as effectually to put a stop

---

[16] Speed.

to the luxury of the lower people, to force the poor to industry, and to provide for them when industrious, the latter part of my labour would be of very little use. And indeed all the pains which can be taken in this latter part, and all the remedies which can be devised, without applying a cure to the former, will be only of the palliative kind, which may patch up the diseases and lessen the bad effects, but never can totally remove it.

Nor, in plain truth, will the utmost severity to offenders be justifiable, unless we take every possible method of preventing the offence. . . . The subject, as well as the child, should be left without excuse before he is punished: for, in that case alone, the rod becomes the hand either of the parent or the magistrate.

All temptations therefore are to be carefully removed out of the way; much less is the plea of necessity to be left in the mouth of any. This plea of necessity is never admitted in our law; but the reason of that is, says Lord Hale, because it is so difficult to discover the truth. Indeed that it is not always certainly false, is a sufficient scandal to our polity; for what can be more shocking than to see an industrious poor creature, who is able and willing to labour, forced by mere want into dishonesty, and that in a nation of such trade and opulence.

Upon the whole, something should be, nay must be done, or much worse consequences than have hitherto happened, are very soon to be apprehended. Nay, as the matter now stands, not only care for the public safety, but common humanity, exacts our concern on this occasion. For that many cart-loads of our fellow-creatures are once in six weeks carried to slaughter, is a dreadful consideration;[17] and this is greatly heightened by reflecting, that, with proper care and regulations, much the greater part of these wretches might have been made not only happy in themselves, but very useful members of the society, which they now so greatly dishonour in the sight of all Christendom.

1.2 An Act for preventing thefts and robberies, and for regulating places of public entertainment, and punishing persons keeping disorderly houses, 1752[18] (Extracts)

This act and the one following incorporated suggestions for reform by the Bow Street magistrate Henry Fielding in his An enquiry into the causes of the late increase in robbers, etc. *(see above).*

---

[17] A reference to the six-weekly trip by cart of condemned felons to Tyburn. For a description of the method of execution, see above, pp. 113–16.

[18] 25 Geo. II, cap. 36. Taken from John Raithby (ed.), *Statutes at large* (1811).

I Whereas the advertising a reward with no questions asked for the return of which have been lost or stolen is one great cause of thefts and robberies, be it enacted that . . . any person publicly advertising a reward with no questions asked for the return of things which have been stolen or lost . . . shall forfeit the sum of fifty pounds for every such offence . . .

II And whereas the multitude of places of entertainment for the lower sort of people is another great cause of thefts and robberies, as there are thereby tempted to spend their small substance in riotous pleasures, and in consequence are put on unlawful methods of supplying their wants and renewing their pleasures, in order then to prevent the said temptation to theft and robberies and to correct as far as may be the habit of idleness which is become too general over the whole kingdom and is productive of much mischief and inconvenience; be it enacted that any house, room, garden, or other place kept for public dancing, music, or other public entertainment of the like kind, in the cities of London and Westminster, or within twenty miles thereof, without a licence had for that purpose from the last Michaelmas Quarter-Sessions . . . in which such a house, room, garden or other place is situate . . . signified under the hands and seals of four or more of the Justices there assembled, shall be deemed a disorderly house . . . And it shall be lawful to and for any constable . . . by warrant . . . to seize every person therein in order that they may be dealt with according to Law. And every person keeping such a house, room, garden or other place without such licence as aforesaid shall forfeit the sum of one hundred pounds to such person as shall sue for the same . . .

III *Licensed premises shall display a notice and not open before five in the afternoon.*

VIII And whereas by reason of the many subtle and crafty contrivances of persons keeping bawdy-houses, gaming-houses or other disorderly houses, it is difficult to prove who is the real owner or keeper thereof, by which means many notorious offenders have escaped punishment, be it enacted that any person who shall at any time appear, act or behave him or herself as Master or Mistress . . . shall be deemed and taken to be the Keeper thereof, and shall be liable to be prosecuted and punished as such.[19]

XI And whereas many persons are deterred from prosecuting persons guilty of felony upon account of the expense attending such prosecutions, which is another great cause and encouragement of thefts and robberies;

---

[19] The use of surrogate managers by owners of shops selling pornographic material in Soho in the 1960s was common.

in order to encourage the bringing of offenders to justice, be it enacted that it shall and may be in the power of the court . . . at the prayer of the prosecutor and on consideration of his circumstances, to order the Treasurer of the County . . . to pay unto such prosecutor such sum of money as to the said court shall seem reasonable.[20]

1.3   An Act for the preventing of the horrid crime of murder, 1752[21] (Extracts)

I   Whereas the horrid crime of murder has of late been more frequently perpetrated than formerly, and particularly in and near the Metropolis of this Kingdom, contrary to the known humanity and natural genius of the British nation, and whereas it is thereby become that some further terror and peculiar mark of infamy be added to the punishment of death, now by Law inflicted . . . be it enacted . . . that all persons who shall be found guilty of wilful murder be executed according to the Law on the day next but one after sentencing unless the same shall happen to be the Lord's day, . . . and in that case on the Monday following.

II   And be it further enacted that the body of such murder so convicted [if in Middlesex or the City of London] be immediately conveyed by the sheriff or sheriffs . . . to the Hall of the Surgeons Company . . . and the body so delivered . . . shall be dissected and anatomized by the said surgeons. And in case such conviction and execution shall happen to be in any other county or place in Great Britain, the judge or Justice of Assize . . . shall award the sentence to be put in execution the next day but one after such conviction except as is before excepted) and the body of such murderer shall in like manner be delivered by the sheriff . . . to such surgeons as such judge or justice shall direct.

III   And be it further enacted that sentence shall be announced in open court immediately after the conviction of such murderer, and before the court shall proceed to any other business . . . ; in which sentence shall be expressed not only the usual judgment of death but also the time appointed hereby . . . , and the marks of infamy hereby directed for such offenders in order to impress a just horror in the mind of the offender and on the minds of such as shall be present, of the heinous crime of murder.

---

[20] A revolutionary clause introducing the notion that the state (in the form of the county) should bear the cost of prosecuting felons.
[21] 25 Geo. II, cap. 37 (Raithby, *Statutes at large*).

V   Provided also that it shall be in the power of such judge or Justice to appoint the body of any such criminal to be hung in chains.[22]

VI   And be it further enacted that . . . the gaoler or keeper . . . shall confine such prisoner to some cell . . . separate and apart from the other prisoners, and that no person or persons shall have access to such prisoner without licence being first obtained for that purpose.

VIII   And be it further enacted that after sentence . . . and until the execution . . . , such offender shall be fed bread and water only, and with no other food or liquor whatsoever.

IX   Any attempt to rescue the condemned prisoner from prison or on the way to the place of execution shall be deemed taken and adjudged to be guilty of felony and suffer death without benefit of clergy.

X   Those attempting to rescue the body from the surgeons to be transported for seven years

1.4   A typical Old Bailey Sessions[23]

20 September, 1752

Ended the Sessions at the Old Bailey when five persons received sentence of death, viz. Randolph Branch and William Descent for robbing and murdering Joseph Brown, a brewer's clerk; Thomas Butler for returning from transportation; John Wilks for a street robbery; and Matthew Lee for a highway-robbery. Two [others] were ordered to be transported for 14 years; forty-seven for 7 years; four to be whipped; and three branded. There were 102 prisoners tried in all.

22 September, 1752

Randolph Branch and William Descent . . . were executed at Tyburn, after which their bodies were delivered to the surgeons, pursuant to the late Act of Parliament.

---

[22] To leave the body to rot in chains in a public place was much feared by felons. For such a case, see p. 164.

[23] *The Gentleman's Magazine*, xxii (1752), p. 429.

1.5 Government funding leads to successful crime-busting, 1753[24]

In 1753 Henry Fielding was very ill, yet, under government pressure, he made his last contribution to law and order in London before handing over to his brother John.

In the beginning of August, 1753, when I had taken the Duke of Portland's medicine, as it is called, near a year, the effects of which had been the carrying off the symptoms of a lingering imperfect gout, I was persuaded by Mr Ranby, the king's premier serjeant-surgeon, and the ablest advice, I believe, in all branches of the physical profession, to go immediately to Bath. I accordingly writ that very night to Mrs Bowden, who, by the next post, informed me she had taken me a lodging for a month certain.

Within a few days after this, whilst I was preparing for my journey, and when I was almost fatigued to death with several long examinations, relating to five different murders, all committed within the space of a week, by different gangs of street-robbers, I received a message from his grace the Duke of Newcastle, by Mr Carrington, the king's messenger, to attend his grace the next morning, in Lincoln's Inn Fields, upon some business of importance; but I excused myself from complying with the message, as, besides being lame, I was very ill with the great fatigues I had lately undergone added to my distemper.

His Grace, however, sent Mr Carrington, the very next morning, with another summons; with which, though in the utmost distress, I immediately complied; but the duke, happening, unfortunately for me, to be then particularly engaged, after I had waited some time, sent a gentleman to discourse with me on the best plan which could be invented for putting an immediate end to those murders and robberies which were every day committed in the streets; upon which I promised to transmit my opinion, in writing, to his Grace, who, as the gentleman informed me, intended to lay it before the Privy Council.

Though this visit cost me a severe cold, I, notwithstanding, set myself down to work, and in about four days sent the duke as regular a plan as I could form, with all the reasons and arguments I could bring to support it, drawn out in several sheets of paper; and soon received a message from the duke by Mr Carrington, acquainting me that my plan was highly approved of, and that all the terms of it would be complied with.

The principal and most material of those terms was the immediately depositing six hundred pounds in my hands, at which small charge I undertook to demolish the then reigning gangs, and to put the civil policy

---

[24] Henry Fielding, *Introduction, The journal of a voyage to Lisbon* (1755).

into such order, that no such gangs should ever be able, for the future, to form themselves into bodies, or at least to remain any time formidable to the public.

I had delayed my Bath journey for some time, contrary to the repeated advice of my physical acquaintance, and to the ardent desire of my warmest friends, though my distemper was now turned to a deep jaundice; in which case the Bath waters are generally reputed to be almost infallible. But I had the most eager desire of demolishing this gang of villains and cut-throats, which I was sure of accomplishing the moment I was enabled to pay a fellow who had undertaken, for a small sum, to betray them into the hands of a set of thief-takers whom I had enlisted into the service, all men of known and approved fidelity and intrepidity.

After some weeks the money was paid at the Treasury, and, within a few days after two hundred pounds of it had come to my hands, the whole gang of cut-throats was entirely dispersed, seven of them were in actual custody, and the rest driven, some out of town, and others out of the kingdom.

Though my health was now reduced to the last extremity, I continued to act with the utmost vigour against these villains, in examining whom, and in taking the depositions against them, I have often spent whole days, nay, sometimes whole nights, especially when there was any difficulty in procuring sufficient evidence to convict them; which is a very common case in street-robberies, even when the guilt of the party is sufficiently apparent to satisfy the most tender conscience. But courts of justice know nothing of a cause more than what is told them on oath by a witness; and the most flagitious[25] villain upon earth is tried in the same manner as a man of the best character who is accused of the same crime.

Meanwhile, amidst all my fatigues and distresses, I had the satisfaction to find my endeavours had been attended with such success that this hellish society were almost utterly extirpated, and that, instead of reading of murders and street-robberies in the news almost every morning, there was, in the remaining part of the month of November, and in all December, not only no such thing as a murder, but not even a street-robbery committed. Some such, indeed, were mentioned in the public papers; but they were all found, on the strictest enquiry, to be false.

In this entire freedom from street-robberies, during the dark months, no man will, I believe, scruple to acknowledge that the winter of 1753 stands unrivalled, during a course of many years; and this may possibly appear the more extraordinary to those who recollect the outrages with which it began.

I was now, in the opinion of all men, dying of a complication of disorders; and, were I desirous of playing the advocate, I have an occasion fair enough;

---

[25] Deeply criminal; extremely wicked.

but I disdain such an attempt. I relate facts plainly and simply as they are; and let the world draw from them what conclusions they please, taking with them the following facts for their instruction.

The one is, that the proclamation offering one hundred pounds for the apprehending felons for certain felonies committed in certain places, which I prevented from being revived, had formerly cost the government several thousand pounds within a single year.

Secondly, that all such proclamations, instead of curing the evil, had actually increased it; had multiplied the number of robberies; had propagated the worst and wickedest of perjuries; had laid snares for youth and ignorance, which, by the temptation of these rewards, had been sometimes drawn into guilt; and sometimes, which cannot be thought on without the highest horror, had destroyed them without it.

Thirdly, that my plan had not put the government to more than three hundred pound expense, and had produced none of the ill consequences above mentioned; but, lastly, had actually suppressed the evil for a time, and had plainly pointed out the means of suppressing it for ever. This I would myself have undertaken, had my health permitted, at the annual expense of the above-mentioned sum.

1.6   The deposition of Sarah Davies, unmarried mother and former sailor, 1751[26]

This is one of the more curious documents in this collection, for it illustrates not only what happened to an unmarried woman who had a child outside of her home parish, and here the treatment of mother and child has not changed significantly over 200 years or more, but also that distinctive eighteenth-century phenomenon of a woman passing herself as a man in order to engage in men's work.

The County of Chester

The examination of Sarah Davies, single-woman, taken upon oath before me, James Croxton, Esquire, one of his Majesty's Justices of the Peace and [of the] Quorum for the said county this twenty-sixth day of December 1751.

This examinate deposeth and saith that she was born in the parish of Saint James in the City of Bristol. That her father, John Davies is a tidewaiter[27] there.

---

[26] Cheshire Record Office, QJF 180/1 FO 8X. The deposition appears as a single unpunctuated piece of prose. The editor has added punctuation and divided the text into paragraphs.
[27] Customs Officer.

That about seven years ago, she dressed herself in men's clothes and went to London and there bound herself apprentice to one Captain John Hasseck for five years by the name of John Davies. That she accordingly went with the said captain as a sailor to Jamaica and was about six months in his service when she ran away from that service and has since been a sailor on board several other ships.

That she was on board a ship on the first of November last which foundered in the Bay of Biscay. That she and thirteen others were taken up by a vessel belonging to Sunderland. That on the eighteenth day of November last, she came ashore at Sunderland aforesaid.

That she travelled wandering and begging from Sunderland aforesaid unto the City of Chester and that on the sixteenth day of this instant December, she went into the town of Eccleston in the said county of Chester wandering and begging.[28] And that on the same day, she was there delivered of a female bastard child which ever since its birth hath been and now is chargeable to the said township of Eccleston.[29]

Taken and sworn the day and year aforesaid
  before me

                                        the mark of
                                             X
  Croxton   Sarah Davies

2   Crime in the eighteenth century

In considering the following statistical data, one should always bear in mind that the figures represent successful prosecutions brought before the courts. They do not include those found not guilty, and those criminals never brought to trial.

2.1   London crime statistics[30]

Felons condemned to death at the Old Bailey, London 1749–71 with a note of those executed or pardoned, transported, or died in gaol

This table reveals the range of serious crime successfully prosecuted in London and the punishments imposed. Note that the proportion of felons condemned to death and then executed is higher than for East Anglia over a similar period (see p. 159).

---

[28] Eccleston is a village three miles south of Chester.
[29] And this, of course, is the issue: who should pay for the support of mother and child?
[30] Abstracted from John Howard, *The state of the prisons in England and Wales* (1777), Table IV.

	Sentenced to death	Executed	Pardoned; transported; died in gaol
Highway robbery	362	251	111
Shop-lifting, riots, etc.	240	109	131
House-breaking	208	118	90
Forgery	95	71	24
Horse-stealing, &c.	90	22	68
Murder	81	72	9
Returning from transportation	31	22	9
Coining	11	10	1
Defrauding creditors	3	3	0
Total	**1121**	**678**	**443**

Transportations of London criminals, 1749–71

These figures include the more serious non-felons and felons pardoned by the king.

Criminals sentenced to transportation directly	5199
Convicted felons whose death penalty was commuted to transportation	401
Total numbers transported	5600

2.2   Crime in East Anglia, 1750–72[31]

These figures for the Norfolk Circuit, which covered East Anglia, reveal a different range of serious crime from that recorded for London and a higher proportion of convicted felons whose sentence was commuted to transportation.

2.3   A child-murderer of a child, 1748[32]

This case reminds us that the horror of a child killing a child is not peculiar to our own age.

Re William York, aged ten years, convicted of murdering Susan Mahew, aged five years

---

[31] Abstracted from Howard, *The state of the prisons*, Table V.
[32] Camden Pelham (ed.), *The chronicles of crime, or the new Newgate calendar* (London, 1887), vol. 1, p. 127.

Crime statistics

Offences carrying the death penalty

Horse-stealing, &c.	202
Burglary & house-breaking	93
Highway robbery; theft from dwelling	65
Other felonious crime	44
Petty treason & murder	20
Returning from transportation	6
Forgery	4
Total of felons condemned to death	**434**

Of these condemned felons:

Executed	117
Reprieved for transportation	308

Other crimes

Grand larceny (sentenced to transportation)	523
Petty larceny (sentenced to transportation)	15
Other crimes (sentenced to transportation)	28
Total	**566**

Summary of punishments

Felons executed	–	117
Felons reprieved for transportation	308	–
Other criminals sentenced to transportation	566	–
Total of those transported	874	874
Total of major punishments		**991**

This unhappy child was but ten years of age when he committed the dreadful crime of which he was convicted. He was a pauper in the poorhouse belonging to the parish of Eye, in Suffolk, and was committed, on the coroner's inquest, to Ipswich jail, for the murder of Susan Mahew, another child, of five years of age, who had been his bedfellow. The following is his confession, taken by a Justice of the Peace, and which was, in part, proved on the trial, with many corroborating circumstances of his guilt.

He said that a trifling quarrel happening between them on the 13th of May 1748, about ten in the morning, he struck her with his open hand, and made her cry: that she going out of the house to the dunghill, opposite to the door, he followed her, with a hook in his hand, with an intent to kill her; but before he came up to her, he set down the hook, and went into the house for a knife. He then came out again, took hold of the girl's left hand, and cut her wrist all round to the bone, and then threw her down, and cut her to the bone just above the elbow of the same arm.

159

That, after this, he set his foot upon her stomach, and cut her right arm round about, and to the bone, both on the wrist and above the elbow. That he still thought she would not die, and therefore took the hook and cut her left thigh to the bone.

His next care was to conceal the murder for which purpose he filled a pail with water at a ditch, and washing the blood off the child's body, buried it in the dunghill, together with the blood that was spilled upon the child's clothes, and then went and got his breakfast.

When he was examined, he showed very little concern, and appeared easy and cheerful. All he alleged was that the child fouled the bed in which they lay together; that she was sulky, and that he did not like her.

The boy was found guilty, and sentenced to death; but he was respited from time to time on account of his tender years, and at length pardoned.

2.4 Sussex smugglers' murder of customs officials, 1748[33]

This infamous case gripped the public imagination because of the sadistic cruelty of the offenders. The murders followed the capture of a shipment of contraband tea and its subsequent recovery by the smugglers from the Customs House at Poole on 6 October 1747. The murders in February 1748 were the bloody culmination of a breakdown in law and order in Sussex caused by smuggling.[34]

Re Benjamin Tapner, John Cobby, John Hammond, Richard Mills, Richard Mills the younger, and others

We do not recollect ever to have heard of a case exhibiting greater brutality on the part of the murderers towards their victim than this. The offenders were all smugglers, and the unfortunate objects of their crime were a custom-house officer, and a shoemaker, named respectively William Galley and Daniel Chater. It would appear that a daring and very extensive robbery having been committed at the custom-house at Poole, Galley and Chater were sent to Starlstead in Sussex, to give some information to Major Battine, a magistrate, in reference to the circumstance. They did not, however, return to their homes, and on inquiry, it turned out that they had been brutally murdered, the body of Galley being traced, by means of bloodhounds, to be buried, while that of Chater was discovered at a distance of six miles, in a well in Harris' Wood, near Leigh, in Lady Holt's Park, covered up with a quantity of stones, wooden railings, and earth.

---

[33] Pelham, *The chronicles of crime*, vol. 1, pp. 127–30.
[34] For a discussion of this case, see Briggs et al., *Crime and punishment in England* (1996), pp. 88–9, and Hay et al., *Albion's fatal tree* (1975), Chap. 3, sec'n iii.

At a special commission held at Chichester, on the 16th of January 1749, the prisoners Benjamin Tapner, John Cobby, John Hammond, William Carter, Richard Mills the elder, and Richard Mills the younger, were indicted for the murder of David Chater; the three first as principals, and the others as accessories before the fact; and William Jackson and William Carter were indicted for the murder of William Galley.

From the evidence adduced, the circumstances of this most horrid murder were proved, and it appeared that the two deceased persons having passed Havant on their road to Stanstead,[35] went to the New Inn where they met one Austin, and his brother and brother-in-law, of whom they asked the road. And they conducted them to Rowland's Castle, where they said, they might obtain better information. They went into the White Hart and Mrs Payne, the landlady, suspecting the object of their mission, sent for the prisoners Jackson and Carter, and they were soon after joined by some others of the gang. After they had been all sitting together, Carter called Chater out, and demanded to know where Diamond, one of those suspected of the robbery, was? Chater replied that he was in custody, and that he was going against his will to give evidence against him.[36] Galley, following them into the yard, was knocked down by Carter, on his calling Chater away, and they then returned in-doors. The smugglers now pretended to be sorry for what had occurred, and desired Galley to drink some rum, and they persisted in plying him and Chater with liquor until they were both intoxicated. They were then persuaded to lie down and sleep, and a letter to Major Battine, of which they were the bearers, was taken from them, read, and destroyed.

One John Royce, a smuggler, now came in and Jackson and Carter told them the contents of the letter, and said that they had got the old rogue, the shoemaker of Fordingbridge, who was going to inform against John Diamond, the shepherd, then in custody at Chichester. Here William Steele proposed to take them both to a well about two hundred yards from the house, and to murder and throw them in. But this was rejected, and after several propositions had been made as to the mode in which they should be disposed of, the scene of cruelty was commenced by Jackson, who, putting on his spurs, jumped upon the bed where they lay, and spurred their foreheads, and then whipped them, so that they both got up bleeding. The smugglers then took them out of the house and Mills swore he would shoot any one who followed or said anything of what had occurred.

Meanwhile, the rest put Galley and Chater on one horse, tied their legs under the horse's belly, and then tied the legs of both together. They now set forward, with the exception of Royce, who had no horse. And they had not gone above two hundred yards, before Jackson called out, "Whip 'em,

---

[35] Near Chichester.
[36] Chater knew Diamond, having worked with him.

cut 'em, slash 'em, damn 'em!" upon which, all began to whip except Steele, who led the horse, the roads being very bad. They whipped them for half a mile till they came to Woodash where they fell off, with their heads under the horse's belly, and their legs, which were tied, appeared over the horse's back. Their tormentors soon set them upright again, and continued whipping them over the head, face, shoulders, &tc till they came to Dean, upwards of half a mile farther. And here they both fell again as before, with their heads under the horse's belly, which were struck at every step by the horse's hoofs. Upon placing them again in the saddle, the villains found them so weak that they could not sit, upon which they separated them, and put Galley before Steele, and Chater before little Sam, and then whipped Galley so severely, that, the lashes coming upon Steele, at his desire they desisted.

They then went to Harris' Well, and threatened to throw Galley in. But when he desired that they would put an end to his misery at once, "No," said Jackson, "if that's the case, we have something more to say to you;" and they thereupon put him on the horse again, and whipped him over the Downs until he was so weak that he fell off. They next laid him across the horse, and little Sam, getting up behind him, subjected him to such cruelty as made him groan with the most excruciating torments, and he fell off again. Being again put up astride, Richards got up behind him; but the poor man soon cried out, "I fall, I fall," and Richards pushed him with force, saying, "Fall, and be damned!"

The unhappy man then turned over and expired; and they threw the body over the horse, and carried it off with them to the house of one Scardefield, who kept the Red Lion at Rake. The landlord remarking the condition of Chater, and Galley's body, the fellows told him that they had engaged with some officers, had lost their tea, and that some of them were wounded, if not dead. This was sufficient, and Jackson and Carter carried Chater down to the house of the elder Mills, where they chained him up in a turf-house. Their companions, in the mean time, drank gin and brandy at Scardefield's, and it being now nearly dark, they borrowed spades, and a candle and lantern, and making him assist them in digging a hole, they buried the body of the murdered officer. They then separated, but on the Thursday they met again with some more of their associates, including the prisoners Richard Mills, and his two sons Richard and John, Thomas Stringer, Cobby, Tapner, and Hammond, for the purpose of deliberating what should he done with their prisoner. It was soon unanimously resolved that he must be destroyed, and it was determined that they should take him to Harris' Well and throw him in, as it was considered that that death would be most likely to cause him the greatest pain.[37]

---

[37] The justification of this was presumably that they considered Chater to be an informer.

During this time the wretched man was in a state of the utmost horror and misery, being visited occasionally by all his tormentors, who abused him, and beat him violently. At last, when this determination had been arrived at, they all went, and Tapner pulling out a clasp-knife, ordered him on his knees, swearing that he would be his butcher. But being dissuaded from this, as being opposed to their plan to prolong the miseries of their prisoner, he contented himself with slashing the knife across his eyes, almost cutting them out, and completely severing the gristle of his nose. They then placed him upon a horse, and all set out together for Harris' Well, except Mills and his sons, they having no horses ready, and saying, in excuse, "that there were enough without them to murder one man."

All the way Tapner whipped him till the blood came; and then swore that if he blooded the saddle, he would torture him the more. When they were come within one hundred yards of the well, Jackson and Carter stopped, saying to Tapner, Cobby, Stringer, Steele, and Hammond, "Go on and do your duty on Chater, as we have ours upon Galley."

It was in the dead of the night that they brought their victim to the well, which was nearly thirty feet deep, but dry, and paled close round. And Tapner having fastened a noose round his neck, they bade him get over the pales. He was going through a broken place; but though he was covered with blood and fainting with the anguish of his wounds, they forced him to climb up, having the rope about his neck. They then tied one end of the cord to the pales and pushed him over the brink; but the rope being short, he hung no farther within it than his thighs, and leaning against the edge, he hung above a quarter of an hour and was not strangled. They then untied him, and threw him head foremost into the well.

They tarried some time, and hearing him groan, they determined to go to one William Comleah's, a gardener, to borrow a rope and ladder, saying they wanted to relieve one of their companions who had fallen into Harris' Well. He said they might take them, but they could not manage the ladder in their confusion, it being a long one. They then returned to the well, and still hearing him groan, and fearful that the sound might lead to a discovery, the place being near the road, they threw upon him some of the rails and gate-posts fixed about the well, as well as some great stones; and then finding him silent, they left him. Their next consultation was how to dispose of their horses; and they killed Galley's, which was grey, and taking his hide off, cut it into small pieces, and hid them so as to prevent any discovery; but a bay horse that Chater had ridden on got from them.

This being the evidence produced, the jury, after being out of Court about a quarter of an hour, brought in a verdict of guilty against all the prisoners: whereupon the judge pronounced sentence on the convicts in a most pathetic address, representing the enormity of their crime, and exhorting them to make immediate preparation for the awful fate that awaited them, adding, "Christian charity obliges me to tell you that your time in this world will be very short."

The heinousness of the crime of which these men had been convicted rendering it necessary that their punishment should be exemplary, the judge ordered that they should be executed on the following day. And the sentence was accordingly carried into execution against all but Jackson, who died in prison on the evening that he was condemned. They were attended by two ministers, and all, except Mills and his son (who took no notice of each other, and thought themselves not guilty because they were not present at the finishing of the inhuman murder), showed great marks of penitence. Tapner and Carter gave good advice to the spectators and desired diligence might be used to apprehend Richards, whom they charged as the cause of their being brought to this wretched end. Young Mills smiled several times at the executioner, who was a discharged marine and having ropes too short for some of them, was puzzled to fit them. Old Mills being forced to stand tiptoe to reach the halter, desired that he might not be hanged by inches. The two Mills were so rejoiced at being told that they were not to be hanged in chains after execution, that death seemed to excite in them no terror; while Jackson was so struck with horror at being measured for his irons, that he soon expired.

They were hanged at Chichester on the 18th of January 1749, amidst such a concourse of spectators as is seldom seen on the occasion of a public execution.

Carter was hung in chains near Rake, in Sussex; Tapner, on Rook's Hill, near Chichester; and Cobby and Hammond, at Selsey Isle, on the beach where they sometimes landed their smuggled goods, and where they could be seen at a great distance east and west.

2.5 Riots in the Strand, July 1749

On Saturday July 1, three sailors from the man-of-war Grafton, *were robbed whilst in a whore-house in the Strand owned by a man called Owen. They returned later that evening, threw out the whores and the house furnishings which they set alight. The following evening, sailors and others attacked whore-houses in the Strand kept by Stanhope and Wood. On the instigation of Saunders Welch, the army were summoned and the mob dispersed, and on the Monday, Henry Fielding, the Bow Street magistrate, examined various prisoners before consigning them to Newgate. Two prisoners were subsequently charged and convicted under the Riot Act of 1715, and one, the strangely named Bosavern Penlez, was executed.*

Newspaper reports of the riots[38]

Saturday 1 July

Three sailors belonging to the *Grafton* man-of-war went into an house of ill-fame near the new church in the Strand where they were robbed of 30 guineas, 4 moidores,[39] a bank note of 20 li., two watches, &c.[40] And obtaining no satisfaction [they] went out, denouncing vengeance. And this night [they] returned with a great number of armed sailors who entirely demolished the goods, cut the feather-beds to pieces, strewed the feathers in the street, tore the wearing apparel, and turned the women naked into the street. Then [they] broke all the windows and considerably damaged an adjacent house. A guard of soldiers was sent from the Tilt Yard, but came too late.

A guard of officer and 60 soldiers were ordered to do duty at Temple Bar to prevent any more riotous proceedings, and nine persons concerned in them were committed to Newgate.

Sunday 2 July

At night the sailors renewed their outrages and committed the same acts of violence on two other houses of ill-fame in the Strand, in presence of a multitude of spectators who huzzard them. Other houses in the Old Bailey and Goodman's Fields were treated in the same manner.

Friday 7 July

A bill of indictment was found at Hick's Hall against four persons for feloniously demolishing the *Star Tavern* in the Strand laid on the statute 1 Geo. I cap. 5, but the evidence not being ready, the trial was deferred to the next Sessions . . .

Thursday 14 September

Ended the Sessions at the Old Bailey, [where] were condemned 19 persons, viz. John Wilson and Bosavern Pen Lez for a riot and pulling down part of a house near Temple Bar . . . [Penlez was executed on Wednesday 18 October]

---

[38] *Gentleman's Magazine*, xix (1749), pp. 329, 426, 474.
[39] A Portuguese gold coin worth 27 shillings.
[40] Note the considerable wealth these sailors were carrying.

Depositions[41]

The deposition of Thomas Munn, beadle of the Duchy of Lancaster

This informant saith that on Saturday the first day of July, [he] was summoned to quell a disturbance which then in the Strand, near the new church, where a large mob was assembled about the house of one Owen, the cause of which [he] was told was that a sailor had been there robbed by a woman. When [he] first came up, the populace was crying out, "Pull down the house, Pull down the house!" and were so very outrageous that all his endeavours and those of another beadle of the same liberty to appease them were in vain. [He] however attempted to seize one of the ringleaders, but he was immediately rescued from him, and he himself threatened to be knocked down. Upon which, [he] sent for the constables and soon after went to his own home.

And [he] saith that between eleven and twelve the same evening, two of the aforesaid rioters, being seized by the constable, were delivered into the custody of this informant, who confined them in the night-prison . . . which night-prison is under [his] house.

And [he] saith further that on the second succeeding night, being Sunday, the second of July, about twelve at night, the mob come to [his] house and broke open the windows, and entered thereat, seized his servant, and demanded the keys of the prison, threatening to murder her if she did not deliver the same. But not being able to procure the same, they wrenched the bars out of the windows with which as [he] has been told and verily believes, they broke open the prison and rescued the prisoners.

And [he] saith that he was the same evening at the watch-house of the said liberty, where two other prisoners were confined for the said riot, and [he] saith that a very great mob came to the said watch-house, broke the windows of the same all to pieces, demanding to have the prisoners delivered to them, threatening to pull the watch-house down if the said prisoners were not set at liberty immediately. After which they forced into the said watch-house and rescued the prisoners.

Deposition of Saunders Welch, gentleman, high constable of Holborn Division

This informant saith that on Sunday morning about ten of the clock on the second of July last, one Stanhope, who then kept a house in the Strand, near the new church, came to [him] and told him that a house had been demolished in the Strand by a great mob, and that he had good reason to fear that the said mob would come and demolish his house, they having threatened that they would pull down all bawdy-houses. Upon

---

[41] Henry Fielding, *A true state of the case of Bosavern Penlez* (1749).

which this informant directed the said Stanhope departed and returned no more to this informant.

And [he] saith that as he was returning the same evening between the hours of eleven and twelve from a friend's house in the City, as he passed through Fleet Street, he perceived a great fire in the Strand. Upon which he proceeded on till he came to the house of one Peter Wood, who told [him] that the mob had demolished the house of Stanhope and were burning his goods, and that they threatened, as soon as they had finished their business there, that they would come and demolish his house likewise. And [he] prayed the assistance of this informant.

Upon which this informant, despairing of being able to quell the mob by his own authority, and well knowing the impossibility of procuring any magistrate at that time who would act,[42] applied to the Tilt Yard for a military force, which with much difficulty he obtained, having no order from any Justice of the Peace for the same. And [he] saith that having at last procured an officer with about forty men, he returned to the place of the riot. But [he] saith that when he came to the Cecil street end, he prevailed upon the officer to order his drum to beat, in hopes, if possible, of dispersing the mob without any mischief ensuing. And [he] saith that when he came up to the house of Peter Wood, he found the mob had in a great part demolished the said house, and thrown a vast quantity of his goods into the street, but had not perfected their design, a large parcel of the goods still remaining in the house, the said house having been very well furnished.[43] And [he] says he has been told there was a debate amongst the mob concerning burning the goods of that house likewise as they had served those of two other houses. And [he] says that had the goods of the said house been set on fire, it must have infallibly have set on fire the houses on both sides, the street being there extremely narrow. And [he] saith that the house of Messrs. Snow and Denne, bankers, is almost opposite to that of Peter Wood.

And [he] saith that at his coming up, the mob had deserted the house of the said Peter, occasioned as he verily believes and hath been informed by the terror spread among them from beating the drum as aforesaid, so that [he] found no person in the aforesaid house save only Peter Wood, his wife and man-servant, and two or three women who appeared to belong to it, and one Lander who was taken by a soldier in the upper part of the said house and who it afterwards appeared at his trial to the satisfaction of the jury, came along with the guard.

And [he] farther says that the said rioters immediately dispersing several of them were apprehended by the soldiers who being produced to Peter

---

[42] Fielding had gone to the country that weekend.

[43] A comment on the quality of London whore-houses; clearly there were big profits in this business.

Wood were by him charged as principally concerned in the demolition of his house. Upon which, they were delivered by this informant to a constable of the Duchy Liberty and were by that constable conveyed under a guard of soldiers to New Prison. And [he] farther saith that he remained on the spot together with part of the guards till about three of the clock the next morning, before which time the mob were all dispersed and peace again restored.

And [he] farther saith that on the Monday morning, about twelve of the clock, he attended H. Fielding, Esq., on of his majesty's Justices of the Peace for the County of Middlesex, who had been out of town during all the preceding riot, and acquainted him with it. That immediately the said Justice sent an order for a party of the guards to conduct the aforesaid prisoners to his house, the streets being at that time full of mob, assembled in a riotous and tumultuous manner, and danger of a rescue being apprehended.

And [he] saith that the above mentioned prisoners, together with Bosavern Penlez, who was apprehended by the watch in Carey street were brought before the said justice, who, after hearing the evidence against them, and taking the depositions thereof, committed them to Newgate. And [he] saith that whilst he attend before the said Justice, and while the prisoners were under examination, there was a vast mob assembled, not only in Bow Street but many of the adjacent streets, so that it was difficult either to pass or repass. And further saith that he . . . received several informations that the mob had declared that notwithstanding what had been done they intended to carry on the same work again at night. Upon which this informant was sent to the Secretary of War to desire a reinforcement of the guard.

And [he] farther saith he was present when the said Justice from his window spoke to the mob, informed them of their danger, and exhorted them to depart to their own habitations. For which purpose, this informant likewise went amongst and entreated them to disperse, but all such exhortations were ineffectual.

And [he] further saith that he was present at the house of the said Justice when several informations were given, that a body of sailors, to the number of four thousand were assembling themselves at Tower Hill and had declared a resolution of marching to Temple Bar in the evening.

And so riotous did the disposition of the mob appear that whole day, to wit, Monday, that numbers of persons as this informant hath been told removed their goods from their own houses from apprehensions of sharing the fate of Owen, Stanhope, and Wood. To obviate which danger, the aforesaid Justice and this informant sat up the whole night while a large party of soldiers were kept ready under arms who with the peace-officers patrolled the streets where the chief danger was apprehended. By means of all which care, the public peace was again restored.

2.6   Raid on a London whore-house, 1752[44]

This case illustrates the difficulties in attempting to control whore-houses.

On the night of the 7th instant., Mr Carne, the High Constable of Westminster, with a warrant from Justice Fielding, stormed a most notorious bawdy-house at the back of St Clement's, and brought the master, with four young women, before the said Justice. The youngest of these girls was fixed upon to give evidence against the others, but could not be prevailed upon that evening. Upon which, she was confined separately from the rest.

And the next morning, being assured of never becoming again subject to her late severe task-master, she revealed all the secrets of her late prison-house, acts of prostitution, &c. The master of the house was committed to gaol; three of the women sent to Bridewell, and the young girl was recommended by the Justice to the parish of St Clement's to be passed to her settlement in Devonshire.[45]

2.7   Raid on London gaming-house, 1752[46]

18 June. The High Constable of Holborn, supported by a party of guards, seized 20 to 30 persons at a gaming-house by the little turnstile, Holborn, some of whom were admonished by Justice Fielding and discharged, some bound in their own recognizances, and some with sureties, and the most notorious sent to prison.

2.8   Riotous attack on a new turnpike, 1752[47]

Note the combination of public and private monies used in an attempt to bring rioters to justice.

8 May. At Selby, Yorkshire, the bellman made proclamation for the inhabitants to bring their hatchets and axes at 12 o'clock that night to cut down the turnpike erected there by Act of Parliament. Accordingly the great gate with five rails was totally destroyed by some riotous persons, for discovery of whom the lords Justices have offered his majesty's pardon to any person concerned, except the bellman, and a reward of £50 on

---

[44] *Gentleman's Magazine*, xxii (1752), p. 27.
[45] According to this the girl came from Devon and was to be passed back to her home parish at the expense of the people of St Clement's.
[46] *Gentleman's Magazine*, xxii (1752), p. 286.
[47] *Gentleman's Magazine*, xxii (1752), p. 237.

conviction. And the commissioners of the turnpike have offered a further reward of £20.

2.9 A gang of hackney-coachmen robbers, 1775[48]

Note that the villains were caught because of a bureaucratic demand to register their cab and, secondly, that it was chance that led the magistrate to note the number.

Lambert Reading was the principal of a desperate gang of hackney-coachmen who robbed Copped Hall, in Essex, not far from London. He had a hackney-coachman in confederacy, who waited for him at Stratford. A magistrate of the county, happening to pass by the coach, was struck at its being there at an unusual hour of the night, from which circumstance he was induced to observe its number.

Hearing, the next day, of the robbery at Copped Hall, he wrote to Sir John Fielding his suspicions, and named the number of the coach. From this information the thief-takers traced Reading to a house in Brick Lane, where they found him in bed with a woman who passed as his wife.

He was surrounded with pistols, hangers, picklock keys, dark lanterns and other apparatus of a housebreaker. He had an opportunity of using some of these arms in his defence, but he was so greatly intimidated that he quietly surrendered himself.

The material result of the search was the recovery of the plate stolen from Copped Hall, which was found hidden in Reading's apartment, in three sacks.

On evidence to this effect, added to other corroborating circumstances, he was convicted and executed.

The other hackney-coachman, whose name was Chapman and who drove for one Conyers, the owner, was taken on the day of Reading's trial; and, being found guilty as an accessory, also received sentence of death, which was afterwards commuted for transportation.

2.10 The forgery of bank notes, 1777[49]

New financial and business methods led to a rise in the number of forgery cases brought before the courts.

---

[48] *The complete Newgate calendar*, pp. 103–4.
[49] *The complete Newgate calendar*, pp. 126–7.

James Elliot had committed forgeries on the Bank of England; but some intricacy appearing in the case, the solicitor had laid five different counts to his indictment, and, though convicted, his case went before the twelve judges, as is customary whenever a doubt arises in the breast of the judge who may try the prisoner.

The following is a sketch of the evidence given upon his trial, which came on at Maidstone, the 24th of July, 1777.

The prisoner had applied to a mould-maker for a pair of fine moulds, in the manner of bills of exchange or notes of hand. He brought three copper-plates, purporting to be notes of the Governor and Company of the Bank of England one for one hundred pounds, one for fifty pounds, and one for twenty pounds and he gave ten guineas for the three.

A copper-plate printer, of the name of Ryland, swore that he had printed off twenty-five fifty-pound notes and twenty-five of the twenty-pound plate, for which Elliot gave him three guineas, though the usual price was no more than one shilling and sixpence per hundred. These notes were produced in court, and Ryland swore they were the same which he printed, and one in particular of the fifty pounds which was filled up, and upon which the indictment was founded.

This note was very defective, and, among other faults, the word pounds was even left out after the word fifty. Upon this, Elliot's counsel started a point of law on this question: whether that could be called a counterfeit where so essential a part was omitted, without which no specific value could be fixed.

The prisoner was, however, found guilty, but his case was reserved for the opinion of the twelve judges. Sentence was accordingly deferred.

On the 5th of March, 1778, he was again called to the bar, and informed that the judges had overruled his motion; and sentence of death was immediately passed upon him.

2.11 Robbery by and subsequent execution of two juveniles, 1791[50]

Here we see the harsh treatment meeted out to recidivist juveniles.

Joseph Wood and Thomas Underwood, two fourteen-year-old boys, executed at Newgate, 6th of July, 1791, for robbing another boy. All the parties in this case were mere children, the malefactors being but fourteen years of age each, and the prosecutor no more than twelve!

---

[50] *The complete Newgate calendar*, p. 187.

Though of this tender age, yet were the two prisoners convicted as old and daring depredators. So often had they already been arraigned at that bar where they were condemned that the judge declared, notwithstanding their appearance (they were short, dirty, ill-visaged boys), it was necessary, for the public safety, to cut them off, in order that other boys might learn that, inured to wickedness, their tender age would not save them from an ignominious fate.

The crime for which they suffered was committed with every circumstance of barbarity. They forcibly took away a bundle, containing a jacket, shirt and waistcoat, from a little boy, then fell upon him, and would probably have murdered him had they not been secured. They had long belonged to a most desperate gang of pickpockets and footpads; but they were so hardened and obstinate that they would not impeach their companions, though the hopes of mercy were held out to them if they would make a confession, so that the villains might have been apprehended.

They were executed at Newgate, the 6th of July, 1791, apparently insensible of their dreadful situation.

2.12   Another case of a woman passing herself off as a man, 1796[51]

Of interest here is the sympathy of the court and its officers towards this woman.

Re A female Trooper, convicted at the Old Bailey, in October Sessions, 1796, of Petty Larceny

This woman was born at Mercival Hall, in Warwickshire, the seat of Mr Stratford, to whom her father was steward, whose name was Brindley. She was apprenticed to a milliner at Lichfield, and married to a shoemaker. Her husband being an idle, dissolute fellow, they were reduced to very indigent circumstances. She left him to come to London. Having had a good education, and writing an excellent hand, she put on men's apparel, and for some time wrote for gentlemen in the Commons; but meeting with a recruiting sergeant at Westminster, she engaged to serve in a regiment of light horse, then being raised, called the Ayrshire Fencible Cavalry. She served upwards of a year with great credit to herself, and was promoted to the rank of corporal. She rode extremely well, and had the care of two horses; but was discovered at Carlisle to be a woman, when she was honourably discharged, after many marks of friendship shown her, not only by Major Horsley, in whose troop she rode, but by the other

---

[51] *The complete Newgate calendar*, pp. 221–2.

officers and many of the inhabitants of Carlisle. She came to
was much reduced, and, through mere necessity, stole the cloak
she was tried and convicted. She acknowledged her crime, and s
the first offence of the kind she had committed, and had meant
satisfaction. The Court passed a light sentence upon her, and she was discharged from Newgate. The two under-sheriffs and the keeper gave her
some money to provide her with a few necessaries, and she left the court,
promising henceforward to seek an honest livelihood in the proper habit of
her sex. She was a masculine-looking woman, of about thirty years of age.

3   Punishment in the eighteenth century

3.1   Dangers of the pillory, 1752[52]

*As can be seen from these few brief newspaper entries, being pilloried could be a
dangerous punishment.*

18 April
Lingard for perjury stood in the pillory near St George's church, Southwark, and was severely pelted with mud, stones and sticks. He waved his
hands in a suppliant manner, but tho' he had a tin seul plate under his cap,
he was cut in the left side of the head, and the blood run down his face.

8 July
Moses Moravia and John Manoury were set in the pillory at the Royal
Exchange, with a paper stuck over their heads denoting their crime, and
were severely pelted.

9 July
Ashley, the gardener stood on the pillory opposite the Sessions House in
the Old Bailey, but was not pelted.

3.2   Unjust treatment of a prisoner by his gaoler, January 1752[53]

Extracts from an anonymous letter published in The Gentleman's Magazine,
*it reveals the weakness in the system which permitted an acquitted prisoner still
to be imprisoned.*

---

[52] *The Gentleman's Magazine*, xxii (1752), pp. 190, 334.
[53] *The Gentleman's Magazine*, xxii (1752), p. 24.

The letter

I am an unhappy person now lying in one of the gaols of this kingdom, to which I was committed about ten months past on accusation of felony, though entirely innocent as afterward appeared on my trial . . .

The grievance I complain of is not my commitment for a crime of which I was not guilty, but the tyranny and oppression of the gaoler. For after I had been declared innocent by the jury, . . . instead of being immediately discharged . . . I was hurried back again to prison there to lie until I could raise 30s to pay the gaoler his fees.

If any situation on earth merits pity, or any evil merits the attention of the legislature, surely it is the case of unhappy prisoners in my circumstances. . . .

If gaolers must have large salaries for the execution of their office, let the public pay them, and let not the sufferings of the wretched be increased by their rapine and inflexibility.

A.P.

Newspaper editor's comment

The order lately made that prisoners acquitted at the Old Bailey should instantly be discharged, is a proof that such an order was deemed equitable and just, and leaves those who have it in their power to render it universal . . .

3.3   The state of prisons in the early 1770s[54]

John Howard was appointed sheriff of Bedford in 1773. He discovered a number of undesirable practices in his county gaol, for which he was responsible as sheriff. This led him to visit most of the county gaols and then the Bridewells (Houses of Correction), and city and town gaols in England. He found considerable variation in the treatment of prisoners and many inhumane practices. He reported his findings to the House of Commons in March 1774 and this led to reforming legislation on the care of prisoners. Howard repeated his inspections, now taking in Welsh prisons and published his findings in 1777. It is from that publication that the following extracts are taken. Howard's national report was the first detailed survey of the condition of prisons and treatment of prisoners.

---

[54] John Howard, *The state of the prisons.*

174

Section I   General view of distress in prisons[55]

There are prisons, into which whoever looks will, at first sight of the people confined there, be convinced that there is some great error in the management of them: the sallow meagre countenances declare, without words, that they are very miserable. Many who went in healthy are in a few months changed to emaciated dejected objects. Some are seen pining under diseases, "sick and in prison", expiring on the floors, in loathsome cells of pestilential fevers, and the confluent small-pox, victims, I must not say to the cruelty, but I will say to the inattention of sheriffs and gentlemen in the commission of the peace.

The cause of this distress is, that many prisons are scantily supplied, and some almost totally unprovided with the necessaries of life.

Food

There are several Bridewells (to begin with them) in which prisoners have no allowance of food at all. In some, the keeper farms what little is allowed them, and where he engages to supply each prisoner with one or two pennyworth of bread a day, I have known this shrunk to half, sometimes less than half the quantity, cut or broken from his own loaf.

It will perhaps be asked, does not their work maintain them? For every one knows that those offenders are committed to hard labour. The answer to that question, though true, will hardly be believed. There are very few Bridewells in which any work is done, or can be done. The prisoners have neither tools, nor materials of any kind, but spend their time in sloth, profaneness and debauchery, to a degree which, in some of those houses that I have seen, is extremely shocking.

Some keepers of these houses, who have represented to the magistrates the wants of their prisoners, and desired for them necessary food, have been silenced with these inconsiderate words, *Let them work or starve.* When those gentlemen know the former is impossible, do they not by that sentence, inevitably doom poor creatures to the latter?

I have asked some keepers, since the late act for preserving the health of prisoners, why no care is taken of their sick: have been answered, that the magistrates tell them *the act does not extend to Bridewell.*

In consequence of this, at the Quarter Sessions you see prisoners, covered (hardly covered) with rags, almost famished; and sick of diseases, which the discharged spread wherever they go, and with which those who are sent to the county gaols infect these prisons.

---

[55] *Ibid.*, pp. 7–17.

The same complaint, *want of food*, is to be found in many county gaols. In about half these, debtors have no bread, although it is granted to the highwayman, the house-breaker, and the murderer. And medical assistance, which is provided for the latter, is withheld from the former. In many of these gaols, debtors who would work are not permitted to have any tools, lest they should furnish felons with them for escape or other mischief. I have often seen those prisoners eating their water-soup (bread boiled in mere water) and heard them say, "We are locked up and almost starved to death."

As to the relief provided for Debtors by the Benevolent Act, 32d of George II. (commonly called the Lords Act, because it originated in their house), I did not find in all England and Wales (except the counties of Middlesex and Surrey) twelve debtors who had obtained from their creditors the four-pence a day, to which they had a right by that Act, the means of procuring it were out of their reach. In one of my journeys I found near six hundred prisoners, whose debts were under twenty pounds each. Some of them did not owe above three or four pounds, and the expence of sueing for the aliment is in many places equal to those smaller debts for which some of these prisoners had been confined several months.

At Carlisle but one debtor of the forty-nine whom I saw there had obtained his groats, and the gaoler told me that during the time he had held that office, which was fourteen years, no more than four or five had received it, and that they were soon discharged by their creditors neglecting to pay it. No one debtor had the aliment in York Castle, Devon, Cheshire, Kent, and many other counties. The truth is, some debtors are the most pitiable objects in our gaols.

To their wanting necessary food, I must add not only the demands of gaolers, &c. for fees, but also the extortion of bailiffs. These detain in their houses (properly enough denominated *spunging-houses*) at an enormous expense, prisoners who have money. I know there is a legal provision against this oppression, but the mode of obtaining redress (like that of recovering the groats) is attended with difficulty, and the abuse continues. The rapine of these extortioners needs some more effectual and easy check. No bailiff should be suffered to keep a public house; the mischiefs occasioned by their so doing, are complained of in many parts of the kingdom.

Here I beg leave to mention the hard case of prisoners confined on Exchequer processes; and those from the ecclesiastical courts: the latter are excluded from the privilege of bail, and the former from the benefit of insolvent acts.

Felons have in some gaols two pennyworth of bread a day, in some three halfpenny-worth, in some a pennyworth, in some a shilling a week: the particulars will be seen here-after in their proper places. I often weighed the bread in different prisons, and found the penny loaf $7\frac{1}{2}$ to $8\frac{1}{2}$ ounces, the other loaves in proportion. It is probable that when this allowance was fixed by its value, near double the quantity that the money will now purchase, might be bought for it: yet the allowance continues unaltered. And it is not uncommon to see the whole purchase, especially of the smaller sums, eaten at breakfast: which is sometimes the case when they receive their pittance but once in two days; and then on the following day they must fast.

This allowance being so far short of the cravings of nature, and in some prisons lessened by farming, to the gaoler, many criminals are half starved. Such of them as at their commitment were in health, come out almost famished, scarce able to move, and for weeks incapable of any labour.

Water

Many prisons have no water. This defect is frequent in Bridewells and town gaols. In the felons courts of some county gaols there is no water. In some places where there is water, prisoners are always locked up within doors, and have no more than the keeper or his servants think fit to bring them. In one place they are limited to three pints a day each – a scanty provision for drink and cleanliness!

Air

And as to air, which is no less necessary than either of the two preceding articles, and given us by Providence quite gratis, without any care or labour of our own; yet, as is the bounteous goodness of Heaven excited our envy, methods are contrived to rob prisoners of this *genuine cordial of life*, as Dr Hales very properly calls it, I mean by preventing that circulation and change of the salutiferous fluid, without which animals cannot live and thrive. It is well known that air which has performed its office in the lungs, is feculent and noxious. Writers upon the subject shew, that a hogshead of it will last a man only an hour, but those who do not choose to consult philosophers, may judge from a notorious fact. In 1756 at Calcutta in Bengal, out of 170 persons who were confined in a hole there one night, 154 were taken out dead. The few survivors ascribed the mortality to their want of fresh air, and called the place, from what they suffered there, *Hell in miniature*!

Air which has been breathed, is made poisonous to a more intense degree by the effluvia from the sick and what else in prisons is offensive. My reader will judge of its malignity, when I assure him, that my clothes were in my first journeys so offensive, that in a post-chaise I could not bear the windows drawn up, and was therefore often obliged to travel on horseback. The leaves of my memorandum-book were often so tainted, that I could not use it till after spreading it an hour or two before the fire.

And even my antidote, a vial of vinegar, has after using it in a few prisons, become intolerably disagreeable. I did not wonder that in those journeys many gaolers made excuses and did not go with me into the felons wards.

From hence any one may judge of the probability there is against the health and life of prisoners, crowded in close rooms, cells, and subterraneous dungeons, for fourteen or sixteen hours out of the four and twenty. In some of those caverns the floor is very damp: in others there is sometimes an inch or two of water, and the straw, or bedding is laid on such floors, seldom on barrack bedsteads. Where prisoners are not kept in underground cells, they are often confined to their rooms, because there is no court belonging to the prison, which is the case in most City and town gaols: or because the walls round the yard are ruinous, or too low for safety: or because the gaoler has the ground for his own use. Prisoners confined in this manner, are generally unhealthy.

Sewers

Some gaols have no sewers; and in those that have, if they be not properly attended to, they are, even to a visitant, offensive beyond expression: how noxious then to people constantly confined in those prisons!

One cause why the rooms in some prisons are so close, is perhaps the window-tax, which the gaolers have to pay: this tempts them to stop the windows, and stifle their prisoners.

Bedding

In many gaols, and in most Bridewells, there is no allowance of straw for prisoners to sleep on; and is by any means they get a little, it is not changed for months together so that it is almost worn to dust. Some lie upon rags, others upon the bare floors. When I have complained of this to the keepers, their justification has been, "The county allows no straw; the prisoners have none but at my cost."

Morals

The evils mentioned hitherto affect the health and life of prisoners: I have now to complain of what is pernicious to their morals; and that is, the confining all sorts of prisoners together: debtors and felons; men and women; the young beginner and the old offender: and with all there, in some counties, such as are guilty of misdemeanours only; who should have been committed to Bridewell, to be corrected by diligence and labour; but for want of food, and the means of procuring it in those prisons, are in pity sent to such county gaols as afford these offenders prison-allowance.

Few prisons separate men and women in the day-time. In some counties the gaol is also the Bridewell: in others those prisons are contiguous, and the yard common. There the petty offender is committed for instruction to the most profligate. In some gaols you see (and who can see it without pain?) boys of twelve or fourteen eagerly listening to the stories told by practised and experienced criminals, of their adventures, successes, stratagems, and escapes.

I must here add, that in some few gaols are confined idiots and lunatics. These serve for sport to idle visitants at assizes, and other times of general resort. The insane, where they are not kept separate, disturb and terrify other prisoners. No care is taken of them, although it is probable that by medicines, and proper regimen, some of them might be restored to their senses, and to usefulness in life.

Gaol fever

I am ready to think, that none who give credit to what is contained in the foregoing-pages, will wonder at the havoc made by the gaol fever. From my own observations in 1773 and 1774, I was fully convinced that many more were destroyed by it, than were put to death by all the public executions in the kingdom.

There then follows a long sub-section on the aetiology of the disease.

Section II   Bad customs in prisons[56]

Garnish

A cruel custom obtains in most of our gaols, which is that of the prisoners demanding of a newcomer garnish, footing, or (as it is called in some London gaols) chummage. "Pay or strip" are the fatal words. I say *fatal*, for they are so to some, who having no money, are obliged to give up part of their scanty apparel; and if they have no bedding or straw to sleep on, contract diseases of which I have known them to prove mortal.

In some gaols, to the garnish paid by the newcomer, those who were there before make an addition; and great parts of the following night is often spent in riot and drunkenness. The gaoler or tapster finding his account in this practice, generally answers questions concerning it with reluctance. Of the garnish which I have set down to sundry prisons, I

---

[56] *Ibid.*, pp. 25–7.

often had my information from prisoners who paid it. But I am aware that the sum is sometimes varied by sets of succeeding prisoners, and the different circumstances of a newcomer. In some gaols, if a felon can pay the debtor's garnish (which is commonly more than that of the felons), he is entitled to partake of the garnish paid afterwards by new-come debtors. In some places, this demand has been lately waved: in others, strictly prohibited by the Magistrates.

Gaming

Gaming in various forms is very frequent: cards, dice, skittles, Mississippi and Porto-bello tables, billiards, fives, tennis, &c. In the country the three first are most common and especially cards. There is scarce a county gaol but is furnished with them, and one can seldom go in without seeing prisoners at play. In London, all the sorts that I have named are in use. I am not an enemy to diverting exercise, yet the riot, brawling, and profaneness, that are the usual consequents of their play. The circumstances of debtors gaming away the property of their creditors, which I know they have done in some prisons to a considerable amount, accomplishing themselves in the frauds of gamblers, who, if they be not themselves prisoners, are sure to haunt where gaming is practised, hindering their fellow-prisoners who do not play from walking in the yards while they do, of which inconvenience I have heard them complain. These seem to me cogent reasons for prohibiting all kinds of gaming within the walls of prison.

Irons

Loading prisoners with heavy irons, which make their walking and even lying down to sleep, difficult and painful, is another custom which I cannot but condemn. In some county gaols the women do not escape this severity, but in London they do, and therefore it is not necessary in the country. The practice must be mere tyranny; unless it proceed from avarice; which I rather suspect; because county gaolers do sometimes grant dispensations, and indulge their prisoners, men as well as women, with what they call "the choice of irons", if they will pay for it.

The author of the letter to Sir Robert Ladbroke on prisons [particularly on Newgate, which was then to be re-built] cites in page 79, the opinion of Lord Coke, Horn's *Mirror of Justice*, &c. against this oppression; and adds afterwards,

> The learned editor of Hale's *History of the Pleas of the Crown* likewise declares, that fetters ought not to be used, unless there is just reason to fear an escape, as where the prisoner is unruly, or

makes an attempt to that purpose; otherwise, notwithstanding the common practice of gaolers, it seems altogether unwarrantable, and contrary to the mildness and humanity of the laws of England, by which gaolers are forbid to put their prisoners to any pain or torment.

Section V   A particular account of English prisons

The bulk of the book consists of Howard's account of the prisons and Bridewells he visited. He begins the section with a description of his method, from which are extracted the principal elements.

Method[57]

In the first page of every county, city, &c. the second article of the Gaoler's or Keeper's emoluments is Fees by which is meant such only as are taken by him and his servants on the admission or discharge of a prisoner. . . .

The next article under Gaoler is Transports. The sum set down to this is what . . . I found was allowed them for conveying convicts sentenced to transportation to the respective sea-ports, and for paying the merchant who contracts what he was supposed to demand for their passage. . . .

Under prisoners in the same page, the number which I found in the respective County-Gaols on my different visits is distinguished into *Debtors* and *Felons &c.* The *&c.* is meant to include two kinds of prisoners, viz. *Fines* and *Petty Offenders*. By *Fines* is understood such as are confined till they pay a sum of money, a *Fine* such as are confined till they find security for good behaviour, and such as are committed for a limited term to mere confinement, or (which is much the same) to hard labour. Of these latter most have been previously whipped or burnt in the hand. The *Petty Offenders* are such as are sent to gaols instead of Bridewells . . . Besides these there are a few *Deserters*. . . .

I have described no prison but from my own examination at the several dates set down before the number of prisoners. I entered every room, cell, and dungeon with a memorandum-book in my hand in which I noted particulars upon the spot. My descriptions will to some readers appear too minute, but I chose rather to relate circumstances than to characterize in general terms. By these the legislature will be better acquainted with the real state of Gaols, and the magistrates will be able to judge whether the prisons over which they preside and to which they commit offenders be fit for the purposes they are designed to answer. . . .

---

[57] *Ibid.*, pp. 147–50.

Newgate[58]

Gaoler: Richard Akerman

Salary	£200
Fees:	
Debtors	8s 10d
Felons	14s 10d
Misdemeanours or Fines	14s 10d
Transports	14s 10d
Licence: for beer and wine	

Prisoners

Allowance to Debtors and Felons a penny loaf a day

Garnish:		
Debtors	5s	6d
Felons	2s	6d

	Debtors	Felons, &c.
1775, March 5	33	190
1776, March 1	38	129
1776, May 17	46	212
1776, Dec. 26	33	152

Chaplain: Revd Mr Villette

Duty: Sunday twice; every day Prayers; once a month Sacrament

Salary:	£35 &c.

Surgeon: Mr Olney

Salary:	£50 for all prisoners

The builders of Old Newgate seem to have regarded in their plan nothing but the single article of keeping prisoners in safe custody. The rooms and cells were so close as to be almost the constant seat of disease and sources of infection, to the destruction of the multitudes, not only in the prison but abroad. The City had therefore very good reason for their resolution to build a new gaol. The plate will give a better idea of it than any description. I give the plan rather to gratify the curiosity of my readers than as a model to be followed. Many inconveniences of the old gaol are avoided in this one, but it has some manifest errors. . . .

    The cells built in Old Newgate a few years since for condemned malefactors, are intended for the same use at present. I shall therefore give some account of them. There are upon each of the three floors five cells, all vaulted, near nine feet high to the crown. The cells on the ground-floor

---

[58] *Ibid.*, pp. 151–5.

measure full nine feet by near six, the five on the first storey are a little larger, on account of the set-off in the wall, and the five uppermost, still a little larger for the same reason. In the upper part of each cell, is a window double grated, near three feet by one and a half. The doors are four inches thick. The strong stone wall is lined all round each cell with planks, studded with broad-headed nails. In each cell is a barrack-bedstead. I was told by those who attended me, that criminals who had affected an air of boldness during their trial, and appeared quite unconcerned at the pronouncing sentence upon them, were struck with horror, and shed tears when brought to these darksome solitary abodes.[59]

The New Chapel is plain and neat. Below are three or four pews for men felons, &c. On each side is a gallery: that towards the women's ward is for them: in it is a pew for the Keeper, whose presence may set a good example and be otherwise useful. The other gallery towards the Debtors Ward is for them. . . .

I once went to prayers there. Mr Villette read them distinctly, and with propriety. The few prisoners who were present seemed attentive, but were disturbed by the noise in the yard.

Staffordshire[60]

Remarks

This gaol is much too small for the number of prisoners and so is the felons' court-yard. The dungeon where the men-felons sleep is about two feet lower than the passage; no steps, a sloping descent. It is too close. No infirmary. An alarm-bell. It is a pity the stream just outside the walls is not within them. I was pleased to see plenty of clean straw in the dungeon, and found it was owing to the generous and exemplary practice of not farming it, but allowing the gaoler to order it whenever wanted, and the county paying for it themselves.

There then follows a list of fees settled at the Quarter Sessions of April 1732. The relevant ones are recorded below.

Staffordshire County Bridewells

Stafford

The house is very dirty. Prisoners always shut up. Keeper's salary, £25: he puts in a Deputy who serves for rent. Allowance same as at the Gaol. No employment.

1775, Nov. 15   Prisoners, 4 men

---

[59] The separation of condemned prisoners from other prisoners was an innovation.
[60] *Ibid.*, pp. 326–9.

County Gaol at Stafford

Gaoler: William Scott
Salary:	none
Fees:	
debtors	17s 4d
felons	15s 10d
Transport	£6 0s 0d each
Licence for beer and wine	

Prisoners

Allowances [for] debtors and felons: each per week 16d bread, and 8d cheese; and in common 3 cwt of coals a week from Michaelmas to May-day.

Garnish:
debtors	2s 1½d
felons	cancelled by the gaoler

	Debtors	Felons
1773, Nov. 19	39	20
1774, April 1	44	17
1775, Nov. 15	40	18

Chaplain: Revd Mr Unett
Duty: Sunday, Wednesday, Friday; a sermon once in about two months.
Salary lately augmented from £20 to £30.

Surgeon: Mr Ward
Salary: none; he makes a bill.

Table of Fees

For the under-keeper or turnkey upon every action or writ	2s 6d
For the under-keeper or turnkey upon discharging of each prisoner	1s 6d

Lodgings

Every prisoner that lies in the Master's side of the Gaol in a bed provided by the Keeper of the gaol shall pay per week if a bed to himself	2s 0d
If two prisoners or more lye together in the one bed then between them all	2s 6d
Every prisoner that lies in the upper rooms or garret in a bed or bedding provided by the Keeper of the Gaol shall pay per week	1s 0d
And if two prisoners lie together then	1s 6d
Every prisoner that lies in the same side and finds his own linen and bedsteads	6d
Every prisoner that lies in the County Chamber shall pay nothing	

Wolverhampton

Only two rooms about twelve feet square, viz. a common day-room and a night-room above for men, women sleep in the day-room. No court-yard; no water; no sewer; no employment. Weekly allowance in bread, fourteen pence; cheese, seven pence; straw, three pence. Keeper's salary, £25; fees, one shilling. Clauses of Act Against Spirituous Liquors not hung up.

The prison is greatly out of repair and so insecure that prisoners, even for the slightest offences, are kept in irons. The county may redress this because they have a large garden close to the prison which they let with an old house on the spot.

1776, Sep. 11   Prisoners, 4 men

Lichfield City Gaol

The rooms too small and close. No yard; no water; no straw. Might be improved upon the ground behind it.

Keeper's salary, £2; Fees, 13s 4d. No table. Allowance, 1s 6d a week.

1773, Nov. 20   Prisoners 2
1776, Jan. 8   Prisoners 1

Chapter 5
Crime in the Nineteenth Century

1 Destitution and Crime, 1891[1]

William Morrison, a chaplain in Wandsworth Prison at the end of the nine-teenth century, was an outspoken commentator on both penal matters and the causes of crime. In the passage below, taken from his Crime and Its Causes *(1891), he argues the familiar Victorian line that there was no significant link between crime and destitution.*

Let us deal first with offences against property. These constitute eight per cent of the annual amount of crime. But according to inquiries I have made, one half of the annual number of offenders against property, so far from being in a state of destitution, were actually at work, and earning wages at the time of arrest. Nor is this surprising. The daily new-spapers have only to be consulted to confirm it. In a very great number of instances the records of criminal proceedings testify to the fact that the person charged is in some way or other defrauding his employer, and when these cases are deducted from the total of offences against property, it considerably lessens the percentage of persons driven by destitution into the ranks of crime. Add to these the great bulk of juvenile offenders con-victed of theft, and that peculiar class of people who steal, not because they are in distress, but merely from a thievish disposition, and it will be manifest that half the cases of theft in England and Wales are not due to the pressure of absolute want.

But what shall be said of the other half which still represents four per cent of the annual amount of crime. According to the calculations just referred to, the offenders constituting this percentage were not in work when the crimes charged against them were committed. Was it destitution arising from want of employment which led them to break the law? At first sight one may easily be inclined to say that it is. These people, it will be argued, have no work and no money. What are they to do but beg or steal? Before jumping at this conclusion it must not be forgotten that there is such a person as the habitual criminal. The habitual criminal, as he will

---

[1] W. D. Morrison, *Crime and its causes* (London, 1891), pp. 82–91.

very soon tell you if you possess his confidence absolutely, declines to work. He never has worked, he does not want work; he prefers living by his wits. With the recollection of imprisonment fresh upon him an offender of this description may in rare instances take employment for a short period, but the regularity of life which work entails is more than he can bear, and the old occupation of thieving is again resorted to. To live by plundering the community is the trade of the habitual criminal; it is the only business he truly cares for, and it is wonderful how long and how often he will succeed in eluding the suspicion and vigilance of the police. Of course, offenders of this class, when arrested, say they are out of work, and will very readily make an unwary person believe that it is destitution which drives them to desperation. But as was truly remarked a short time ago by a judge in one of the London courts, nearly all of these very men are able to pay high fees to experienced counsel to defend them. After these observations, it will be seen that the habitual criminal, the man who lives burglary, housebreaking, shop-lifting, and the theft of every description, is not to be classed among the destitute. Criminals of this character constitute, at least two per cent of the delinquency annually brought before the courts.

Respecting the two per cent of offenders which remain to be accounted for, it will not be far from the mark to say that destitution is the immediate cause of their wrongdoing. These offenders are composed of homeless boys, of old men unable to work, of habitual drunkards who cannot get a steady job, or keep it when they get it, of vagrants who divide their time between begging and petty theft, and of workmen on the tramp, who have become terribly reduced, and will rather steal than enter the workhouse. The percentage of these offenders varies in different parts of the country. In the north of England, for instance, there are comparatively few homeless boys who find their way before the magistrates on charges of theft; in London, on the other hand, the number is considerable, and ranges according to the season of the year, or the state of trade, to between one and three per cent of the criminal population. Why does London enjoy such an evil pre-eminence in this matter? In my opinion it often arises from the fact that house accommodation is so expensive in the metropolis. In London, it is a habit of many parents, owing to the want of room at home, to make growing lads shift for themselves at a very early age. These boys earn just enough to enable them to secure a bare existence; out of their scanty wages it is impossible to hire a room for themselves; they have to be contented with the common lodging-house. In such places, these boys have to associate with all sorts of broken-down, worthless characters, and in numbers of instances they come by degrees to adopt the habits and modes of life of the classes among which their lot is cast. At the very time parental control is most required, it is almost entirely withdrawn; the lad is left to his own devices and, in too many cases, descends into the ranks of crime. The first step in this downward career begins with the loss of employment: this sometimes happens through no fault of his own, and is simply the result of a temporary slackness of trade; but in most instances a job is lost for want of punctuality or some other boyish irregularity which can only be properly corrected at home. To lose work is to be deprived of the means of subsistence; the only openings left are the workhouse or crime. It is the latter alternative which is generally chosen, and thus, the lad is launched on the troubled sea of crime.

It must not be understood that all London boys drift into crime after the manner I have just described. In some instances, these unfortunates have lived all their life in criminal neighbourhoods, and merely follow the footsteps of the people around them. What, for instance, is to be expected from children living in the streets such as Mr Charles Booth describes in his work on *Life and Labour in East London* (1889).[2] One of these streets, which he calls St Hubert Street, swarms with children, and in hardly any case does the family occupy more than one room. The general character of the street is thus depicted.

> An awful place; the worst street in this district. The inhabitants are mostly of the lowest class, and seem to lack all idea of cleanliness or decency . . . The children are rarely brought up to any kind of work, but loaf about, and, no doubt, form the nucleus for future generations of thieves and other bad characters.

In this street alone there are between 160 and 170 children. These children do not require to go to lodging-houses to be contaminated. They breathe a polluted moral atmosphere from birth upwards, and it is more than probable that a considerable proportion of them will help to recruit the army of crime. It is not destitution which will force them into this course, but their up-bringing and surroundings.

In addition to homeless boys who steal from destitution, there are, as I have said, a number of decrepit old men who do the same. There is a period in a workman's life when he becomes too feeble to do an average day's work. When this period arrives employers of labour often discharge him in order to make way for younger and more vigorous men. If his home, as sometimes happens, is broken up by the death of his wife, his existence becomes a very lonely and precarious one. An odd job now and again is all he can get to do, and even these jobs are often hard to find. His sons and daughters are too heavily encumbered with large families to be

---

[2] Charles Booth had been a Liverpool merchant but his growing concern for the poor led him to conduct a study of the London poor, published in 17 volumes between 1889 and 1903. This work was one of the most ambitious surveys ever undertaken and a factor in changing attitudes towards poverty and welfare at the turn of the century.

capable of rendering any effective assistance, and the union[3] looms gloom-ily in the distance as the only prospect before the worn-out worker. But it sometimes happens that he will not face that prospect. He will rather steal and run the risk of imprisonment. And so it comes to pass that for a year or two before finally reconciling himself to the union, the aged workman will lead a wandering, criminal life on a petty scale; he becomes an item in the statistics of offenders against property.

Habitual drunkards form another class who sometimes steal from desti-tution. The well-known irregularity of these men's habits prevents them, in a multitude of cases, from getting work, and unfortunately, they cannot keep it when they do get it. Employers cannot depend upon them: as soon as they earn a few shillings they disappear from the workshop till the money is spent on drink. It is at such times that they are arrested for being drunk and disorderly. As they can never pay a fine they have to go to prison, but long before their sentence has expired they have lost their job, and must look out for something else. If such men do not find work many of them are not ashamed to steal, and it is only when trade is at flood-tide that they can be sure of employment, no matter how irregular their habits may be. At other times they are the first to be discharged and the last to be engaged. It is not really destitution, but intemperance which turns them into thieves. That they are destitute when arrested is perfectly true, but we must go behind the immediate fact of their crimes. When this is done, it is found that the stress of economic conditions has very little to do with making these unhappy beings what they are. On the contrary, it is in periods of prosperity that they sink to the lowest depths.

Summing up the results of this inquiry into the relations between desti-tution and offences against property, we arrive as nearly as possible at the following figures, so far as England and Wales are concerned:-

Table 5.1

Proportion of offences against property to total offences	8%
Thus divided:-	
Proportion of offenders in work when arrested	4%
Proportion of offenders, habitual thieves	2%
Proportion of offenders, homeless lads and old men	1%
Proportion of offenders, drunkards, tramps	1%

---

[3] Morrison is here referring to the poor law union, i.e. the workhouse.

2 Men and Women Compared, 1873[4]

Women have always committed less crime than men and the Victorian period was no exception – in 1857, for example, they were responsible for just over one quarter of indictable offences. In the passage below, one of the earliest historians of crime, L. O. Pike, attempts to explain this fact by reference to his notions of the biological and social differences between men and women. He also suggests that social change was acting to decrease the gap. In doing so, he relies on a series of assumptions and prejudices shared by many of his contemporaries.

The sex which is physically weaker is less prone to all those actions which are now styled criminal than the sex which is physically stronger. There are at present, in England, nearly four males to one female apprehended for all offences, great and small, and nearly five males to two females committed to prison. In France and in Germany the disparity is at least as great, if not greater. Inherited tendencies, no doubt, have their influence upon this striking disproportion, for although women certainly aided in some of the forcible entries, were sometimes the receivers of stolen goods, in the Middle Ages, and may even have taken some part in the wars of tribe against tribe in still earlier times, the men are always the chief actors in deeds of enterprise and danger. Thus women are less criminal than men not only because they are physically weaker now, but because they were physically weaker generations ago. The habit of mind has descended with the habit of body, and the cumulative effect of ages is seen in modern statistics.

Nevertheless, great though the excess of male over female criminal offenders still remains, the prevalence of town-life seems to have a perceptible effect in diminishing this disproportion. If the men grow more like the women in ceasing to commit the greater crimes, the women grow more like men in their disposition to commit the lesser crimes. More causes than one may contribute to this result. Prostitution – essentially a town custom – may afford opportunities for robbery, especially to the lowest class of prostitutes, who are probably associated by indissoluble bonds with the habitual criminals of the male sex. But prostitution is only one phase of a great social fact. The prostitute is engaged in that terrible struggle for existence from which civilization has not freed us, however much the blows and the bloodshed may have been diminished. She has taken what appears to her the easiest path by which she may earn her own bread. But other women have taken innumerable other paths with the same object in view; and in proportion as they have rendered themselves independent of men for their subsistence, they have thrown off the

---

[4] L. O. Pike, *A history of crime in England*, vol. 2 (London, 1873), pp. 526–30.

protection against competition and temptation which dependence on men implies. It follows that, so far as crime is determined by external circumstances, every step is made by woman towards her independence is a step towards that precipice at the bottom of which lies a prison.

A remarkable illustration of this fact is to be found in the number of female Irish criminals in England. In Ireland, as everywhere else, the number of male criminals is greater than the number of female, though (from causes which could not be made apparent without a very close examination of Irish history) the difference is considerably smaller than in England. But while the females of Irish birth committed to prison in Ireland are but thirty-seven per cent of the whole number of persons of Irish birth so committed, the females of Irish birth committed to prison in England are more than forty-three per cent of the whole number of persons of Irish birth so committed. The women who are most enterprising, who are most capable of earning a subsistence for themselves, and who, perhaps, are the least domesticated, are the women who come from Ireland to seek their fortune in England. The same rule holds good in the case of those women who leave the rural districts to seek their fortune in the towns, or who migrate from one part of Great Britain to another. They are, like the rest of the immigrants into our cities, more active and energetic than their fellow-villagers, or they resort to the towns for prostitution because they have lost their chastity in their native place.

The progress made by women towards a life of complete independence is, however, as yet but slight. The great increase in the number of houses which necessarily accompanies a great increase in the population causes a demand for women to perform those domestic duties for which they have an instinctive aptitude. The girl who might otherwise have remained beneath her father's roof, becomes a servant in a town; but the change does not always in that case very greatly affect her habits or her future life. The work which she does for her master is not very different in kind from the work which she would have done for her father; she has, while in service, little of the anxiety of the daily struggle for existence; and when she marries she is as little independent as she would have been had she left her father's house for her husband's without any intermediate period of servitude. The Census returns show that in 1871 the great bulk of the grown women in England and Wales were still employed in domestic occupations. But, though small in proportion to the whole female population, there is, nevertheless, a number (which, taken by itself, is by no means inconsiderable) of women earning, or attempting to earn, their daily bread by daily labour, and competing not only with their fellow women but some extent also with men. The more enduring they may be in body and the more masculine in mind, the greater, obviously, is their prospect of success in this unequal struggle. But while the women who survive and continue to support themselves approximate more or less closely to the male in energy and resolution, those who are too impatient to persevere, or are unsuccessful from other causes, commonly yield to the temptation to seek a readier means of subsistence by prostitution. Thus, on the one hand, there arises a class of women hardened in the school of adversity, and differing little from men in the natural tendency to commit crime, so far as the tendency is connected with self-reliance and courage – on the other hand, a class of women whose natural weakness leads them astray when they are without the protection of a home and feel themselves to be outcasts. It is probable that female criminals abound most in the latter class, but it is also only reasonable to suppose that the less women differ from men in their occupations, the less will be the difference in the number of male and female criminals.

3   Juvenile Offenders, 1819 and 1875

Although there is much modern concern about the links between youth and crime and about youth gangs, neither of these are restricted to the twentieth century. The following passages originate from either half of the nineteenth century. In the first, Stephen Lushington, barrister and reformist parliamentarian, gives evidence to the Select Committee on the State of Gaols. He describes his interest in the subject and also his discovery of what he believed to be the existence of a network of youth gangs in London. In the second, William Hoyle uses newspaper coverage of youth gangs from Manchester in the 1870s, known as "scuttlers", to prove his argument that crime was not falling but actually getting worse.

3.1   London Youth Gangs, 1819[5]

Have you from your observation any means of informing the community of the number of juvenile offenders likely to exist in the metropolis?

Of course, it is impossible to do that with any accuracy but I have formed my estimate from observations for a good many years past: I have been one of the committee of the Refuge for the Destitute[6] since 1805, excepting one year, and I have also been on the committee of the Prison Discipline Society,[7] and I have had occasion during that time, to direct my

---

[5] Evidence of Stephen Lushington, D. C. L. to the *Select Committee on the State of Gaols, etc.*, P. P. Sess. 1819, vol. vii, pp. 162–4.

[6] Such refuges were commonplace in London, offering food and accommodation to vagrants.

[7] A society established by the Quaker, William Allen, to campaign for reform of the prison system.

attention repeatedly to the subject. I have made an estimate in my own mind of the number, without reference to any of the accounts laid before parliament. My sources of information are various, arising from innumerable little items which compose the whole sum. I estimate the number of juvenile delinquents under seventeen, in London, Westminster and Southwark, and the immediate environs, at about 8000. I would beg to add, that I know of the existence of gangs in various places. For instance, there is a gang near Paddington, lately met with, and by mere accident, which, I believe, chiefly meet in the lower part of Gray's Inn-Lane, and I know there are several gangs in Spitafields. Judging from all these circumstances, and supposing that the numbers in the Borough, in the lower part of Westminster, and Whitechapel, would bear something of the same proportion, I have made my calculation upon that basis. I would beg leave to add, when the committee for inquiring into juvenile delinquency first commenced their labours, inquiries were made of boys, about the number of thirty, and those thirty alone gave the names of eight hundred of their accomplices: the committee afterwards proceeded to investigate as far as two thousand cases, or very nearly that amount. They then stopped, conceiving they had carried the investigation as far as was necessary under the circumstances.

In speaking of those eight thousand, do you speak of persons who you suppose are actually engaged in the commission of felonies of different descriptions?

Of felonies, I will not specifically say, but I believe, out of the eight thousand, many of those support themselves by what they call being upon the cross.

Were the gangs you speak of composed entirely of boys?

I think very few, if any, were above the age of seventeen.

In what numbers generally?

Very various. It is impossible to say, the gangs separate themselves so much: of course when they go out on their depredations they cannot go in large bodies.

Have the gangs any communication with each other?

No, I do not think that the gangs in the different parts of the town have any general communication.

Have you any means of knowing how they dispose of the stolen property?

No, not to give the committee any accurate information: I have, in a particular instance, been enabled to obtain it back, but I could not trace it.

Do these two thousand cases extend over any particular district, or over the whole of London?

The information relating to these cases came chiefly from Newgate, Coldbathfields, and the Borough compter.

Has each gang a leader, or any particular bond of union?

In some cases they may have, but I do not think generally.

Do you not find they are connected with men generally?

Certainly, there is a connection, because they dispose of the property they have purloined by means of men, but that connection is not to be ascertained, unless one were to extort the information from them by means of promises.

Have you ascertained by their confession that they have adult accomplices?

Yes, they have adult accomplices. From their confession, they have receiving accomplices, who receive and dispose of their property, but I understand the question to be whether I could trace receiving houses: that I cannot do.

Do the same individuals continue long to form the same gang?

I should say, certainly.

Do you generally find the same gangs meeting together at the same place?

They are found generally resorting to the same houses, and connected together in their depredations.

Did you ever happen to get any accurate information with respect to any individual gang?

With respect to the Spitalfields gang, an occasion arose very lately, when I was at the home where they met. Upon that occasion, I saw a very considerable number of them myself.

Of what ages?

I should say from fifteen to twenty, but there were two or three men among them.

At a public house?

Yes, at a public house.

Will you name the public house?

The Virginia Planters, in Spitalfields.

Will you be good enough to relate the circumstances that led you to have intercourse with this gang, and what you observed among them?

The circumstances were in consequence of what occurred respecting Knight, who was executed about ten weeks ago. It happened about two days before his execution, that Mr Bedford, one of the society of friends [Quakers], who is secretary to the committee, called upon me, and requested me to go into Newgate. I accompanied him: Knight had been convicted of robbing a man in Whitechapel of his watch. Upon seeing him, he protested his innocence, and said there was a person in Newgate who well knew the person who had taken the watch, and could inform us. When Knight was withdrawn, we had this other boy down and, upon examining him, I found he belonged to another gang in Spitalfields, and that he had been there informed of the fact. In the course of the evening, Mr Bedford requested me to go with him to follow up the inquiry, which I did. We went to the house where the gang were assembled between nine and ten o'clock at night (no previous intimation had been given of our intention to go) and we passed the rooms, where twenty to thirty were met together. I, on entering the house, spoke to the landlord, and desired that

I might speak to some of the boys. They came into me and, on mentioning the subject I came upon, one came forward and said he knew perfectly well the individual who had committed the offence as well as the person who had received the watch and where the watch was. I had in vain attempted to see the prosecutor, but early in the next morning I did see him, and ascertained from him whether the evidence, as taken down in the Newgate calendar, was correct. According to his belief, it certainly was: so the next morning the boys were produced, one of them came forward and said that he was the person who actually did commit the robbery, the other boy stated that he had received the watch and it was produced. I would go on to state, that I had occasion to go to this house two or three times afterwards and I ascertained there were several gangs in the neighbourhood of Spitafields, amounting to a very considerable number, their principal resort being at the house I mentioned.

Will you state to the Committee all the information you derived at that meeting, with respect to the conduct of all the individuals there, and any others to whom their information directed you?

I made many inquiries as to the number of the gangs and the manner in which they carried on their depredations. They told me that that particular robbery had been committed by four of them, who had gone out for the express purpose. I afterwards took great pains to find whether those persons had any means of employment, any means by which they might have been saved from the consequence of their present situation, and a very large sum of money was raised by certain individuals for the express purpose of giving these boys an opportunity of leaving their course of life.

That applies to the whole number assembled there?

Yes, a certain sum of money was raised to be paid by the Refuge, if the boys would consent to remain there for one year. Enough was raised to pay for ten or fifteen. In consequence of this being done, upon a subsequent occasion, I went down and stated it to them. There were not many assembled in the room at that time: they made an application that I would come again and, upon going a second time, a certain number volunteered to come into the Refuge. The majority declined, stating that they could not submit to the confinement in the Refuge. Some did come, but I am sorry to add that only two consented to remain, one of whom is doing very well indeed.

Did you understand that this was a house in which boys engaged in those habits were accustomed to meet?

It was.

Exclusively, or nearly so?

Not quite so: there were persons there at one of the meetings considerably above the age of twenty, perhaps twenty-four or five. I would beg leave to add, upon one occasion, when I was going down, there was a great riot, so much so as to make it a question whether it was prudent to enter, but I did enter and I was received with great civility: at that time a great many assembled on the outside of the house, as well as in.

What is the age of the youngest of the gang, which you say consisted of twenty or thirty?

I should say, sixteen.

Are not the landlords of public houses of this description generally known by the name, which is technically called "fencers", or receivers of stolen goods?

I have heard so, but I do not know of my own knowledge.

When you went into those houses, did the boys freely communicate to you upon the nature of their offences?

Perfectly and with perfect freedom.

Not only in respect of the one transaction alluded to, but also to their general conduct?

Yes, I told them that I was well aware that every individual in that room maintained himself by dishonesty, and none of them attempted to deny it: some lamented it; some were very much affected; and some stated that they had not a friend in the world.

Did you trace any of them to their parents?

Some of them.

Do you suppose they were connected with them?

No.

Then apparently they were carrying on those depredations on their own account?

Yes.

Did they state the reason for living this life?

The two reasons given were bad company and distress. Those are the reasons universally given. If you ask the question, it is universally given, I believe, by them all.

Had their parents expelled them, or turned them adrift?

No, some of them were living partly with their parents.

Did they appear to be connected with any women?

They all are.

Had they the women with them?

No.

Did you obtain any information as to the course of their proceedings; whether they met at stated hours, or what were their plans?

I do not think they met at stated hours, but according to the circumstances of the individual, if they have no employment at the time. Some of them have employment and when they have not, they go there, or to a ground where they gamble, close by.

Have they any rule for the introduction of strange boys?

I do not know.

Would it be easy to obtain from those boys a list of the places where they generally harbour?

I do not think it would.

Could you trace those boys to any other house?

There is another house which they had been in the habit of frequenting, but they had had some quarrel at that time with that house.

Do you happen to know whether it is a licensed house?

Yes.

Does it exist at the present?

Yes, I believe so.

What refreshment were they in the habit of having in the house at all?

As I passed by the room where they met, they were drinking and smoking but I cannot tell what it was they were drinking.

Were they gambling?

I am nearly positive upon one occasion they were playing at cards.

Could you ascertain whether they carried any part of the stolen goods to their parents?

I do not believe that any of those boys did.

What do they do with them?

They dispose of them to the receivers of stolen goods.

Is the money received distributed amongst the whole gang, or does each take his own share?

As I learned, among the number who go out to commit the individual robbery.

Had they any leader or president there?

No, I did not understand they had.

Do you know whether any of those had been long in Newgate or in any other gaols?

Most of them have been in gaol.

3.2   Manchester Youth Gangs, 1875[8]

Five youths were charged with having stabbed a boy named England and an old man named Charles Flynn. Evidence was given showing that on Saturday night, about half-past eight o'clock, the prisoners, who belong to a gang of "scuttlers", came along Prussia Street, Ancoats, and meeting a boy they asked him if he was a scuttler, saying that if he was they would stick a b— knife into him. They, however, passed on, and shortly after they met the old man Flynn, whom they knocked and hustled about. When the old man tried to get away Rigby tripped him up, and Melia stabbed him in the back with a large table knife, inflicting a wound about an inch deep. The wound bled profusely. Gerrard kicked the old man,

---

[8] *Manchester Evening News*, 29/11/1875, quoted in W. Hoyle, *Crime in England and Wales in the nineteenth century: an historical and critical retrospect* (London, 1875), pp. 67/8.

and threw a brickbat[9] at him. The other prisoner, Burns, followed this up by striking the old man on the back with a small hammer, saying to a large crowd which had gathered that if anyone attempted to interfere he would "do" for them. After this outrage the prisoners went a little further, and meeting the boy England they seized hold of him, and Melia stabbed him on the right side of the head with a knife. The prisoners were apprehended during the evening by Sergeant Chambers and Police-constables Plimsoll and Tomlinson, of the B Division of the City Police Force. One of the constables said that he had known the prisoners for six months as disorderly characters in the neighbourhood of Prussia Street, Oldham Road. The prisoner Melia was sent to prison for four months, with hard labour; and the other prisoners were summarily committed for two months each.

4   Burglars and Burgling, 1894[10]

The fears that surrounded discussion of crime in the nineteenth century were often tinged with fascination. In the extract below, the public interest in crime is shown by the establishment of the Scotland Yard museum in a passage admiring the skills of the burglar.

Of all the more hazardous – though thoroughly romantic – professions, none is more interesting than that of burgling. The art of burgling and housebreaking has positively developed into a fine art, and, although we do not admire the members of the craft, yet every individual representative of it is undeniably interesting. There is something irresistibly tantalising, yet at the same time fascinating, about your average burglar. Those of nervous temperament may look under their beds for a whole twelvemonth – from the 1st of January to the 31st of December. But he is never there. He is a playful fellow – a merry man; he likes his joke, for on the very night you forget to peep under the couch where Morpheus receives you for a few hours, he is bound to be there, and the next morning you find all your drawers ransacked. At first you put it down to the dog, but when you discover that something like a cart-load of valuables has disappeared, you come to the conclusion that no representative of the canine world who ever barked or picked up an honest bone could possibly help himself so freely and with so liberal a hand.

The New Scotland Yard Museum will provide much practical information on the ways and means which our friend the enemy utilizes for the purpose of thus annoying you. Your enterprising burglar shall have what he thoroughly deserves – a complete chapter to himself, and illustrates

---

[9] A brickbat was a brick broken in half.
[10] *The Strand Magazine* 7, 1894, pp. 273–84.

with his own weapons of warfare into the bargain. Not that we expect he will be much gratified at the publicity here given to his methods publicity which is all to the advantage of his enemy, the householder, for whom to be forewarned is to be forearmed.

5   Garotting, 1862[11]

The end of transportation brought with it the problem of how to treat those who had previously been exiled. The replacement, penal servitude, saw a fixed period of custodial punishment followed by one where convicts were released on licence or "ticket of leave". The prospect of hardened criminals stalking the streets brought a sense of apprehension in the late 1850s and early 1860s. When it appeared that there was a new type of crime, garotting, this apprehension turned into a panic.[12] The passage below, taken from the Illustrated London News, *gives a lucid portrayal of this panic and laments the priority given by English law to protecting property over the person.*

The uppermost topic of the week – that upon which conversation has been more general, and thought more in earnest, than any other – is the frequency and the frightful audacity of crimes of violence in the streets of the metropolis. London has been almost as panic-stricken by prowling gangs of ticket-of-leave men as though a score of tigers were known to be at large. No man out of doors feels sure of his life. In broad daylight, in the most public thoroughfares, at times and in places the most unlikely, men are suddenly throttled or knocked on the head and rifled of any valuables they may chance to have about them. It is as if we had been, by some magical art, thrown back into the middle of the last century, and made the denizens of some Italian city infested with bravos. For aught we can tell, death may be lurking for us under any one of the gateways we have to pass. No one, when leaving his home in the morning for his place of business, is secure against being lodged in a hospital before night, maimed for the remainder of his days. Fear, of course, exaggerates the danger. Nevertheless, the danger is real, and exists in fact as well as fancy. Such a state of things has taken the town by surprise. For a brief interval people have been fairly staggered. Everybody is arming himself with some deadly weapon. There is a momentary tendency – only momentary, we hope – to throw away as useless and deceptive the lessons which it has taken us more than a century to learn, and to regret that our laws are not as savage as they were before Romilly laboured to tone down their harshness or

---

[11] *Illustrated London News,* 6/12/1862.
[12] Garotting was the act of using an implement, such as a piece of wire, to temporarily strangle a person from behind, whilst an accomplice affected a robbery.

Howard to soften somewhat the intolerable cruelty of prison discipline.[13] The impulse, however, is probably as exceptional as the crime which has excited it. Neither the one nor the other is likely to outlive many weeks.

Taking it for granted, as surely we may consider ourselves entitled to do, that this exceedingly disagreeable and disconcerting phenomenon will speedily disappear, and that the very extravagance of the evil will ensure its quick suppression, it yet remains for us, as a practical people, to search for the causes which have conduced to the eruption. The ugly symptoms are, no doubt, bad enough in themselves; but it were wise, nevertheless, to look at them as protests against some remoter and deeper wrong latent in the body politic. We are not disposed to controvert the position that crime, like disease, occasionally takes an epidemic form; that it is some-times wayward in its course; or rather, is governed in its forms of manifesta-tion by unaccountable fashions. To some extent, perhaps, we may be at a loss to assign reasons for its sudden outbreak in this or that particular form, or may set down its prevalence under any special guise as due, in part at least, to that imitative propensity which plays as powerfully upon criminals as upon any other portion of the population. But we may reas-onably infer that, underlying this law, which more or less is universally operative, there must be some more specific causes to the combined action of which this alarming type of epidemic crime may be pretty clearly traced; and, if so, the mere suppression of it should not content us; for crime, like disease, has always some lesson to impart, and will be apt to reappear again and again, until that lesson has been learned and reduced to practice.

Before proceeding to consider the proximate causes which appear to us to have prepared the way for the singular outbreak, the virulence of which has put the whole metropolis on the *qui vive*,[14] we shall offer a remark or two on somewhat that lies back of them, partly inherent in our system of law, but rendered still more remarkable by magisterial administration. Whether it be owing to the keen appreciation of property by the British people, to their dominant commercial habits, or to remoter antecedent circumstances, the fact is undeniable that crimes against the person are not dealt with by English law with anything like the severity which is systematically meted out to crimes against property. It is, we think, still less to be denied that our police magistrates, especially in London, ordin-arily intensify, by their administration, this serious defect of our criminal code. The ruffian whose ferocious temper has maimed his victim for life, or who, in the indulgence of his brutal passion, has given the bodily

---

[13] Samuel Romilly was a Member of Parliament who had attempted a reduction in the number of offences carrying the death penalty during the first twenty years of the nineteenth century. John Howard had been an ardent campaigner for the improvement of prison condi-tions during the 1770s and 1780s.

[14] On alert.

constitution a shock from the effects of which it can never recover, commonly escapes with a lighter penalty than the dishonest but often needy wretch who feloniously appropriates to his own use goods to the value of £5 belonging to another. It is almost impossible to read a column or two of police reports without being struck with the ridiculously low appraisement which the magistrates ordinarily put upon the features and limbs of her Majesty's subjects, and with the small legal sacrifice at which brutes in the human form may indulge their barbarity upon the persons of others. Now, whilst such continues to be the case – that is, so long as the laws and their administration make so light of offences against the person as compared with offences against property – it seems inevitable that there should grow up in the soil of our criminal population an unnatural amount of recklessness as to the extent of bodily injury, short of death, which it may be found necessary to inflict with a view to secure a trifling booty. We fear the desperados who prey upon society, especially in our crowded towns, have learned to take the measure of their own crimes from the estimate put upon them by the public administration of justice, and, observing the slight account which is taken of murderous assaults, as such, are in the habit of calculating that they may be safely resorted to for the sake of obtaining plunder without greatly increasing the severity of their sentences if captured and convicted, whilst considerably diminishing the chances of both capture and conviction. It is the robbery which appears to constitute the offence, and to carry with it the main proportion of punishment; the assault is regarded merely as an aggravation, and, in the allotment of penalties, is almost overlooked. The mischievous educational influence of this high legal appraisement of property above person, operating as it has done for successive generations, has necessarily fostered a predisposition to crimes of violence which only wanted fitting opportunity to burst out, as at present, with a virulence truly alarming.

6 Thieves and Swindlers[15]

Henry Mayhew's work was the most well known of nineteenth-century commentaries on criminality. A journalist, he worked for the Morning Chronicle *in the 1840s and 1850s, investigating and categorizing the London poor through a series of tours and interviews. His writings were published in the newspaper and, subsequently, in printed volumes. Those on crime were collected in the fourth volume. In the extract below he describes dolly shops, just one of the varied ways through which stolen property could be disposed.*

---

[15] H. Mayhew, *London labour and the London poor*, vol. 4 (London, 1861), pp. 373–4.

6.1   Receivers of Stolen Property

When we look to the number of common thieves prowling over the metropolis – the thousands living daily on beggary, prostitution, and crime – we naturally expect to find extensive machinery for the receiving of stolen property. These receivers are to be found in different grades of society, from the keeper of the miserable low lodging-houses and dolly shops in Petticoat Lane, Rosemary Lane, and Spitafields, in the East End, and Dudley Street and Drury Lane in the West End of the Metropolis, to the pawnbroker in Cheapside, the Strand, and Fleet Street, and the opulent Jews of Houndsditch and its vicinity, whose coffers are said to be overflowing with gold.

6.2   Dolly Shops

As we walk along Dudley Street, near the Seven Dials – the Petticoat Lane of the West End – a curious scene presents itself to our notice. There we do not find a colony of Jews, as in the East end, but a colony of Irish shopkeepers, with a few cockneys and Jews intermingled among them. Dudley Street is a noted art for old clothes, consisting principally of male and female apparel, and second-hand boots and shoes.

We pass by several shops without sign-boards – which by the way is a characteristic of this strange by-street – where boots and shoes, in general sadly worn, are exposed on shelves under the window, or carefully ranged in rows on the pavement before the shop. We find a middle-aged or elderly Irishman with his leather apron, or a young Irish girl brushing shoes at the door, in Irish accent inviting customers to enter their shop.

We also observe old clothes stores, where male apparel is suspended on wooden rods before the door, and trousers, vests, and coats of different descriptions, piled on chairs in front of the shop, or exposed in the dirty unwashed windows, while the shopmen loiter before the door, hailing the customers as they pass by.

Alongside of these we see what is more strictly called dolly or leaving shops – the fertile hot-beds of crime. The dolly shop is often termed an unlicensed pawnshop. Around the doorway, in some cases of ordinary size, in others more spacious, we see a great assortment of articles, chiefly of female dress, suspended on the wall: petticoats, skirts, stays, gowns, shawls, and bonnets of all patterns and sizes, the gowns being mostly of dirty cotton, spotted and striped; also children's petticoats of different kinds, shirt-fronts, collars, handkerchiefs, and neckerchiefs exposed in the window. As we look into these suspicious-looking shops we see large piles of female apparel, with articles of men's dress heaped around the walls, or deposited in bundles and paper packages on shelves around the shop, with strings of clothes hung across the apartment to dry, or offered for sale. We find in some of the backrooms, stores of shabby old clothes, and one or more women of various ages loitering about.

In the evening these dolly shops are dimly lighted, and look still more gloomy and forbidding than during the day.

Many of these people buy other articles besides clothes. They are in the habit of receiving articles left with them, and charge 2d or 3d a shilling on the articles, if redeemed in a week. If not redeemed for a week, or other specified time, they sell the articles, and dispose of them, having given the party a miserably small sum, perhaps only a sixth or eighth part of their value. These shops are frequented by common thieves, and by poor dissipated creatures living in the dark slums and alleys in the vicinity, or residing in low lodging-houses. The persons who keep them often conceal the articles deposited with them from the knowledge of the police, and get punished as receivers of stolen property. Numbers of such cases occur over the metropolis in low neighbourhoods. For this reason the keepers of these shops are often compelled to remove to other localities.

The articles they receive, such as old male and female wearing apparel, are also resetted[16] by keepers of low coffee-houses, and lodging-houses, and are occasionally bought by chandlers, low hairdressers, and others.

They also receive workman's tools of an inferior quality, and cheap articles of household furniture, books, etc., from poor dissipated people, beggars, and thieves; many of which would be rejected by the licensed pawnbrokers.

They are frequently visited by the wives and daughters of the poorest labouring people, and others who deposit wearing apparel, or bed-linen, with them for a small piece of money when they are in want of food, or when they wish to get some intoxicating liquor, in which many of them indulge too freely. They are also haunted by the lowest prostitutes on like errands. The keepers of dolly shops give more indulgence to their regular customers than they do to strangers. They charge a less sum from them, and keep their articles longer before disposing of them.

It frequently occurs that these low traders are very unscrupulous, and sell the property deposited with them when they can make a small piece of money thereby.

There is a pretty extensive traffic carried on in the numerous dolly shops scattered over the metropolis, as we may find from the extensive stores heaped up in their apartments, in many cases in such dense piles as almost to exclude the light of day, and from the groups of wretched creatures who frequent them – particularly in the evenings.

The principal trade in old clothes is in the East End of the metropolis – in Rosemary Lane, Petticoat Lane, and the dark by-streets and alleys

---

[16] Received, knowing them to be stolen.

in the neighbourhood, but chiefly at the Old Clothes Exchange, where huge bales are sold in small quantities to crowds of traders, and sent off to various parts of Scotland, England, and Ireland, and exported abroad. The average weekly trade has been estimated at about £1500.

7   Poaching, 1833[17]

In the early nineteenth century, poaching was perceived as becoming increasingly violent and organized. In the following article from the Chester Chronicle, *three incidents from different areas of the country are placed next to each other. The levels of violence surrounding these were far from usual and one can see the fears generated by the press through their selective coverage. The tone of the article is noticeably antagonistic to the poachers themselves.*

About two o'clock on Sunday morning, while the Earl of Wilson's game-keepers were on the watch in Heaton Park,[18] they perceived five men employed in shooting pheasants in one of the plantations. On the approach of one of the keepers, the men made off. They were pursued by the keepers, overtaken, and after a desperate resistance, in which the poachers kicked – purred[19] – and bit, in the true Lancashire fashion, one of them was secured. He was brought before the magistrates at Manchester, on Monday, and sentenced to be imprisoned three months to hard labour, and at the termination of that period, to find two sureties in five pounds each,[20] not to offend in the same way for twelve months, in default of finding such sureties, his term of imprisonment was extended to six months.

On the night of the 30th last, a gang of determined poachers met near Denbigh,[21] to the number of twelve, armed with guns and bludgeons, for the purpose of destroying the game on the preserves of Lord Dinorben, at Lleweny, near Denbigh. They were heard in the wood between one and two in the morning of the 31st by the keepers, and when they found the latter on the alert, they determined not to be taken even at the hazard of their own lives. One of the keepers had a dog which the poachers shot, and no sooner had they done so than they fired several shots at the keepers which fortunately did not take effect. Two of the keepers (out of nine) being armed with guns, were compelled to fire in their own defence, and having fired once each, they rushed upon the poachers and a most desperate conflict took place, by which four of the poachers' guns were

---

[17] *Chester Chronicle*, 8/2/1833.

[18] Heaton Park lies to the north of Manchester.

[19] A term specific to Cheshire, referring to kicking with boots and clogs.

[20] Two people prepared to guarantee the defendant's behaviour by agreeing to forfeit five pounds each, should the defendant reoffend within the stipulated period.

[21] Denbigh is in North Wales, close to the border with Cheshire.

broken and two left behind. Two of the keepers, Edward Parry and Robert Jones, were most brutally maltreated by the poachers with guns and sticks, and left in the wood for dead. The ruffians then escaped, and the keepers found the wounded men in a state of insensibility from loss of blood. They were immediately conveyed to a cottage in Lleweny Yard, where they still remain without hope of recovery. Five of the party have been taken and committed by the aldermen of Denbigh to take their trial at the next Ruthin Assizes, and it is confidently hoped that the other seven, who have at present absconded, will not long escape.

During Wednesday night one of the watchers on the estate of Sir G. Heathcoate, Baronet of Nermanton, about six miles from Stamford,[22] on going his usual rounds about eleven at night, heard the discharge of three guns. He immediately made his way back to communicate the fact to Sir Gilbert's head keeper, named Peach, and the second keeper, named Morris. On this, Peach, Morris and another keeper, named Johnson, with two assistants, went to the wood in pursuit of the gang. On arriving at the wood the keepers heard the party walking from end to end, discharging several guns in their progress, and the pheasants falling down from the trees, but the night being dark they could not distinguish them. Peach and his companion were lying down, on which they rose, and Peach accosted them. Hearing this, the rest of the party ran to the spot, Morris exclaiming: "Come on, lads, here they all are!" Instantly, a gun was fired by one of these cold-blooded murderers; and Peach fell to the ground, and cried, "O Lord, I'm shot."

Morris, seeing his friend fall to the ground, rushed towards the man who shot him, when another of the party cried out: "Curse him, shoot him too!" which was instantly obeyed, another gun being levelled at his head and discharged, the contents lodging in his left ear, temples, and hat, and two shots in the corner of his eye. On this, Morris dropped on his knees, and a pistol which he held in his hand fell from his grasp. However, he was able immediately to rise again, and commenced looking and feeling for his pistol and hat, which was blown off his head by the discharge of the gun. At this instant two more of the gang (making a total of five) came over the wall, and seeing poor Morris, whom they had witnessed shot, on his legs, one of them cried: "Curse him, shoot him again," and another gun was pointed at him and fired, and the contents perforated through his coat and shirt, spreading over the small of his back, but fortunately was only sufficiently strong to slightly mark the skin, without inflicting any serious wound. The keeper's assistant, seeing these dreadful and deliberate acts of bloodshed and murder, fell back to a distance completely dismayed, as all except Morris were unarmed; but Morris now hearing the

---

[22] Stamford lies on the border between Lincolnshire and Cambridgeshire.

heart-rending moans and cries of Peach, after being shot for a second time, went to his assistance, on which Peach exclaimed: "John, they've killed me!" At this time the murderous ruffians stood and calmly looked on to witness and hear what took place between the two helpless objects of their vengeance, and then deliberately walked off from the wood at a slow pace. Peach and Morris, now left weltering in their blood, were again joined by their assistant, who witnessed the departure of the poachers, and it was found necessary to fetch a cart and horse to convey them to their homes at Empingham. Peach lies in a very dangerous and almost hopeless state but Morris is in a fair way of recovery.

8 Whitechapel Murders, 1888[23]

The Whitechapel murders remain a part of popular folklore due to the infamy of Jack the Ripper and the mystery surrounding his identity. They were the first set of crimes to receive saturation coverage from the press across the whole of the country. Fascinating as some people may find this, the victims of the murders were real people and there was widespread anxiety amongst the residents of the area. In the passage below, from The Times, *speculation about the murders reaches a high point with the receipt of two communications by the police, purportedly from the murderer himself. At the end, it is reported that the anxieties had been translated into questions about police effectiveness.*

The excitement caused by the murders committed early on Sunday morning in Berner Street, Commercial Road and Mitre Square, Aldgate, has in no way abated. In the East-End, statements and rumours of the most extraordinary nature were in circulation yesterday respecting conversations which certain persons, male and female, had had with two or three suspicious-looking men an hour or so before the crimes were committed, the purport of the statements in question being to connect the latter individuals with the outrages. Nothing, however, can be extracted from these statements of sufficient importance to form any clue. A few arrests have been made by the Metropolitan Police, but none had been made by the City Police up to a late hour last night. The authorities are now fully on the alert in the localities of the murders, and, as stated below, it has been decided by the City Police to offer a reward for the discovery of the assassin.

It is satisfactory to announce that one discovery at least has been made which, in the hands of efficient detectives, should prove an important clue to the lurking place of the murderer – for the belief is now generally

---

[23] *The Times*, 2/10/1888.

entertained in official quarters that to one person alone is attributable the series of crimes which in the last few weeks have horrified and alarmed the public.

It appears that, after perpetrating his foul work in Mitre Square, the miscreant retracted his steps towards the scene of the crime which he had committed an hour or so earlier. As stated in the particulars given in *The Times* of yesterday, part of the attire of the unfortunate woman who was butchered in Mitre Square consisted of a portion of a coarse white apron, which was found loosely hanging about the neck. A piece of this apron had been torn away by the villain, who, in proceeding to his destination further east after leaving the City of London boundary, presumably used it to wipe his hands or his knife on, and then threw it away. It was picked up in Goulston Street very shortly after the second murder had been committed and it was brought to the mortuary by Dr Phillips soon after the body had been removed there. It was covered with blood and was found to fit in with the portion of apron which had been left by the murderer on his victim. Goulston Street, it may be stated, is a broad thoroughfare running parallel with the Commercial Road and is off the main Whitechapel Road, and the spot where the piece of apron was picked up is about a third of a mile from Mitre Square. By the direct and open route it is 1550 feet, but it can be approached through several small streets, making the distance about 1600 feet. These measurements were taken yesterday.

The only other clues in the possession of the police are two pawn-broker's tickets, which were found lying close to the spot where the Mitre Square murder was discovered and a knife, which was picked up by a police constable in the Whitechapel road early yesterday morning. It is described as black-handled, ten inches long, keen as a razor and pointed like a carving knife. The pawn-tickets are believed to have belonged to the woman. They were in a small tin box and related to pledges which had been made in August of a pair of boots and a man's shirt. The tickets had been made out in two names – Emily Birrell and Anne Kelly – and the articles had been pawned for 1s and 6d, respectively, with Mr Jones of Church Street, Spitalfields, who, however, cannot identify the woman as having made the pledges.

Photographs of the ill-fated creature were taken at the city mortuary in Golden Lane both before and after the post mortem examination, after which the features – which, as already reported in *The Times*, had been brutally cut about – were rendered more life-like by the doctors. Up to a late hour last night, however, the body had not been identified, though several persons, having missed relatives or friends, have been taken to see it by the police.

Yesterday morning, shortly after ten o'clock, an interview respecting the Mitre Square murder took place between Mr McWilliam (the inspector of the City Detective Department), Superintendent Foster, and Inspector

Collard and the city coroner, who has arranged to hold the inquest on Thursday morning, it being hoped that the woman may be identified on the meantime. The plans taken by Mr F. W. Foster, of Old Jewry, of the scene of this outrage immediately after it was discovered were submitted to the coroner and Mr Foster will be one of the witnesses at the inquest.

The following is a description of a man seen in company with a woman who is supposed to be the victim of the murderer. The man was observed in a court in Duke Street, leading to Mitre Square, about 1.40 a.m. on Sunday. He is described as of shabby appearance, about thirty years of age and five feet, nine inches, in height, of fair complexion, having a small fair moustache and wearing a red neckerchief and a cap with a peak.

Two communications of an extraordinary nature, both signed "Jack the Ripper", have been received by the Central News Agency, the one on Thursday last and the other yesterday morning. The first – the original of which has been seen by Major Smith, the assistant commissioner of the City Police – was a letter, bearing the E.C. postmark, in which reference was made to the atrocious murders previously committed in the East End, which the writer confessed, in a brutally jocular vein, to have committed; stating that in the "next job" he did he would "clip the lady's ears off" and send them to the police, and also asking that the letter might be kept back until he had done "a bit more work". The second communication was a postcard, and as above stated, it was received yesterday morning. It bore the date, "London, E., October 1", and was as follows:

> I was not codding, dear old Boss, when I give you the tip. You'll hear about Saucy Jacky's work tomorrow. Double event this time. Number one squealed a bit; couldn't finish straight off. Had not time to get ears for the police. Thanks for keeping the letter back till I got to work again.

The postcard was sent to Scotland Yard. No doubt is entertained that the writer of both communications, whoever he may be, is the same person.

Many adverse remarks have been made concerning the want of vigilance on the part of the police in connection with the outrages but it should be remembered, as urged by them, that the women are of a class who know that they are liable to punishment if detected and who, therefore, go alone to the places where they agree to meet their male companions. Shortly after the first horrible murders were committed some weeks ago, special precautions were taken by the City Police authorities with a view to detect the criminal or criminals, several plain-clothes constables being ordered on the beats in the district which has now become so notorious. Instructions were given to the constables to watch any man or woman seen together in suspicious circumstances, and especially to observe any woman who might be seen in circumstances of a similar nature. At about the time when the Mitre Square murder was being committed two of the extra men who had been put on duty were in Windsor Street, a thoroughfare about 300 yards off, engaged, pursuant to their instructions, in watching certain houses, it being thought that the premises might be resorted to at some time by the murderer. Five minutes after the discovery of the murder in Mitre Square, the two officers referred to heard of it, and the neighbourhood was at once searched by them, unfortunately without result. It is believed that had any man and woman been in company with each other going to Mitre Square they must have been observed, and that the man in that case would have been detected and captured. The supposition of the police is that the murderer and the ill-fated woman went to the place separately, having made an appointment. The general impression is that no man in his right senses could have perpetrated such a series of dreadful crimes. Some of the doctors who have been engaged in the examination of the bodies believe it quite possible that the murders may have been committed in from three to five minutes.

9   Workplace Crime

The nineteenth century saw new working relationships and new ways to commit crime. The newspaper paragraphs below give examples of the attempts of textile capitalists to stem the appropriation of their materials, their use of the master and servant laws to impose new disciplines, and outbreaks of violence in the factory. The incidents that have been chosen also show the ways in which the magistracy mediated the competing claims before them.

9.1   Macclesfield, 1829

Silk manufacturers are subjected to considerable loss by the various ways in which the workpeople occasionally defraud them of their materials. One principal way has been as follows: the manufacturers deliver out the silk to the weaver's upon wooden bobbins, and charge them with the gross weight. When the weavers return the materials woven, the piece is weighed and if its weight and that of the empty bobbins (allowing for the weight of the warp and a reasonable weight for waste) corresponds with the gross weight delivered out, it is correct; but many of the fraudulent workmen distract some portion of the silk, and to make up the gross weight, place the empty bobbins in some damp place, or soak them in water to obviate this source of fraud. Some of the manufacturers have hit upon the expedient of making their bobbins of japanned tin but some of these bobbins on being returned were weighed by themselves, and found to be of greater weight than they should be. It was discovered that a very small hole had been bored through the tin into the hollow part of the bobbins, and a quantity of old cotton waste thrown in.[24]

9.2   Macclesfield, 1831

At the Guildhall yesterday a quantity of unwrought silk was produced before the Mayor, and T. Critchley, Esq., by Burgess the constable, who stated that he had traced it, on Tuesday last, to the possession of Josiah Bailey, and suspecting that it had been stolen, he sent Sutton (assistant constable) to fetch it. The defendant appeared, and the silk having been separated into lots stated, that he had purchased the four sorts consisting of Italian Raw, Bengal Tram, China and Brussia, from William Challinor Painter with a larger quantity, on the 4th of October last. He produced the invoice, and Painter, being brought forward said that the defendant had dealings with him at that time, and that the Italian Raw and Bengal Tram might be part of what he sold him but that he did not sell him any China or Brussia. The Court not deeming the account of possession satisfactory, fined him in the penalty of £20, one half to be given to the funds of the Dispensary, and the other half to the informer.[25]

9.3   Stockport, 1832

Ann Keeley, a weaver in the employ of Mr S. Radcliffe, cotton manufacturer, was charged by her master with stealing calico from his mill on Friday. For a considerable time past property of this nature has been missing from the factory, and, in order to detect the criminal, Mr Radcliffe determined to keep a strict lookout. On going into the throstle room, he perceived the defendant who had only been in his service two days, with huge pockets, and after a little further search, found a quantity of calico (which had been torn off a piece) in her pocket. Her father being a hawker of such articles, that fact weighed criminally against her, and she was taken into custody. The amount of the theft was trifling, but it was the system against which Mr Radcliffe complained; and after she had begged her master's pardon, and saying in court she would never do the like again, she was discharged.[26]

---

[24] *Macclesfield Courier*, 26/12/1829.
[25] *Macclesfield Courier*, 22/10/1831.
[26] *Stockport Advertiser*, 9/11/1832.

9.4 Stockport, 1838

Catharine Dunn, weaver, in the employ of Messrs Hole, Lingard and Cruttenden, was charged with stealing oil. James Lighton, an overlooker of looms in the room wherein Dunn worked, stated that on Thursday she borrowed his oil can (which had just been filled) for the purpose, as she assigned, of oiling her looms, and he let it to her. When she returned the can it was empty. Elizabeth Swann, a tenter, gave evidence to the effect that she saw Dunn empty the overlooker's can of oil into a bottle, and put it in her basket, where it was found by the police officer, and to whom she admitted taking it, adding that she wanted to sharpen a razor with it. Mr Slack [magistrate], observing that the value of property stolen was so small, asked Mr Vickers whether he pressed the case – Mr Vickers answered in the affirmative. The present case was not so much a question of value as one of protection. The oil had been valued at 2d at least, but he was inclined to believe that this system of pilfering was carried on to some extent in cotton mills. He, therefore, considered the present case important, since employers had no protection but in the honesty of their servants. He well recollected the observations of the chairman at a recent Knutsford Quarter Sessions, who in his charge to the grand jury, directed their particular attention to this – that they were not to ignore bills of indictment because the property stolen was small in value. The distinction between petty and grand larceny no longer existed, and therefore the principle remained the same, whether the property be of a great or a trifling value. Mr Slack was aware that their duty would be to commit the thief for trial, but thought that the ends of justice might possibly be as well served by the present exposure as putting the county to the expense of prosecuting such a trifling felony. Of course, if the case was pressed, the Bench had no alternative. Mr Vickers, replied that, for the due protection of the property of the firm, he was constrained to press the case. [The defendant was committed for trial where she was found guilty and sentenced to six months in prison].[27]

9.5 Stockport, 1828

John Saxon charged a number of his workpeople with absenting themselves from their work, on Monday last. Mr Saxon stated that he had received a considerable order of twist, and that it has to be executed in a given time, and if not ready at the time agreed upon, it would be returned to his hands; consequently he could not stop his mill during the wakes.[28]

---

[27] *Stockport Advertiser*, 6/4/1838.
[28] Wakes were traditional week-long festivals.

The defendants said in their defence, that the whole of the factories in the town were stopped during the wake, except the complainants', and they considered they were only doing as others did at such times. The magistrates however, differed in opinion with the latter, and told them any employer had a right to please himself as to play time, and it was no justification of conduct, that because others were idling at the wake, that they in a body should leave their work to do the same. [Defendants had to pay costs and expenses and return to work.][29]

9.6   Stockport, 1840

Several weavers recently in the employ of Messrs Hole, Lingard and Cruttendon, have been during the week summoned before the magistrates, for leaving their service without notice. The legal representative of the firm, Mr Vaughan, said that so far from having any vindictive motive for bringing forward the cases, he would consent to withdraw all further proceedings on the defendants returning to their work, giving the usual notice, and paying the costs.[30]

9.7   Stockport, 1871

Thomas Irlam, an overlooker at Messrs Leigh's Mills, Portwood, was summoned for assaulting a little girl named Cromwell, while at work on the 20th last. The girl was represented by her aunt. The defendant did not deny correcting the girl, because she had been guilty of disobedience, and the aunt instructed him to do so in order to make the girl into a good back tenter. He merely boxed her ears. Mrs Cromwell admitted having given some such authorization, and the summons was accordingly dismissed.[31]

9.8   Stockport, 1871

Margaret Greek was summoned by Owen McDermott for assault. They are employed at a mill in Portwood, and on Wednesday morning, the complainant, in putting some bobbins in the defendant's box, against her wish, broke her ends through letting the bobbins go on her reel. She threw a bobbin at him, which hit him on the forehead, and he retaliated by throwing one at her, but missed her – case dismissed, and costs divided.[32]

---

[29] *Stockport Advertiser*, 17/10/1828.
[30] *Stockport Advertiser*, 7/2/1840.
[31] *Stockport Advertiser*, 27/01/1871.
[32] *Stockport Advertiser*, 2/06/1871.

9.9   Stockport, 1872

Thomas Monks, an overlooker at Howard's Mill, was summoned by Mary Ann Shaw for what the law calls an assault while at work as a back tenter in the card room, on Monday, because she applied for some oil, and he "clouted her". The defendant said he merely pushed her aside for the impertinent way in which she spoke to him. Being a new overlooker he met with a little annoyance and opposition from some of the hands. The magistrates said such a trifling case ought never to have been brought to a court. It might have been settled in the mill. But as an assault had been proved, they would only impose the lowest penalty – the costs.[33]

10   Peterloo, 1819[34]

Peterloo was one of the major confrontations between protesters and the state, yet it cannot be described as either a popular disturbance or a riot. There had been a series of meetings in 1819 to demand political reform. In August, a crowd of unprecedented size (60,000) gathered peacefully in St Peter's Fields, Manchester, to hear the radical speaker Henry Hunt. There was no indication of unrest or riotousness yet the Manchester and Cheshire yeomanry were determined to stop it. In the two extracts below, a spinner describes the actions of the yeomanry and a magistrate describes the fears of authority preceding the riot.

10.1   Abraham Wrigley – examined by Blackburne[35]

I was a cotton spinner living at Oldham in 1819. I went with the Oldham people to Manchester on the 16th August. In the course of our progress, nothing was done to excite a disturbance. I was about five or six yards from the hustings with my back to the constables. I saw the yeomanry advance. Before that time the people conducted themselves in a very decent manner; all appeared to be harmony and conviviality. The yeomanry had got close up to me before I could see them. When they first came up to the place where I stood, they were cutting away with their swords at the people. When they came up to me, I stood, as I observed before, with my back to the constables. The constables that stood next to me began to strike the people with their truncheons; and one of the constables standing nearest to me pushed me forward close to the cavalrymen's

[33] *Stockport Advertiser*, 15/03/1872.
[34] "Redford against Birley and Others", in *Reports of state trials*, new series, vol. 1, 1820–23, H.M.S.O., pp. 1091–3 and 1172–3.
[35] Counsel for the plaintiff.

horses; and I received a blow on the hat, which I conceived to be one of the cavalrymen's swords. It knocked it off.

Did you observe anybody else?

Yes; I saw many that were struck by the cavalrymen in that situation.

Did you see the effect the blows had on them?

I saw blood flowing very copiously from the heads of some of them, after their hats were struck off; they struck them over the head.

Which way did you get away?

I was forced back by the pressure of the crowd, in the way where the constables stood; that is, to my back. I was forced against the higher part of the houses that formed Windmill Street.

Well?

In that situation, the houses in Windmill Street have cellars.

Holroyd, J. *You are now speaking about other people in the cellars?*

Yes; there were some cellars: the houses have mostly cellars in that street; there was an iron railing to prevent accident, which was broken down by the pressure.

Iron railings opposite the cellaring?

Yes.

Well?

I was then forced into a backyard of Windmill Street.

Holroyd, J. *I do not know whether this is material.*

Did you observe anything more of what happened?

After we were driven through the yard, followed by the constables, a great many constables followed and struck several of the people. We were then compelled to make our escape over a fence, not being safe, a very high fence of boards. From there, I got down to a backyard. I got into a brickyard towards Lower Maley Street. I came on the fields again in ten minutes after I was forced away.

What did you see?

I was coming on the top of Windmill Street; I met an old man, whom I knew, bleeding profusely from, apparently, a sabre wound received on his forehead.

Was the blood from his forehead?

Yes.

Did the blood come from a wound in his forehead?

Yes.

What more? I observed to him.

What did you see? After I had seen him, I came down to that part of the ground where I had been, in order to obtain my hat or get another.

You came back to get another hat? Had you seen anybody else that had lost their hats?

Many.

What did you see?

When I came back, I observed that most of the people had fled, and that the cavalry were riding about and forming in a sort of column, and the constables near them.

Did you see anything more?

I saw the constables striking the people who had got away, infirm people.

10.2   William Hutton – examined by Serjeant Hullock[36]

I am a magistrate of the county of Lancaster. I was elected chairman of the committee of magistrates. It was appointed about the 18th July in consequence of the disturbed state of the country, to provide for the peace of the country. As a magistrate, I had opportunities of becoming acquainted with the state of the country. I knew that in every town and in almost every village there were union societies, conducted by committees, corresponding with each other by means of delegates. I should have added there was a general panic throughout the district from these and other circumstances. We derived information of what was going forward in the adjoining districts. It produced a rapid increase of alarm for the public safety. From time to time we received what we considered as positive information of drilling or training in several parts, and it was conveyed to us frequently by gentlemen of the highest respectability. The great mass of the people, all degrees and all classes, were under the greatest apprehension. After we were apprized of the proposed meeting of the 16th, our meetings were almost permanent. For myself I did not return home, though I lived within twelve miles. I was detained all night solely for the purpose of attending this committee. I cannot speak to other magistrates being detained. I only know they were late in the evening, and early in the morning. I am quite certain that the last night or two Mr Trafford was added to the magistrates. Mr Hay, I believe, resided there permanently. We were assisted by the gentlemen of the town of Manchester. There was a committee formed. It was formed at a committee of public safety, with whom we were in constant communication. It was composed of some of the principal gentlemen of the town and neighbourhood of Manchester. We met on the Sunday together; directions were given that we should meet directly after church. We made such arrangements as we thought requisite to meet what we deemed impending danger. We assembled at the Star about nine o'clock in the morning of the 16th; nine was the hour appointed, and we met sooner. I think it was about eleven when we went to Mr Buxton's house. It commanded a perfect view of the area. I think every member of the committee was present but one. There was one who had attended at the New Bailey, who happened not to be present

---

[36] Counsel for the defence. A serjeant was the equivalent of a Queen's Counsel.

– Mr Entwistle.[37] All the others who had attended were present, except Mr Trafford. I think there was a paper handed to the magistrats – a declaration of the apprehensions of the inhabitants, and the danger to the town from such a meeting. I think that paper was brought to me, as chairman of the committee of magistrates.

11   Riots at Bristol, 1831[38]

The reform of parliament and elections had been a divisive issue since the end of the Napoleonic Wars. At the beginning of 1831 the Tories had lost power to the Whigs, political radicalism was more organized than it had ever been and the country was the scene of agricultural and industrial disturbances, following three years of economic depression. Nevertheless, traditionalists were determined in their opposition to reform. The Bristol riots were the most destructive of a series of incidents which had followed rejection of the second reform bill in the House of Lords. Sparked by the return of the conservative Charles Wetherall to the city and exacerbated by the actions of commander in charge of the army, Lieutenant-Colonel Brereton, the riots lasted three days and saw the destruction of much of the city centre. The passage below gives a detailed account of the rioters' targets, the means by which the authorities attempted to reimpose order and the attitudes of the Gentleman's Magazine *itself to the rioters.*

This great commercial city has been the theatre of the most disgraceful and diabolical outrages that have been perpetrated in this country since the riots of London in 1780. The destruction of life and property is most lamentable; and Bristol will doubtless feel the terrible effects for some time to come. The mob who perpetrated this devastation was the lowest of the low – fellows who knew no distinction, their hands uplifted against all parties – who had no other end in view than to gratify their natural thirst for plunder, violence, and bloodshed. It appears that Sir Charles Wetherell, the Recorder of Bristol, having announced it to be his intention to arrive in that city on Saturday the 29th of October last in his judicial capacity, great fears of disturbance were entertained, in consequence of his conduct on the reform question being regarded by the populace with a feeling of perfect abhorrence. At the time appointed, dense masses of the lower orders poured out from St Phillip's, Lawford's Gate, etc., to meet the unpopular Recorder, and several persons assembled at Totterdown, awaiting his approach.

At half-past ten his arrival was announced. He was attended by four to five hundred special constables, with bludgeons or staves. The moment he came within sight of the populace, execrations, yells, and groans were

---

[37] The New Bailey was the name of the local magistrates' court and gaol.
[38] *Gentleman's Magazine*, November 1831, pp. 459–60.

216

uttered. Several volleys of stones were thrown. This was continued all the way to Broad Street. The Recorder reached the Guildhall, and proceeded to open the Commission; but, from the groans and yells, not a word could be heard. Afterwards Sir Charles proceeded to the Mansion house, amidst continued groans. Several thousand persons were collected round the Mansion house. A slight scuffle ensued between the mob and the special constables. A general rush was then made by the people to the Quay, where they armed themselves with bludgeons. They were met on their return by the special constables, who completely routed them. The crowd, however, still increased, and several windows were soon broken.

At five o'clock the Riot Act was read, immediately after which every window, frames and all, in the Mansion house was smashed to pieces. The 14th Dragoons now arrived, and saved the Mansion house from destruction. At eight o'clock the crowd was still increasing in numbers and fury, and the special constables were quite overcome. At this critical moment, Sir Charles Wetherell made his escape in disguise. In spite of the troops, the mob continued to increase, and they cheered the soldiers with great enthusiasm. Things continued thus until twelve o'clock at night, about which time, a party of rioters proceeded to the council chamber, the windows of which were broken. The cavalry were here ordered to charge, and the people were pursued to a considerable distance, several of them receiving severe sabre wounds. The military prevented the reassembling of the populace during the night.

On Sunday morning the mob again assembled in Queen Square, but everything remained quiet; and it being hoped that the danger had subsided, the troops withdrew, in order to take some refreshment having been on duty more than twenty-four hours. The moment they disappeared, the mob recommenced their outrages. The upper rooms of the Mansion house were now entered, and the valuable furniture, etc., was either plundered or destroyed in the most wanton manner. The cellars were broken open, and a vast quantity of wine was carried off, and drunk or destroyed by the mob. People of all ages, and of both sexes, were to be seen greedily swallowing the intoxicating liquors, while the ground was strewed with persons in the last and most beastly state of intoxication. The troops (the 14th Light Dragoons) speedily reappeared but the mob attacked them with a shower of stones and brickbats, which the men were unable to resist and, no magistrates being present to direct their proceedings, the commanding officer withdrew them, and they were replaced by a body of the 3rd Dragoon Guards.

At about two o'clock in the day, a party of the mob went to the Bridewell,[39] rescued the prisoners, and set the building on fire. About

---

[39] "Bridewell" is another term for house of correction.

the same time a stronger party went to the New Gaol, when, having procured hammers from an adjoining shipyard, they broke the various locks to pieces, and liberated the criminals, to the amount of more than a hundred. This done, the building was fired, and the conflagration was awful in the extreme. The work of destruction here completed, the various tollhouses were next consumed, after which the Gloucester county prison, Lawford's Gate, the Bishop's Palace, Canon's Marsh, and the Mansion house were all set on fire and destroyed! By twelve o'clock at night, the whole mass of houses, from the Mansion house to the middle avenue of the square, including the custom house and all the brick buildings in Little King Street, were one immense mass of fire. In this manner the mob swept away one whole side of the square, and then proceeded to another, commencing with excise office at the corner. From there the flames extended to the houses of the parallel streets, including many of the principal wine and spirit stores. Forty-two offices, dwelling houses and warehouses were completely destroyed, exclusive of public buildings. The scene throughout was appalling in the extreme. Having got entire possession of the custom house, the population drank to excess, and many parts of the road near that building were inundated with rum, etc. Ten or twelve persons, in a state of drunkenness, were burnt in the houses and buildings which they themselves set fire to. The whole city appeared to be panic-stricken.

On Monday morning, the shops remained unopened, and the military were shortly afterwards withdrawn, and the inhabitants, armed with staves, took upon themselves the maintenance of the public peace. The number killed and wounded does not exceed one hundred. Of the dead, as far as could be ascertained, six were burnt, two shot, two died of sword wounds, and two of excessive drinking. Of the wounded, ten were injured by shots, forty-eight by sword cuts, two by drinking, and thirty-four from other causes. Most of these were residents of Bristol or the neighbourhood. The number committed is one hundred and eighty, fifty of whom are capitally charged with rioting and burning. A subscription has been raised for the immediate relief of the sufferers by fire, many of whom have lost their all. At a subsequent meeting, a series of resolutions were passed, praying the government to inquire into the conduct of the magistrates and the commanding officer of the district.

Partial disturbances have existed in different parts of the country. At Bath, the mob made an attempt to prevent the yeomanry cavalry leaving the city for the purposes of assisting in the suppression of the riots at Bristol. The inn where the captain of the corps stayed was almost pulled down. At Worcester, on the 2nd of November, it was found necessary to call in the military to preserve the public peace, the mob having taken advantage of a fire which broke out in a back street, to congregate for purposes of mischief. Twenty-nine of the rioters were apprehended. On the 7th, some rioting took place at Coventry. One factory was burnt down, and the military and special constables were called out to suppress the disturbances.

12   Vagrancy in the Nineteenth Century

There had been vagrancy laws in England dating back to the early modern period, but the nineteenth century was to see a widening of state powers through the inclusion of new offences within their scope and more efficient law enforcement. The passages below relate to this from different angles. The first, taken from the Gentleman's Magazine, *gives an indication of hardening attitudes towards poverty at the end of the Napoleonic Wars. The three clauses of the Vagrancy Act, which make up the second passage, show the array of offences that were covered under the law and the gradation of punishments. The third and fourth passages are newspaper accounts of cases in which the Vagrancy Act was used, highlighting the targeting of young and incapable.*

12.1   Beggars, 1814[40]

It is to be observed, that every beggar may be classed under one of two descriptions of persons. He is either in distress and an object of charity, or he is an imposter and deserving of punishment. It is a scandal upon our benevolence, if one is allowed to wander abroad, and to live upon the precarious aims of casual bounty; and it is a disgrace to the legislature if the other shall be permitted to practise upon the weakness of tender natures, or to subsist in dishonesty and plunder. Such are the provisions made for the poorer classes of the community in this happy country, by the established laws of the land, that unless shame, or some distress of the mind, shall intervene to obstruct the course of these laws, no man can die from absolute want; nor can ignorance of the means of benefiting by these merciful institutions be urged by anyone, with even a plausible appearance of justice, because the poor, although little learned in matters of higher moment, have, I might almost say, an intuitive knowledge of their own immediate rights and privileges. There is not, I believe, a pauper in any direction, from the centre to the extreme boundary of the kingdom, who does not know, that the poor are provided for by the laws; and that every one has a legal settlement in some parish or other, in which he may demand relief in his necessity, with a certainty that his demand will not be resisted, and must be complied with.

---

[40] *Gentleman's Magazine*, September 1814, pp. 228–9.

At the present crisis, these observations deserve more than a common notice. The disembodying of many militia regiments; the reduction of the army in general; and the dismantling of a large portion of our navy, will necessarily throw a mass of population upon the internal resources of the country, for which at first she will find it difficult to make an adequate provision. Those persons are greatly deceived, who imagine that all or even the greater part of the hands so thrown out of employment will immediately find occupation or maintenance in the improved or improving state of our manufactures. Great numbers of deserving poor creatures will be reduced to absolute want, but an equal number, probably, will take advantage of this unavoidable calamity and, under the shadow of it, will practise the most shameful impositions, and commit the most daring depredations.

As a means, therefore, of substantially relieving real distress, and punishing fraud and dishonesty, instead of indiscriminate and injudicious almsgiving, I recommend a strict though liberal construction and execution of the Laws. Let vagrants of every description [and all itinerant beggars are properly classed under this head, of offenders against "*bonos mores*", and the "decency of life"] be diligently watched, and promptly apprehended. The magistracy is administered by men of talents and integrity, and those will, in all cases, provide for the wants of the distressed poor and honest man; and by the wholesome correction or restraint, prevent crimes or punish the offenders.

Yours, &c.

W.A.A.

12.2   The Vagrancy Act, 1824[41]

Clause Three [Idle and Disorderly Persons]

And be it further enacted, that every person being able wholly or in part to maintain himself or herself, or his or her family, by work or by other means, and wilfully refusing or neglecting so to do, by which refusal or neglect he or she, or any of his or her family whom he or she may be legally bound to maintain, shall have become chargeable to any parish, township or place; every person returning to and becoming chargeable in any parish, township or place from whence he or she shall have been legally removed by order of two Justices of the Peace, unless he or she shall produce a certificate of the churchwardens and overseers of the poor of some other parish, township or place thereby acknowledging him or her to be settled in such other parish, township or place; every petty chapman or pedlar wandering abroad and trading, without being duly licensed, or otherwise authorized by law; every common prostitute wandering in

---

[41] 5 Geo IV cap. 83.

the public streets or public highways, or in any place of public resort, and behaving in a riotous or indecent manner; and every person wandering abroad, or placing himself or herself in any public place, street, highway, court or passage, to beg or gather alms, or causing or procuring or encouraging any child or children so to do, SHALL BE DEEMED AN IDLE AND DISORDERLY PERSON within the true intent and meaning of this Act; and it shall be lawful for any Justice of the Peace to commit such offender (being thereof convicted before him by his own view, or by the confession of such offender, or by the evidence on oath of one of more credible witness or witnesses) to the house of correction, there to be kept to hard labour for any time not exceeding one calender month.

Clause Four [Rogues and Vagabonds]

And be it further enacted, that every person committing any of the offences hereinbefore mentioned, after having been convicted as an idle and disorderly person; every person pretending or professing to tell fortunes, or using any subtle craft, means or device, by palmistry or otherwise, to deceive and impose on any of His Majesty's subjects; every person wandering abroad and lodging in any barn or outhouse, or any deserted or unoccupied building, or in the open air, or under a tent, or in any cart or waggon, not having any visible means of subsistence, and not giving a good account of himself or herself; every person wilfully exposing to view, in any street, road, highway or public place, any obscene print, picture or other indecent exhibition; every person wilfully, openly, lewdly and obscenely exposing his person in any street, road, or public highway, or in the view thereof, or in any place of public resort, with intent to insult any female; every person wandering abroad and endeavouring by the exposure of wounds or deformities to obtain or gather alms; every person going about as a gatherer or collector of alms, or endeavouring to procure charitable contributions of any nature or kind, under any false or fraudulent pretence; every person running away and leaving his wife, or his or her child or children, chargeable, or whereby she or they or any of them shall become chargeable to any parish, township or place; every person playing or betting in any street, road, highway or other open and public place, at or with any table or instrument of gaming, at any game or pretended game of chance; every person having in his or her custody or possession any pick-lock key, crow, jack, bit or other implement, with intent feloniously to break into any dwelling house, warehouse, coach house, stable or outbuilding, or being armed with any gun, pistol, hanger, cutlass, bludgeon or other offensive weapon, or having upon him or her any instrument with intent to commit any felonious act; every person being found in or upon any dwelling house, warehouse, coach house, stable or outhouse, or in any enclosed yard, garden or area, for any unlawful purpose; every suspected person or reputed thief, frequenting any river, canal or navigable stream, dock or basin, or any quay, wharf or warehouse near or adjoining thereto, or any street, highway or place adjacent, with intent to commit felony; and every person apprehended as an idle and disorderly person, and violently resisting any constable or other peace officer so apprehending him or her, and being subsequently convicted of the offence for which he or she shall have been so apprehended, SHALL BE DEEMED A ROGUE AND A VAGABOND, within the true intent and meaning of this Act; and it shall be lawful for any Justice of the Peace to commit such offender (being thereof convicted before him by the confession of such offender, or by the evidence on oath of one or more credible witness or witnesses) to the house of correction, there to be kept to hard labour for any time not exceeding three calender months; and every such pick-lock key, crow, jack, bit and other implement, and every such gun, pistol, hanger, cutlass, bludgeon or other offensive weapon, and every such instrument as aforesaid, shall, by the conviction of the offender, become forfeited to the King's Majesty.

Clause Five [Incorrigible Rogue]

And be it further enacted, that every person breaking or escaping out of any place of legal confinement before the expiration of the term for which he or she shall have been committed or ordered to be confined by virtue of this act; every person committing any offence against this act which shall subject him or her to be dealt with as a rogue and vagabond, such person having been seen at some former time adjudged so to be and duly convicted thereof; and every person apprehended as a rogue and vagabond, and violently resisting any constable or other peace officer so apprehending him or her, and being subsequently convicted of the offence for which he or she shall have been so apprehended, SHALL BE DEEMED AN INCORRIGIBLE ROGUE within the true intent and meaning of this Act; and it shall be lawful for any Justice of the Peace to commit such offender (being thereof convicted before him by the confession of such offender, or by evidence on oath of one or more credible witness or witnesses) to the house of correction, there to remain until the next general or Quarter Sessions of the peace; and every such offender who shall be so committed to the house of correction, shall be there kept to hard labour during the period of his or her imprisonment.

12.3   Vagrancy and Youth in Chester, 1840[42]

Five lads named Ainsworth, George Hughes, Thomas Williams, John Williams and Richard Hall were charged with being implicated in stealing

---

[42] *Chester Chronicle*, 10/1/1840.

two pairs of shoes from a shoe stall under the exchange on Saturday night. The stall belonged to a man named Rowlands and three of the prisoners were seen standing near to it. Immediately afterwards two pairs of shoes were missing. Harrison and Brown, two of the police, went in quest of the parties, and ascertained that Ainsworth had been offering a pair of shoes in pawn at Mr Burton's who refused to take them in. He then observed them all together in Watergate Street Row, when he took them into custody, and found the property on Ainsworth. Evidence was given that connected the whole of them with the transactions and also to the effect that they were idle persons, who followed no occupation, and had no visible means of obtaining a livelihood. Rowlands the person who had lost the property, did not appear, and would not prosecute; therefore they were all five committed under the Vagrant Act to the house of correction for one month, and to be kept to hard labour.

12.4   Vagrancy and Frequent Offenders in Knutsford, 1860[43]

Nancy Robinson, of no occupation, Stockport, was indicted for being an incorrigible rogue and vagabond, at Nether Knutsford [Quarter Sessions] on the 13th September on which day she left the gaol, after serving her prison of imprisonment for a felony committed in this town. Constable Jebb said he apprehended the prisoner at Knutsford, where she was making a great disturbance. She was drunk, very disorderly, and was going about the streets soliciting prostitution. He apprehended her, and lodged her in the lock-ups, where she became still more enraged, smashing everything she could lay her hands on, including a great number of glazed lamps. Mr Douglas, late police officer, proved several convictions against the prisoner, as a thief, rogue and vagabond.

[43] *Stockport Advertiser*, 26/10/1860.

Chapter 6

The Nineteenth-century Police

1   Traditional Policing, 1806[1]

Patrick Colquhoun, a stipendiary magistrate in London from 1792, has received much attention from historians because of his role in establishing the Thames River Police in 1798 and the publication of his ideas in A treatise on the police of the metropolis. *The passage below, taken from this book, typifies a common view of the period that the police needed to be placed on a more professional footing.*

When robberies or burglaries have been committed in or near the metropolis, where the property is of considerable value, the usual method at present, is to apply to the City Magistrates, if in London; or otherwise, to the Justices at one of the Public Offices, and to publish an Advertisement offering a reward on the recovery of articles stolen and the conviction of the offenders.

In many cases of importance, to the reproach of the Police, resource is had to noted and known receivers of stolen goods for their assistance in discovering such offenders, and of pointing out the means by which the property may be recovered. This has on many occasions been productive of a success to the parties who have been robbed, as well as to the ends of public justice for, however lamentable it is to think that magistrates are compelled to have recourse to such expedients, while the present system continues, and while robberies and burglaries are so frequent, without the means of prevention, there is no alternative on many occasions but to employ a thief to catch a thief.

It is indeed so far fortunate, that when the influence of magistrates is judiciously and zealously employed in this way, it is productive in many instances of considerable success, not only in the recovery of property stolen, but also in the detection and punishment of atrocious offenders.

Wherever activity and zeal are manifested on the part of the magistrates, the peace officers, under their immediate direction, seldom fail to exhibit a similar desire to promote the ends of public justice. And when it is

---

[1] P. Colquhoun, *A treatise on the police of the metropolis* (London, 1806), pp. 383–6.

considered that these officers, while they conduct themselves with purity, are truly the safeguards of the community, destined to protect the public against the outrages and lawless depredations of a set of miscreants who are declared enemies of the state, making war upon all ranks of the body politic who have property to lose; they have a fair claim, while they act properly, to be esteemed as "the civil defenders of the lives and properties of the people".

Everything that can heighten in any degree the respectability of the office of constable adds to the security of the state, and the safety of the life and property of every individual.

Under such circumstances, it cannot be sufficiently regretted that these useful constitutional officers, destined for the protection of the public, have been (with a very few exceptions) so little regarded, so carelessly selected, and so ill supported and rewarded for the imminent risks which they run, and the services they perform in the execution of their duty.

The common law, as well as the ancient statutes of the kingdom, has placed extensive powers in the hands of constables and peace officers. They are, in this point of view, to be considered as respectable, and it is the interest of the community that they should support the rank and character in society, which corresponds with the authority with which they are invested. If this were attended to, men of credit and discretion would not be so averse to fill such situations, and those pernicious prejudices that have prevailed in vulgar life and in some degree among the higher ranks in society, with regard to thief-takers, would no longer operate, for it is plain to demonstration that the best laws that ever were made can avail to nothing if the public mind is impressed with an idea that it is a matter of infamy to become the casual or professional agents to carry them into execution.

This absurd prejudice against the office of constable, and the small encouragement which the major part receive, is one of the chief reasons why unworthy characters have filled such situations; and why the public interest has suffered by the increase of crimes.

2   London Police, 1812[2]

Despite the criticisms of commentators such as Colquhoun, not everyone felt that the police were inadequate for the demands placed upon them. In the extract below from a parliamentary report on the London police and watchmen, the dominant emotion is one of calm reflection and there is a recognition of the moves which the existing police had made to improve themselves.

---

[2] *Report on the nightly watch and police of the metropolis, 1812*, P.P. 1812, vol. ii, pp. 95–6.

Your committee first direct their enquiries to the state of the nightly watch. They were induced to pursue this course in their investigations, as well as from a desire to conform to the order in which the several subjects submitted to their consideration are classed by the House in terms of their appointment, as, from conceiving this branch of the subject to be of itself of high importance, and in consequence of late occurrences, to be pressed upon their attention with more urgency than any other.

Had they found the defects in this part of the system of our police to have been such, at this moment, as to have demanded the immediate interposition of the legislature, they would have hastened to have made an early report, but they had the satisfaction of observing that the apprehensions which had been excited had produced such a degree of activity and vigilance in many parishes and districts, and such a conviction that the former means of security was insufficient, that all immediate alarms on this head had been in a great measure removed.

In some parishes, indeed, the zeal and energy of the inhabitants appears to have been most exemplary and meritorious; they have agreed to take upon themselves, in rotation, the duties of superintendents of the nightly watch, to visit and inspect the watchhouses, the constables, beadles, patrols and stationary watchmen, so as to ensure the perpetual vigilance and activity of every class of persons on duty during the night, within their parish. And a system of the nightly watch, thus introduced by the voluntary exertions of the householders, has been so effectual, that your committee think it necessary only to recommend such measures to be enforced by legislative enactment, as would give an uniformity and permanency to such a system, and secure its activity by a constant superintendence and control.

Your committee finding, that, owing to these and similar means of security, no immediate dangers were to be apprehended, were desirous, indeed they felt it to be their duty, to endeavour to obtain a more detailed as well as a more comprehensive view of the various circumstances which influence and affect the state of the metropolis as to its police, the manner in which the local limits are divided, the various laws applicable to such divisions, the various public bodies, or individuals in whom powers are vested, for the purpose of watching over and regulating the means by which its security and good order is to be maintained, and the mode in which such powers are executed.

3   Calls for Police Reform, 1828[3]

The following extract from the conservative journal the Quarterly Review *argues that the police had failed to keep pace with the social changes of the recent past*

[3]   *Quarterly Review* **36**, 1828, pp. 494–6.

and that a new power was needed if the law was to be imposed effectively. In its proposals, the term "police" is used in a general and ambitious sense to cover prevention, detection, and pre-trial adjudication.

We have no sort of doubt that the primary defect in our present system, and the proximate cause of the immense majority of criminal acts committed, is no other than our want of an organized power – a criminal force throughout the kingdom, with functions well defined, vigilant, active, and prompt to give effect to whatever authorities are recognized by the constitution for the repression of crime. It is the safety of sinning that is now the great scourge of society. With so many chances of escape, punishment, however severe, loses half its terrors, its intimidative effects being in the ration of its certainty.

The insufficiency of the existing means for the repression of crimes cannot justly be ascribed to a want of judicial power, since there is so much that still lies dormant in our books, but rather to an indiscriminate adherence to ancient forms and institutions, not as they were, in their origin, vigorous, and even more than adequate to their occasion, but as they now are, in their decay, and when they have become the mere shadows of antiquity. When we look at the mutual suretyship by which every man became responsible by the state for the conduct of his neighbour; at the hue and cry with which the suspected felon was pursued with horse and horn from vill to vill;[4] at the power of the sheriff who could rouse and arm a whole county in an instant; and feel that all these have passed away, and nothing has been devised in their place. When we consider, too, that the same judicial apparatus that was in use in the reign of Edward III, for the preservation of order and upholding public and private security, is now, when worn out and utterly inadequate, employed to control a population of nearly thirteen millions, one-tenth of which is in a state of pauperism, and consequently on the confines of crime, who can for a moment remain insensible to the necessity of remodelling the police in this country?

Police, in our view of the subject, when rightly understood, its limits and functions well defined, is the base on which the men's liberties, properties, and social existence repose. Its functions may be divided into three branches, the executive, the ante-judicial, and the judicial. The first is partly dependent, and partly independent, of the two last; its operations are preventative or protective; those of the antejudicial, detective; of the judicial, corrective. The character of the preventative should be watchfulness, constant but cautious, over the first approaches to crime, or, rather, its earliest manifestations, so as to leave to the evil disposed no hope of accomplishing their wicked designs. The principle of the preventive branch

---

[4] "Vill" was a traditional legal term for township.

of its operations, strictly so termed, for all penal laws may be said, by intimidation, to prevent, is founded on the good that thereby accrues to the offender, to the subject and to the state: to the offender, as being the more merciful; to the subject, the more just, ensuring safety to his person and property (for the penalties that are consequent on crime, are, in their nature, intimidative and not compensative); to the state, as more honourable and economical, first, from an improvement in its moral condition, and last, by diminishing the number of offenders, and the necessity of long, and to the country expensive, confinement. The instant and preventive has failed to interpose itself between the imagining and execution of an act, the detective steps in, and its service is of a threefold kind: first, to secure the offenders, whether principles or accessories; second, to find out and collect the scattered pieces of evidence that tend to establish their guilt; third, to search for, and procure the stolen property. The character of the detective[5] is promptitude, as, by the smallest delay, all traces of the offender and proofs of his guilt may be lost. When the detective has succeeded in its object, it submits the results of its operations to the judicial, the acts of which are also threefold: judgements preliminary, appellatory, and final. By the first is determined the nature of the offence, as constituted by the evidence; if a provable one, but not within its competence to decide, its business is to condense and arrange the proofs, and hand them over, together with the criminal, to be dealt with by the superior tribunals; and in this light, police may be considered as the handmaid to the criminal courts. If the offence is within its competence, it determines the truth of falsehood of the allegations, and discharges or punishes the offenders accordingly, subject, in all cases, to certain judicial formalities, and, in some, to the revision of higher authorities.

The injuries, which it is the duty of police to avert or punish, arise in two ways: first, from natural causes, such as fires, inundations, storms, contagions, etc.; secondly, from human; and these are classed according to the degree of moral turpitude; there are some offences, which are universally denominated crimes or misdemeanours, and as universally considered fit objects of public vengeance. There are others of a more trivial nature, caused, whether intentionally or otherwise, either by mischievous, rash, or negligent conduct, or by the want of regard to conveniency, decency, or good order. These last are particularly the objects of the judicial branch of the police – they are such as are of hourly occurrence, more or less interfering with the enjoyment of our rights, and but for some direct power, to which much discretion must unavoidably be allowed, immediately to punish them, would infallibly escape punishment altogether.

---

[5] This is one of the earliest uses of the term "detective".

4 Rural Policing, 1835[6]

In calling for reform of the police, the following petition from the magistrates of Monmouthshire to the Royal Commission on County Rates highlights a feeling that crime was increasing. In contrast to the document above, however, there is also a sense of panic at the nature of these new crimes. Conditions of pay and the quality of superintendence are again emphasized.

To the Honourable the Commons of the United Kingdom of Great Britain and Ireland, in parliament assembled. The humble petition of the under-signed acting magistrates within the several districts or divisions of Newport, Bedwelty, Christchurch and Caerlon, comprising 47 parishes in the county of Monmouthshire. Humbly showeth,

That several serious crimes and depredations have of late been committed, and are daily increasing to an alarming extent, in the different parishes, townships, and hamlets within the above-named divisions. That the parochial and other constables within the said divisions are for the most part incompetent to the discharge of their duties imposed on them, and that able and competent persons are unwilling to serve the office, in consequence of the loss of time and expense incurred in so doing; for which little or no remuneration is allowed, though they are usually selected from those classes who are indebted to their daily labour for their means of support. That, from the manner in which they are chosen and called upon to act, they cannot be put under any general system of efficient control, or be rendered subservient to the purposes of preventing offences, or detecting them when committed. That in general they merely consider their duty to be to act in executing warrants, or serving summonses where required, on which occasions they are entitled to a small fee, but are not usually paid for any other trouble they may take, or for any expense or loss of time they may incur.

That it is highly expedient to adopt some general system of preventative police throughout the country, and to have in each division of the country at least one active and intelligent officer, who should under the direction of the magistrates, have the general superintendence of the constables throughout the division; and to whom, as well as to the constables, a fair and proper remuneration should be made out of the poor rates in each parish or the county stock in general; by which means able and efficient men may be induced to undertake the duty, and to qualify themselves for the proper discharge of it.

---

[6] *Royal commission on county rates*, P.P. 1836, vol. xxvii.

Wherefore your petitioners humbly pray that your Honourable House will be pleased to adopt such measures as to your wisdom shall see fit for forming an efficient police throughout the country for the prevention of crime and detection of offenders, and for placing the same on your petitioners, as in duty bound, will ever pray.

5 The Cheshire Police Acts, 1829–52[7]

The Cheshire Police Act was an example of reform that did not rely on the Metropolitan Police as a model. The Cheshire magistrates had attempted to create a force appropriate to their locality by using the traditional divisions of the county (hundreds) as units of organization. Each hundred was to have its own superintendent (special high constable) who was to look over those constables appointed and report to the local magistrates on their duties and the state of crime in their area. The passage below is taken from the evidence of Edwin Corbett, one of the Cheshire magistrates, to the 1852 Select Committee on Police. He explains why the county had not chosen to have a chief constable and defends the Cheshire model in the face of some critical questions.

Will you state what the system of police was, under that first Act?

Under this first Act, and it is similar now, we have no general superintendent of police, but we have one special high constable for each hundred, or each petty sessional division. In the hundred of Macclesfield, there are three high constables; that is a very populous manufacturing part of the county. The petty sessional divisions are divided into three, and there is one for each division; we have one high constable for each of the other hundreds in the county. The appointment of the constable is rested upon the recommendation of the magistrates in Petty Sessions to the Quarter Sessions, and then they are appointed for certain townships, but at the time of the passing of this Act there was considerable jealousy on the part of some gentlemen in Cheshire. In 1829 there was a good deal of opposition made to the bill, in consequence of their thinking it not right that the townships should be charged for the payment of the constables except with their own consent. The impression was that there should be limited payment in each township. I beg to observe, that the parishes in Cheshire are many of them extremely large; the townships are similar to parishes in other counties, in every respect; the poor rates, highway rates, and everything else, there being a jealousy in charging the township, without the approbation of the township itself. The payment of each township

---

[7] *Evidence of Edwin Corbett to the select committee on a uniform system of police in England, Wales and Scotland, P.P. 1852/3, vol. xxxvi.*

was limited to £20 pounds, and the consequence was that the force was very ineffective and I can show by the population and the value of the property in particular townships, some townships were unfairly charged, to make up the salary of £50 a year to the constable. Therefore, I suggested to the magistrates in Quarter Sessions last year, that it would be very desirable to pay the constables by a hundred rate. I can state many instances where it operated very unfavourably; and perhaps it would be as well that I should state the particulars now before I go on, if it is the wish of the committee. I can show an instance where a township is valued at a very large sum, namely, at £63,000 a year; and another township is attached to that which is only assessed at £16,000; it would be impossible to put any rate upon that township proportionately to make up the salary for the constable. Therefore, we went to Parliament last year, and we obtained another Act which makes it a hundred rate, and not a township rate, and we find it works remarkably well. It was originally paid out of the poor rate; now by the hundred rate, the hundreds are assessed according to their proportion, and I think it seems to have given very general satisfaction as a system of working the police. I have got a letter from the clerk of the peace which he wrote to me unmasked, in which he says that it acts a great deal better than where the constables are under a superintendent for the whole county. They are therefore separate jurisdictions, the high constables being of course in constant communication with the magistrates of the hundred. The police of every hundred is entirely a separate thing, the constables under the Act of 1829 were forced to be appointed to particular townships. Now they are appointed for the whole hundred, and the magistrates appoint the particular districts to which they are immediately to give their attention; for instance, in some cases, two constables will have a jurisdiction in the same township. We do that from local knowledge, so as to make the police as effective as possible.

In your opinion you would prefer a system of constabulary separate in each hundred in your county, under a superintendent, to having a consolidated county police under one head?

I think it decidedly operates better.

Will you state to the committee the reasons why you think so?

I think you have always a responsible officer upon the spot, and a man who is acting under one general superintendent in the county is not in a position to be so responsible to his superiors, though there should be a superintendent of police, for not doing his duty I do not think he would be so independent a person. He could not act upon his own authority if he was under a superintendent.

Did you say that you thought the circumstances of the county of Chester rendered this institution admissible, although it might not be admissible elsewhere?

I think it is the best system of the police, in my opinion, that can be established.

Are you of opinion that in an entirely rural county a division of hundreds, with a separate police in each division would be better than having the police all under one authority?

I think so because the officers are all under the superintendence of resident magistrates. From the reports which the men are obliged to make, the magistrates see whether those people are active and attend to their duty. They see the magistrates constantly, and I think they are better acquainted with what is going on than one superintendent of police in a county could be with what his subordinates are doing.

Do you mean practically that magistrates are acquainted with all the movements of these constables from week to week?

No, not exactly; I know, as far as my hundred goes, we hear from time to time whether the constable is visiting his different posts from different parties, and from personal inquiries.

Do you know whether your county's patrol at night?

Yes, they do.

Who ascertains whether they perform their duties at night?

The only way in which it is done is this: they are obliged to keep regular routes of what they do, and of such parties as they meet; they are received by the high constables every week, and if he has any reason to believe they are not doing their duty, he then would go to those parties whom the constable says he has met upon the road; that is frequently done. I mean from different residents in different parts of the country, where the constables have attended upon their duties. They go round to farm houses. An instance was mentioned to me the other week, that a man had not locked up his cheese room; fortunately there were no rogues there, but there might have been; and the constable called him up, and told him of it.

6 Police Reform, 1852–3[8]

Edwin Chadwick was one of three commissioners who wrote an 1839 report on establishing a rural constabulary. He was an unashamed advocate of rationalization and centralization who was also active in other areas of reform, particularly public health and the poor law. In the passage below Chadwick is found reflecting on the need for reform and the changes that had taken place since the proposals of 1839 had become law. Predictably, he laments the fact that not all areas had adopted the provisions of the Act.

Were you one of the commissioners in 1839 who were appointed to inquire into the best means for establishing a county force?

---

[8] *Evidence of Edwin Chadwick to the select committee on a uniform system of police in England, Wales and Scotland*, P.P. 1852–3, vol. xxxvi.

I was. In 1835, when were carrying out the organization of the parishes into unions, under the Poor Law Amendment Act, there were frequent riots, instigated, as was ascertained, by those who thought they would lose money by the change of system; as by small farmers, who expected they would have to give more wages on the discontinuance of the allowance system, and by small shopkeepers, who expected the loss of the parish supplies. There were riots in Suffolk, Sussex, and several other counties. On these occasions, we were requested to send down a force for the preservation of the peace, and the ground of the application initially was, the utter inefficiency of the local constabulary. On these occasions it was my duty to go to the Home Office and I generally had to communicate with the Home Secretary to make arrangements for sending a sufficient force, generally of police, sometimes of military, or of coast guardsmen. This experience of local deficiencies of means for the preservation of peace (of which, indeed, we had previous experience in the agricultural riots and fires of 1830) as well as for the ordinary service of a constable in various counties, appeared to make it my duty to represent Lord John Russell, who was then Home Secretary, the importance of the issuing a commission to inquire whether the like deficiencies prevailed throughout the country. In consequence of these representations a commission was issued in 1836 to the present Speaker of the House of Commons, the late lamented public officer, Sir Charles Rowan, and to myself. The result of the investigations of that commission was the recommendation of the establishment of a paid constabulary or police force in the counties of England and Wales. It was one of the primary conditions of that recommendation, that by whatsoever county it was adopted, it should be a constabulary for the whole county, including the boroughs. We stated emphatically "that any administration of a paid constabulary on a less scale than for a whole county, does not comprehend a sufficiently wide basis for ultimate and complete efficiency and economy, either as to the county regarded separately, or in its general relation to the rest of the kingdom."

Have you had occasion to observe the practical operation of the 2 & 3 Vict. c. 93 which is commonly called the Rural Police Act, since it was passed?[9]

I have had frequent occasion; I was much consulted by magistrates about its introduction into several counties, and I have, of course, watched its operation with great interest. Moreover, in taking part in the consideration of the new local administrative organization to observe the deficiencies of organization and action of the police force in towns for sanitary as well as other purposes.

Has the result of that Act been in accordance with the views and the expectations of the commissioners?

---

[9] This Act was passed in 1839. It was also known as the County Constabulary Act and the County Police Act.

They have. I mean that, considering the measure has been carried out partially, and exclusively of the proper centres of the working of a police – the towns – the working of the fragmentitious county forces, has, on the whole, been much more satisfactory than we anticipated.

In what respect?

Most prominently first, in the immediate and marked difference between those districts where there is a police force, and those where there is none; and in the next place, although we were prepared for the introduction of much eventual economy by the action of a properly constituted force, we were not prepared for the extent to which even the partial county forces instituted have been, by the collateral services which they have rendered, been made nearly, if not entirely, self-supporting.

You think it is a defective measure, because it has not been uniform?

Yes: because it was adopted in only part of the counties; because it was not arranged for concurrent action with contiguous counties or upon any general system; but, above all, because within the counties, the most important centres and portions of a properly acting county force, the town forces, are left separate and uncombined; which state of separation commonly means, a state of hostility as well as inaction for any general purposes. I am clearly of opinion that, if the proper amalgamation of the borough forces were effected with the rest of the county forces, the proportionate expenses might be lessened, whilst, without any increase of expense, the efficiency and public service of the force would be more than doubled. I am very confident that, even now, if there was an amalgamation of the forces existing in some of the counties where the County Constabulary Act has been adopted, very small, if any, additional forces would be required, most probably none eventually, for the purposes of penal administration.

To take the example of the county of Lancaster: there are now in the county only 355 policemen, but there are, in Manchester, between four and five hundred; in Liverpool, upwards of 700, and in the whole of the county, according to the last returns, a force of nearly 2000 police constables. By the end of the last returns there were 1393 policemen in the boroughs, and in the whole county 1918 men. There were originally 500 policemen in the county under the County Constabulary Act but at the spring sessions of 1842 the magistrates, acting no doubt on such information as their own districts, exhaustive of the larger towns, gave them, which was such as the event displayed, determined to reduce the force to 350, and on the first day of the month the reduction took place. From the 9th to the 12th of the same month there was a general outbreak in the towns, which spread throughout the whole of the rural districts, put all the property at the mercy of the mobs, which only wanted leaders with ability commensurate with the powers at their disposal to have done widespread and irreparable mischief. Now I was in the county at the time, and I observed the outbreak as a constabulary force commissioner; and I had no doubt whatsoever, that had the whole of the force in the county been under one proper organization, that every large town, which was then driven to rely on military force, would have been secure without any addition, and that the outbreak would have been repressed at its commencement.

To advert to a more recent and smaller instance, the borough of Blackburn had been under the county police force, when 22 policemen were stationed there. It obtained a town council, where they reduced the force to eleven. At the recent election riots, disgraceful to the whole country, occurred; the town was in possession of the mob, and it became necessary to send for a military force. Now the 22 county policemen, if they had remained there, would, in all probability, have suppressed the riots at the outset. But if they had not sufficed, a hundred more might have been sent, as similar forces were sent with effect to Bury and Wigan from the existing county force.

7 Police Violence, 1829, 1831 and 1843

The new police were poorly trained and up to a third of the early recruits left their respective forces within a year. A symptom of this was the accusation of over-zealous behaviour almost as soon as the first officers set foot on the streets of London. The three extracts, taken from contrasting sources, describe the types of incident which produced such sentiments. The first highlights the fate of a "respectable" man whose actions were misinterpreted. The second suggests that a working-class man had died as a result of police brutality, alleging that the law did not protect the poor in such circumstances. The third gives a satirical sketch of a superintendent coaching his officers to pick on those who could not defend themselves.

7.1 Incident in Pimlico, 1829[10]

On Sunday morning, between nine and ten o'clock, a most disgraceful occurrence took place at Pimlico, by two of the new policemen dragging a most respectable gentleman to the watchhouse, and from the effects of the treatment he received it is very improbable he will ever recover. The name of the person alluded to is Mr Hudson, an elderly gentleman, about 70 years of age, residing at 14, Ranelagh Grove, clerk of the works of the Royal Mews, Pimlico. He has lately been in very ill health, which has brought on a temporary aberration of mind, but of this he was fast recovering and, although it was considered necessary some person should be with him, he was perfectly harmless and nothing like violent in his disposition. On Sunday morning he went out to take a walk with his son, and he

---

[10] *The Times*, 6/10/1829.

had a favourite dog with him when, passing by a public house, several persons came out with another dog, which immediately flew at Mr Hudson's dog. The old man laid hold of his dog and endeavoured to take it away, when he was pushed down and ill-treated by several men from the public house and two of the new police came up and seized him, alleging that he was drunk. The son represented to the policemen who his father was and the nature of his infirmity, and requested them to make inquiry in the neighbourhood, where he was well known, as to the truth of his statement. The old gentleman became greatly excited by the rough treatment he received and was literally dragged along the street until his arm was nearly dislocated. The son, indignant at his father's treatment, declared to the officers that his father had not tasted anything but water for the last three months, and offered to take his father to the watchhouse himself, as he would go quietly with him. This they refused and threatened to knock him down if he dared to interfere with them in the execution of their duty. The son, finding all expostulation in vain, begged they would allow him to call a coach, which was consented to, and they all drove to the watchhouse together, where charge was given. Mr Frith, a respectable inhabitant of Smith's Square, Westminster, offered himself as bail for Mr Hudson's appearance, which was refused, and a representative of the circumstances was made to Mr Gregorie, the resident magistrate at Queen Square, of Mr Hudson's state of health, which had greatly increased in violence since he had been taken to the watchhouse. Mr Gregorie immediately sent Hull, one of the officers of Queen Square, to order his immediate liberation, which mandate, it is needless to say, was complied with. Mr Hudson was removed to his house in a most dreadful condition, being in a state of raving madness from the treatment he had received. It was found necessary immediately to call in medical aid, and he was visited by Mr Nursey, a surgeon of his majesty's household, and also Sir Gilbert Blane. It was also found necessary to put on a strait waistcoat, and lash him, in which state he remained yesterday. Mr Firth came to Queen-Square office, and informed Mr Gregorie of the state of Mr Hudson's health, and the occasion of his non-appearance, and we understand the charge against him was erased.

7.2   Alleged murder by one of the new police[11]

On Tuesday evening, an inquisition was taken at St Thomas's Hospital, on view of the body of Charles Sweet, aged 28, alleged to have received his death blow from a police constable of S division, on the day of the coronation. William Clarke deposed, that he knew the deceased, who was a brewer's servant. On the day of the coronation they went together to see

---

[11]   *Poor Man's Guardian*, 24/9/1831.

the procession, and about three o'clock in the afternoon arrived opposite the Horse Guards, where a great crowd of persons had assembled to see their Majesties pass. Witness and the deceased stood in the foremost rank, having a dense multitude in the rear. A number of police constables of the S division were stationed at this spot, with whom the people conversed in a familiar and good-humoured way, so that no violence was apprehended. Having stood in this situation for about twenty minutes, a detachment of Life Guards advanced through the gates towards the people, when the constables instantly commenced thrusting the people back with their staves, and striking over the heads in a most violent and dangerous manner. Witness and deceased found it impossible to move back in consequence of the pressure behind them; notwithstanding this, a police constable came up, and without any previous warning struck the deceased a violent blow on the head with his staff, and the poor fellow fell as if shot, into his arms. With such force was the blow given, that the deceased's hat was completely cut through, and his forehead laid open, from which the blood gushed in a stream. Witness, with assistance, bore the deceased out of the crowd (who cried shame on the policeman), and took him to the nearest surgeon, when the wound having been dressed he was carried to the Westminster Hospital.

Witness, in the following morning (having taken the policeman's number and letter, 116 S), preferred a complaint before the Commissioners at Whitehall, when, after a long investigation, the policeman, whose name is William Kinsman, was dismissed the service, and the deceased was presented with 40s, by way of compensation for the injury.

The deceased after remaining a week in the hospital was discharged as cured, and he went home to his wife. Witness called to see him several times afterwards, when he complained of the effects of the blow, and appeared by no means recovered. After he had been at home about a week, he became so completely delirious that it was found necessary to remove him to this hospital – Mr Richard Whitfield, apothecary to the institution, stated, that the deceased was admitted on the 22nd inst. He examined him, and found that he was labouring under erysipelas[12] of the face and neck, attended with strong delirium, and notwithstanding every attention was paid him, the delirium continued to increase, and he died on Sunday. There were the remains of a wound on the left side of the head which appeared healed. The head was examined after death, but no fracture of the scull could be detected, and there was nothing in the appearance of the brain which could sufficiently account for his death.

Coroner: *"Do you think erysipelas was brought on by the blow?"*

Witness: "I should think not, as I understand the deceased was discharged from the Westminster Hospital as completely cured."

---

[12] Erysipelas is a skin disease which causes red inflammation, headaches and nausea.

Coroner: *"Does not erysipelas frequently arise from local injuries long after they have been received?"*

Witness: "Not in a case like this, where a patient has been discharged as cured."

On hearing this sentence, the first witness (Clarke) stepped forward and stated that it was his firm conviction that the deceased had never recovered from the blow, and that shortly before he became delirious he had complained to him of its effects. The coroner here suggested to the jury the propriety of adjourning, if they thought further medical advice necessary, which might easily be procured from the Westminster Hospital. They might also have the testimony of the deceased's wife if they thought it requisite. A juryman here said that it would save a deal of trouble if they could come to a verdict at once. He, for one, was satisfied by Mr Whitfield's evidence, that the deceased had died a natural death, but expressed a conviction that the deceased had been treated with unnecessary violence. The witness Clarke, upon hearing this announcement, quitted the room, declaring that the deceased had been murdered, and that he had been wasting his time for nothing.

Here was a jury of "middle men" sitting in judgment on a "property protector", who had murdered a mere working man. Had his poor victim been a "lord", would these jurymen have been so satisfied without further medical advice and investigation; had he been a "middle man", would they have come "to a verdict at once to save a deal of trouble"? Had the murderer (for murderer he certainly was, whether legal or not, direct or indirect) been a poor working man, and his victim a gentleman, who had rudely pushed him by, and wrongfully provoked his blow, how much advice would they not have required – how much trouble would they not have taken to fix a criminal charge upon him – though but as an example? Good God! What is there in us that property alone can make our lives either dear or valueless? Curses on thee, demon, at every turn thy damned tyranny arrests our horror!!

7.3   Hackney Police, 1843[13]

Hackney witnessed a series of splendid police manoeuvres a few days ago, under the direction of Mr Superintendent Fallaloo. After the whole of the lanthorn evolutions had been gone through, the cape exercise was splendidly executed. A stuffed figure was then introduced, to enable the men to go through the usual manoeuvres with a person found drunk and incapable of taking care of himself. The figure was first let to fall heavily on its face, and the police then executed the beautiful kicking movement, as if to

---

[13] *Punch* **6**, 1843, p. 132.

rouse the drunken man in a state of consciousness. After this the whole of the staff exercise was performed on the head and body, with great spirit. Orders were then given to raise the figure, which was done in good style, followed by the usual evolution of letting it fall heavily down again. The legs and arms were then cleverly seized, and the figure carried off (with the head hanging downwards) to the station house – the police beating time with their staves on the legs, arms and knuckles. At the end of this manoeuvre the men were complimented by Superintendent Fallaloo, who finished the review by directing a grand charge on an apple-stall. The attack lasted only two minutes, and was a most brilliant affair, ending in the demolition of the basket, the distribution of the contents, and the capture of the fruit-woman.

8   The Growth of the Metropolitan Police, 1856–70

The following passages give two descriptions of the Metropolitan Police, one in 1856 and the other in 1870. Both suggest that the police had evolved considerably since the original legislation of 1829. They highlight new controls and organized lines of communication but also the local peculiarities of police work and the constant demands on the policeman's time.

8.1   The Metropolitan Police, 1856[14]

At the present time the Metropolitan Police Force consists of a chief commissioner, Sir Richard Mayne, two assistant commissioners, Captain Labalmondiere and Captain Harris, 18 superintendents, 133 inspectors, 625 sergeants, and 4954 constables, making a total of all ranks of 5734. The machinery by which this comparatively small force is enabled to watch by night and day every ally, street, and square of this vast metropolis, nay, tries every accessible door and window of its 400,000 houses, patrols 90 square miles of country, exercises a surveillance over the 8000 reputed thieves who prey upon its inhabitants, and keeps in awe the 40,000 or 50,000 people who form "the uneasy classes" of the metropolis, is not very complicated. The Metropolitan Police district extends from Charing Cross 15 miles in every direction, and includes the whole of Middlesex and large portions of Surrey, Hertfordshire, Essex, Kent, Buckinghamshire and Berkshire, for which seven counties the Commissioners are magistrates and the police are sworn constables. The River Thames is also under its jurisdiction, from Chelsea to Barking Creek, including all its wharves, docks, landing-places and dockyards. The entire district has a circumference of 90 miles, and extends over an area of upwards of 700 square miles, 100 of which,

---

[14] *Quarterly Review* **99**, 1856, pp. 164–7.

forming what is called the interior area, is covered with our great Babel of brick and mortar. This wide extent of ground is mapped out into 18 divisions, each of which is watched by a detachment of men, varying in number according to the extent of the area, the exposed nature of the property, or the density of the population.

Each division is separated into subdivisions, the subdivisions into sections, and, last of all, the sections into beats. Of the main divisions, A, although one of the smallest in the area, is by far, the most important: it is the seat of the central authority located at Scotland Yard. Its police are much finer men (taller on the average than the Guards), and their duties are more responsible than those of any other division. They attend upon the Sovereign, the Parliament, the theatres, the parks, and all other places of public resort, such as Epsom and Ascot races, the flower shows, Crystal Palace, etc. The A division is, in fact, to the general body of the Metropolitan Police what the Guards are to the army. To enable it to perform those extra duties, it has a reserve force of 250 men, drafted off on ordinary occasions in companies of fifty each to the B, C, D, G and M divisions; upon this reserved force it draws when necessary.

The other divisions are pretty much alike in the nature of their duties, which are simply those of watching. Certain modifications, however, arise from the character of their districts; thus a constable on duty at Whitechapel, if suddenly removed to Westminster or Marylebone, would find himself considerably at fault, inasmuch as a familiarity with fights in courts,[15] disputes with tramps, and the coarse language of low lodging-houses, is not a good school for the amenities required among a more fashionable population. In all the divisions exactly the same organization is maintained and the same amount of arduous work is performed. Two-thirds of the entire force is on duty from nine or ten in the evening till five or six in the morning. Not long since the night police were condemned to patrol the streets for nine hours, without sitting down or even leaning their weary limbs against any support. This severe labour was found incompatible with the maintenance of due vigilance towards the end of the watch. The men are, therefore, now kept on duty only eight hours. Day work is divided into reliefs, and extends from six in the morning to nine at night. Notwithstanding its greater severity, there are men who prefer the stolid unimpeded walk in the night, in which they go through their work like machines, to the more bustling and exciting day-patrol. The sergeants or inspectors make the round of the districts to see that the constables are duly parading their beats.

If a door or window is discovered in an unsafe condition, its insecurity is immediately made known to the inmates; and if the constable fails to

---

[15] i.e. inner courtyards.

detect the circumstance during his tour, and it is afterwards observed by his sergeant or the succeeding constable, he is reported and fined for his neglect. Continued inattention is visited by dismissal. Offences of every kind are severely punished, as appears from the fact that, between the years 1850 and 1856, 1276 policemen were turned out of the force. Of these 68 were criminally convicted. Thus the men are kept up to their work, and collusions with thieves are rendered exceedingly difficult. Every morning a sheet of "Occurrences" is forwarded to the Chief Commissioner at Scotland Yard, which contains the full particulars of all matters worthy of notice which have taken place during the night throughout the metropolis, and a record of all property lost or stolen, from a gold pin to a chest of plate, is kept in the same central establishment.

In case any affair of unusual importance occurs, a murder or a great robbery, the intelligence is conveyed by the constable who first becomes cognizant of it to the central station of his division; from this point the news is radiated by policemen, carrying what are termed route-papers, or papers of particulars of the offence, on the backs of which are marked the hour at which they were received at the different divisions through which they passed. In this manner, information can be circulated in two hours to all the stations, excepting those belonging to the exterior of suburban districts. In these reports are given the names of the constables who were on the beats in which the offences took place, the sergeants in charge of the sections, and the names of the constables whose particular business it was to trace the offenders as far as possible. We understand, however, that the electronic telegraph is now shooting its nerve-like threads to all the divisional stations in the metropolis, and, when the new agent is brought to bear, the communication will be almost instantaneous. Thus, in the case of robbery, every constable will be made acquainted with the particulars without a moment's delay, and the police-net will be thrown at one cast over the entire metropolis. Thieves will no longer be able to get away with their plunder, ere a hue and cry has been raised after the property. In cases of riot of a formidable nature, the telegraph will be able to concentrate 5000 men in a couple of hours upon any spot within five miles of Charing Cross.

Towards the outskirts of the metropolis, in the exterior or suburban districts, the widely scattered constables chiefly perform the duties of a rural police. The great distances they have to traverse necessitates the use of horses. Here, accordingly, we find the mounted police, the successors of the old horse-patrol established in 1805. The strength of this force, men and officers included, is only 120. They are furnished with powerful nags, and are armed with swords and pistols. Indeed, the foot-police, whose beats lie in unfrequented rural districts, are allowed side arms – a precaution which the fate of the policeman, who was brutally murdered in a field at Dagenham, in Essex, some years since, proved to be by no means unnecessary.

8.2   The Growing Duties of the Metropolitan Police, 1870[16]

Although the primary object of the Metropolitan Police was the establishment of an efficient day and night patrol, the organization of so well-disciplined a body of active, steady, and intelligent men, spread over the whole metropolis, was found so convenient as to induce the authorities to call upon them from time to time to undertake new duties, with a view to the improved convenience, comfort, and security of the inhabitants; and it is not saying too much to aver that they have, on the whole, performed them with discretion, judgement and efficiency.

Among the more important of such new duties entrusted to the police is the regulation of the traffic of the metropolis. The increase in the number of carriages, cabs, omnibuses, vans, and vehicles of all kinds, has been so great of late years that, without the most careful regulation, the principal thoroughfares would, for the greater part of each day, be the scene of disorder, danger, and inextricable confusion. As it is, the principal thoroughfares are crowded with traffic from morning till night, and being for the most part insufficient in width, they can only be kept clear by dint of constant attention on the part of the police.

As might be expected, the greatest glut of traffic is in the thoroughfares leading to and from the city – not fewer than three quarters of a million of persons entering it daily, mostly for purposes of business. The pressure is greatest towards the centre, and where the thoroughfares are the narrowest – at the Mansion House, in the Poultry, at Temple Bar, in Holborn, at Aldgate, and especially on London Bridge. About 60,000 persons cross the bridge daily on foot, and over 25,000 vehicles; and it is only by the constables stationed at the ends of the bridge, by which it is divided into four distinct streams passing in opposite directions, that the thoroughfare is kept clear; though, notwithstanding all the care that can be taken, blocks are still of frequent and unavoidable occurrence.

Since the abolition of the office of Registrar of Hackney Carriages, the regulation of the public conveyances of the metropolis has also been entrusted to the Chief Commissioner in Scotland Yard, under whose direction six Inspectors of Public Carriages perform the duties pertaining to the office, as prescribed by the various Acts. They inspect all carriages plying for hire, all omnibuses and cabs (of which there are over 7000), and ascertain that they are in a fit condition for public use. The Commissioner licenses the drivers and conductors, on proof of good character being produced, as well as the watermen at carriage standings; and he also fixes the standings for hackney carriages. All property left in public carriages must immediately be taken by the drivers and conductors to the office in Scotland Yard, where it may be reclaimed by the public. In 1868, the number of persons

---

[16] *Quarterly Review* **129**, 1870, pp. 102–5.

informed against because of violations of the law – such as furious driving, cruelty to horses, demanding more than the legal fare, want of proper license or ticket, causing improper obstruction of thoroughfare, and such like offences – was 4785, and in 4166 of the cases convictions were obtained.

Another duty of the police is the inspection of common lodging-houses under the Act of 1851. All cases requiring attention are reported to the Commissioner for instructions. In 1868, proceedings were taken in 59 cases, in 49 of which convictions were obtained.

The police have also of late years been charged with carrying out the Act for abating the smoke nuisance, in which their labours have been attended with marked success. Since the passing of the Act in 1853, 15,335 cases of nuisance have been reported by the police, in 11,405 of which the nuisance was abated when the proprietor was cautioned by order of the Commissioner or when alterations had been made in the furnaces after examination by the inspecting engineer. It was found neces-sary to prosecute in 1827 cases, in 1635 of which convictions were obtained, and fines levied varying from 1 shilling and costs to £40. But there were 505 cases still pending at the end of 1869. The nuisance of smoke has thus been greatly abated not only on the land, but also on the river.

Another howling nuisance, as well as a great cause of waste amongst the poorer classes, which the police have of late years been called upon to abate, has been the nuisance of dogs – fighting dogs, rat dogs, curs and mongrels. In the course of fifteen months, ending the 28th of February last, they succeeded in seizing no fewer than 20,871 of these animals, 12,257 of which were destroyed. Of the remainder, 4644 were restored to their owners; 3649 were sold to the Dogs' Home, Holloway, at two pence per head; 270 were sold by auction; and 51 escaped.

Another duty of the police is to take up lost and missing persons, and restore them to their friends. Of 5195 persons reported as lost or missing in the metropolis district in 1868, 2805 were so restored. They were also instru-mental in the course of last year in restoring lost property to the owners, of the value of £21,924, independent of stolen property, or property left in metropolitan stage and hackney carriages, the amount of which was con-siderably greater. Last year also, the police carried to the hospitals 1347 cases of street and other accidents, besides 732 persons suffering from other causes. And in 1868 they were instrumental in preventing not fewer than 324 suicides.

9   Police Charge Book, 1868[17]

One of the most important activities for the police within the criminal justice system was the arrest of offenders. Giving a complete record of all those arrested by Chester Police during the first three weeks of June, 1868, Table 6.1 reveals

---

[17] Chester Police Force, *Police Receiving Book*, DPO/5, Chester City Record Office.

Table 6.1 Chester Police Charge Book, 1868

Date	Day	Time	Age	Occupation	Charge	Sentence
1 June	Monday	12.00 a.m.	47	miller	Drunk and Disorderly	Fined 5s
1 June	Monday	1.00 a.m.	29	labourer	Assault on Wife	Adjourned
1 June	Monday	4.00 p.m.	27	labourer	Assault	Fined 10s
1 June	Monday	4.00 p.m.	45	widow	Assault	Discharged
1 June	Monday	7.00 p.m.	23	baker	Desertion	To join Army
2 June	Tuesday	12.00 a.m.	20	prostitute	Being a Common Prostitute	Imprisoned 7 days
2 June	Tuesday	1.00 a.m.	21	clerk	Malicious Damage to Property	Discharged
2 June	Tuesday	1.00 a.m.	18	clerk	Malicious Damage to Property	Discharged
2 June	Tuesday	1.00 a.m.	20	clerk	Malicious Damage to Property	Discharged
3 June	Wednesday	10.00 a.m.	28	labourer	Assault	Fined 10s
3 June	Wednesday	10.00 a.m.	24	labourer	Assault	Fined 10s
3 June	Wednesday	10.00 a.m.	14	labourer	Assault	Fined 10s
4 June	Thursday	11.00 a.m.	25	labourer	Assault	Discharged
4 June	Thursday	11.00 a.m.	19	labourer	Assault	Discharged
5 June	Friday	11.00 p.m.	47	labourer	Forgery	Remand
5 June	Friday	1.00 a.m.	24	weaver	Concealed on Premises	Discharged
5 June	Friday	1.00 a.m.	23	factory hand	Concealed on Premises	Discharged
5 June	Friday	1.00 a.m.	17	servant	Concealed on Premises	Discharged
5 June	Friday	1.00 p.m.	60	married	Drunk and Disorderly	Fined 5s
5 June	Friday	3.00 p.m.	60	labourer	Theft	Bound over
6 June	Saturday	1.00 a.m.	25	labourer	Drunk and Disorderly	Fined 5s
6 June	Saturday	11.00 a.m.	48	widow	Assault on Watchman	Fined 5s

Date	Day	Time	Age	Occupation	Offence	Sentence
6 June	Saturday	6.00 a.m.	50	married	Drunk and Disorderly	Fined 5s
6 June	Saturday	10.00 p.m.	34	labourer	Theft	Imprisoned 3 months
7 June	Sunday	12.00 a.m.	30	married	Disorderly Conduct	Discharged
9 June	Tuesday	11.00 a.m.	35	dryer's assist	Desertion	Discharged
10 June	Wednesday	1.00 a.m.	21	prostitute	Drunk and Disorderly	Fined 5s
10 June	Wednesday	1.00 a.m.	39	prostitute	Drunk in the Street	Imprisoned 7 days
10 June	Wednesday	10.00 a.m.	32	gent	Assault on Wife	Bailed
10 June	Wednesday	1.00 p.m.	55	fisherman	Drunk and Disorderly	Fined 5s
10 June	Wednesday	11.00 p.m.	64	married	Drunk and Disorderly	Fined 5s
10 June	Wednesday	12.00 a.m.	27	prostitute	Drunk and Disorderly	Fined 5s
11 June	Thursday	2.00 a.m.	16	prostitute	Sleeping on Premises	Discharged
11 June	Thursday	2.00 a.m.	22	prostitute	Sleeping on Premises	Discharged
11 June	Thursday	12.00 p.m.	29	married	Assault on Watchman	Discharged
11 June	Thursday	7.00 p.m.	17	single	Vagrancy	Imprisoned 14 days
11 June	Thursday	10.00 a.m.	25	labourer	Drunk and Disorderly	Fined 5s
13 June	Saturday	12.00 p.m.	29	prostitute	Soliciting Prostitution	Told to leave Chester
13 June	Saturday	9.00 a.m.	18	single	Concealed on Premises	Discharged
13 June	Saturday	7.00 p.m.	50	labourer	Drunk and Disorderly	Fined 5s
13 June	Saturday	11.00 p.m.	20	puddler	Theft	Imprisoned 14 days
14 June	Sunday	12.00 a.m.	63	labourer	Drunk	Fined 5s
14 June	Sunday	1.00 a.m.	62	needlemaker	Drunk and Disorderly	Fined 5s
14 June	Sunday	2.00 a.m.	22	prostitute	Being a Common Prostitute	Imprisoned 1 month
14 June	Sunday	2.00 a.m.	16	labourer	Drunk and Fighting	Fined 5s
14 June	Sunday	2.00 a.m.	16	confectioner	Drunk and Fighting	Fined 5s
15 June	Monday	4.00 p.m.	25	labourer	Assault on Watchman	Bound over
16 June	Tuesday	12.00 a.m.	24	tailor	Drunk and Damaging Property	Fined 5s

Table 6.1 Cont'd

Date	Day	Time	Age	Occupation	Charge	Sentence
16 June	Tuesday	12.00 a.m.	22	labourer	Assault on Watchman	Discharged
17 June	Wednesday	11.00 a.m.	50	labourer	Assault on Watchman	To raise sureties
17 June	Wednesday	1.00 p.m.	20	prostitute	Assault	Imprisoned 1 month
18 June	Thursday	1.00 a.m.	52	private detective	Drunk and Abusive	Fined 5s
18 June	Thursday	11.00 a.m.	42	broker	Theft	Committed to Assizes
20 June	Saturday	12.00 a.m.	27	prostitute	Disorderly Prostitute	Discharged
20 June	Saturday	1.00 a.m.	21	labourer	Drunk and Assaulting Police	Fined 10s
20 June	Saturday	5.00 p.m.	32	labourer	Drunk and Disorderly	Fined 10s
20 June	Saturday	6.00 p.m.	21	labourer	Assault	Fined 10s
20 June	Saturday	8.00 p.m.	20	labourer	Drunk and Fighting	Fined 5s
20 June	Saturday	8.00 p.m.	26	labourer	Drunk and Fighting	Fined 5s
20 June	Saturday	8.00 p.m.	41	married	Resisting Arrest	Discharged
20 June	Saturday	9.00 p.m.	22	labourer	Drunk and Disorderly	Fined 5s
20 June	Saturday	9.00 p.m.	38	painter	Drunk and Disorderly	Fined 5s
20 June	Saturday	11.00 p.m.	21	mason	Abusive Language to Watchman	Bound over
20 June	Saturday	11.00 p.m.	?	labourer	Drunk and Disorderly	Fined 5s
21 June	Sunday	1.00 a.m.	20	labourer	Assault on Watchman	Fined 5s
21 June	Sunday	1.00 a.m.	72	pauper	Drunk and Disorderly	Set to work

that this was most likely to involve public order incidents which would receive either a discharge or light sentence.

10   Chief Constable's Report, Staffordshire, 1865[18]

Under the County and Borough Police Act of 1856, every chief constable had to write a report on the state of crime in their area. This was sent to the Home Office and to the local magistrates, if a rural force, or the watch committee, if an urban force. In addition to returning statistics on crime, they were also an opportunity for chief constables to praise their force and offer constructive criticism. The extract below contains a series of observations by the Chief Constable of Staffordshire.

My Lords and Gentlemen,

I have the honour to report for your information that the Constabulary Force under my command gives a total of all ranks of 437:

Table 6.2   Staffordshire Police Force Numbers, by region, 1865

	Mining	Rural	Pottery	Headquarters and Reserve	Stafford and Tamworth Boroughs
Deputy Chief Constable	1				
Chief Superintendents	0	1	1		
Superintendents	3	3	3	1	
Inspectors	4	4	2	1	
Sergeants	19	16	15	2	1
Constables	138	100	91	7	7
Additional Constables	12	1	4	0	0
Total	**177**	**125**	**116**	**11**	**8**

2078 prisoners have been in custody during the three months ended the thirty-first of May last, namely:

Committed	746
Summarily Convicted	744
Reprimanded and Discharged	588

---

[18] *Report of the Chief Constable of the Constabulary Force of the County of Stafford, 1865*, C/ PC/1/1/1, Staffordshire Record Office.

24,644 miles have been conveyed at a cost of £119 17s 3d. The maintenance of prisoners has cost £107 1s 2d.

I share with some of my brother Chief Constables the difficulty which exists in gathering suitable men to fill the vacancies constantly occurring, and it will be my duty to bring this question prominently before the police committee, and the court, on an early day.

I have had a report of the apprehension this morning at Cradely Heath, of two burglars (one a ticket-of-leave man) by Sergeant Powner of the Staffordshire Force, a Constable Taylor and Chatham of the Worcestershire Force. The struggle was a desperate one. The police and prisoners are very seriously injured. Constable Taylor dangerously so. The conduct of the officers engaged is as praiseworthy, as the capture of two such notorious and desperate characters is satisfactory. The cordial co-operation of the two forces is most important, and will no doubt meet the high approval of the magistrates of both counties.

As empowered by the 3rd and 4th Victoria, chapter 88, sections 10 and 11,[19] I certify that Police Constable George Harvey, first class, now fifty-three years of age, who has served twenty years of age and upwards in the constabulary force of this county, is incapable, from infirmity and body, to discharge the duties of his office. I therefore recommend that a sum of £26 per annum, the same not being more than two-thirds of his pay, be granted him out of the police superintendent fund, on his retirement.

I have received an application form from The Patent Nut and Bolt Company, Limited, of the London Works, Smethwick, for an additional constable at their charge; also from S. M. Peto, Bart., for two additional constables at his charge – all to be stationed at or near Smethwick – and now apply for approval of such appointments, according to the 3rd and 4th Victoria, chapter 88, section 19.

11   Chief Constable's Orders, 1858–70[20]

Much of the material used for the history of the police is taken from documents produced in a public sphere, such as watch committee minutes, parliamentary papers or the official reports of Chief Constables. The following source, being an internal document of the Chief Constable of Cheshire's (Captain Johnnes Smith) orders to his superintendents, provides a much more candid view of police operations. In his orders he is as prepared to confront weaknesses as he is to praise his force. The first order is taken from a book marked "confidential", the rest from the main instructions.

---

[19] The County and Borough Police Act, 1856.
[20] *Cheshire County Constabulary Confidential Instructions 1866–75*, CJP/2; *Cheshire County Constabulary Chief Constable's Orders 1856–72*, CJP 4/1, Cheshire County Record Office.

21/12/1867

Superintendents will as far as practicable have secretly prepared a list of all Irish in the several towns in their divisions, particularly of such as may be connected with Fenianism, and will whenever any such latter are in custody for drunkenness or any other offence be most careful in the search of their persons and residences and will moreover in all such occasions when they are known to be prominent Fenians have photographs taken of them.

23/4/1857

Discretionary power is granted by the Chief Constable to Superintendents to allow any men of their divisions to appear in plain clothes where the exigencies of the service may demand it.

13/11/1858

In consequence of a late combination amongst publicans and other characters to subscribe in order to obtain the aid of foreign attorneys to prosecute the police for performing their duty, the Chief Constable thinks it most advisable that a defence fund should be at once formed to meet such cases.

7/3/1864

P. C. James Spann, no. 5 Division, is promoted to 2nd Class for clever capture of a notorious character, with stolen property in his possession, during the hours of night duty and after a severe struggle.

17/6/1867

In all important cases of murder or others of a like serious nature, whenever the solicitor for the prosecution declines to call evidence or prepare necessary plans because of the expense, the Chief Constable desires that immediate reference be made in order to secure authority for such expense – and in any such cases competent legal advice will be at once engaged to conduct the examination before magistrates instead of as in some late cases an incompetent police officer undertaking what is so far beyond his ability, and so inflicting a serious injury on public justice.

19/2/1870

It becomes the duty of the Chief Constable, in consequence of certain abuses that have come to his knowledge, to warn the constabulary that, if from this date any of them are discovered to accept money at sessions and assizes from magistrates' clerks, beyond what is allowed to them from the magistrates' clerks, other or beyond what they are legally entitled to, dismissal will be the penalty.

12   Memoirs of a Chief Constable[21]

William Chadwick was a Chief Constable who had risen through the ranks, beginning his police career in the Metropolitan Police before moving to the Cheshire Constabulary and becoming Chief Constable of the borough of Stalybridge in 1862. The two extracts below are taken from his autobiography. In the first, he talks with pride about how he dealt with a hostile crowd in stopping a prize fight take place. In the second he reveals resentment at the growing trend towards appointing outsiders to the post of Chief Constable.

12.1   Raids on Prize-fighters, etc.

In the old days when prize-fighting, cock-fighting, bear-bating, dog-fighting and other brutal sports were the common pastimes of the people, and laws began to be enacted to suppress them, raids were often made by the police as a matter of necessity.

Prize-fighting was in practice to a considerable extent, as well as dog-fighting, in Longdendale and one the Coombs, above Charlesworth.

In 1855 there were eight men besides Mr Little in the Hyde Division, and many a rough job they had about Woodhead. One Sunday night information was given at the Hyde police station of a prize-fight which was about to come off the next morning at Woodhead, betwixt Harry Carter of Ashton, and a man named Smith, of Sheffield. A messenger was at once despatched to Dukinfield, which was received there at midnight, ordering me and my brother officer, Dalgliesh, to proceed to Woodhead as quickly as a horse could take us, and also to take constables from Staley and Hollingworth with us. Accordingly, we procured a horse and light cart, and getting the before-mentioned officers out of bed, proceeded through Tintwistle betwixt three and four o'clock in the morning, each man armed with pistols and cutlass. On the way we passed a large number of greengrocers' carts from Ashton, with backers in them, as well as some scores of men on foot. On arriving at Woodhead, we found Mr Little amongst a large crowd of roughs, who were swearing vengeance against him. He had come from Newton by the same train as them, but unnoticed until the train arrived at Woodhead Station, when he jumped out of the train, went to the luggage van, secured the ropes and stakes intended for forming the ring for the fight to take place in, and put them into the porter's room before the mob were aware of his presence. They threatened to

---

[21] William Chadwick, *Reminiscences of a chief constable* (London, 1900), pp. 115–19 and 143–4.

break into the place and take them out, but the bold front shown by the officers induced them to hesitate, and they left the station, when Mr Little put the ropes, etc., into a passing train and sent them to Hyde.

The mob, however, were not for returning home without the two men fighting, and they went from place to place, followed by the whole of the officers, deep snow being on the ground. They several times attempted to commence operations on the borders of all three counties of Cheshire, Derbyshire and Yorkshire, but moved away at the approach of the police. This went on for several hours, when the police officers got quite out of patience, and at last, ascertaining that the man Smith was in a light cart which was passing, a dash was made and the horse stopped, upon which Smith jumped out and attempted to bolt, but officer Madem aimed a blow which brought him to mother earth. He was at once secured and handcuffed to me, and I dragged him into a public house amidst a shower of stones. A rush was made to rescue, when the whole of the officers drew their swords (none of which had hitherto been seen by the mob), which caused a regular stampede. The mob, however, rallied again, and stoned the officers who kept guard in front of the house. One party went round to the back of the house, where they could see me and my prisoner Smith, through the windows, which were low ones, and protected by iron stanchions. As they came up, I very quietly pulled out a loaded pistol, and, pretending not to notice their approach, quietly examined the priming, upon which one of these brave heroes called, "He's going to shoot," when another rush was made across the field. The mob of roughs dispersed, and I took my prisoner to Woodhead Station, and thence to Hyde, where he was taken before a magistrate and bound over to keep the peace.

12.2   Promotion and Favouritism

A policeman's lot, although not generally considered a happy one, is pretty much what he himself makes it. The career of "Robert" can be "may be marred" in a measure proportionate to his merit and ability. Still, as everywhere else, favouritism may spoil many of his chances of promotion. In the appointment of Chief Constables nowadays, influence appears to be a greater factor than merit. It is a question of having friends in court. In the English counties more than three-fourths of the chief constableships are held by "outsiders", of the military class; while the English cities and boroughs favour the civil element in the proportion of eight to one, and in that proportion place practical ability before social standing in appointing their Chief Constable. This state of matters raises a suspicion that in the counties the selection of gentlemen of social standing as Chief Constables, to the disparagement of able men who have been trained to the work, is made for the benefit of certain classes, rather than in the interest of police efficiency. Those Chief Constables who have been served their apprenticeship in the ranks, and gained their proud position by merit and ability, are better able to efficiently discharge the responsible duties to learn after appointment. The experienced chief is naturally in close sympathy with his men, understands the difficulties and temptations they have to contend with from personal experience, and is able to point out the numerous pitfalls and stumbling blocks that surround the constable on his beat. He will also have an extensive knowledge of the criminal classes and their habits.

I remember some years ago meeting with a number of gentlemen in a small borough in which a new Chief Constable had been appointed a few hours before. Amongst the unsuccessful candidates was a captain, who, on being asked if he had any knowledge or experience of police duties, replied: "Oh, no! It is a matter of getting the appointment, as I am told that there can always be a man got to look after the business for about 30s a week."

The superintendents of counties, and Chief Constables of boroughs, recommended their men for promotion, and although they are often accused of favouritism, I do not think such a thing is practised to any great extent, inasmuch as these superior officers are responsible for the good management of their departments, and it is only likely they will try to secure the best men they can get. There have been cases where the recommendations of a Chief Constable have been ignored through the nominee not having friends in court. More than probable, owing to influence and the "back door" policy, such promotion was made before the Watch Committee actually met together, and when the meeting did take place everything was cut and dried.

I well remember on one occasion being present at a Watch Committee meeting where the merits of a constable were being discussed. One gentleman remarked, "I think him a fairish officer, as he interferes with nobody so long as they will let him alone."

If favouritism were carried on to any great extent, it would constitute a great drawback to the good discipline of police forces.

13   Metropolitan Detectives, 1850–94

When first established, the Metropolitan Police had no detectives, although the force existed side-by-side with the Bow Street Runners until 1839. In 1842, a detective branch was established with eight officers. This was expanded in 1868 to fifteen, only for a scandal in 1878 to force a major reappraisal of the detective branch. Subsequently, detection was placed on a new footing and the number of officers expanded to 800 men by 1883. The passages below trace the changes in police detection across this period and all suggest elements of continuity and change. The first comes from the pen of Charles Dickens, the novelist who held a particular fascination of the police detective. He portrays the detectives of 1850 as distinctly more bright than the average police constable. The second, from 1856, briefly describes changes since 1829. The third is indicative of changing attitudes towards the police of the continent, comparing unfavourably the London police to their continental counterparts. The fourth passage, which appeared seven years before the adoption of fingerprinting techniques by the Metropolitan Police, argues that the techniques for identifying suspects in 1894 had barely got beyond "personal recognition".

13.1   Thieftaking, 1850[22]

If thieving be an Art (and who denies its more subtle and delicate branches deserve to be ranked as one of the Fine Arts?), thieftaking is a science. All the thief's ingenuity; all his knowledge of human nature; all his courage; all his coolness; all his imperturbable powers of face; all his nice discrimination in reading the countenance of other people; all his manual and digital dexterity; all his facility in expedients, and promptitude in acting upon them; all his Protean cleverness of disguise and capability of counterfeiting every sort and condition of distress; together with a great deal more patience, and the additional qualification, integrity, are demanded for the higher branches of thieftaking.

If an urchin picks your pocket, or a bungling "artist" steals your watch so that you find it out in an instant, it is easy enough for any private in any of the seventeen divisions of London Police to obey your panting demand to "Stop thief!" But the tricks and contrivances of those who wheedle money out of your pocket rather than steal it; who cheat you with your eyes open; who clear every vestige of plate out of your pantry while your servant is on the stairs; who set up imposing warehouses, and ease respectable firms of large parcels of goods; who steel the acceptances of needy or dissipated young men – for the detection and punishment of such imposters a superior order of police is requisite.

To each division of the Force is attached two officers, who are denominated "detectives". The staff, or headquarters, consists of six sergeants and two inspectors. Thus the Detective Police, of which we hear so much, consists of only forty-two individuals, whose duty it is to wear no uniform, and to perform the most difficult operations of their craft. They have not only to counteract the machinery of every sort of rascal whose only means of existence is avowed rascality, but to clear up family mysteries, the investigation of which demands the utmost delicacy and tact.

---

[22] *Household Words* **1**, 1850, p. 368.

13.2   Metropolitan Detectives, 1856[23]

Let us now revert to the Detective Police. When the metropolis force was established in 1829, the old Bow-street officers, not caring to work with the new system, retired from public life and set up a private practice in hunting out offenders, in which occupation some of them continue to this day. For fifteen years there was no establishment of detectives connected with the police; but the inconvenience of not possessing so necessary a wheel in the constabulary machinery induced Sir James Graham, who had perhaps a leaning towards this branch of the profession, to revive the fraternity. The force consists of three inspectors, nine sergeants, and a body of police termed "plain-clothes men", whose services can be held at any moment. There are about six policemen in each division who take upon themselves the duty of detectives when wanted, which affords a total number of 108 auxiliaries, upon whom the inspectors and sergeants can rely to carry out their orders with silence and address. In all great gatherings these men are distributed among the crowd, dressed according to the character of the assembly. Thus, at an agricultural meeting, smock-frocks are worn, or the dress of a small farmer; at a review, the habiliments of a decent mechanic in his Sunday best. In this respect they follow the principle of Nature, who protects her creatures from observation by giving them coats of a colour somewhat similar to that of the soil they inhabit: to the arctic fox, a fur white as the surrounding snow; and to the hare, a coat scarcely distinguishable from the brown heath in which she makes her form. It is the general rule to station these plain-clothes men as near as possible to the policemen of their own division, in order that they may be assisted in capturing prisoners.

13.3   British and European Detectives Compared, 1883[24]

There can hardly be a doubt but that certain recent events, both in England and Ireland, should teach us that we ought in this country to take a new departure as regards the detection of crime. With the most efficient police in Europe, so far as the maintenance of public order is concerned, it is a curious fact that as regards a detective force we are very little if at all better off than our grandfathers were half a century ago, when they had to rely upon Townsend, the famous Bow-street runner, as the one only man

---

[23] *Quarterly Review* **99**, 1856, pp. 174–5.
[24] M. Laing Meason, "Detective Police", *The Nineteenth Century* **13**, 1883, pp. 756–7.

in England who could hunt out thieves or murderers and bring them to justice. It is very true that we have, both in London and the provinces a considerable number of what are called detective officers; but except that these individuals wear plain clothes instead of a uniform, they differ little or nothing from the ordinary constables of the force. Not only to the dangerous classes, but to the Londoner of any experience, our "plain clothes officers", as they are called, are as well known as if they were clad in blue tunics and helmets. In fact they don't pretend to be what they certainly are not, a secret body of public servants, whose mission it is to detect crime, to spot down criminals, and, without making themselves known to those they are always fighting against, to put the authorities on the right track as to how and where criminals are to be found, and the crimes they have committed brought to light.

It is only fair to state that a great deal of the crime committed in London meets with the punishment it deserves. But, with a few rare exceptions, the criminals are invariably laid hands on by the ordinary police, in the everyday way of duty. Considering the immense districts of outlying houses the force has to watch over, more particularly in many of the suburbs, and taking into consideration how easy of access all our habitations are, it is marvellous to note how wonderfully the Metropolitan Police must do its duty. When we remember the almost interminable streets and roads, many of them composed of detached and semi-detached houses, that the police have to watch over in those ever-extending western suburbs of London, and we recollect how easy of access nearly all these buildings are, it seems little short of a miracle that cases of burglary are not twenty times more numerous than they are within the Metropolitan Police district.

But beyond this it is impossible to praise the manner in which lives or property are guarded. To those who take any interest in the subject, it is very evident that when once a crime is committed in London, when once the thieves get fairly off with the property they have taken, or if the unknown murderer manages to keep out of the way for a few hours after he has killed his victim, the detection of crime seems to be a problem which our so-called detectives have not the capacity in most cases to solve. And it is the same with great as with smaller affairs. Is there a capital in all of Europe where the Hatton Garden robbery and the attempt to blow up the Government Offices in Westminster would have remained mysteries of which it seems impossible to discover the sources? In Paris, St Petersburg, Vienna, Rome, or Berlin, the thieves who stole the several thousand pounds' worth of precious stones in the former instance, or the perpetrators of the outrage in the latter, would in all probability have been in the hands of the police twenty-four hours after either crime was committed.

13.4   Identifying Suspects, 1894[25]

By the Prevention of Crimes Act of 1871, it was provided that a register should be kept of "Habitual Criminals" – that is to say, of every person convicted on indictment of a crime, a previous conviction of a crime being proved against him. The register was at first established at Scotland Yard, under the charge of the Commissioner of Metropolitan Police, but was afterwards transferred to the Home Office, Sir Edmund Du Cane, Chairman of the Directors of Convict Prisons, being appointed Registrar. Of late years it has included the names of all convicts released under sentences of penal servitude. From this register are annually compiled the Habitual Criminals Register, and the Register of Distinctive Marks. Copies of both these are distributed to all police forces, but they do not appear to be consulted to any great extent, or at least with much advantage. Considerable delay takes place in the publication, the register for each year being seldom, if ever, published before the following September, and therefore, as the Report of the Committee points out, "An habitual criminal's name is not available for the police in the registers until a period of from nine to twenty months after his release, though this is precisely the time at which he is most likely to be wanted." The Register of Distinctive Marks tells very little or too much. In many cases it states that a prisoner has no distinctive mark, whilst in other cases, as, for instances, that of a tattooed ring on the second finger of the left hand, it enumerates nearly thirty persons bearing that mark, and leaves the puzzled policeman to make his choice between them.

The shortcomings of these registers caused the Metropolitan Police to keep its own records of the names and distinctive marks of convicted criminals, and to supplement them with albums of photographs of all convicts, and (since 1887) of a large number of other habitual criminals. At first these photographs were arranged chronologically, but are now divided according to the age and stature of the persons, and the class of crime that each criminal affects. By means of these registers a prisoner can perhaps, with luck, be identified in a few minutes, but the search may be a long one, and Inspector Neame, of the Convict Supervision Department, stated before the Committee that "His men would search for days rather than lose a 'good man'." On March 1, 1893, twenty-one officers searched for twenty-seven prisoners, and made seven identifications. The total time spent was 57½ hours, or an average of more than two hours for each prisoner sought for, and more than eight hours for each identification. This is not excessive when one reflects that, in default of other indices, recourse must

---

[25] Edmund R. Spearman, "Known to the Police", *The Nineteenth Century* (September 1894), pp. 357–9.

be had to the photograph albums, which contain the portraits of some 70,000 recent criminals, or to the more ancient records extending to 1864, and containing the portraits and descriptions of some 45,000 other criminals.

Personal recognition is, however, the main thing on which the English detective or prison warder relies. The remanded prisoners of the entire London district are sent to Holloway, and they are there inspected by detectives and warders from other Metropolitan prisons to see if they can be identified as old offenders. Thirty police officers from various quarters of London visit Holloway Prison three times a week, and each week they obtain, on average, four identifications. Apart from the great waste of time – about ninety hours for each identification – the method is an objectionable one.

With all this elaborate provision the habitual criminal often manages to escape identification in England, and, worse still, wrongful identifications are sometimes made by too positive prison warders and police officers. The Home Office Report sets forth at length a series of judicial blunders of this kind which have cropped up of recent years. The Report also explains the weak place in the armour of identification. It is impossible to classify photographs and bodily marks so as to easily pick out the right description amongst tens of thousands of cases. Therefore the Home Office Committee conclude that

> even with more photographs and more exact descriptions, we are agreed that the present system will leave much to be desired. What is wanted is a means of classifying the records of habitual criminals, such that, as soon as the particulars of the personality of any prisoner (whether description, measurements, marks, or photographs) are received, it may be possible to ascertain readily, and with certainty, whether his case is already in the register, and if so, who he is. Such a system is not, we believe, attainable merely as a development of the existing English methods; if it is to be found at all it must be found in the application of some scientific method as those on which we have now to report.

Chapter 7

Criminal Justice in the Nineteenth Century

1 Law Reform

In the first forty years of the nineteenth century the whole shape of criminal justice in England was brought into question through debates on the criminal law. On the one side were those who trusted the judiciary and defended the existing law as giving the discretion that prosecutors and the courts needed. On the other were those who portrayed this discretion as a lottery, arguing that the deterrent effects for criminals were negligible. This latter group called for consolidation and an alleviation of the severity of the law together with its more consistent application. In the passages below, the arguments for and against change are put forward by two writers: the first, taken from the works of William Paley – Archdeacon of Carlisle at the time of writing the Cambridge textbook Principles of Moral and Political Philosophy *(1785) – who argued that the law already provided a powerful, wide-ranging deterrent; the second is taken from a speech by Henry Brougham, a former Lord Chancellor (1830–34), editor of the radical journal* Edinburgh Review *and active civil-law reformist. He ridiculed the traditionalists, arguing for an approach to prevention which encompassed efficient implementation of the law and more attention to general morality.*

1.1 *William Paley, 1830*[1]

There are two methods of administering penal justice. The first method assigns capital punishment to few offences, and inflicts it invariably. The second method assigns capital punishment to many kinds of offences, but inflicts it only upon a few examples of each kind.

The latter of which two methods has long been adopted in this country, where, of those who receive sentence of death, scarcely one in ten is executed. And the preference of this to the former method seems to be founded in the consideration, that the selection of proper objects for capital punishments principally depends upon circumstances, which, however

---

[1] William Paley, *The works of William Paley, D. D., with additional sermons etc. and a corrected account of the life and writings of the author* (London, 1838), pp. 429–32.

easy to perceive in each particular case after the crime is committed, it is impossible to enumerate or define beforehand; or to ascertain however with that exactness which is requisite in legal descriptions. Hence, although it be necessary to fix by precise rules of law the boundary on one side, that is, the limit to which the punishment may be extended; and also that nothing less than the authority of the whole legislature be suffered to determine that boundary, and assign these rules; yet the mitigation of punishment, the exercise of lenity, may without danger be intrusted to the executive magistrate, whose discretion will operate upon the numerous, unforeseen, mutable, and indefinite circumstances, both of the crime and the criminal, which constitute or qualify the malignity of each offence. Without the power of relaxation lodged in a living authority, either some offenders would escape capital punishment, whom the public safety required to suffer; or some would undergo this punishment, where it was neither deserved nor necessary. For if judgment of death were reserved for one or two species of crimes only (which would probably be the case if that judgment was intended to be executed without exception), crimes might occur of the most dangerous example, and accompanied with circumstances of heinous aggravation, which did not fall within any description of offences that the laws had made capital, and which consequently could not receive the punishment their own malignity and the public safety required. What is worse, it would be known beforehand, that such crimes might be committed without danger to the offender's life. On the other hand, if to reach these possible cases, the whole class of offences to which they belong be subjected to pains of death, and the execution of the laws will become more sanguinary than the public compassion would endure, or than is necessary to the general security.

The Law of England is constructed upon a different and a better policy. By the number of statutes creating capital offences, it sweeps into the net every crime which, under any circumstances, may merit the punishment of death; but when the execution of this sentence comes to be deliberated upon, a small proportion of each class are singled out, the general character, or the peculiar aggravations, of whose crimes, render them fit examples of public justice. By this expedient, few actually suffer death, whilst the dread and danger of it hang over the crimes of many. The tenderness of the law cannot be taken advantage of. The life of the subject is spared as far as the necessity of restraint and intimidation permits; yet no one will adventure upon the commission of any enormous crime, from a knowledge that the laws have not provided for its punishment. The wisdom and humanity of this design furnish a just excuse for the multiplicity of capital offences, which the laws of England are accused of creating beyond those of other countries. The charge of cruelty is answered by observing, that these laws were never meant to be carried into indiscriminate execution; that the legislature, when it establishes its last and highest sanctions, trusts to the benignity of the Crown to relax their severity, as often as circumstances appear to palliate the offence, or even as often as those circumstances of aggravation are wanting which rendered this rigorous interposition necessary. Upon this plan, it is enough to vindicate the lenity of the law, that some instances are to be found in each class of capital crimes, which require the restraint of capital punishment, and that this restraint could not be applied without subjecting the whole class to the same condemnation.

1.2   The Inefficiency of Simply Penal Legislation, 1857[2]

It appears expedient to lay before the union a statement of the considerations which, above forty years ago, mainly induced me to press upon the attention of the legislature and the country, the necessity of combining other measures with those of penal infliction, in order to prevent the commission of crimes. The education and moral training of the people, and the making punishment subservient to the reformation of offenders, offered the best means of saving society from the pollution it is exposed to: first, from ignorance and the immoral habits which it engenders; next, from the injudicious treatment and neglect of those who have fallen into criminal courses. A due reflection upon the point to which I refer, opens us nearly the whole subject of criminal police and, truly, we cannot easily overrate its importance. It concerns neither more nor less than the peace, the morals, nay, the very existence of society, threatened as it is by the frightful progress of crime, while the inefficacy of the means that the laws afford for restraining evil-doers becomes every day more deplorably manifest. Let us calmly consider this subject, and then ask whether the known facts, the result of our past experience, do not warrant a grave suspicion that all our efforts to prevent the commission of crimes have hitherto been made in a wrong direction?

I begin with the startling fact, that, having conferred both with my brethren at the Bar, with experienced judges, with experienced magistrates exercising the functions of police, with secretaries of state, the heads of the police department, I have uniformly found their opinion to be unfavourable, when asked if punishment had any great and steady effect in deterring offenders from following the example of the parties punished?

Next, I observe that the dread of punishment must always depend upon the certainty of its following the commission of the offence, inasmuch as, while the slightest infliction which should be quite sure speedily to visit the offender, would, in most instances, suffice to deter him, the heaviest would fail to influence him if not believed to be inevitable, or expected to

---

[2] Lord Brougham, *The works of Henry, Lord Brougham – historical and political dissertations*, vol. 8 (London, 1857), pp. 239–44.

be remote, and the degrees of uncertainty and of remoteness being always increased by the party's own imagination, the passion which afforded the temptation would also make him sanguine in his hopes of escape. Now, nothing like certainty and celerity ever can, in the nature if things, be attained in the connection which the law would establish between guilt and punishment. That connection is evidently not a necessary one and, though we may diminish much of its uncertainty, still enough will always remain to flatter the hopes of the guilty-minded and to weaken the force of the law in restraining him.

I grant that much has of late years been done to lessen the chances of escape. The mitigation of the severity which once disgraced our criminal code has rendered it much easier to find prosecutors, witnesses and jurors, who may be disposed to put the penal laws in execution. The amendments in the rules of pleading and of evidence have diminished the chances of guilt escaping. The greater frequency of trials has shortened the interval between apprehension and punishment. The improvement of the police in great towns establishing a more vigilant superintendence of wrong-doers, has, by the late act, been extended to other districts.[3] The better selection of magistrates has amended the administration of the criminal law, and especially of the police, or preparatory process. But even if these reforms, with the others still wanted of a public prosecutor and stipendiary justices, should make our criminal code as efficacious as any human laws can be, and render the magistrate as far as is possible a terror to evil-doers, there is still an obstacle that never can be removed, to the complete success of a system which rests upon terror alone as the means of repressing crime. Even if the certainty of punishment were made far greater than it ever can be rendered by any improvements in that system, all would be in vain, and for this plain reason, that men, while considering whether or not they shall break the law, are not in a calm and calculating mood – they are under the influence of passions or feelings, or of wishes and hopes, which silence the voice of reason as well as of conscience, making them alive only to the prospect of gratification and to the hope of impunity.

Again, in reasoning upon the tendency of punishment and the motive to offend, we have always committed one serious error. We have considered crimes as insulated, and we have regarded each offence as originating in an occasional gust of passion, or view of interest. We have argued as if all criminals were alike in their nature and all spectacles of punishment, or exhortations to wrong-doing, were addressed to the same minds. Now, nothing can be more certain than that the great majority of all the offences committed in every civilized community are the result of immoral character, or gross ignorance, of bad habits, and that the graver sort are committed

---

[3] Brougham is here referring to the County and Borough Police Act of 1856.

after a series of faults less aggravated in their character. It follows, as a necessary consequence from this proposition, that when the example of penal infliction is addressed to the offender, its deterring effect is very much lessened because it is addressed to a mind which evil habits have entirely perverted. Thus, the guiltily disposed person is to be not merely deterred by a fear of punishment, but to be reclaimed from a course of thinking, feeling, and acting, into which he had fallen.

It is no doubt to be set on the other side of the account that the knowledge possessed by the community of punishments, being by the law denounced and being by the administration of that law actually inflicted, tends to produce a habit of thinking and feeling in the people, and, by connecting in their minds the punishment with the offence, may create a general aversion to evil practices. This in truth is the only effect produced by punishment. But for this, it would be wholly inoperative, and would indeed be only an aggravation of the evil occasioned by crimes. But it is also certain that this habit has to struggle with other propensities, which are generally found to be more powerful. Ignorance, evil association, indulgence in lawless passions, first of a less and afterwards of a more hateful kind, the familiar contemplation of vicious excesses, the observation, often the actual experience, of escape from penal visitation, the spectacle of the law so often failing to be effectually executed – all engender bad habits, against which the habit of regarding vice as connected with punishment, contends in vain and fruitless conflict. Hence, the only possible efficacy of the penal code, however wisely framed or ably enforced, becomes feeble to its purpose, the repression of offences. For against the habit of reflecting on the criminal act as a thing punishable, is to be further set the temptation to do it as a thing desirable. Thus, the habit already enfeebled by the other circumstances just enumerated, is immediately overpowered by the interest or the passion of the hour.

2   Rural Magistrates, 1836[4]

Despite changes in the law, the magistrate sitting on his own retained considerable discretion as to how he conducted his business. In some cases, such as that described below, this was combined with a haphazard geographical distribution of Justices, allowing individuals to ignore their fellow magistrates.

Communication from E. Simeon, Esq., Oxford.

I must inform you that I have been, and am, very differently situated from most of the country magistrates in consequence of being fourteen

---

[4] *Evidence of E. Simeon to the royal commission on county rates*, P.P. 1836, vol. xxvii.

miles from the nearest Oxfordshire Petty Sessions, held at Henley. I have been in the habit of transacting all the business of this neighbourhood, for the last ten years, without the intervention or assistance of any clerk. When I first began to act, it was hinted to me that I ought to take regular fees, and hand them over to the clerk of the Petty Sessions at Henley; but, as I did all the labour myself, I declined laying a tax upon my neighbours which most of them could ill afford; and no fee of any sort has ever been levied or received by me, or my authority, either directly or indirectly.

3   Societies for the Prosecution of Felons, 1832[5]

Prosecution Associations were established to provide a collective means for the apprehension and prosecution of thieves. They generally consisted of farmers or tradesmen who each paid a subscription to a fund that was administered by a treasurer. Should a theft occur involving one of the members, the rest of the association would go in pursuit of the offender and the funds would be used to pay for the prosecution expenses, including the employment of a solicitor. Increasingly during the nineteenth century, the social occasion of the annual dinner became more important than the original business of the association. Below are two key clauses from a standard set of articles of agreement.

Fourth – That each member of the society shall keep an exact description in writing of every horse, mare, gelding and colt belonging to him, specifying the colours, ages, height, and other marks of each horse, mare, gelding, colt, cattle, sheep, or other live property, or any goods, property or effects to be stolen from any member of this society, he or she shall without delay give notice personally or in writing to the treasurer, who shall call a committee, and the treasurer and such committee shall order if they think it requisite, as many members as may be necessary to proceed on such routes as they shall appoint; first giving them proper descriptions of the property stolen, and (if known), of the suspected offender or offenders, and that each member on receiving such order shall go on horseback in person, or send one sufficient man on horseback along the roads and route allotted to him, and shall therein use his utmost diligence in making strict enquiry after the offender or offenders and stolen property; and if he shall hear of the same beyond the limits of his route, he shall with all expedition continue pursuit, and endeavour to apprehend and secure the offender or offenders and stolen property, so long as any intelligence shall be obtained of him, her, or them; and that the expenses of such pursuit, and such satisfaction as shall be deemed reasonable by the treasurer and

---

[5] *Articles of agreement for the Audley Association for the Prosecution of Felons, 1832.* D4842/15/4/32, Staffordshire Record Office.

committee, shall be paid by the treasurer out of the general stock of fund of this society. . . .

Seventh – That the treasurer after any live or other property is stolen, shall on receiving notice thereof with the approbation of a committee disperse hand-bills, notifying the robbery, and shall also advertise the same in such newspapers as he and such committee shall think most proper; and likewise upon the discovery or apprehension of any offender or offenders, use every effectual means for his, her or their commitment, prosecution and conviction, and shall pay to any person not being a member of the society, upon such discovery or apprehension, the following rewards on conviction (that is to say).

For any person or persons convicted of a capital offence, the sum of £5 5s 0d.

For any person or persons convicted on any offence, and sentenced to transportation, the sum of £3 3s 0d.

For any person or persons convicted of any offence, and not subjecting him, her or them to transportation, the sum of £1 1s 0d.

To every toll-gate keeper giving information of any offender or offenders, who shall thereby be convicted, the sum of £1 1s 0d.

4   Paying for Prosecutions, 1836[6]

Although parliament had gradually provided legislation to reimburse prosecutors for the expense incurred in bringing cases, there were still activities which required individuals to spend their own money. The letter below highlights the fact that the expenses of arrest were only compensated if the case proceeded beyond the magistrates' courts.

Communication from T. Alcock, Esq., Kingswood, Epsom.

With reference to the constabulary force in the county [of Essex] I would submit that it is not only a very inefficient police, but that magistrates are placed in great difficulty with particular reference to the expenses and charges for apprehending offenders and procuring witnesses. Where no commitment takes place upon examination of a prisoner brought up on suspicion, magistrates have not the power to order any expenses. A constable, too, being directed to pursue a man on suspicion of felony, may be put to considerable expense in endeavouring to apprehend the same, and, having failed to do so, is obliged sometimes to go uncompensated. This, of course, is a great preventive to the discovery of offenders. I have known, however, a sum of £50 ordered to be paid out of the county purse

---

[6] *Evidence of T. Alcock to the royal commission on county rates*, P.P. 1836, vol. xxvii.

for the expenses of constables and witnesses in a single case; and at another time I have known constables obliged to submit to a loss of many pounds, who remain unsatisfied at this moment. Such, indeed, is the uncertainty of fair and reasonable recompense, that it is difficult to procure the zealous services of a constable unless there is other reward offered than the law allows him. It would tend much, in my opinion, to the well-being of the country at large, if a regular police were established by government throughout the kingdom.

5   Submission, 1849[7]

To those people or organizations with sufficient funds, the system of private prosecution provided significant discretion. The advertisement below was placed in a provincial newspaper. It consists of a compromise between a man and the London and North Western Railway Company in which the defendant admits the crime and promises not to offend again in return for the abandonment of charges by the company.

Whereas, I, the undersigned, John Sumner, of Heaton Norris, in the county of Chester, did, on the 26th day of August, at Heaton Norris, wantonly throw a stone over the pavement of a bridge, which stone fell upon a railway carriage then travelling on the London and North Western Railway, and the passengers were thereby endangered, for which offence proceedings at law have been commenced against me, by order of the said railway company; but such proceedings have kindly been stayed, on my making a public submission, and paying the costs incurred, and promising not to offend again.

I do hereby publicly express my contrition for my offence, and my thanks to the prosecutors for their clemency, and I promise not to offend again; and I hereby agree to pay the expenses incurred, and that this my submission shall be published by printed bills, or in any other manner.

6   Judge's Correspondence with the King, 1819[8]

For the first forty years of the nineteenth century, when thousands of death sentences were being passed but the number executed declined sharply, information sent to the king regarding judge's reprieves and requests for mercy were an integral part of the criminal justice system. The extracts below dating from 1819,

---

[7] *The Stockport Advertiser*, 7/9/1849.
[8] *Judge's correspondence with the king*, H/O 6/4, Public Record Office.

four different types of approach can be seen. The first merely lists those who had their sentences commuted and gives an overview of the types of offence which carried the death penalty. The second uses age and behaviour since conviction as pleas in a petition for mercy; the third refers to the low levels of horse theft as a reason to recommend a prisoner for mercy; and the fourth blames a boy's behaviour on his upbringing and associates, suggesting an alternative punishment.

6.1   Northern Circuit, 1819

To the King's most excellent Majesty. May it please Your Majesty.

We do most humbly represent unto Your Majesty that at the last Assizes and General Delivery of the Gaols held for the northern circuit the following persons were capitally convicted of the crimes hereafter specified, but some reasonable circumstances appearing on their respective trials they were aforesaid reprieved in order to be represented unto Your Majesty as fit objects of Your Majesty's most gracious mercy upon the following conditions, that is to say,

At the Castle of York in and for the County of York, 6th March 1819.

Thomas Parker, John Crawthorne, Matthew Charlton and Charles Castles of burglary, Thomas Hickman and William Hickman, Matthew Smith and Francis Rhodes of highway robbery, Richard Jackson and George Jackson of sheep stealing and Thomas Robinson of feloniously stealing and taking from the possession of Matthew Dobson he being a person employed to convey letters sent by the post from Wetherby for and towards Harrogate and Knaresborough all in the said county from bags of letters sent by the said post – to be severally transported beyond the seas for the term of their natural lives.

John Staley of forgery – to be imprisoned and kept at hard labour in the house of correction at Wakefield in and for the West Riding of the county of York for two years.

William Ward of burglary, James Greenwood and John Roberts of horse stealing and Hannah Atkinson, widow, of feloniously uttering false and counterfeit money well knowing the same to be false and counterfeit, after having been convicted of being a common utterer of false and counterfeit money – to be severally imprisoned and kept to hard labour in the same house of correction for two years.

John Thorpe of feloniously killing a sheep with a felonious intent to steal the carcass thereof – to be imprisoned and kept to hard labour in the same house of correction for one year.

George Dalton of horse stealing, John Delocate of feloniously stealing three heifers, William Morrell of feloniously wilfully and of his malice aforethought shooting at Joseph Scott, and William Brown of feloniously breaking and entering a dwelling house in the daytime and Catharine

Collier they being therein and feloniously stealing goods therein of the value of five shillings – to be severally imprisoned and kept to hard labour in the same house of correction for one year.

And Robert Steals of horse stealing and Thomas Bayley of feloniously and privately stealing goods of the value of five shillings in a shop – to be severally imprisoned and kept to hard labour in the house of correction at Beverley in and for the East Riding of the said county for one year.

They were tried before me,

George Wood

6.2   Petition for Mercy, Cheshire, 1819

We, the undersigned, most humbly, but most earnestly petition your Royal Highness in behalf of Samuel Hooley now under sentence of death in Chester Castle, for breaking into the dwelling house of Eleanor Baldwin, in company with three other persons.

We are tempted to hope that your Royal Highness may be induced to extend the prerogative of your mercy to the unhappy criminal, in consideration of his youth, he not having yet arrived at man's estate; and from the circumstance that no particular act of atrocity marked his crime.

We have also to urge in his behalf, that during his confinement at Chester he has conducted himself entirely to the satisfaction of William Hudson, the gaoler, and we have the testimony of the Reverend William Law, the minister of our Parish, who has visited him in his confinement, that he is fully awakened to a sense of his guilt, is truly and devoutly penitent.

We are further enduced to offer this humble petition to your Royal Highness' motive from our feeling for the sufferings and agony of an aged and respectable parent, who is mourning over the ignominious fate which awaits his deluded son.

May we then, on every account, entreat your Royal Highness to save the wretched and persistent sufferer Samuel Hooley from death. Oh may it please your Royal Highness to mitigate in punishment to transportation for life – to any other punishment he would submit without a murmur – only may his life be spared.

We, the undersigned, who are all inhabitants, or intimately connected by property and local interests with the parish of Bowden (in which the wretched Samuel Hooley was born and bred) write in offering this our earnest petition to your Royal Highness, being assured that the benevolence of your nature will be as truly gratified by granting mercy, as we can be by the receiving this important favour at your hands –

Bowden, Cheshire September 9, 1819

Stamford and Warrington Grey, George H. Chester, James Thomas Law (Vicar of Bowden), Oswald Leicester (Minister of Altrincham), Hugo Worthington, Charles Lowndes, William Cass

6.3   Clemency for a horse-thief, Ely, 1819

To his Royal Highness the Prince Regent may it please your Royal Highness.

Whereas Jeremiah Hill was tried before me the Chief Justice of the Isle of Ely at the assizes held at Ely for the said isle on the 16th of February last, and was found guilty of stealing one mare the property of James Hart and received judgment of death, but I have respited the execution of the said judgment until the pleasure of your Royal Highness be known concerning the premises; and I now humbly recommend the said Jeremiah Hill to the clemency of your Royal Highness and that you will be graciously be pleased to grant him a pardon upon condition that he may be transported for life: and I humbly certify to your Royal Highness that my reason for asking this recommendation is that the crime of horse stealing does not prevail in the isle, it being now many years since any one was tried for that crime within the Isle of Ely.

Given under my hand this ninth day of March in the year of our Lord, 1819.

Edward Christian C.J.L.

6.4   Juveniles and Philanthropy in Somerset, 1819

My Lord,

At the assizes holden at the Castle of Taunton in and for the county of Somerset on Saturday the 27th day of March last, John Weston was tried and convicted of a felony in privately stealing from the person of the prosecutor a purse containing £20.

He is only twelve years old, is one of a gang of pickpockets who travel about the county to fairs, etc., for the purpose of committing their depredations, by three or four of whom he was accompanied at the time of committing the offence for which he was tried and it appeared that the only chance of preventing his coming to an untimely end and of making him a useful member of society was to endeavour to procure his admission into the Philanthropic Society's Reform and with this view he was sentenced to be imprisoned and kept at hard labour in the house of correction at Witton, which adjoins Taunton, for six calendar months.

From the information which I received in consequence of the inquiries which have been made since my return to town, I find that this is not his first offence, that he was convicted of a felony in Warwickshire about two years ago and imprisoned for three months and that it is necessary to separate him not only from his former associates in crime but also from his own family who are living at Birmingham and his case having been laid before the Philanthropic Society they have agreed to receive him if his Royal Highness the Prince Regent will be graciously pleased to permit them so to do and they have made a conditional order for his admission.

Under these circumstances, I beg humbly to recommend the prisoner to the consideration of his Royal Highness as a proper object for a pardon on the condition of his being received into the Philanthropic Society's Reform.

I have the honour to remain, my Lord, your Lordship's most obedient humble servant,

George Holroyd

7 The Justice of the Peace, 1837[9]

Justices of the Peace were amateurs who rarely held any legal knowledge prior to taking up office. In making their decisions they had traditionally relied on their common sense, the advice of their clerks, and publications such as R. Burns's Justice of the Peace. *In publicizing the first issue of a new journal, the extract below makes clear the wide array of tasks over which Justices and their clerks were expected to be competent, and promises to provide a national resource of legal information.*

In offering this paper to the attention of that body to whose service it will be exclusively devoted, it is incumbent upon the publisher briefly to explain the purposes it is designed to answer.

While the agency of the press is resorted to by several of the other orders of society, as the clergy, the medical, and a branch of the legal profession, for protecting their interests, and supplying the information properly belonging to each of them, it is a matter of some surprise that so large and influential a part of the community, as that, comprising Justices of the Peace, clerks of the peace, clerks of Petty Sessions, town clerks, and parochial officers, is yet without this universal medium of communication; especially when it is considered that to most of them, it is of primary importance to be furnished with the earliest and most correct intelligence upon the many, and often complicate questions with which they have to deal.

To supply this deficiency, it is proposed to establish this paper, which, to enumerate some of its advantages, holds out to Justices, clerks of the peace, and clerks of Petty Sessions, the certainty of the speediest information

---

[9] *The Justice of the Peace* **1**, 1837, p. 1.

upon all subjects falling under their respective cognizance, of the decisions which take place in the courts at Westminster, and of Quarter Sessions, throughout the kingdom; of reports of cases in Petty Sessions, where such may be of any utility; of other matters of an interesting or important nature in either of these courts, as well as in their respective counties at large; and in addition, during the sitting of parliament, an outline or analysis of every bill introduced there, affecting their judicial, or ministerial functions and duties: to town clerks, besides such of the matter it shall contain as may be useful to them, every timely information that may be deemed serviceable towards the effectual discharge of their office, with notices of all controversial cases in the courts at Westminster and elsewhere, in any way connected with Borough affairs, and the decisions thereon: to guardians, clerks of unions, and parish officers, reports of all transactions and decisions as well as under the poor law commission, or otherwise, relating to the management of the poor, or to their respective offices.

To the foregoing will be added, accounts of the proceedings of the tithe commissioners for England and Wales, and any practical matter under the registration, marriage, highway, and enclosure Acts, together with accurate reports of the decisions of the revising barristers upon points under the reform Act.

And from time to time will be given every important proceeding respecting savings' banks, friendly societies, government annuity societies, and loan societies, with notices of the formation of new societies under the different statutes relating to them, and decisions upon practical points that have been submitted to the certifying barrister.

It will also be the aim of this paper faithfully to bring to the notice of its readers, such new publications as may appear, upon any of the subjects within its sphere of enquiry, and generally to become a vehicle of the most extensive, correct, and useful intelligence to that part of the public whose interest it espouses.

Having thus briefly explained the views and objects of this undertaking, the publisher respectfully hopes to receive, from an order of men so considerable and intelligent, that countenance and support, which its utility may deserve.

8   Letters by Defendants, 1857–88[10]

In addition to letters by judges, there were also many pleas for mercy by defendants themselves. Outside of capital cases, these have received very little attention, yet they provide one of the few sources through which the voices of defendants

---

[10] All the letters below come from the Chester Quarter Sessions files kept at Chester City Record Office.

can be heard. The following ten letters have been chosen because of the variety of defence arguments and pleas that they reveal. The first five were written by those who could not raise sureties to keep the peace[11] or afford to pay a fine. Both of these were a common cause of imprisonment. The rest of the letters were written before trial and consist of appeals to personal circumstances together with attempts to discredit the prosecutors. All were written by defendants who had been previously convicted and they illustrate the pressures which such people faced.

8.1   Letter from James Barrington, July 1857

Honoured Sir

By reference to the calender you would perceive that I am committed to prison for the term of six months in default of finding two sureties for the several sums of six pounds – likewise in my own person for those sums collectively. The five months imprisonment which I have already endured – the exigencies of my wife and family – the resolution which I have formed of leaving Chester and the certainty of occupation under my late employer at Wolverhampton are facts which I humbly beg to submit for your merciful and mitigating considerations. I presume to add that the moral and religious impressions which I've received at this house of correction are likely to have a salutary effect upon my future conduct.

8.2   Extract of letter from Ellis Crimes, July 1857

I have written to my friends and I cannot get the three five pounds to pay it but if you will be so kind to let me pay it at so much per month I would feel greatly obliged to you Sir. If not, will you please give me some imprisonment in default of the fine, Sir, and I will promise faithfully that I will never come before you again Sir. I can get bail to keep the peace for the twelve months Sir.

8.3   Extract of letter from John Hay, October 1857

The charge was an assault preferred against me by a disorderly female who came to my house to enquire for a person. I told her the person was not there. When she denied it, she then began abusing me with the most abusive language. I ordered her to go away several times but she refused

---

[11] The raising of sureties was a way of guaranteeing a person's behaviour, by making the people listed (usually the offender and two other people) liable to pay a fixed sum to the authorities should the defendant re-offend.

to go. I then took her by the shoulders and turned her away as she was disturbing the whole neighbourhood, she alleging that I had used violence with ejecting her from my house but I beg most emphatically to state that no such violence was used beyond what her resistance demanded.

8.4   Extract of letter from Richard Davies, July 1865

Sir, I am very sorry to say that through me being a stranger in Chester, as I only came here to follow my trade which is a carpenter, and through me not having any friends citizens, I cannot get bail and, Sir, I resort to the expedient of imploring your favour to be kind enough as to grant me my liberty upon my own recognizances, as my trade is now very brisk. I can soon get work to provide for my wife and children if I was at liberty.

8.5   Letter from Richard Rowland, January 1865

Sir,
   I respectfully beg to lay my case before you, humbly hoping, as I used no violence to any one but during a few words which occurred between myself and my wife. Being excited at the time, I made use of threats I never intended to put into execution and having been already six weeks in prison by which I have suffered great loss in my business, which I shall probably lose by being imprisoned, and having always occupied a respectable position in this city, I hope your honour will mercifully consider my case . . . I have no friends willing to become sureties for me.

8.6   Letter from Mary Ann Chamberlaine/Noyes, January 1863
[A 38-year-old woman accused of stealing a shawl and dress from the shop of Richard Cartwright (draper, Bridge St) at Chester Quarter Sessions]

Sir,
   It is with painful feeling that I address you as I feel ashamed of the situation in which I am now placed to appear before you. Sir, I sincerely beg for mercy as it was in an unguarded moment when I was suffering from illtreatment from my husband's relations and under the influence of drink that I did what I now so painfully feel. Sir, I beg for mercy as during the time I was away my conduct was good and when I returned to Chester I married and did all I could to reform my past life but my husband's

relations were all against me and always upbraiding me for my past life and, had I not been under the influence of drink, I should not have been standing here before you. Sir, I sincerely beg for mercy and beg that you will give me one more trial for the sake of my husband.

[Defendant received a sentence of four years' penal servitude]

8.7 Letter from Thomas Dolan, October 1888 [A 27-year-old hawker, accused of stealing ginger beer and glasses from the shops of Mary Kirkham, Harriett Allmark and Samuel Lloyd at Chester Quarter Sessions]

Dear Sir,

These charges that there is against me I do not know anything about. I had been out of town working about two months and working when I came home again. I got amongst a few friends and got the worst for drink. I had been drinking about three days. It was on the third night when I got into this trouble. On the morning of the 23rd of August, I was going down Foregate Street. I met Detective Hughes when he stopped me and asked me whether I knew anything about going into one or two shops in Boughton and calling for any ginger beer and not paying for it. I told him if I did, I knew nothing about it. I would not do such a thing as that if I knew anything about what I was doing. He then asked me would I go with him to see the Chief Constable and I went. He said there wont be much about it. It isn't much, so I don't remember anything about it, Sir.

Dear sir, I have been now waiting nine weeks and three days in prison for my trial. Dear sir, it is a very paltry charge to send for sessions. I must conclude with the case against me. I pleaded guilty before the Magistrates so I am guilty sir.

[Defendant received a sentence of two months' imprisonment]

8.8 Letter from Ralph Minshull, January 1871 [A 40-year-old butcher, accused of theft by false pretences from John Davies Siddall (Bridge Street) at the Chester Quarter Sessions]

Dear Sir,

I am a labouring man and I have endeavoured to obtain an honest living since my former conviction five years ago, until this unfortunate occurrence, to which I plead guilty.

Although I did not go with the full intention to defraud the prosecutor; but being employed by W. R. Littler for to empty the prosecutor's ashpit which I did, and after finishing it, I asked the prosecutor for the money in question, which he gave to me and I intended to return it again when I had received from Mr Littler the pay that was due to me for emptying the ashpit. I am grieved and sorry for what I have done, and I hope and trust that your Honour will take a merciful view of my case, on account of my wife and six children, and my endeavours to lead an honest life for the past five years.

[Defendant received a sentence of six months]

8.9   Letter to the Recorder and Jury from Thomas Knight, July 1857 [A 23-year-old labourer, accused of stealing a watch from John Evans at Chester Quarter Sessions]

Dear Sirs,

I humbly crave your perusal of this simple petition hoping I may meet with your kind consideration. I plead guilty gentlemen to receiving the watch but not to stealing it. But gentlemen I would rather plead guilty to both than take the time of the court up with this painful case. I wrote to the Governor of the Liverpool prison in which I had the misfortune to be confined and informed him of the parties I came to Chester with as he was known by the officers of the above prison but I have not been able to know whether he has been found or not. There is no proof gentlemen to show that what I state is correct but if I may be believed though a prisoner what I have said is true. Mr Clark Duke or any of the officers will if necessary give me a character as to how I conducted myself when discharged from the above prison and how I let no opportunity pass without applying for situations. Mr Duke entrusted me with property belonging to the prison and when I could not gain a maintenance by them was kind enough to write to the chairman of the town council for the restoration of my licence and I was told by the chairman that it would be granted only when the number allowed was completed and I found my character so stained with being in prison that I was unable to get any situation. I now gentlemen throw myself upon you kind mercy hoping that what I have said may have met with your kind consideration and that after looking into my distressing circumstances you will be as lenient as my unfortunate case will allow and I beg leave to state that as soon as my imprisonment has expired I have determined to "enlist" sooner rather than throw myself again upon the precipice I now stand. I now conclude gentlemen hoping that I may not despair of your good and kind mercy at this most distressing moment.

I am gentlemen a most penitent and distressed youth,

Thomas G. Knight

[Defendant was sentenced to six years' penal servitude]

8.10   Letter from three accused robbers, October 1871

[Peter O'Brien (28, labourer), James Bird (27, tailor) and W. Bradshaw (25, tailor) were accused of robbing Robert Duncan (collier) of a razor and some money at Chester Quarter Sessions, October 1871. Each of the defendants had several previous convictions.]

"Sir, please put the following questions to the Prosecutor."

1. What money did he have when he left the pub to accompany the two women to the private room, that they and he went too? (He had a florin and a shilling; the shilling he gave to Betsy McIntyre, the Mrs of the room, for the use of it, and the florin he gave to the prisoner, O'Brien, for to fetch half a gallon of ale, and the shilling change, that he received out of the florin, He gave to Mary Galloen to have connections[12] with her.)
2. How much money did he give to the prisoner Bird in the room?
3. What amount of money had he, when he left the room, to return a second time to the public house and if he called for any drink? (He said that he had no money on entering the public house the second time and he begged sixpence from O'Brien, to pay for his lodgings.)
4. If he saw the prisoner, Bradshaw, anywhere in his company during that day? (He stated before the magistrates that he had never seen Bradshaw anywhere until he saw him in the court.)
    Sir, I wish to understand, that all this took place, before the prosecutor went anywhere near Dee Lane, the place were he said he was robbed.
5. If he remembers being locked up in a cell along with a young man, and saying to him thus: I should like to know what I am here for

---

[12] i.e. sexual intercourse.

I have not robbed anyone, but there are two men in here [meaning the lock-ups] that I have been drinking with today, and perhaps I am charged on suspicion with them, for something they have done, because I was in their company?

6. When he was brought out of the cell next morning, into the police office, if the razors and other articles were not shown to him, and by whom? (Sir, the prosecutor was in the police office when the prisoners O'Brien and Bird were brought in, but he did not charge them with robbing him, he did not make any charge until he was giving his evidence before the magistrates.)

Peter O'Brien   James Bird   W. Bradshaw

[All three defendants were sentenced to seven years' penal servitude.]

9   Low Attorneys, 1854[13]

In a system which relied on private civilians to organize their cases with little information from official sources, there was always the risk that some prosecutors would fall prey to those who exploited legal ignorance for their own ends. In giving evidence to a select committee which was to recommend the employment of a public prosecutor, a clerk highlights the activity of unscrupulous attorneys.

It is astonishing with how much mischief you have to put in Staffordshire. It is very well known there, that though the costs are at a very low rate, there is a perfect hunt for the prosecutions by low attorneys, and by those persons who practise in the names of attorneys but who are not attorneys; the consequence is that they get hold of the prosecutors who are poor, and incompetent to carry on the prosecution; they tell them that they will conduct the prosecution; it gets into their hands, and they never take the least trouble about it, any more than giving counsel a copy of the depositions with the fee on the back of the brief, and they let the case take its chance at the assizes.

10   The Police Courts, 1870[14]

The press gave a high level of coverage to the police courts in the second half of the nineteenth century. This is illustrated by the passage below, which is taken from a single column of one edition of the Staffordshire Advertiser. *Note the*

---

[13] *Evidence to the select committee on the public prosecution bill*, P.P. 1854/5, vol. xii.
[14] *Staffordshire Advertiser*, 24/12/1870.

range of offences covered and the way in which the journalists used carefully chosen subheadings and local knowledge to embellish mundane cases. Newspapers reported aspects of the magistrates' courts not covered by official records, such as the interventions of solicitors and conversations between magistrates and witnesses.

10.1   Stafford

A juvenile offender – Thomas Harvey, of Bank Top, Manchester, a lad who goes about the country singing, was charged with stealing a clothes' brush, the property of Mrs Thomas Turner, ironmonger, and was sentenced to two months' imprisonment.

Theft from an employer – John Ward, of the Backwalls, pleaded guilty to stealing a shilling the property of Mr John Taylor, shoe manufacturer, to whom he was apprenticed. He confessed to the prosecutor that he had at various times taken between £7 and £8 from a drawer in the office. Police-sergeant Lester said the prisoner had got into bad company and learnt to smoke and drink. Although his wages were only 4s a week he had paid 22s into a money club at the Spread Eagle public house in Eastgate Street, having deposited 8s at one time. He pleaded guilty and was sentenced to three months' imprisonment.

The Bench called the attention of the police to a very dangerous nuisance caused by boys and girls sliding in the streets, and directed them to use their best endeavours to put a stop to the practice. They fined a lad 1s and costs for playing at tip-cat,[15] another game very dangerous to passers-by.

10.2   Cannock

Fowl stealing – Joseph Whitehouse, of Wryley Bank, and William Snape, of Pelsall, commonly called the "Pelsall Prince", were charged with stealing five fowls, the property of Mr Sampson Sambrook, Shoal Hill, near Cannock. Mr Dale (from the office of Messrs Duignan, Lewis and Lewis, Walsall) appeared for the prisoners. The prosecutor deposed to seeing four hens and a cock safe between five and six o'clock on the evening of the 12th instant: he missed them on the following morning. Police-sergeant Barnes arrested the prisoners. On searching the house of Whitehouse the next day he discovered two hens and a cock, the heads of which had been

---

[15] A game in which a player uses a stick to hit one end of a piece of wood on the ground so that it jumps up. The wood is then hit as far as possible.

cut off, and in the house of Snape one hen and the remains of another. He also discovered footmarks leading from the direction of the high road towards the fowlpen of the prosecutor. The marks corresponded with the boots worn by the prisoners. The prosecutor identified the head of one of the fowls stolen. The prisoners, who have both been previously convicted, were committed for trial at the sessions.

10.3   Lichfield

Bridget Smith and Stephen Freeman were each fined 10s and costs for assaulting Mr James Grimley, landlord of the Duke of Cambridge, and refusing to quit his house on the 18th last.

10.4   Tamworth

Poaching – Francis Cox, John Wingfield, Thomas Burdett and John Thompson, all of Fazely, pleaded guilty to trespassing in search of game upon land belonging to Captain Levett, of Pickington, in the occupation of Mr C. Cox. There were three previous convictions against Wingfield for various offences, and he was fined £1 and 6s 3d costs. The three others were each fined 10s and 6s 3d costs.

10.5   Burton-on-Trent

Thomas Roberts, railway servant, was fined 20s and costs for trespassing in pursuit of game on land over which Mr F. Gretton has the right of shooting.

John Staton, an old offender, was fined 30s and 9s 6d costs for a similar offence at Branstone. Mr Stevenson appeared for the prosecution, and Mr Williams for the defendant.

Frederick Trowell, of Etwall, and George Thacker, of Linton, were each fined 1s and 12s 6d costs, for removing offensive matter[16] during prohibited hours at Burton.

Theft by a girl – Sarah Doman, a girl 13 years of age, pleaded guilty to stealing a half-sovereign and three cigars, the property of her master,

---

[16] i.e. sewage.

Mr J. W. Weaver, of the Railway Inn, Borough Road. During the temporary absence of Mrs Weaver to another part of the house, the prisoner extracted the half-sovereign from a purse upon the kitchen table, and called the attention of her mistress to it, and attempted to cast suspicion upon a customer in the house. Inspector Hatton was called in, and after inquiry he took the prisoner into custody. Three cigars were found in her possession, but she stoutly denied taking the money, and it was not until she was searched at the lock-up that the half-sovereign was found in her possession. She was sentenced to one month's imprisonment and three years in a reformatory.

Moses Siddals, a newspaper hawker, charged with refusing to maintain his wife and child, was ordered to contribute 5s per week towards their maintenance. Mr Coxon appeared for the Guardians,[17] and Mr Wilson for the defendant.

Larceny and assaulting the police – Christopher Ling, maltster, was sentenced to fourteen days' imprisonment for stealing twelve herrings, the property of Thomas Coates, fishmonger. The prisoner was further charged with another maltster named Isaac River, with assaulting police constables Williams, Callaghan, and Devay, while in the execution of their duty, and they were each fined £1 and costs, or one months' imprisonment.

The adjourned case against Arthur Goodhead, for embezzlement, was today dismissed. Mr Wilson appeared for the prisoner.

An order of removal was granted in the case of Joseph Vale, aged 77, from Burton to Austrey in the Tamworth union.[18]

10.6   Stone

Assault – Richard Light, of Oulton, was charged with assaulting Mary Jackson. From the complainant's evidence it appeared that Light's mother was very ill, and she had been requested to attend to her. She did so until the defendant came into the bedroom and began swearing at her, and threatened to burn his mother's bed under her to save any further medicine. He then began to beat her about the arms and shoulders. She screamed out, and assistance came. The defendant was fined 5s and costs, and the Bench severely reproved him for his unseemly conduct in his dying mother's bedroom.

---

[17] These Guardians were officers of Poor Law Union.
[18] i.e. the Tamworth Poor Law Union.

Alleged cruelty by a step-mother – Joseph Arrowicks, of Coton, charged his wife with cruelty to a child three years old, the offspring of a former wife, by pushing it violently into a chair on the 22nd of August. The wife said the child was very dirty and had provoked her. The bench dismissed the case.

Charge of assault – Job Carr, of Barlaston, charged George Slynn and James Day with assaulting him on the 10th last. The complainant stated that as he was coming from Tittensor the defendants met him, pulled him down, beat him until the blood came, and then carried him into Latham's house, where they lodged. Mr Latham, for the defence, said Carr was drunk and coming up singing near their house, when he fell down, and George Slynn went out and fetched him into the house. The bench dismissed the case, telling Carr that when persons acted the part of the Good Samaritan towards him he should not charge them with assault.

Alleged thefts – Mr Paul Prince, of Coton, charged Alfred Bromley, of the same place, with larceny. The prosecutor said he had bought a dozen traps for rabbits from Stone, and in September he lost three of them. John Shakespeare, gamekeeper of the Earl of Shrewsbury, deposed that on the 27th last he was watching in the cover adjoining where Mr Prince has the shooting, when he saw the defendant come to the ditch where witness was, and stoop down to a hole in cover. Witness sprang out and said, "Bromley, I have caught you at last," and the prisoner dropped the trap, which Mr Prince identified as his property. Mr Brough, who appeared for the prisoner, urged that it being five o'clock in the evening Shakespeare could not see very well, and that it was a case of mistaken identity. The prisoner was committed to trial to the Sessions.

10.7   Newcastle

Patrick Murphy pleaded guilty to charges of having, while drunk and disorderly, assaulted Police-sergeant Marriott and Police-constable Pegg. He was fined 10s and costs, or 21 days' imprisonment.

A boy named Thomas Whittaker was fined 1s and costs for having assaulted another youth, named Philip Elliot, on the 14th December.

10.8   Hanley

Alleged fraud by a debtor – John Hughes, grocer and beerseller, Tunstall, was charged with having (within four months of the commencement of a liquidation, by arrangement, of his affairs) by false representations and other fraud, unlawfully obtained from Josiah Lester Thomas, provision merchant, Hanley, goods to the amount of £12 9s 2d on credit, and had not paid for the same. Mr E. Tenant appeared for the prosecution. The case was adjourned for a fortnight, a meeting of the creditors taking place meanwhile.

10.9   Longton

A refractory policeman – George Watson, a Police-constable stationed at Longton, was charged with neglect and violation of duty on the night of the 19th last. Police-sergeant Macrory stated that about half-past ten on Monday evening he heard a great noise in the messroom. On going to inquire the cause he found the defendant very drunk and making a great disturbance, kicking and knocking everything about in the most violent manner. He ordered him to bed, but he refused, and continued his violent conduct. Superintendent Kelly, subsequently finding that Watson was totally unfit for duty, and still refused to go to bed, locked him up. The Bench said they were sorry that a policeman should place himself in so disgraceful a position, and sentenced him to a month's imprisonment.

William Lockett and John Perkins, charged with playing at pitch-and-toss at Longton, were each ordered to find sureties for their good conduct and for the next three months and pay costs.

Mr Garnham, inspector of nuisances, preferred a complaint against Samuel Elkin for unlawfully taking the town manure. The defendant did not appear and the evidence not being sufficiently conclusive as to his identity, except that he had a wooden leg, a warrant was ordered to issue against him.

10.10   Tunstall

The highway robberies and indecent assaults – Michael Fury was charged on remand with robbing and indecently assaulting Elizabeth Colclough, at Tunstall, and Elizabeth Thornhill, at Bradwell Wood, the latter offence taking place as far back as November, 1868. The depositions were completed and the prisoner was committed for trial at the next Assizes on all the charges. An application to admit bail was peremptorily refused. Mr Salt was for the prosecution.

Larceny at Tunstall – Richard Cooper and Mary Cooper were charged with stealing a pair of trousers, the property of James Griffiths. On Wednesday evening the female prisoner went to pledge a pair of trousers at the shop of Mr Hadfield, stating that they belonged to her husband. The fact of tradesman's private ticket being found upon the trousers led to the pawnbroker's assistant suspecting that they had not been honestly come by. So it turned out, as the woman subsequently admitted that she had stolen the trousers from Mr Griffiths' shop. Superintendent Baker asked for the husband to be discharged as he seemed in no way connected with the theft, and he was at once liberated. The wife was committed to prison for seven days as a vagrant, the prosecutor recommending her to mercy.

Unfeeling conduct of a mother – Mary Greenwood came up, on remand, charged with being drunk and assaulting her child, about eight years of age. The poor child is a great cripple and dumb, and the mother, who was brutally ill-treating it when drunk in the streets at Tunstall, was given into custody. Superintendent Baker had the child properly taken care of, and subsequently it was placed in the union workhouse, where it now remains. The mother was ordered to find a surety in £10 to keep the peace for three months, which will be tantamount to that term of imprisonment. She was said to have come from Lancashire, and had no doubt gone about begging with the child.

Edwin Ragguley came up on three charges, one preferred by Mr Bennett, the governor of the workhouse, of absconding with the clothing; the second of doing wilful damage to the amount of 20s to three doors at the house of Thomas Allen, in Tunstall; and the third, of being drunk and disorderly in Tunstall. For the first offence, the defendant was committed to prison for 14 days; for the wilful damage, in default of payment, he was sentenced to a further period of 14 days; and on the charge by the police, he was fined 10s and costs, or a third 14 days. He is thus sent to prison for six weeks.

Ann Bates, a notoriously old offender, who has just come out of gaol, where altogether she has spent some years of her wretched life, was again committed for a month for vagrancy at Kidsgrove.

10.11 Wolverhampton

Music licences – This was a special sitting for hearing applications for music licences. Mr H. Underhill (Town Clerk) applied for such a licence to Molineux House and grounds. He said that the playing of musical instruments would be kept at least 100 yards from the Waterloo Road, would be wholly confined to string instruments, and the number of the band would not exceed seven persons, who would cease playing at sunset. Mr Underhill pointed out that the Act gave the Justices power to grant the licence under any conditions they thought fit to impose, and for every breach of such conditions the licensee would be liable to a fine of £5 and costs. The application was granted on condition that a string band of seven performers only played, that they did not play within 100 yards of adjoining premises, and that they ceased playing at sunset – A licence was also granted to Mr Sparrow for music and dancing at the Albion Grounds, Dudley Road, the amusements to cease at sunset – The upper room of the Horse and Jockey inn, Bilston Road was licensed for music and dancing; and Mr W. Brett, of the Concert Hall, Cheapside, had his music licences renewed – Fourteen other applications from innkeepers in the town were refused.

11   The Old Bailey, 1862[19]

The passage below, written by Henry Mayhew and John Binny, describes the layout of the most prominent trial court in England: the Old Bailey. Thinking about the physical settings in which trials and hearings took place is one way to study the atmosphere and power-relations of the courts. As can be seen, each participant in the trial process had their place and these were carefully arranged within the courtrooms.

The sessions house is situated adjoining to Newgate [prison]. The older wing is uniform with it in external appearance and was the ancient sessions house. In former times there was only one High Criminal Court held there, but the business is now divided among three and sometimes a fourth is held in the grand jury room, all within the same building in the Old Bailey. The heavier offences are tried here, such as forgery, arson, coining, manslaughter, murder, etc. At one or other the Recorder and the Common Serjeant[20] are seated on the bench and other judges of the State.

The old courtroom, which is represented in the engraving, is only about 50 feet square. There are six small movable desks, on which the judges take their notes and write their communications, comfortably seated on cushioned seats of a crimson colour. The panelling behind them is covered with crimson cloth sadly faded. Over the centre of the bench there is a tasteful wooden canopy, surmounted with the Royal Arms beautifully carved. A sword of justice, with a gold handle and ornamental scabbard is usually suspended under the canopy during the sittings of the court. Opposite to the bench, on the other side of the courtroom is the dock, a

[19] H. Mayhew & J. Binny, *The criminal prisons of London and scene of prison life* (London, 1862), pp. 607–8.
[20] The common serjeant was an officer particular to London, appointed by the Corporation of London as an assistant to the Recorder.

small enclosure, 13 feet by 19, where the criminals stand to take their trial. The jury box, consisting of two long seats, is situated on the right hand of the judges. The clerk of arraigns occupies a desk beneath the bench and fronting the dock. The attorneys are seated around a table, in the area of the court, covered with green cloth and the counsel in wig and gown, their official costume, occupy three seats alongside. Behind the latter there are several seats for the reporters, with others for friends of the judges, and for a portion of the jury in waiting. The prisoners enter the dock by a staircase behind communicating with the cells beneath. The governor of Newgate occupies a seat at the corner of the dock, by the side of the prisoners and their attendants. Behind and above the dock there is a small gallery for the public, where heads are seen peering over as in the engraving, and there are usually a number of solicitors, barristers, witnesses and policemen clustered around the area, and to be seen in the various passages.

There are seven doors entering into the old courtroom: two of them on the side next to Newgate, one of them in the area being for witnesses, and another more elevated being a private entrance for the judges. On the opposite side there were two doors, one for the jury and counsel, and the other a private entrance for the judges and magistrates who take their seats on the bench. There is another door behind the bench by which any of the judges are able to retire when disposed and, on each side of the dock, there is another door for the entrance of the witnesses, solicitors, and jury.

This courtroom is lighted by three large windows towards Newgate, and by three smaller sombre windows on the opposite side.

12   The Law Courts, 1891[21]

The following sketch of the English law courts was published in 1891. It outlines the structure of the court system of the late nineteenth century and compares it with that of the previous centuries. In tracing the changes that had taken place, the author gives a polemical portrayal of the role of the police and the deteriorating position of defendants within the courts.

So far as its procedure is concerned, our criminal law has hardly changed since the time of the Conquest, and in the opinion of many lawyers as well as laymen who have studied the matter, it is high time that some improvements were introduced. It is not our intention here to review the whole field of criminal administration. The work is too vast for the limits of this

---

[21] A. Guest, "The State of the Law Courts", *The Strand Magazine* 11, 1891, pp. 84–92.

article. We may, however, briefly direct attention to those matters wherein we think that improvement might be effected.

The criminal courts in this country consist of the Petty Sessions, as they are generally termed in boroughs, the police courts, the Courts of Quarter Sessions, and the assize courts. In the large cities, such as Manchester, Newcastle, etc., there are stipendiary magistrates who are appointed by the Home Secretary at the instance of the local town council, which provides their salaries. The metropolis is divided for the purpose of police administration into various districts, every police-court having two magistrates, each of whom sits three days a week, the busiest days being Mondays and Tuesdays.

The work of the London police magistrates is of an exceedingly diversified character, consisting principally of charges of drunkenness, petty larceny, assaults on the police or on private individuals, and indictable offences in which they take the preliminary hearing, and, is satisfied that there is a prima facie case, commit the accused for trial. In addition to this, they have a vast number of duties recently imposed upon them by the Legislature, such as school board prosecutions and cases under the Sanitary, Tramway and Public Carriage, Building, and Employers and Workmen's Acts, as well as various other matters which it is unnecessary to detail. Altogether the work is of a singularly repulsive character, and it is for this reason, perhaps, that many of the magistrates pride themselves on getting through the greatest possible number of cases in the shortest time. But this system of administering justice at high pressure is not entirely satisfactory. Most of the magistrates are remiss in the matter of taking depositions and notes of evidence. Indeed, this is very seldom done at all except in cases of indictable offence. The rapidity with which some of the cases are disposed of is almost absurd. For instance, in some courts when a prisoner is charged with being drunk and disorderly, the magistrate does not even give him time for defence, the trial occupying about two minutes and consisting of something like the following: Officer (kissing the book): "I found the prisoner outside the Green Lion public house last night at twelve o'clock. He was drunk and disorderly, and I took him into custody." Magistrate (interrupting): "Five shillings, or seven days."

There is no appeal, and no note is taken by means of which a possible injustice might be investigated.

Undoubtedly, the magistrates ought to take notes in every case, so that, on the event of a miscarriage of justice, they might be submitted to the Home Secretary.

One of the gravest defects in the administration of justice by police magistrates results from the almost implicit reliance that they place upon the uncorroborated testimony of a single Police-constable. We shall probably not be accused of exaggeration when we assert that the police are, as a rule, hard swearers. The very *esprit de corps*, which in itself is a commendable feature of the force, leads the constables often recklessly to support each other's evidence. Besides this, whenever the police make a charge against any individual they at once jump to the conclusion that he is guilty, and there is nothing that they desire so much as a conviction.

To such an outrageous degree has the acceptance of police evidence extended that the public have come to look upon it as next to useless to defend themselves against a police charge. No better illustration of this is to be found than in the complaints against omnibus and tramway drivers for loitering. One well-known magistrate was in the habit of doubling the fine where a defence was offered, and, conviction being inevitable, the public drivers now invariably plead "guilty" by the instruction of their employers. They pay the fine without demur, rather than incur the expense and delay of what would certainly be a futile defence, be the real merits of the case what they may.

Not very long ago a well-known metropolitan magistrate entertained the strongest possible aversion to bicycles and tricycles, and whenever he had before him a dispute between a cyclist and a constable, or, indeed, any other person, it was almost a certainty that he would decide in favour of the latter.

The fact that charges against Police-constables are rare is largely due to the hopelessness of success. The Treasury, in our judgement very unfairly, places at the disposal of the policeman the best legal advice and he is represented by a clever criminal lawyer, while a poor man bringing a charge has to rely upon his own unaided resources, or, perhaps, on one of those fifth-rate solicitors who haunt the purlieus of the police courts, and whose advocacy is too often detrimental to the interests of their client. It is a serious fault in the system that the magistrates should always have the same division of police before them. Frequently seeing the same officers, they become predisposed in their favour, the more so as they find that a great acceleration of business is thereby attained. Many of the magistrates, indeed, through being too mindful of their own convenience in this respect, have gradually become mere slaves of the police. The magistrate is practically the only protector of the public against the indiscretions of the police, and if he invariably sides with that body against the public, whose servant he is, he undoubtedly fails in his duty.

The Quarter Sessions are established in all the counties, including the county of London, and other county boroughs, as well as in certain Quarter Sessions boroughs. In the small boroughs where there are no Quarter Sessions, the appeal from Petty Sessions goes to the Quarter Sessions of the county in which the borough is situate. Besides its appellate jurisdiction, the Quarter Sessions constitutes a court for the trial of those criminal cases that are not within the exclusive jurisdiction of the High Court. In London the court is presided over by a salaried officer known as the assistant-judge; in some boroughs the recorder presides, and in the counties there is usually an unpaid Justice called the chairman. All the cases are heard before a jury. The Quarter Sessions in the provinces are usually attended by a numerous Bar, chiefly composed of the younger men on each circuit, together with a few more experienced barristers who have never emerged from criminal work. A prisoner unable to employ a solicitor to instruct counsel is entitled to secure the services of a barrister by handing a guinea over the dock, and many young advocates do a brisk trade in what are termed "dockers". It would be a great gain if the state were to provide for the proper defence of prisoners, who are undoubtedly at a great disadvantage when opposed by astute criminal lawyers.

The judges of the High Court go on assize four times a year to try those more serious cases which are outside the jurisdiction of the Quarter Sessions, and also to deliver the gaols of such prisoners as, whatever their offence, have been committed for trial since the previous Quarter Sessions.

And while the judges are away on assize, the Common Law work of the metropolis is absolutely at a standstill. Even at the assize court it is doubtful whether adequate justice is always done; it certainly depends in a great degree on the individual temperament of the judges. The extraordinary disparity between the sentences passed by different judges for offences of the same gravity gives rise to continual comment. It seems strange, indeed, that the judges and chairmen of Quarter Sessions have not conferred together to lay down some approximate rule as a guidance in the measure of punishments. Some judges are in the habit of inflicting almost uniformly light sentences, while there are others who are remarkable for their severity. Lord Coleridge has, in a praiseworthy manner, always discountenanced those barbarious sentences of penal servitude for trumpery larceny which have sometimes shocked the public conscience.

There is another grave defect in the administration of the criminal law, but to this – as it has been of late widely discussed – we need to do no more than briefly advert. We refer to the fact that England stands almost alone in not according to persons charged with offences the right to give evidence on their own behalf.[22] Recent legislation has given this privilege in offences of a certain class; but these cases are rare, and they merely accentuate the absurdity of closing the mouth of the prisoner in the majority of criminal charges. Lawyers of experience generally concur in the view that, if a prisoner were always permitted to give evidence on his own behalf, the innocent would be materially assisted. It is a curious fact that the present practice is a survival of an older system under which a defendant in a civil cause were also ineligible as a witness. The disability has been removed in the one case, and there is a strong feeling among those who should best know, in favour of its abolition in the other.

---

[22] This situation was soon to be reversed with the Criminal Evidence Act, 1898. 61 & 62 Vict. c. 36.

13 Reform of the Police Courts, 1908[23]

Thomas Holmes had worked as a Police Court Missionary[24] in London over a 21-year period and was secretary of the Howard Association for prison reform at the time of writing his book Known to the police *(1908). In the following section, in a tone contrasting markedly with the passage above, he reminisces about the Police Courts of the early 1880s. He portrays the period 1880–1900 as one of major change, arguing that squalid conditions, corrupt policemen, officious magistrates and unprincipled solicitors had all disappeared.*

The conditions at London police-courts in those days [1880s] were bad, past conception. No words of mine can adequately describe them, and only for the sake of comparison and encouragement do I attempt briefly to portray some of the most striking features of those days. Even now I feel faint when I recall the "prisoners' waiting-room", with its dirty floor, its greasy walls, and its vile atmosphere.

The sanitary arrangements were disgusting. There was no female attendant to be found on the premises. Strong benches attached to the walls provided the only seats; neither was there separation of the sexes. In this room old and young, pure and impure, clean and verminous, sane and insane, awaited their turn to appear before the magistrate; for the insane in those days were brought by local authorities that the magistrate might certify them, and they sat, too, amongst the waiting prisoners.

The sufferings of a decent woman who found herself in such company in such a room may easily be imagined; but the sufferings of a pure-minded girl, who for some trifling offence found herself in like position, cannot be described. The coarse women of Alsatia made jests upon her, and coarse blackguards, though sometimes well dressed, vaunted their obscenity before her. Deformed beggars, old hags from the workhouse – or from worse places – thieves, gamblers, drunkards, and harlots, men and women on the verge of delirium tremens – all these, and others that are unmentionable, combine to make the prisoners' room a horrid memory. Things are far different to-day, for light and cleanliness, fresh air and decency, prevail at police-courts. At every court there is now a female attendant; the sexes are rigidly separated. Children's cases are heard separately; neither are children placed in the cells or prisoners' room.

In those days policemen waited for the men and women who had been in their custody, and against whom they had given evidence, and, after their fines were paid, went to the nearest public house and drank at their

---

[23] Thomas Holmes, *Known to the police* (London, 1908), pp. 13–20.

[24] Police Court Missionaries were employed to look into cases that came up before the magistrates, offering help both to those being tried and also to anyone involved in a case who appeared to be facing particular social or financial difficulties.

expense. Hundreds of times I have heard prisoners ask the prosecuting policeman to "Make it light for me", and many times I have heard the required promise given and an arrangement made. Sometimes I am glad to think that I have heard policemen give the reply: "I shall speak the truth"; but not often was this straightforward answer given.

In this respect a great change has come about, for policemen do not hold a conference with their prisoners in the waiting room, and it is now a rare occurrence for a policeman to take a drink at his prisoner's expense.

And this improvement is to be welcomed, for it is typical of the improvement that has been going on all around. Gaolers in those days were "civil servants", and were not under police authority; now they are sergeants of the police, and under police discipline and authority. The old civil servant gaoler looked down from his greater altitude with something like contempt upon the common policemen, and this often led to much friction and unpleasantness. Now things work smoothly and easily, for every police-court official knows his duties and to whom he is responsible.

But a great change has also come over the magistrates – perhaps the greatest change of all. Doubtless the magistrates of those days were excellent men, but they were not only officials, but official also.

It was their business to mete out punishment, and they did it. Some were old – too old for the office. I have seen one sleeping on the bench frequently, and only waking up to give sentence. Once, while the Justice nodded, his false teeth fell on his desk; he awoke with a start, and made a frantic effort to recover them. No doubt these men were sound lawyers, but they were representatives of the community as it then existed; there was no sentimentality about them, but they were rarely vindictive.

The legal profession, too, has changed. Where are the greasy, drunken old solicitors that haunted the precincts of police-courts twenty-five years ago? Gone. But they were common enough in those days, and touted for five-shilling jobs, money down, or higher prices when payment was deferred. With droughty throats and trembling limbs, they hastened to the nearest public house to spend what payment had been given in advance. Here they would remain till their clients were before the magistrate, and would then appear just in time to say: "I appear for the prisoner, your worship." Horrid old men they were, the fronts of their coats and vests all stained and shiny with the droppings of beer. Frequently the magistrate, unable to tolerate their drunken or half-drunken maunderings, would order them out of court; but even this drastic treatment had little effect upon them, for the next day, or even the latter part of the same day, they, apparently without shame or humiliation, would inform his Worship that they were in So-and-so's case, and ask at what time it would be taken – as if, forsooth, their engagements were numerous and important.

The bullying solicitor, too, has disappeared or mended his ways. No longer is he allowed to bully and insult witnesses or prosecutors, and cast scurrilous and unclean imputations on the lives and characters of those opposed to him. Generally these fellows were engaged for the "defence".

They one and all acted on the principle that to attack was the best defence. I once heard an athletic young doctor ask a solicitor of this kind, who had been unusually insulting, to meet him when the case was over, assuring him also that he would receive his deserts – a good thrashing. The pompous ignorant solicitor, with neither wit, words, action, utterance, nor the power of speech – he, too, has gone. One wondered at the strange fate that made solicitors of such men; wondered, too, how they passed the necessary examinations; but wondered most of all why people paid money for such fellows to defend them. Invariably they made their client's case much worse; they always declined to let "sleeping dogs lie", and were positively certain to reveal something or discover something to the disadvantage of the person whose interests they were supposed to be upholding. I remember one magistrate, sitting impatient and fidgety while the weary drip of words went on, calling out suddenly: "Three months' hard labour, during which you can ruminate on the brilliant defence made by your solicitor!"

All these have passed, and police-courts have been civilized; for law is more dignified, and its administration more refined. Magistrates are up to date, too, and quite in touch with the new order of things and with the aspirations of the community.

Bullying, drunken, and stupid solicitors have no chance to-day. In all these directions great changes have come about, and great progress has been made.

14 Magistrates and the Poor, 1903[25]

A. C. Plowden had been a recorder, stipendiary magistrate in the London police courts and a barrister in the trial courts. In the extract below he argues that the magistrate's role in the police courts went beyond the mere distribution of justice. He saw the activity of advising the poor as playing an important part in fostering trust of the law and improving the image of the magistracy.

Readers of the newspapers who are interested in the police court will have noticed that magistrates, besides disposing of cases, have to listen to a considerable number of applications in their courts.

The people who make them are mostly in humble circumstances, and the general grasp they have of the limits within which the law can help

---

[25] A. C. Plowden, *Grain or chaff: the autobiography of a police magistrate* (London, 1903), p. 26.

them is remarkable. It is very seldom they have the means to employ a solicitor. At the same time, as is only natural, there are many whose knowledge is less exact, and who seem to think there is no wrong or trouble in life which cannot be redressed at the hands of a magistrate.

It would be an ungracious act to deal too brusquely with these poor people. The borderland between offences which are purely moral and those which come within the purview of law is more easily defined than explained, and humble folk who take their stand on the Decalogue[26] may be pardoned if they fail to understand why it should be criminal to break the eighth commandment and not the seventh. And with many others who perhaps have not considered the subject at all it is easy to understand that in the daily ordering of their lives social and domestic difficulties will constantly arise for which it may be thought, not unreasonably, that the law will provide a remedy.

But what specially appeals to the magistrate is the touching faith which seems to be reposed in him personally. If the law can help, well and good; if it can't, surely the magistrate will be able to comfort in some way or other, and give welcome advice. It is impossible to turn a deaf ear to these people, and thus the custom has grown up in all the courts not only to grant process for legal wrongs, but to advise generally wherever a sympathetic answer or the application of a little common sense or knowledge of the world is likely to give relief.

If there are days when the regular business of the court is somewhat impeded by dealing with these irrelevancies, the balance is more than restored by the strengthening of the bond between the magistrate and the public, and the greater confidence which is felt in the administration of justice.

A police court is the tribunal of all others which is most in touch with the people. In the higher courts of the land the issues are too high and mighty for popular comprehension. The sittings, too, are interrupted by circuits and suspended by the vacations. With the police courts it is different. The sittings are continuous. The courts are open every day of the year, excepting only Good Friday and Christmas Day, and the cases which come before the magistrates are mostly simple, and easily understood by the people.

The magistrates, too, by the mere fact of their own constant attendance become familiarized in their several districts. It is natural their advice should be sought, and it is all to the good of the law which they administer, as tending to make it more gracious and popular, that they should lend a sympathetic ear to grievances honestly put forward and believed in, even though they fall short of a legal wrong.

---

[26] The Ten Commandments.

And there is this to be said about irrelevant applications, that they frequently reward attention by revealing rich surprises in human nature. They bring to the surface the most extraordinary beliefs and superstitions, diversities of thought and conduct, which seem to lie quite outside the ordinary experience of life.

Chapter 8

Punishment in the Nineteenth Century

1 Gloucester Prison, 1819[1]

Sir George Onesiphorus Paul was one of a group of magistrates who set about reforming prisons at the local level at the end of the eighteenth and beginning of the nineteenth century. He oversaw the building of a new county gaol and four houses of correction. In the passage below, he outlines his philosophy to a parliamentary committee on solitary confinement and the use of labour within the prison.

Are you an acting magistrate in the county of Gloucester?
I am.
Were the present gaol, penitentiary house and houses of correction built and the system adopted there carried into effect under your particular recommendation?
Yes.
Have you had an opportunity of examining the effects of that system, and up to what period?
I attended to the effect for seventeen years, up to the period of 1809. The principle of my system of imprisonment is to make a discriminate and distinct use of the several species of prisons, which are sanctioned by the common, or ordained by statute law.
How have the prisoners been employed?
In a great variety of works of simple manufacture.
How have the prisoners been confined during the day?
All of them have worked alone so long as there were separate cells for the purpose.
What laborious work have they had?
Since the gaol was finished, the only laborious work has been walking in a vertical wheel, for the purpose of raising water for the prison, which wheel is necessarily kept going the greater part of the day. In this wheel two prisoners make a joint effort, without being able to see or to converse with each other. The prisoners are taken from their cells in pairs, and work about twenty minutes; after they come out of the wheel they are generally, more or less, in a state of perspiration, and as it would be

---

[1] *Evidence of G. O. Paul to the report of the select committee on the state of gaols, etc.*, P.P. 1819, vol. vii, pp. 401–4.

improper to put them into their cells in that state, they therefore walk in the yard for another twenty minutes. These prisoners are then returned to their day cells, and others, in succession, pursue the same course.

Did that working in the wheel find employment for all the prisoners in the course of the day, who were in a fit state of health?

Yes, generally, in this degree, with the exception of old men or boys, and others who were unfit for such labour.

Did you consider that as beneficial to the prisoners with regard to health?

I have every reason to believe it greatly conduced to their health.

Did it operate as a punishment, or was it undertaken with cheerfulness?

I never observed any disposition to murmur at these or any other orders which were given to the prisoners in this prison.

Was work of any other kind found for all prisoners in the penitentiary?

Yes, some employment or other has been found for all, as a necessary concomitant to seclusion.

Do you conceive constant employment to be essential for persons confined in solitude?

I believe that solitude, with occupation or employment, and with due attention to its effects, will reform the most hardened criminal; but without such occupation and such attention it ought never to be applied for such a length of time as prisoners in the penitentiary house are generally confined.

Are you aware that the governor has been in the habit, for the last seventeen or eighteen years, of leaving persons, who have been sent there for a month, in perfect solitude without any occupation?

I understand that the governor has suffered prisoners to remain in solitude without employment, when confined for short terms, as in houses of correction. I may presume that even this solitude has been relieved by congregating them with their fellow prisoners at the morning chapel and on their evening parade: this practice, although it may be usefully applied in special cases, I am not at present disposed to admit into the general rules of discipline.

For what time do you think it might be allowed?

The effect of solitude depends on the character of the patient; but generally, I should say, not more than a month, without some occupation of mind or body. I beg to add, that the employment of the prisoners has principally been on manufactures on account of the county, by purchasing the raw material, and abiding by the risk of sale of the manufactured goods. The late improvements in machinery have so diminished, or rather so annihilated the objects of work by hand, that the power of supporting a system of hard labour in prison, to be productive of emolument, is entirely out of the question. The principle, therefore, of this part of our discipline, is rather to give employment than to punish by hard labour, as intended by former laws: by preventing solitude from pressing too severely on the mind; by accustoming prisoners to find relief and gratification in employment and thus to dispose them of habits of industry; and finally, by providing a variety of useful trades, and adapting them to the respective dispositions of prisoners, to enable them to maintain themselves on their return to society; for these several purposes the employment of prisoners in a penitentiary is essential, but subservient to the great purpose of reformation by seclusion.

What share of the earnings are the prisoners allowed?

They are not allowed any money save of earnings in the penitentiary house. The prisoners are furnished by the public with everything conducive to their health, both as to food and clothing: the use of other extraneous supply is forbidden by the law, and would, in my opinion, be injurious in practice.

2   New South Wales Government and General Orders, 1814[2]

Transportation had received criticism almost as soon as it was made an official form of punishment in 1714. Some regarded it as too easy on the criminal, others as cruel and barbaric. Furthermore, as the colonies matured, each presented their own set of problems. The orders below were an unsuccessful attempt by the New South Wales government to stem the lawlessness of the colony.

His Excellency the Governor, viewing with the greatest regret and abhorrence the frequent commission of robberies and murders which for some time past have rendered the situation of the well-disposed and industrious settlers of the country truly distressing, feels it his duty to adopt such regulations as appear to him best suited, in co-operation with the ordinary course of the laws, either to repress the further commission of such crimes, or to bring the perpetrators to more speedy and effectual punishment.

With a view to this desirable object, and in the hope, at the same time, to ameliorate the condition and improve the morals of the male convicts, who are new or may hereafter be assigned[3] as government-men to the free settlers or landholders, whether on or off the stores, and of those convicts also who have the indulgence of tickets of leave,[4] His Excellency has framed the following regulations, for the mutual guidance and government of the

---

[2] "Government and General Orders, New South Wales", Appendix to *The report of the select committee on the state of gaols, etc.*, P.P. 1819, vol. vii, pp. 407–9.

[3] This was the system whereby, after an initial period in a penal colony, convicts were assigned to settlers, who gave them work.

[4] After a set period of time, depending on the sentence, convicts were released on a ticket of leave. This allowed them to move freely throughout their colony but not to return to Britain.

persons possessed of government servants, and of those servants themselves; the magistrates and other peace officers within the several districts of the colony being hereby strictly enjoined to enforce, according to their authority, the fullest compliance with them.

It having come to the knowledge of the Governor, that the practice of remunerating government-men for their extra time and labour, either by permitting them to employ certain portions of their time for their own benefit wherever they may choose to engage themselves, or to cultivate grain and rear pigs and other animals, in lieu of giving them the wages prescribed by the established regulations of the colony, His Excellency cannot avoid calling the attention of the public to the consideration of the ill consequences necessarily resulting from either the one commutation or the other: those persons who have been in the habit of giving up portions of their time to their government-men in lieu of wages, must be aware that they thereby enable idle and disorderly persons, in the class of assigned convicts, to pass into parts of the country where their persons are not known; whilst the latter, availing themselves of that circumstance, commit the most flagrant and atrocious acts, under the idea that they will thus avoid detection. That robberies very frequently escape punishment by the sudden retreat of the perpetrators from that part of the country where they committed their depredations, is too notorious to be controverted. This fact fully evinces the necessity for doing away the practice.

These government-men, who have the indulgence of cultivating ground and rearing stock, instead of receiving their prescribed wages, frequently become the receivers of stolen grain and provisions, which, being blended with that of their own rearing, baffles detection, and justice is thereby often defeated.

1. Under the consideration of these evils, it is now His Excellency's the Governor's order of command, that from and after the 30th instant, all settlers and others having the services of the government-men of any denomination, whether on or off the shores, shall retain them altogether in their own service, and pay them agreeably to the government regulations established in the year 1804, and in no other way whatsoever.

2. Settlers or others, who do not require the entire services of the men assigned to them, or who cannot afford to pay them for their extra labour, are required to return them forthwith to the principal superintendent of convicts at Sydney, or to the magistrates of the districts to which they respectively belong.

3. The complaints, either of neglect of duty or of ill-treatment on the part of the government-men or their employers, are to be made to the district magistrate, whose duty it will be to punish and redress mutually the ill-behaved and injured party.

4. All the male convicts, whether assigned or settlers, or on tickets of leave in each district, are to assemble and be mustered by the district constable every Sunday morning at ten o'clock, in such central part of the district as shall be pointed out by the magistrate, and to proceed from thence, under the direction of the constable, to the nearest church or place of divine worship, in case there shall be one within three miles of the muster. On these occasions it will be expected that the assigned servants, and persons on tickets of leave, shall be not only punctual in their attendance, but also clean and decent in their appearance; and any of them who shall attend either unshaved or intoxicated, or absent themselves, except in cases of sickness or other unavoidable cause, are to be reported by the constable to the magistrate of the districts, who is to reprimand for the first offence, and punish every subsequent one by placing the offender in the stocks for one hour.

5. Ticket-of-leave men are to muster on the right of the assigned government-men and if there should be no place of worship where they assemble, they are to be dismissed there, after answering to their names, and to such questions as the constable shall find necessary to put to them. Settlers or others deriving the advantage of assigned servants, are particularly called upon to render every assistance in their power to the due execution of this order, whereby they will show themselves worthy of further indulgence; whilst on the contrary, if it should appear that they throw any difficulty in the way of it, such conduct will be punished by the withdrawing altogether from their service those convicts already assigned to them.

6. The district constables are to keep books, in which they are to enrol the names of all the government-men within their respective districts, and the names of the persons in whose employment they are, whether as assigned government-men, or persons on tickets of leave. The form of this muster roll will be furnished forthwith to the magistrates of the colony, and they are to give them to the district constables. Each Sunday's muster, with the list of absentees, and of those appearing in any way neglectful of the enjoined form, either as to dress, cleanliness or sobriety, is to be submitted on the Monday following to the magistrate of the district, whose orders thereon are to be carried strictly into effect by the constables. It is to be expected that the magistrates will from time to time attend the musters personally, in order to their being held according to the true intent of the order.

7. For the purpose of avoiding as much as possible the necessity for resorting to corporal punishments, His Excellency has deemed it advisable to establish government gaol-gangs at the three principal townships in the interior, namely Paramatta, Windsor and Liverpool;

and to these places of punishment convicts found guilty of serious offences are to be sent, to be employed at hard labour for a limited period of weeks or months, according to the measure of their offences, instead of undergoing corporal punishment, and in order to brand their ill conduct with a public mark of disgrace, and to distinguish them from the better behaved, they are to be clothed in a party-coloured dress, half black and half white, which they are to wear at all times during the time they are sentenced for. For this purpose the respective gaolers will be furnished with the prescribed dresses, and they are to take charge of the clothes which the convicts shall bring with them, until such time as they shall be discharged, when they are to be returned to them, and the gaol dresses received back into their stores. The gaol-gang at Paramatta is not to consist of more than ten, that at Windsor of more than eight, and that at Liverpool of more than six convicts, all of whom are to be lodged in their respective gaols every night, and to be daily employed (Sundays excepted) under government overseers, in the repair of the roads leading them into towns, and in the improvement of their streets, or in such other public work as the magistrates may consider more necessary.

8. The foregoing gaol-gangs, as also that established at Sydney, are to receive and commence wearing their party-coloured dresses on Sunday the 2nd day of October next ensuing, and are never to be permitted to appear in any other during the term of their respective sentences, unless a remission of their sentences, in consequence of good conduct, should be extended to them.

9. It being a matter of great importance, as well for the sake of encouraging and rewarding the meritorious, as for restraining and punishing the idle and ill-behaved, that the Governor should be made fully acquainted with the characters of the inhabitants at large, and more especially with those of the convicts of both sexes, in whatever manner they may be employed. His Excellency directs, that the several magistrates shall transmit him (through the office of his secretary to the government) quarterly returns of all fines and punishments ordered by them, on delinquents of every description, residing in their respective districts. Those reports are to specify the names and situations in life of the offenders, and their usual places of residence, with the offences committed by them, and the sentences passed on them. All remissions of punishments are also to be reported. For the town and district of Sydney, it will be the duty of the superintendent magistrate of the police to make these reports. The first return of these quarterly reports is to be made in the first week in January next, comprehending all the magisterial proceedings for the quarter, which will commence on the 1st of October next; and the Governor

recommends in the strongest manner to the magistrates to inflict corporal punishment as seldom as possible, but to substitute in its stead, confinement in the stocks for petty crimes, and either solitary confinement or hard labour in the gaol-gang, according to their judgment of the degrees of the offence, still keeping in view the general conduct and character of the delinquents.

10.   It is His Excellency the Governor's desire that these government and general orders shall be read, during the time of divine service, by the chaplain, at their respective churches or places of public worship on Sunday the 18th, and on Sunday the 25th of the present month of September.

By command of His Excellency the Governor

(signed) J. T. Campbell-Scott

3   Female Convicts, 1829[5]

In addition to being a punishment, transportation was also a system of labour supply for the colonies. The following letter illustrates this through a discussion of the problems associated with female convicts.

Sir,

His Majesty's Government having given their consideration to the representations contained in your dispatch of the 18th February last, as to the difficulty which has been experienced in disposing of the female convicts, the settlers refusing to receive them as assigned servants, and the Government not possessing fit places within which to confine them, I am induced to recommend to your consideration the adoption of a regulation for remedying this inconvenience. It has appeared to me that, by compelling every settler to take off the hands of government one convict woman for every two, or even for every three convict men who may be assigned to him, there would be effected not only a saving of the heavy expense which the maintenance of all unassigned prisoners occasion to the public, but a great moral improvement of the unfortunate females themselves, and a material advance towards the prevention of those mischiefs which their exportation was intended to remedy.

Although it is to be apprehended that the measure may, at first, be unpopular, by the obligation on the part of the settler to take charge of

---

[5] Despatch from Sir George Murray to Lieutenant-General Darling, Downing Street, 17 July 1829. Appendix to *The report of the select committee on transportation*, P.P. 1837/8, vol. xxii, p. 224.

a proportion of these women, yet I am willing to hope that the good sense of the majority of the inhabitants will point out to them the prospective benefits to be derived to the community from it; and I am therefore desirous, if you see no serious objection, that the experiment should be tried. You will consider yourself at liberty to modify the proposed arrangement in any way which you may deem expedient, particularly by diminishing the number of the females, as compared with the male prisoners, whom the settler is to be bound to take, if you should think it unadvisable to fix the proportion at the rate I have mentioned.

I am, &c.

(signed) G. Murray

4 Crime and Transportation, 1838[6]

Sexual deviance was not a subject the Victorians liked to discuss and sodomy was a capital offence until 1861, yet the delivery of thousands of men to Australia in close quarters, and the gender imbalance within the colonies themselves, raised fears about this and other "unnatural crimes". In his contribution to the parliamentary enquiry on transportation the Very Revd Ullathorne tells of his suspicion that homosexuality was commonplace.[7] In doing so, he provided another argument for why transportation was not effective as a punishment.

With regard to the crimes committed in the penal colonies, in a work which is written by you, you say, "There is another class of crimes too frightful even for the imagination of other lands; which St Paul, in detailing the vices of the heathens, has not contemplated; which were unknown to the savage, until taught by the convict – crimes which are notorious – crimes that, dare I describe them, would make your blood to freeze, and your hair to rise erect in horror upon the pale flesh." Now, it is my faithful duty, as Chairman of this Committee, one of whose chief objects is to enquire into the moral state of the penal colonies, to call upon you to give a full and clear explanation of the meaning of the passage which I have just read. I am convinced that no false delicacy on your part will induce you to withhold information which you have been placed in a position to obtain. You must perceive, I think, that you will perform your duty as a priest, and render an important service to the community, by unfolding

---

[6] *Evidence of The Very Revd William Ullathorne to the select committee on transportation*, P.P. 1837/8, vol. xxii, pp. 14–26.

[7] The word "homosexuality" was not used until the 1890s. Before this, it was subsumed under the general heading of unnatural crime unless it involved the specific activities of sodomy or buggery.

the horrors to which I have referred, in order that, convinced of their magnitude and extent, the Committee may be induced to make the most strenuous efforts to amend that system which had produced such enormities. I need hardly ask you whether, in the passage to which I have referred, you allude to unnatural crimes; I would inquire whether you believe those crimes to be common in the colony?

Before I enter into the subject, I beg leave to state, that it was intimated to me that I should be examined on this subject, I have seriously considered the subject, and I beg leave particularly to state to the Committee, that it is only a hope that something will be devised for preventing such horrible crimes, which will induce me to say anything at all upon the subject. I have gone through a great deal of pain and torture of mind in consequence of the horrors which I have witnessed in the colonies, and particularly in the penal settlements, and I have such an intense conscientious feeling upon that subject, and of the results of those evils, in the thorough breaking up of the moral man, which ensues from the crime, that I would do anything that is lawful; I would even deliberately give my life if I could in any manner lawfully contribute towards the removal of that evil. The crime, I believe, sometimes prevails on board ships going out from England; but I do not think it prevails in ships going out from Ireland. I believe, that where it is introduced on board the ships from England, it is most commonly introduced by persons from the hulks in England. I believe, likewise, that the putting together such a number of persons on board ship, and the crowding even of boys together, is a cause of much crime of that kind.

Are those crimes supposed to be common in the hulks of this country, do you mean to say?

Yes.

On the voyage, you do not say that they are so common?

Not so common during the voyage, as they are under certain circumstances in the colony.

Under the circumstances in the colony, in the barracks?

I believe, and am convinced, that wherever a number of bad men are brought together and continue together for any length of time, and are crowded together, there is a very great deal of that crime.

Do you derive your impression of the frequency of crime in the hulks[8] here from the statements of convicts with whom you have conversed in the colony, who have been in the hulks?

I derive my information from convicts arriving in the colony, and occasionally from persons who have been in the hulks, but more frequently from the other persons who have been on board ship, and of course are aware that such is the case.

---

[8] The prison ships which held the convicts for the first nine months of their sentence.

In the barracks of Sydney did you say that those crimes were supposed to be common?

I believe that they exist, and that they are not uncommon in the barracks at Sydney.

Are the boys permitted to associate with the men?

At night I believe they are separated from the men, but during the day they mix with them; and I have already mentioned a case where a boy was, very soon after he arrived, assailed, and first taught the crime, of which he had no idea previously.

Is it not the fact that the boys are designated by female names in the barracks?

I believe it is not infrequent.

Are unnatural crimes common in country districts amongst the convicts?

I believe that where they do exist on farms, it is where a number of them are brought together on the large farms.

That they are not uncommon amongst the shepherds, who are separated?

I do not think that they are so common amongst the shepherds as they are amongst a much more dissolute set, the stockmen.[9]

Are they common amongst these stockmen?

I believe that there is a great deal of that kind of crime among the stockmen.

Is it supposed that they have introduced those crimes amongst the natives?

Yes.

You stated that your information, with regard to the existence of unnatural crimes, resulted from persons who had been at the hulks, and from other persons in the ships, who were aware that such crimes were committed; you do not mean sailors, but convicts?

I mean convicts; persons on board the hulks are put on board ships in which there are convicts from other places.

You do not know what proportion of the convicts pass through the hulks before they are transported?

I could not state the proportion.

Are those crimes common in the penal settlements of Norfolk Island and Moreton Bay?

I believe they are very common.

What proportion do you suppose are guilty of those crimes in Norfolk Island?

When I was there, at the close of 1835 and the beginning of 1836, there were two prisoners sentenced to death; they were attended by another person, a Protestant, who was in the habit of reading prayers and instructing persons there, and it was publicly stated by those two persons, that one of the prisoners had declared that two-thirds of the island were implicated. I believe that there is considerably less of it now than there was at the time.

---

[9] Stockmen looked after cattle.

That statement refers exclusively to Norfolk Island?
It does.

Do you think that those crimes will ever entirely cease in the gaols and barracks, as long as men and boys are crowded together in the manner you describe?

I think it is impossible that they should cease so long as they are crowded together. When I returned from Norfolk Island, I suggested what I thought would be a measure of preventing them to a considerable extent; I proposed that the prisoners should each be separated from the other by a sort of boarded partition; that there should be two lamps, one suspended at each end of the apartment; and that there should be likewise two watchmen in each apartment, one at each end; and that no communication should be allowed whatever between the convicts, and no words spoken during the night. I thought that there was a more effectual means of preventing it; but that will not prevent it being done in other places where the men are together; it will be necessary, whenever the men are employed together, during the day, that they should always be under the eye of the inspector.

Do you think that those crimes will ever cease among the convicts not in confinement as long as the proportion of men to women is so great as it is at present in the whole colony? I believe in Sydney it is two and a half to one, and in the country districts almost four to one?

Yes, I believe that is about the proportion; I think the temptation to crime will be very great as long as the disproportion is so considerable.

5   A Day on Board the *Defence* Hulk, 1862[10]

The prison hulks began as a short-term measure to relieve the pressure on inadequate gaols brought about by the sudden ending of transportation to the United States of America in 1775. After the revival of transportation they continued to be used as a substitute for gaol places, being mainly used as a floating prison for transportees before they left for Australia. The following description comes from a book published in 1862, almost ninety years after the original crisis. It describes the layout of the hulk and the atmosphere at dawn.

On reaching the top deck we found it divided, by strong iron rails (very like those in the zoological gardens, which protect visitors from the fury of the wild beasts) from one end to the other, in two long cages as it were, with a passage between them. In this passage a warder was pacing to and fro, commanding a view of the men, who were slung up in hammocks,

---

[10] Mayhew & Binny, *The criminal prisons of London*, pp. 208–13.

fastened in two rows, in each cage or compartment of the ship. There was also a little transverse passage at the end of each ward, that allowed the officer on duty to take a side view of the sleepers, and to cast the light of his bull's-eye[11] under the hammocks, to assure himself that the men were quiet in their beds.

The glimmering little lanterns attached to the railings, so that the warder on duty could trim them without entering the wards, were still alight. The glazed hats of the men hung up overhead, reflecting the pale beams; and the men themselves were still snoring in their dingy hammocks.

In these two compartments or wards were 105 convicts, parted off into sections, D1, D2, and A1 and A2. And a curious sight it was to look upon the great sleeping mass of beings within them! The hammocks were slung so close to one another that they formed a perfect floor of beds on either side of the vessel, seeming like rows of canvass boats. But one or two of the prisoners turned on their sides as we passed along the deck, and we could not help speculating, as we went, upon the nature of the felon dreams of those we heard snoring and half-moaning about us. How many, thought we, are with their friends once more, enjoying the ideal liberty! – how many are enacting or planning some brutal robbery! – how many suffering, in imagination, the last penalty of their crimes! – how many weeping on their mother's breast, and promising to abandon their evil courses for ever! – and to how many was sleep an utter blank – a blessed annihilation for a while to their life-long miseries!

The convicts here arranged were first-class men – there being manifest advantages in the top deck over the middle and lower ones. We followed the warder towards the stern of the ship and, at the extremity of this deck, we crossed a grating and reached the hatchway leading to the middle deck.

The middle deck was arranged on the same plan as that of the top one, excepting that the passage between the swinging hammocks was wider. Here 129 men were sleeping in the divisions or wards called E1, E2; B1, B2. Here, too, the officer was parading between the wards or cages, and splashing about chloride of lime that stood in buckets between the wards. It was still very dark and the groaning, coughing and yawning of the sleeping and walking prisoners had anything but a cheerful effect on the mind. The air was close and unpleasant, but not remarkably so, considering that it had been exhausted by the breath of so many men since nine o'clock on the previous night, when they turned in.

We still had another deck to visit; so we followed our warder and descended the hatchway to the lower deck, which was higher, and had a broader passage than the two upper ones through which we had just passed. This deck was arranged to accommodate only 240 men but, at

---

[11] Lantern.

the time of our visit, it contained only 190 sleepers, arranged in sections thus, F1, F2 and F3 on one side and C1, C2 and C3 on the other. This spacious deck stretches right under the fore-part of the poop,[12] the barred port-holes admitting but little light. Still, the air is fresher than in the decks above, which receive the ascending heat from the 190 sleepers for, by means of broad openings in the stern and bows of the ship, a constant stream of fresh air is carried through the vessel. Altogether there were, at the time of our visit, 424 convicts stowed between the decks.

The men seem to be comfortably covered, having two blankets and a rag each. The tables used for meals are unshipped, and lean against the bars of the passage. The men's boots are under their hammocks and their clothes lie upon the benches.

Having passed through this gloomy scene we reach a narrow white-washed passage, at the head of the lower deck, and entering by a side door, we come to the solitary cells. We follow the bull's-eye carried by the warder. Presently he stops, and placing his lantern against a rude opening in the bulkhead, throws its light upon a man in one of the cells within, who is sentenced to "forty-eight hours". Having inspected the sleeper, who is lying huddled in his brown rug upon the ground, for there are no hammocks allowed in this cell, he darkens the place once more and proceeds to the second.

In solitary cell No. 2, the man is sleeping in his hammock and the scuttle is not darkened. As the light from the bull's-eye falls upon his face, the prisoner blinks his eyes and calls, "All right!" as he rolls in his bed.

We now pass on to a cell in the bows of the ship. Here the hammock hides the man's face from our view, so we advance across immense white-washed timbers or "knees", that stand up as solid as milestones, and so on to the opposite cell in the bows. This one is empty; but the next contains a prisoner who is in for three days, on bread and water, for refusing to work in the boats. We then return to the lower deck, through a door at the opposite side to that which we entered the solitary cell-passage. There are five such cells in all – two on either side and one in the bows.

6 Execution for Arson, Lincoln, 1831[13]

Despite the fact that consolidation of the law during the 1820s had drastically reduced the number of statutes carrying the death penalty, executions were still being held at the rate of one per week in England and Wales in 1831. The newspaper article below describes one such occasion and justifies the use of the

---

[12] The raised structure at the back of the ship.
[13] *The Times*, 5/8/1831.

death penalty in the case of arson. The writer of the article pays particular attention to the response of the criminals to their fate.

On Friday 1st, Richard Coolling, aged 26, and Thomas Motley, aged 20, the two infatuated and misguided young men who were convicted of arson at our late assizes paid the forfeit of their lives to the offended laws of their country on the new drop of our gaol. Much as we are opposed to punishment by death, we cannot deny the wisdom of the legislature in thus visiting a crime so easy of perpetration, so difficult of detection, so dreadful in consequences, and which we fear nothing but the most rigorous means can check. The prisoners both acknowledged the justice of their punishment, and by their demeanour showed that they had prepared their minds for the event. During the time of confinement, Motley, who appeared to be from his simplicity almost incapable of distinguishing between right and wrong, acknowledged that it was their intention, before firing the stackyard of Mr Wilson at the instigation of Coolling, whom he represented as the instigator and planner of the whole, to have set fire to the premises of Mr Thimbleby, of Kirby, and of Mr Kirkham of Hagnerby, but that circumstances prevented him. It was deemed prudent to search Coolling immediately after his conviction: to this he offered some resistance, but being compelled to submit, a knife was found concealed in the lining of his waistcoat. He maintained a brutal hardihood throughout, and said to Mr Brockleby the day previous to the execution, "You shall see tomorrow. I can go to the gallows without a tear or a groan." When questioned as to the ground of his courage, whether it originated in the consciousness of a well-spent life or in belief of having made his peace with God, he said, "that he and Motley had stolen some fowls two or three times; but," said he, "why should I confess to man, it is quite sufficient if I confess to my Maker." Seeing his father, who had come to take leave of him, apparently distressed, he said, "Why, father, you take on and fret a deal more about it than I do; it can't be helped now, it is no use making a fuss about it." He maintained the same degree of recklessness to the last.

When they were brought into the gaol yard, we could not help noticing the different demeanour of the two men, Coolling came forth with a stern scowl upon his countenance, eyeing the awful ceremony and preparation with apparent contempt, and walked across the courtyard with a firm and undaunted step. Motley was equally collected, but his was the mild placidity of resignation to his deserved fate by repentance and prayer: he had obtained the comforting assurances of pardon from him to whom the cry of a broken and contrite heart was never raised in vain, and never do the rays of divine mercy appear so resplendently beautiful as when reflected from the last tear of repentance on the cheek of the dying culprit.

After the religious duties had been performed, both men shook hands with those around them, and ascended the scaffold without a murmur or any indication of fear. Whilst the executioner was drawing the cap over poor Motley's eyes and adjusting the rope, the brutally indifferent gaze of Coolling at the dreadful preparation was truly horrifying. He then underwent the same ordeal, and about two minutes after twelve earthly justice was appeased, and their souls were ushered into the presence of Omniscience. Motley died without a struggle, but Coolling was dreadfully convulsed.

7   The Last Public Execution, 1868[14]

The last public execution took place in 1868. Michael Barrett was hung for his part in the Fenian attempt to rescue members of the organization from Clerkenwell Prison in which fifteen people were killed. By this period, executions were rare but were still capable of drawing large crowds. In the article below, a journalist from The Times *gives a vivid description of the crowd and reflects on the behaviour of Barrett himself as he goes to his death.*

The execution differed little from other similar exhibitions. On Monday the barriers were put up, and on Monday night a fringe of eager sightseers assembled, mostly sitting beneath the beams, but ready on a moment's notice to rise and cling to the front places they had so long waited for. There were the usual cat-calls, comic choruses, dances, and even mock hymns, till towards 2 o'clock, when the gaiety inspired by alcohol faded away as the public houses closed, and popular excitement was not revived till the blackened deal frame which forms the base of the scaffold was drawn out in the dawn, and placed in front of the door from which Barrett was to issue. Its arrival was accompanied with a great cheer, which at once woke up those who had been huddled in doorsteps and under barricades, and who joined in the general acclamation. The arrival of the scaffold did much to increase the interest, and through the dawn people began to flock in, the greater portion of the newcomers being young women and little children. Never were these more numerous than on this occasion, and blue velvet hats and huge white feathers lined the great beams which kept the mass from crushing each other in their eagerness to see a man put to death. The crowd was most unusually orderly, but it was not a crowd in which one could trust. It is said that one sees on the road to Derby such animals as are never seen elsewhere; so on an execution morning one sees faces that are never seen save round the gallows or near a great fire. Some laughed, some fought, some preached, some gave tracts, and some sang hymns; but what may be called the general good-humoured disorder of the crowd remained the same, and there was laughter at the preacher

---

[14] *The Times*, 27/5/1868.

or silence when an open robbery was going on. None could look on the scene, with all its exceptional quietness, without a thankful feeling that this was to be the last public execution in England.

Towards 7 o'clock the mass of people was immense. A very wide open space was kept round the gallows by the police, but beyond the concourse was dense, stretching up beyond St Sepulchre's Church, and far back almost, into Smithfield – a great surging mass of people which in spite of the barriers kept swaying to and fro like waving corn. Now and then there was great laughter as a girl fainted and was passed out hand over hand above the heads of the mob, and then there came a shuffle and a fight and then a hymn and then a sermon and then a comic song, and so on for hour to hour, the crowd thickening as the day brightened, and the sun shone out with such a glare as to extinguish the very feeble light which showed itself faintly through the glass roof above where the culprit lay. It was a wild, rough crowd, not so numerous nor nearly so violent as that which thronged to see Muller or their pirates die. In one way they showed their feeling by loudly hooting a magnificently attired woman who, accompanied by two gentlemen, swept down the avenue kept open by the police, and occupied a window afterwards right in front of the gallows. This temporary exhibition of feeling was, however, soon allayed by coppers being thrown from the window for the roughs to scramble for. It is not right, perhaps, that a murderer's death should be surrounded by all the pious and tender accessories which accompany the departure of a good man to a better world, but most assuredly the sight of public executions to those who have to witness them is as disgusting as it must be demoralizing even to all the hordes of thieves and prostitution it draws together. Yesterday the assembly was of its kind an orderly one, yet it was such as we feel grateful to think will under the new law never be drawn together again in England.

The sheriffs with the under-sheriffs arrived at the prison shortly after seven o'clock and, according to custom, spent the interval until eight o'clock in their official apartment connected with the courthouse. There they were joined by the governor of Newgate, the prison surgeon and the ordinary. A few representatives of the press to whom tickets of admission had been given were also present. The convict Barrett had retired to rest about ten o'clock on the previous evening, and having spent a somewhat restless night, rose at six o'clock yesterday morning, dressed himself, and engaged in prayer. Shortly afterwards he was joined in his cell by the Reverend James Hussey, attached to the Roman Catholic chapel in Moorfields, who had attended him regularly since his conviction, and who remained with him to the last. It is understood that he received the sacrament one day last week, and again yesterday morning. Towards eight o'clock the sheriffs paid him a visit, accompanied by the governor, and then retired to a part of the prison leading to the scaffold, where the rest of the authorities and the public representatives had already assembled. By a predetermined arrangement, and contrary to the usual practice, the convict was not pinioned in the press-room, as it is called, but in his own cell and, this process over, he was conducted to the drop by a private way, accompanied by his priest and attended by the executioner and three or four warders, the prison bell and that of St Sepulchre's Church, hard by, tolling all the while. Then sheriffs and under-sheriffs who, with others, stood in a group in a gloomy corridor behind the scaffold, just caught a glimpse of the doomed man as he emerged with his attendants from a dark and narrow passage and turned a corner leading to the gallows. He was dressed in the short claret-coloured coat and the grey striped trousers, both well worn, by which he had become familiar to all who were present during his protracted trial. His face had lost the florid hue it then wore, and in other respects he was an altered man.

With the first sound of the bells came a great hungry roar from the crowd outside, and a loud, continued shout of "Hats off", till the whole dense, bareheaded mass stood, white and ghastly-looking in the morning sun, and the pressure on the barriers increased so that the girls and women in the front ranks began to scream and struggle to get free. Amid such a scene as this, and before such a dense crowd of white faces, Barrett was executed.

His clergyman came first. Barrett mounted the steps with the most perfect firmness. This may seem a stereotypical phrase, but it really means more than is generally imagined. To ascend a ladder with one's arms and hands closely pinioned would be at all times difficult but to climb a ladder to go to certain death might try the nerves of the boldest. Barrett walked up cooly and boldly. His face was as white as marble, but still he bore himself with firmness, and his demeanour was as far removed from bravado as from fear. We would not dwell on these details but from the singular reception he met as he came out upon the scaffold. There was a partial burst of cheers, which was instantly accompanied by loud hisses, and so it remained for some seconds, till as the last moment approached the roars dwindled down to a dead silence. To neither cheers nor hisses did the culprit make the slightest recognition. He seemed only attentive to what the priest was saying to him and to be engaged in fervent prayer. The hangman instantly put the cap over his face and the rope round his neck. Then Barrett turning spoke through his cap and asked for the rope to be altered, which the hangman did. In another moment Barrett was a dead man. After the bolt was drawn and the drop fell with the loud boom which always echoes from it, Barrett never moved. He died without a struggle. It is worthy of remark that a great cry rose from the crowd as the culprit fell – a cry which was neither an exclamation nor a scream but it partook in its sound of both. With the fall of the drop the crowd began to disperse but an immense mass waited till the time for cutting-down came, and when 9 o'clock struck there were loud calls of, "Come on, body snatcher!" "Take away the man you've killed!" etc. The hangman appeared and cut down the body amid such a storm of yells and execrations as has seldom been heard even from such a crowd. There was nothing more then to be seen, so the concourse broke up with its usual concomitants of assault and robbery.

8   Prison Discipline

Gaol-keepers held a wide array of tools for disciplining their inmates. In the passages below, their use of such tools is described in contrasting ways. The first extract is taken from a gaol-keeper's journal and is a matter-of-fact record of the different uses of the punishment cell within the prison. The second is taken from an impassioned novel by Charles Reade in which the keeper of the gaol is cast as a cruel villain intoxicated with his own power. The third, from a chaplain's description of Stafford Gaol, gives a more sympathetic portrayal of the prison official but raises concern about the effect of rigid prison discipline on the inmate.

8.1   Huntingdon County Gaol Journal 1833–4[15]

13 October 1833
Locked up Mary Austen for disorderly conduct in the chapel this morning.

20 October
Locked up Edward Raynor for conversing with other prisoners when confined in their cells.

22 October
Locked up Joseph Raynor for conversing with other prisoners and for neglecting his work on the tread wheel.

6 November
Locked up Edward Tokins for conversing at dinner time with other prisoners when locked up in separate cells.

9 November
Locked up Edward Arthur for making a loud noise in his cell after he had been confined therein for the night.

7 January 1834
Locked up George Hopkins for irreverent and disorderly conduct in the presence of the chaplain at the time of instruction this morning.

---

[15] *Gaol Keeper's Journal 1833–8, Huntingdon County Gaol*, HCP/2/320/1, Huntingdon County Record Office.

3 February
Locked up Thomas Lyon for negligently performing his work and attempting to break the crank machine.

7 February
Locked up Thomas Lyon for being very lame when employed at the hand crank machine.

11 February
Locked up Richard Gurton for making use of indecent language towards his fellow prisoners.

17 February
Locked up Joseph Hill for talking to other prisoners when at work after being ordered not to do so.
   Locked up George Hopkins for profane swearing.

24 February
Locked up William Theobald for violently resisting the keeper and his officers when conducting him into the receiving room of the gaol.

1 March
Locked up Henry Winslade for insolent behaviour towards the keeper who directed the prisoner to be released at the expiration of two hours' confinement in the refractory cell which he refused to comply with.

15 March
Locked up Joseph Hill for refusing to do such work as he was able to perform.
   Locked up John Buck and John Giddings for fighting.

31 March
Locked up Thomas Lyon for stealing his fellow prisoner's bread.

4 April
Locked up Thomas Lyon for throwing stones thereby displacing the loose bricks upon the boundary wall.
   Put Thomas Lyon in the lunatic securing straps one hour for riotous conduct in the refractory cell in the presence of the visiting justices.

7 April
Locked up Thomas Lyon for refusing to work on the tread wheel and for using profane language towards the turnkey.

8.2   It is Never Too Late to Mend, 1853[16]

Discipline before all. Not because a fellow is sick is he to break discipline. So the sick lay in their narrow cells, gasping in vain for fresh air, gasping in vain for some cooling drink, or some little simple delicacy to incite their enfeebled appetite.

The dying were locked up at the fixed hour for locking up, and found dead at the fixed hour for opening. How they had died – no one knew. At what hour they had died – no one knew. Whether in some choking struggle a human hand might have saved them by changing a suffocating position or the like – no one knew.

But this all knew, that these our sinful brethren had died, not like men, but like vultures in the great desert. They were separated from their kith and kin, who, however brutal, would have said a kind word and done a tender thing or two for them at that awful hour. Nothing was allowed them in exchange, not even the routine attentions of a prison nurse; they were in darkness and alone when the king of terrors came to them and wrestled with them: all men had turned their backs on them, no creature near to wipe the deus of death, to put a cool hand to the brow, or soften the intensity of the last sad sigh that carried their souls from earth. Thus they passed away, punished lawlessly by the law till they succumbed, and then, since they were no longer food for torture, ignored by law and abandoned by the human race.

They locked up one dying man at eight o'clock. At midnight the thirst of death came to him. He prayed for a drop of water, but there was none to hear him. Perched and gasping, the miserable man got out of bed and groped and groped for his tin mug, but before he could drink the death agony seized him.

When they unlocked him in the morning, they found him a corpse on the floor with the mug in his hand and the water spilled on the floor. They wrenched the prison property out of its dead hand, and flung the carcass itself upon the bed as if it had been the clay cast of a dog, not the remains of a man.

All was of a piece. The living tortured, the dying abandoned, the dead kicked out of the way. Of these three, the living were the most unfortunate, and among the living Robinson and Josephs. Never since the days of Cain was existence made more bitter to two hapless creatures than to these – above all, to Josephs.

His day began thus: between breakfast and dinner he was set five thousand revolutions of a heavy crank; when he could not do it, his dinner was taken away and a few crumbs of bread and a can of water given him instead. Between his bread-and-water time and six o'clock, if the famished

---

[16]   C. Reade, *It is never too late to mend* (London, 1853).

worn-out lad could not do five thousand more revolutions, and make up the previous deficiency, he was punished *ad libitum*. As the whole thing from first to last was beyond his powers, he never succeeded in performing these preposterous tasks. He was threatened, vilified and tortured every day and every hour of it.

Human beings can bear great sufferings if you give them periods of ease between, and beneficent Nature allows for this. When She means us to suffer short of death, She lashes us at intervals. Were it otherwise, we should succumb under a tenth of what we suffer intermittently.

But Hawes [the governor of the gaol], besides his cruelty, was a noodle. He belonged to a knot of theorists into whose hands the English gaols are fast falling; a set of shallow dreamers who, being greater dunces and greater asses than four men out of every six that pass you in Fleet Street or Broadway at any hour, they think themselves wiser than Nature and her author. Josephs suffered body and spirit without intermission. The result was that his flesh withered on his bones; his eyes were dim, and seemed to lie at the bottom of two caverns; he crawled stiffly and slowly instead of walking. He was not sixteen years of age, yet Hawes had extinguished his youth and blotted out all its signs but one. Had you met this figure in the street, you would have said, "What, an old man and no beard?"

8.3   *Stafford Gaol*[17]

The question of prison discipline has, since the days of the great prisoners' friend, John Howard, who lived in the latter part of the last century, engaged the attention of many philanthropists and criminal code reformers, and very numerous have been the beneficial effects of their agitations. At the present time prison discipline could not be improved in many material points, but it should be more tempered with humanity, and the supply of food should certainly be more plentiful. A muscular individual was recently discharged from Stafford gaol, and he had once had the reputation of being one of the strongest men in England, and a great "bruiser", but after two years in prison and the terribly insufficient food provided for him, together with the heavy labour tasks imposed upon him, he felt no stronger than a baby, and he was daily in dread of his mind giving way. Harsh treatment not only affects prisoners themselves but also those who have charge of them. When a man has been shut up he is not done with. Society owes prisoners something for depriving them of their liberty, and the duty of society should be "cure" and not "kill" or create in prisoners a feeling of revenge for the wrongs they may, or imagine they have, suffered at its hands. The great endeavour should be to find out how far

---

[17] W. Payne, *Stafford gaol and its associations* (Hanley, 1887), pp. 13, 19, 22–7.

humane conduct is compatible with justice, and not to what limits justice can proceed without absolutely overwhelming its victims.

Much however may be said in favour of the prison officials of Stafford gaol. As far as the memory can go, the governors and deputy governors of this gaol have been men of unimpeachable character. They would not countenance wrong or over-harsh treatment of the prisoners placed under their care. The law is laid down for them, and as regards prison regulations, they have no alternative but to administer it. Some of the warders, too, are men of high principles and sound integrity. But they have hardships to endure, and to what extent their naturally humane and kindly feelings are destroyed by the cruelties of the prison system, of which they are merely the instruments and interpreters, is not generally known. While some warders are of a naturally cruel and vindictive nature, others are so only from necessity and compulsion. The warder, as a rule, must necessarily lead a "dog's life". He has long hours, pay not so large as that received by the average artisan, and has to submit to rules and regulations which are both severe and unjust. No doubt reforms in prisons are almost as much needed for the warders as for the prisoners. If their life was made more tolerable, they would be able to do their duty with much more satisfaction than they are at present able to do. When warders are engaged they are "supposed" to be men of good character and good physique, endued with the courage of a lion and the patience of a Job. While fully obeying the harsh injunctions of prison discipline, they are, nevertheless, expected to be humane. Their lives are in continual jeopardy, and frequently one or other of them is attacked by some ferocious prisoner, at whose mercy they are placed. It is they who are prisoners in the bondage of the State, which is a harsh and merciless taskmaster. It is they who, through no fault of theirs, but owing to stern necessity, are the white slaves of the State; and if only the public knew one hundredth part of what they are called upon to endure, they might, perhaps, hope for some improvement in their condition. But the authorities take very good care that the public shall not know anything about the working of the gaol, or more than they think fit. Vindictive and cunning prisoners can wreak their vengeance upon them at every possible opportunity. They stand from day to day, staring fixedly, and without a moment's cessation for many weary hours at a time, at groups of prisoners, on each of whom they must throw their whole attention.

9   Pentonville, 1848[18]

Pentonville, opened in 1842, was widely held to be a model for prisons elsewhere in England, although very few local gaols had the resources to respond to its

---

[18]   *Quarterly Review* **82**, 1848, pp. 182–4.

example. The following passage reflects the fascination of the prison to the public and portrays Pentonville as a temple of controlled, efficient discipline.

What a contrast to the pandemonium of associated criminals does the visitor perceive who enters for the first time the walls of the model prison at Pentonville! Instead of the noise and bustle of the old Newgates – absolute stillness; a few silent warders only scattered here and there in the large and lofty corridors containing a triple tier of cells, which range the whole length of these galleries! In spite of the blaze of daylight which should enliven, and the scrupulous cleanliness which should raise notions of comfort, it is impossible not to feel the oppression of resistless power; it is in vain, on a first visit, that you are solicited to inspect the minutiae of the admirable mechanism by which the architect (Colonel Jebb)[19] has contrived to secure the complete isolation of 500 individuals from each other. They are fed at the same moment, rest at the same hour, are out in masses in the open air. They are catechized in the school, and respond in the chapel – yet man knows not man. There is contiguity, but no neighbourhood; and the very names of the prisoners are lost in the mechanism which assigns numbers in their stead.

It requires the aid of sense to confirm the testimony of others, that the prison is really tenanted; the impulse is irresistible to ascertain the fact. A small aperture is so contrived in the door of each cell as to permit the visitor to see its inmate without himself being seen; and he can now traverse a corridor and remark the intensity of still life. All are profoundly engaged – one plying his trade, another busy with his slate, a third fixed and motionless over his Bible. The shoemaker is squatting cross-legged and stooping over his last; the tailor raised on his table with implements and materials about him; the weaver hardly distinguishable amid the framework of his active machinery; the basket-maker in his corner, distant an arm's length from the heap of osiers from which ever and anon he is selecting that to which he is about to give form and shape. It is not here, as in the solitary occupations of the world, that the artisan can beguile his labour with snatches of some favourite melody; nothing must break the silence of the cell. Its inmate soon learns to concentrate all his energies on his work, which becomes to him a solace – a necessity. Unconscious that any eye is upon him, as he now appears, so he will be found at any interval of days, weeks, or months.

If the visitor be still disposed to linger and observe, he will presently see a long file of prisoners emerging from their cells, in such a pre-arranged order that each man is fifteen paces apart from his fellow, and so masked as to render mutual recognition impossible. Thus accoutered and marshalled,

---

[19] Jebb was surveyor-general of the prison system at the time this article was written but he was a Royal Engineer when he designed Pentonville.

and shod as to prevent sound, one half of the prisoners [250] proceed rapidly to the chapel, the interior of which is so arranged as to preclude even the tallest man from overlooking the one in the next slip. The pulpit is placed high, so as to command a perfect view of every convict, but inter-communication is further prevented by wardens perched up on elevations, each with a full inspection of his own section of prisoners. Here at last is the silence broken – by the congregated sound of the simple melodies of our hymns; and there are few places where they strike so impressively on the heart as when they are poured forth amid the suggestive influences of the prison. The service done, a dial-plate turns round presenting certain letters and numbers, which correspond to the sectional numbers and letters of the prisoners; as these appear, the peak of each cap is again let down so as to mask the features, and the chapel is as silently and quickly emptied as it had before been filled.

10   Fines, 1844[20]

For cases of assault and public order, a fine was the most common official sen-tence but, in the one third of cases in which the defendant could not afford to pay, it led to punishment in prison. In the middle of the nineteenth century, there were few magistrates prepared to give defendants extra time to gather the money or to pay by instalments and this led to accusations that there was one system of justice for the rich and one for the poor. The Punch *article below uses satire to make such a point.*

10.1   Police Justice – The Luxury of Wealth

Yesterday, the Hon. Augustus Toppingham, a person of gentlemanly exter-ior, was brought before Mr Honneycombe, charged with a very gross and violent assault on Grace Mittens, a most respectable and meek-looking woman, whose face, however, retained marks of a severe blow, she having lost four of her front teeth by the violence of the accused.

Police Constable Lynx deposed that he was, on Monday night, on his beat in Coventry Street, when he heard the screams of a woman. He ran, and discovered the complainant lying on the pavement, and the accused at the bar shouting and hallooing, and swearing he was a gentleman, and no mistake. Whereupon, after much difficulty, the constable took the prisoner into custody.

Grace Mittens (the complainant) deposed that she was employed in a dressmaker's establishment. She had been kept late at work on Monday night, and was returning home, when the person at the bar accosted her,

---

[20] *Punch*, vol. 7, 1844, p. 243.

placing his arm round her waist. She told him to go about his business, when, with his clenched fist, he struck her so violently on the mouth, that he dislodged four or her front teeth.

Mr Honeycombe asked the prisoner what he had to say for himself.

The prisoner said he had been out dining.

Mr Honeycombe observed that that could be no excuse for such ungentlemanly atrocity. It was a most shameful and cowardly assault upon a defenceless, virtuous girl, and he certainly would fine the prisoner in the sum of five pounds, or two months' imprisonment.

The fine was immediately paid, and the *gentleman* drove from the office in his cab.

John Briggs was charged before Mr Honeycombe with having committed an assault upon Mr Jessamy Bloom, a person of somewhat genteel appearance.

It appeared that the prisoner and his wife were proceeding home on Thursday night. They had had a few words. In fact, the prisoner was a little the worse for liquor and his wife was walking a few paces on advance of him. The complainant meeting the woman, addressed her in a very rude and unseemly way, at the same time throwing his arms round her. Whereupon the prisoner, rushing forward, struck the complainant and knocked him into the road.

Charlotte Briggs deposed to the above facts. She had been very grossly assaulted by the complainant before he was struck by her husband.

Mr Honeycombe said he had no doubt that an assault had been committed, a very gross assault. Nevertheless, people must not take the law into their own hands: there would be an end to all things, if people took the law into their own hands. He wished to know what the prisoner had to say for himself!

The prisoner said that, seeing his wife assaulted, he could not help doing what he had done; he was not sure that he should not do the like again under the same circumstances.

Mr Honeycombe observed, that he had no doubt that the complainant had very grossly misconducted himself. Nevertheless, the prisoner had committed an assault and the sentence was that he must pay a fine of £2 or undergo six weeks' imprisonment.

The prisoner had not a farthing, and was – *removed in the prison van.*

11   Penal Theories

Philosophies of punishment were closely related to beliefs about criminality. If criminality was caused by the environment, there was more hope that the offender could be reformed than if it was caused by genetic characteristics. In the three passages below we see contrasting explanations of why people turned to crime together with comments on how best they should be treated by the penal system. The first passage is taken from one of the earliest espousals of the theory of phrenology, the "science" of measuring character by looking at the shapes of heads. The second passage relates to young offenders and argues strongly that crime was caused by the environment in which some young people grew up. The third passage puts forward the theory of atavism, whereby the physical and emotional development of offenders was held to be lower than the average of the society around them. The author, Havelock Ellis, argues against the philosophy of the late nineteenth-century prison authorities by calling for the treatment of offenders to be individualized.

11.1   Phrenology[21]

In examining the heads of criminals in jail, I have found the most daring, desperate and energetic to possess large brains. When great size and an unfavourable combination occur together, the officers of justice are reduced to despair in attempting to correct the offender. They feel a strength of character which they cannot subdue, and an evil bent which they cannot direct. The result, generally, is a report from the police that the individual is incorrigible. His first capital offence is prosecuted to extremity, and he is hanged for the sake of protecting society from further mischief. In professional pursuits, also, the men who are indisputably paramount to their fellows not merely in cleverness, but in depth and force of character, have large heads; and this holds, not only in the learned professions, but in mercantile avocations. I have observed that individuals who, born in indulgence, have arisen to wealth, by conducting great and extensive establishments, have uniformly brains above an average size; and that mercantile travellers who succeed in procuring orders, and pushing a trade amidst a keen and arduous competition, are distinguished by the same quality. Such men make an impression, and act with a confidence of power, which gives effect to all they say or do. In a school, if the children care nothing for the master and treat him with disrespect, and if he fail, after using every severity, to maintain discipline and subordination, he will be found to have a small brain. In the domestic circle, if the mistress of a family (while in good health) is easily overcome, annoyed and oppressed with the cares and duties of her household, the origin of the evil will be found in too small a head.

Account of Mr Combe's Phrenological Examination of Heads of Criminals in the Jail of Newcastle-on-Tyne, October 1835
On Wednesday 28th October, Mr Combe, accompanied by the following gentlemen, visited the jail: Dr George Fife, assistant-surgeon to the jail

---

[21] G. Combe, *System of phrenology*, 4th edn (Edinburgh, 1836), pp. 690–91 and 896–8.

(who is not a phrenologist); Benjamin Sorsbie, Esq., alderman; Dr D. B. White; Mr T. M. Greenhow, surgeon; Mr John Bird, surgeon; Mr George C. Atkinson; Mr Edward Richardson; Mr Thomas Richardson; Mr Wm. Hutton; and Captain Hooke.

Mr Combe mentioned that his chief object was to show to such gentlemen present as had attended his lectures in Newcastle the reality of the fact which he had frequently stated, that there is a marked difference between the development of the brain in men of virtuous dispositions, and its development in decidedly vicious characters, such as criminals usually are; and that the moral organs generally are larger in proportion to the organs of the animal propensities, in the former than in the latter; and he requested that a few striking cases of crime might be presented, and that the heads of the criminals should be compared with those of any of the gentlemen present indiscriminately.

This was done; and Dr Fife suggested that it would be further desirable that Mr Combe should write down his own remarks on the cases, before any account of them was given, while he himself should, at the other side of the table, write down an account of their characters according to his knowledge of them; and that the two statements should then be compared. Mr Combe agreed to this request; and the following individuals were examined.

P.S., aged 20

Mr Combe wrote as follows: anterior lobe well developed; intellectual powers are considerable. The organ of imitation is large, also secretiveness; acquisitiveness is rather large. The most defective organ is conscientiousness. Benevolence and veneration are large. The lower animal organs are not inordinate. My inference is, that this boy is not accused of violence; his dispositions are not ferocious, or cruel, or violent; he has a talent for deception, and a desire for property not regulated by justice. His desires may have appeared in swindling or theft. It is most probable that he has swindled: he has the combination which contributes to the talents of an actor. – Dr Fife's remarks: A confirmed thief; he has been twice convicted of theft. He has never shown brutality; but he has no sense of honesty. He has frequently attempted to impose on Dr Fife; he has considerable talent; he attended school, and is quick and apt; he has a talent for imitation.

T.S., aged 18

Mr Combe wrote: destructiveness is very large; combativeness, secretiveness, and acquisitiveness are large; intellectual organs fairly developed; amativeness[22] is large; conscientiousness rather moderate; benevolence is full, and

---

[22] Propensity to love or sexual passion.

veneration rather large. This boy is considerably different from the last. He is more violent in his dispositions; he has probably been committed for assault connected with women. He has also a large secretiveness and acquisitiveness, and may have stolen, although I think this less probable. He has fair intellectual talents, and is an improvable subject. – Dr Fife's remarks: crime, rape, ****, no striking features in his general character; mild disposition; has never shown actual vice.

J.W., aged 73

Mr Combe's observations: The coronal region is very defective; veneration and firmness are the best developed; but all are deficient. Cautiousness is enormously large; the organ of combativeness is considerable, and amativeness is large; there are no other leading organs of the propensities inordinate in development; the intellect is very moderate. I would have expected to find this case in a lunatic asylum rather than in a jail; and I cannot fix upon any particular feature of crime. His moral dispositions generally are very defective; but he has much caution. Except in connection with his amativeness and combativeness, I cannot specify the precise crime of which he has been convicted. Great deficiency in the moral organs is the characteristic feature, which leaves the lower propensities to act without control. – Dr Fife's remarks: a thief; void of every principle of honesty; obstinate; insolent; ungrateful for any kindness. In short, one of the most depraved characters with which I have been acquainted. – Note by Mr Combe: I have long maintained that where the moral organs are extremely deficient, as in this case, the individual is a moral lunatic, and ought to be treated as such. Individuals in whom one organ is so large as cautiousness is in this old man, and in whom the regulating organs of the moral sentiments are so deficient, are liable to fall into insanity, if strongly excited, owing to the disproportion in the cerebral organs. It is common to meet with such cases in lunatic asylums; and as the criminal law has gone on punishing this individual during a long life (for he has been twice transported), and met with no success in reclaiming him, but left him in jail, under sentence for theft, at seventy years of age, I consider these facts a strong confirmation of my opinion that he ought to have been treated as a moral patient from the first.

11.2   The Child Criminal, 1881[23]

What shall we do with the child-criminal? We say, do not send him to prison, if you would not hinder the advance of civilization and humanity; for, despite the arrogant utterances of magisterial pomposity which have

---

[23] Elizabeth Surr, "The Child Criminal", *The Nineteenth Century* (April 1881), pp. 650–52.

reached us from some of the provinces, we cannot be satisfied that all the fiats of our justices were unexceptionally wise which condemned 7416 children in the year just expired to breathe the tainted atmosphere of prison life. Hundreds of these offenders under twelve years of age, some of them little fellows barely able to bring their matted heads and tearstained faces to the level of the dock – creatures of neglect rather than of crime, living only to struggle, because every struggle was needed to live. Only very recently we heard a magistrate aver that children brought before him for theft and other offences were sometimes so small he was obliged to order them to be "lifted up" that he might see them, and that occasionally so great was their terror of being locked up in prison cells that the gaol officials humanely placed them in the infirmary, fearing if they did otherwise, the children might fall into fits through fright and be found dead in the morning. And if a large percentage of such children are adept in the pilfering art, it is because many of them have no alternative but to steal, if they would not starve. The children of the very poor are not naturally more predisposed to dishonesty than the cherished children of the affluent, but their temptations to the commission of this sin are more pressing and abundant in proportion to their larger need. The babe born of a besotted woman in a dismal den, where no ray of sunlight penetrates the rag-stuffed window, is quite as guileless, tender, and innocent a creature, as susceptible in time of good impressions, and as capable of attaining moral excellence, under efficient training, as the infant in costly cradle, whose father is a peer of the realm. Let those two children change places and conditions. Take the course wrap from the beggar's berceaunette[24] with holy and happy surroundings, and

> Shed in rainbow hues of light
> A halo round the Good and Right
> To tempt and charm the baby's sight.

Let it, as it grows, associate only with well-taught and well-bred children, sheltered carefully from contact with the vicious and the mean, and we hesitate not to affirm that when the child becomes a man you shall fail to trace upon his honest brow the faintest stain of infamous origin, or brand of ignoble birth. On the other hand, let the infant of high degree, by some terrible mischance, inhale only the impure atmosphere of vicious indigence among the brutal and miserable. Let him suffer from hunger, cold, experiencing none of the countless endearments which should ever fall to the lot of early childhood. A little creature, never without care, let him as he older grows listen only to the corrupt conversation of the depraved and the abandoned.

---

[24] Wicker cradle.

With ready and obedient care
To learn the tasks they teach him there –
Black sin for lesson, oaths for prayer.

Let him be cuffed, and kicked, and scolded, till he becomes almost insensible to rating[25] and callous to blows. Let him be driven out into the cold street to steal, if he cannot beg the breakfast that none provide him, and see then if, despite his noble birth, he will not prefer to pilfer rather than suffer the pangs of hunger. Mark if he will not seize the milk-can on the doorstep (meant to be presently taken in) and gulp down its contents as rapidly and cunningly as any low-born delinquent, and make off with feet as nimble to escape capture. Only leave the child among evil companions to pursue a pernicious course unchecked, and though he first saw the light in a ducal mansion, all too soon he may develop into the degraded felon, with slouching gait and hangdog expression of countenance. Vice is a heritage as surely and equally bequeathed to the children of the so-called "better classes" as to the offspring of the poor; and if the former have no recollection, as they grow older, of the fields "where cockles grow instead of barley", it is that they were early led from them by virtue's path into healthier pastures, led by holy teachers, wise counsellors, and good companions. Crime contains contagion that is speedily communicated by contact, and let us not then too hastily censure an unfortunate child for sickening morally amid the pestilential exhalations of a dissolute locality. But when he has so sickened, and the malady is virulent enough to taint a whole district, let us be less anxious to deal out punishment to the sin-stricken child than to discover how best we may treat and isolate him, with the double object of preserving others from infection, and securing his own moral restoration. Therefore we rejoice that the public mind is stirring and the public voice protesting against the mistaken policy of committing young offenders to gaol in the belief that such a measure must be remedial of crime. Crime, which might be nipped in the bud, becomes crime full-blown, if the young plant be placed in a hothouse of moral unhealthiness; therefore it is not desirable that naughty little children with the imitative faculty strong and active within them should be early acquainted with the evil ways of adult criminals. It is not for us to make young eyes and ears familiar with the debasing sights and sounds which must occasionally be seen and heard wherever full fledged gaol-birds congregate; for the impressionable heart of childhood is even more yielding to the hideous stamp of vice than to the softer imprint of virtue, and vainly we shall essay hereafter to obliterate the deep disfiguring scar. We are aware that greater care has been exercised of late in isolating children as

---

[25] Severe rebuke.

322

far as possible from adult criminals; but despite precautionary measures, young offenders often acquire in a gaol much objectionable knowledge.

11.3   The Criminal[26]

Criminality, therefore, cannot be attributed indiscriminately even to the lowest of races. It consists in a failure to live up to the standard recognized as binding by the community. The criminal is an individual whose organization makes its difficult or impossible for him to live in accordance with this standard, and easy to risk the penalties of acting anti-socially. By some accident of development, by some defect of heredity or birth or training, he belongs as it were to a lower and older social state than that in which he is actually living. It thus happens that our own criminals frequently resemble in physical and psychical characters the normal individuals of a lower race. This is that "atavism" which has been so frequently observed in criminals and so much discussed. It is the necessarily anti-social instinct of this lowlier organized individual which constitutes the crime.

In the criminal, we may often take it, there is an arrest of development. The criminal is an individual who, to some extent, remains a child his life long – a child of larger growth and with greater capacity for evil. This is part of the atavism of criminals. Mental acuteness is often observed among criminal children; it is rare among criminal adults. There is evidently arrest of development at a very early age, probably a precocious union of the cranial bones. Among savages, also, the young children are bright, but development stops at a very early age. All who have come very intimately in contact with criminals have noted their resemblance to children. Thus that profound and sympathetic observer Dostoyevsky, in his *Recollections of the Dead-House*, summing up some of the light-hearted easy-going characters of the convicts, says: "In one word they were children, true children, even at forty years of age." And elsewhere he quotes a saying concerning the exile: "The convict is a child; he throws himself on everything he sees."

The key to the failure of the prison, and a chief clue to its reform, lies in the system of administering definite and predetermined sentences by judges who, being ignorant of the nature of the individual before them, and therefore of the effect of the sentence upon him, and of its justice, are really incompetent to judge. Enough has been said of long sentences, the justice of which, it is obvious, must be quite a matter of chance. But the short-term imprisonments reveal quite as clearly the inadequacy of the system. The newspapers constantly tell of old offenders who have been in

---

[26] Havelock Ellis, *The criminal* (London, 1890), pp. 206–7, 214, 257–8.

prison for over a hundred short periods. In a recent report of the Prisons Board of Ireland, the case of a woman is mentioned who was committed to Grangegorman prison thirty-four times during 1888, and never received a sentence for a larger term than fourteen days. This woman had been committed 146 times in previous years, so that she has undergone in all 180 imprisonments.

Society must say, in effect, to the individual who violates its social instincts: so long as you act in a flagrantly anti-social manner, I shall exercise pressure on you, and restrain, more or less, the exercise of your freedom. I will give you a helping hand, because the sooner you begin to act socially the better it will be for both of us. I shall be glad to leave you alone, and the sooner the better; but so long as I see that you are a dangerous person, I shall not entirely leave my hold on you.

That is the only attitude towards the criminal which is at once safe, reasonable and humane. If, holding this lamp, we turn to our prison, we see at once how incompatible with such an attitude is the system of determining beforehand the exact period of the delinquent's detention. Many a man imprisoned for life, to his own misery, the ruin of his family, and the cost of the State, might with absolute safety to the community be liberated today; it is unnecessary to speak further of the thousands for whom society, inside or outside prison, has done nothing, and whom it liberates, with full knowledge that they proceed at once to prey upon itself. The great fault of our prison system is its arbitrary character. It is a huge machine working by an automatic routine. The immense practical importance of criminal anthropology lies in this: that it enables us to discriminate between criminal and criminal, and to apply to each individual case its appropriate treatment.

12   Penal Servitude, 1885[27]

The following passage was written by Edmund Du Cane in the middle of his term as the chairman of the prison commission from 1877 to 1896.[28] It is taken from his book The punishment and prevention of crime. *It gives an outline of his penal philosophy, with particular reference to solitary confinement. His belief in that punishment should be uniformly applied contrasts with that of Havelock Ellis.[29]*

---

[27] E. Du Cane, *The punishment and prevention of crime* (London, 1885), pp. 155–61.

[28] The prison commission was made up of a chairman and two sub-chairman and was responsible for the running of the convict prisons. The convict prisons were those that were established for the sentence of penal servitude, the successor to transportation.

[29] For a further discussion of Du Cane, see *Crime and punishment in England*, pp. 228–33.

A sentence of penal servitude is, in its main features, and so far as concerns the punishment, applied to exactly the same system to every person subjected to it. The previous career and character of the prisoner makes no difference in the punishment to which he is subjected, because it is rightly considered that it is for the courts of law, who have, or should have, a full knowledge on these points, to consider them in awarding the sentence; and if any prisoner were subjected to harsher or milder treatment in consequence of any knowledge the prison authorities might have of his previous character, it might be that he would practically be punished twice over on the same account, and on information much less complete that the court of law would have at its command. The government would also always be liable to charges of showing favour to or prejudice against certain particular prisoners; and any feeling of this kind would be fraught with danger and inconvenience.

It is also considered, and justly, that the judge or court who passes the sentence should know, or should be able to know, the exact effect of the sentence, and this would be impossible if any discretion rested with the executive officers as to the mode of carrying out the punishments.

A sentence of penal servitude is divided into three principal stages. During the first stage, which endures for nine months in all cases, the prisoner passes his whole time – excepting the period allotted to prayers and exercise – in his cell, apart from all other prisoners, working at some employment of an industrial or remunerative character. During the second he sleeps and has his meals in a separate cell, but works in association under a close and strict supervision, at employment suited to him. The third period is that during which he is conditionally released from prison but kept under the supervision of the police, and liable, for any infraction of the conditions of his release, to be returned to prison, there to fulfil the portion of his sentence which remained unexpired at the time of his release. A stage, intermediate between the public works and the conditional release, is applied to women, who may be sent for nine months before their release on license to "refuges" – establishments managed by private persons, who interest themselves in preparing the women for discharge, and in procuring suitable situations for them.

It is not possible here to state in detail the rules laid down for the treatment of prisoners in the three stages, but an outline of the objects which are aimed at may be given.

The first stage is one of severe penal discipline, during which the prisoner's mind is thrown in upon itself, and the prisoner cannot fail to feel that, however agreeable may have been his previous life, probably one of idleness and excitement, he pays dearly for it by the dull monotony, hard work, a diet which is sufficient, but no more than sufficient, and deprivation of every luxury he has been accustomed to indulge in; and, above all, by the absence of freedom, and the constant supervision which is his present condition, and which form his prospects for some years to come.

During this time he becomes open to lessons of admonition and warning; religious influences have full opportunity of obtaining access to him; and he is put in that condition where he is likely to feel sorrow for the past and to welcome the words of those who show him how to avoid evil for the future.

I have said that this stage of a prisoner's sentence endures for nine months, and it may naturally occur to any one to ask, if its effects are both penal and reformatory, such as I have described and believe them to be, why the same treatment should not be followed throughout the whole of the sentence? The reason is, that it has always been held that we must bear in mind that the prisoner should not only be punished and *taught* what is right, but should be returned to society fitted both morally and physically to fulfil his proper duties in the battle of life.

It cannot be expected that this object would be fulfilled by his perpetual seclusion in a cell for years, with no communication with his fellows, an artificial state of existence absolutely opposed to that which nature points out as the condition of mental, moral, and physical health, and entirely unlike that which he is prepared to follow on his discharge from prison.

When the system of separate confinement was first established in the model prison at Pentonville, in 1842, the duration of the period of separate confinement was fixed at eighteen months.[30] It was carried out with considerable rigour, and results showed themselves which could not be neglected. It was shown incontestably, as the Reports of the Commissioners demonstrated, that the minds of the prisoners became enfeebled by long-continued isolation; and, after various trials, the present term of nine months was fixed on as the longest to which prisoners could, with advantage, be subjected to this stage of the discipline. No doubt a modified system of separate confinement suitable to longer periods might be introduced, and it would then be possible to legalize sentences between the two years which is the maximum sentence of "imprisonment", and the five years which is the minimum sentence of "penal servitude"; and this course, which was recommended by the Lords' Committee of 1864, would be easy now that the prison system throughout the country has been made uniform by being placed under the Government.

Keeping in view the principle that during his imprisonment the convict is to be prepared and enabled to lead a reformed life when he is discharged, attention is paid, more especially during the first period, both to his moral, mental and literary education.

---

[30] As the first passage in this chapter shows, the isolation of prisoners from each other predated this in the local prisons.

Every prison has its staff of ministers of religion, who, in prisons which contain large numbers, are not permitted to have any other duties, and who, therefore, can devote their whole time to the improvement and advantage of the prisoners placed under the spiritual care.

The advantage of thus inculcating religious feelings will not be contested by any one; and not withstanding the doubts which have arisen from injudicious exaggerations of the results of these influences, and by misconception of the true position of and functions fulfilled by the chaplains of prisons, it is certain that these advantages are much appreciated by prisoners, and that the exertions of the ministers of religion bear perhaps as much fruit as in the world outside.

The prison library and educational departments are in charge of the chaplain. Books are supplied to the prisoners, both of a purely religious and of an instructive character; and those who are uneducated are taught by a staff of schoolmasters at least the elements of reading and writing; those who have already some knowledge have opportunities and encouragement to improve themselves. As a knowledge of reading and writing affords so much opportunity for mental and moral improvement, and may have so important an effect on a prisoner's well-being in after life, inducements are offered to prisoners to exert themselves to attain it, by rendering some of the consequent privileges a prisoner may gain conditional on his being able to read and write; and after he has been under instruction a sufficient time, he is obliged, if he wishes to enjoy the privilege of communicating by letter with his friends, to do it himself, and without assistance. Of course, exceptions to these rules are made in the cases of men who, from age or mental incapacity, cannot be expected to acquire even the elements of knowledge.

Half-yearly examinations are held, to show the progress each prisoner makes, the result of which may be seen in the Yearly Reports of the Directors of Convict Prisons, and it is found that many prisoners who had not been able either to read or write when convicted, had learned to do both while in prison; and most of the remainder had made advances in the knowledge which they previously possessed.

13   Five Years' Penal Servitude, 1878[31]

In the late nineteenth century there was a spate of publications of prison memoirs. This means that we do not have to take the word of the authorities themselves regarding the nature of prison regimes. In the extract below, an anonymous

---

[31] W. H. Thomson, *Five years' penal servitude by one who has endured it* (London, 1878), pp. 175–8.

author who had served a sentence of five years' penal servitude describes the system of work at Dartmoor. Du Cane's emphasis on equal treatment of all seems somewhat distant.

When the chief has received all the returns of the numbers in each gang, also from the infirmary, and from "No. 5", the punishment cells, and entered them in his book, he adds up the total; and if it agrees with the number known to be in prison, the word is given for the gangs to march off. The outside gangs go first, the red-collar men who attend to the farm leading off. These are generally old men who have a knowledge of horses, cows and farm life. They are dressed in blue, with red cuffs and collars, and are considered a privileged gang.

Dartmoor privileges are very questionable. For instance, one of the privileges of this red-collar gang is that they go out to feed the horses and cows before breakfast, and they are the only gang, except hospital orderlies and one-third of the cooks, that have any work to do on Sundays.

After them march the quarrymen, who labour in the granite quarries; the turf-cutters, road makers and bogmen generally; and then old Mr Dicks' gang, who go about the place emptying the latrines both in the prison and in the town outside, and carrying their loads on to the land, where it is utilized by the gardening and agricultural gangs.

The gardeners really are a privileged gang, and generally consist of well-conducted men who are doing the last twelve or six months of their time. A large amount of very fine vegetables are grown here, the best of which are sent to market.

There are also the laundry gang; for, there being no women at Dartmoor, all the prisoners' clothes were washed by prisoners, and a strong gang it was. One of the best warders in the whole establishment had charge of it, and though a very different man in appearance, he always reminded me of Paddy at Millbank, by the care he took of his men. He was liked by the care he took of his men. He was liked generally, and many a man schemed to get into little Welsh's gang.

Another "soap-suds" gang followed them – the cleaners, who kept all the prison halls, the long stone passages, and chapel floors clean. Their warder was just the reverse of Mr Welsh, and was such a tyrannical old fidget that his men were always begging the chief warder to remove them into some other gang.

Then follow the artisan gangs – blacksmiths, masons or stone-cutters, and carpenters. In the carpenters' gang are also the painters, glaziers, tin-workers, and a few others.

The shoemakers come next, two very strong gangs. A great deal of work is done here by these men. All the boots for the Metropolitan Police are made by the convicts at Dartmoor, as well as for the various convict prisons. With the shoemakers are the saddlers and harness-makers.

Next comes the tailors' gang, with whom are incorporated the book-binder and school orderly.

The last gang is that of the oakum-pickers and stocking-knitters. The cooks and bakers do not parade with the other gangs outside, nor do the hospital orderlies.

The artisan and outside gangs march off to their work at once; some of the latter have two miles to march to get there.

As each gang goes out the warders take their firearms, and a certain number of civil guards are sent off to attend them, while the rest of the guards go on picket duty. The parade ground is now left at liberty for the indoor gangs – shoemakers, tailors, and oakum men, who fall in two and two and have half-an-hour's exercise before going to their work.

14   Reformatories and Industrial Schools, 1913[32]

The official separation of young offenders from the rest of the prison population was first made possible in 1854 with the passage of the Reformatory School Act. Reformatories were originally intended for those aged sixteen or under who would otherwise have had a prison sentence. Industrial Schools, brought into being in 1857, had a much broader scope, taking in those children deemed to be at risk due to behaviour such as begging, not attending school, or involvement in petty crime. Some were even sent at the request of their parents. Both institutions were intended to have a more reformist purpose than prisons but those committed could expect a much longer stay than they would have had in prison. The extract below, from the book Young delinquents *by Mary Barnett, discusses the occupational training of girls in the early years of the twentieth century. It reveals both a new concern with the individual and a variation of quality among the institutions. It also illustrates the way in which the girls were trained for "female" occupations.*

In the matter of industrial training there is practically no variety in the schools other than housework, laundry-work, and a certain amount of needlework and dressmaking. As regards the efficiency of the training, however, there is considerable difference. Many schools still appear to believe in the potency of hard labour, and the wholesale nature of much of the work affords unlimited opportunities for carrying out such a policy. Such work as this, which fails to rouse any interest or to demand any individual skill, has the result of turning out the "institution girl" who is the despair of her mistress, and is at the best a competent machine. There are many large schools where the work is better arranged, and where

---

[32] M. G. Barnett, *Young delinquents: a study of reformatory and industrial schools* (London, 1913), pp. 139–41.

everything possible is done to arouse the girls' interest, and to avoid any risk of making the work distasteful to them. It is now being realized that housewifery is an art, and theory is essential to practice; more enlightened managers are therefore introducing housewifery classes, and this is a great step towards the abolition of the machine-like methods which still exist in many schools.

It has often been found in the past that a servant trained in an institution has little or no idea of the methods of an ordinary household, because, unless she has had an opportunity of waiting on the superintendent and mistresses [of the schools], her training has been confined to scrubbing and the most elementary housework. In many schools, because work has had to be found for the girls, there has been little or none of the domestic machinery used which exists in the average household. It has been found occasionally that the girls do not even know how to use a broom, not only because of the absence of carpets in the schools, but also owing to the everlasting scrubbing which was considered a wholesome discipline and a satisfactory means of employment. At Nazareth House [reformatory] each girl learns to "turn out" and dust a model sitting-room and bedroom. Both rooms are kept well supplied with ornaments of every description, which accustom the girls to be careful in their work, with the result that when they go to service they do not make havoc of everything which is of a somewhat fragile nature. Some such scheme as this exists in several schools and helps to make the training far more efficient.

The laundry is usually a source of profit to the schools, and the quickest girls reach a considerable degree of proficiency in it and are able, on leaving, to obtain good posts in public or private laundries. Here again the managers are seeing the wisdom of allowing their girls to learn the theory of the work, but even then it has always to be remembered that it is not really healthy work, and therefore no girl should be kept at it for many hours together. If the work comes from outside, the laundry comes under factory legislation and the conditions are inspected by the factory inspectors. For the big, strong girls in reformatories it is generally found to be the most suitable work.

Glossary

affeerers elected manorial officials who set the level of individual amercements (fines) at manor courts.

ale-tasters elected manorial officials who regulated the food and drink trade in a village or town.

amercement financial punishment set by custom or by-law in manor courts.

Archdeacon's Court lowest level of church court.

assignment the system of assigning transportees to private employers in Australia.

Assizes twice-yearly royal court held in each county normally at the county town. Presided over by visiting Westminster judges, it dealt *inter alia* with the more serious criminal cases.

bench the collective term for a group of magistrates presiding at either Quarter Sessions or Petty Sessions.

benefit of clergy the right of a cleric to be tried in a church court; this right became extended to criminals who could read. Felons successfully claiming benefit of clergy were branded on the brawn of the left thumb, not executed. A reading test was imposed to establish clerical status. Branding acted as a proof of first conviction. On the second the offender was hanged.

benefit of the belly women convicted of a felony who successfully claimed to be pregnant had the death sentence respited until after the birth of the innocent child. Often this reprieve was turned into a full pardon.

Borough courts very like manor courts in their procedures but located in towns.

Bow Street Runners set of policemen attached to a number of London magistrates' offices from the 1750s to the 1830s, organized by the magistrates and famous for thief-taking.

bridewell another term for a House of Correction.

burglary house-breaking with intent to thieve, originally at night.

canting criminal argot of the sixteenth and seventeenth centuries.

chap-books cheap popular literature of the early modern period.

coin-clipping paring coin to collect the silver or gold clippings.

coining the illicit casting of metal to make fraudulent coinage.

common scolds a person (usually a woman) accused of being quarrelsome.

common serjeant medieval equivalent of a QC.

Consistory Court the bishop's court.

constable elected or appointed peace-keeping officer.

cony-catcher sixteenth-century criminal; the "cony" was the victim.

convict someone subjected to the sentence of transportation or penal servitude.

convict prisons prisons managed at a national level for those serving the sentence of penal servitude.

copyholder peasant farmer who held his land by copy of a manor court roll.

corporal punishment punishment which inflicted pain on the body, most commonly whipping.

counsel the barrister(s) charged with conducting a prosecution in court.

Court leet manor court with criminal jurisdiction.

Court of Requests an equity court which heard *inter alia* complaints by ordinary people about miscarriages of justice.

crank the mechanism by which criminals were required to turn heavy weights as part of hard labour.

embezzlement the fraudulent diversion of money, etc. to one's own account or benefit.

enclosures the assignment of formerly common land to private owner-ship, often involving hedging it around.

felony a serious crime subject to the death penalty.

Fenians members of a group of Irish nationalists committed to the over-throw of English rule by physical force.

game laws ancient laws protecting the rights of the propertied classes to hunt specified species of animal and birds for sport.

garrotting highway robbery by throttling the victim.

grand jury the county jury which decided whether or not there was a case to answer. (See **trial jury**.)

grand larceny stealing goods to the value of one shilling or above.

Habeas Corpus Act under this legislation a writ could be issued requir-ing that a person accused of a crime be present in court at the time of his trial and that they be not convicted *in absentia*.

hard labour imprisonment with heavy bodily toil imposed upon con-victs. (See *crank* and *treadmill*.)

High Commission ecclesiastical court.

Home Office the branch of the civil service responsible for law and order.

housebreaking theft from a dwelling place in the daytime, involving forced entry.

house of correction a type of prison dating from the late sixteenth cen-tury that from its inception attempted to inculcate the work ethic into its inmates.

hundred sub-division of a county, sometimes called a wapentake.

hulks the hulls of superannuated ships moored in river estuaries as tem-porary prisons but in fact in use for many years.

Inns of Court the organizations of London lawyers, now just barristers.
Justice of the Peace magistrate.
King's Bench westminster court with criminal jurisdiction.
magistrate later term for a Justice of the Peace.
magistrate's clerk legal advisor and record keeper for magistrates.
manor court local customary court.
Manorial steward the presiding judge at a manor court.
misdemeanour minor criminal offence.
overseers of the Poor locally elected or appointed officials charged with looking after the poor on behalf of a parish.
peculiar a parish (or other benefice) outside of the bishop's jurisdiction.
Peine forte et dure punishment designed to make a defendant enter a plea.
penal colony a colony established for the punishment of transportees.
penal servitude longer sentences of imprisonment with hard labour, which replaced transportation. (See **hard labour**.)
penance shaming punishment imposed by church courts.
penitentiaries the new prisons of the nineteenth century which sought not simply to offer retribution and to deter but to reform.
petty larceny stealing goods valued at less than a shilling.
Petty Sessions court presided over by JPs meeting more frequently than Quarter Sessions – usually monthly – normally on a hundred basis.
pillory wooden framework into which an individual was locked upright for public ridicule for a set period of time.
Police Commissioners the two men, answerable to the Home Secretary, responsible for managing the Metropolitan Police.
press-gang body of men charged with securing by force individuals to serve in the navy or the army.
probation the release of criminals especially first offenders on licence and under supervision to complete their sentence in the community as long as they exhibit good behaviour.
procure to provide the sexual services of another person, usually a woman.
Quarter Sessions court which met four times a year in each county. Presided over by JPs. Dealt with cases that were more serious than those handled by Petty Sessions but less serious than those which came before the assizes.
Quakers a Christian group renowned for their active engagement with social issues in the nineteenth century.
receiving the acceptance of stolen goods with a view to selling them to others.
recidivism re-offending after a period of imprisonment; relapsing into criminal behaviour.
recognizance legal instrument binding an individual to obey the order of a court.
recusant Catholic who refused to go to the Anglican church.

reeve manorial official.

reformatory school institution established for young offenders in 1854 as an alternative to imprisonment.

remand prisoners prisoners in custody awaiting trial.

Royal Commission an official investigation into pressing social and administrative issues, involving the testimony of expert witnesses covering the whole country.

Select Committee special committee of MPs drawn together to consider proposed legislation and parliamentary issues.

sidesmen or questmen assistants to the churchwardens.

statutory crime offences created and defined through legislation.

Star Chamber equity court dealing mainly with riots.

stews brothels.

stocks a device which clamped the legs of a person between two planks. Used as a punishment for minor offences and sometimes, in remote villages, as a holding device before an accused person was brought to court.

sureties money deposited with the court by a defendant and two associates as insurance against future misbehaviour.

Ten Commandments God's law given to Moses on Mount Sinai (Exodus 20).

tickets of leave tickets issued to convicts, licensing them to free movement within set terms.

tithes ecclesiastical tax of one-tenth of the produce and harvest of the land paid for the support of the clergy and parts of the church.

tithings groups of neighbours in a village having mutual responsibility to report on each other's misdemeanours.

Tourn a minor county court held twice a year and presided over by the sheriff.

treadmill appliance for producing motion by the stepping on and off movable steps attached to a revolving cylinder; used in prisons as a form of hard labour.

treason criminal act against the sovereign and the sovereignty of the state.

trial juries juries sworn to try a case.

Tyburn public place of execution in London.

upright-man gang-leader of early modern criminals.

vestry the laymen charged *inter alia* with upholding church law in a parish. Later it became the group of people taking political decisions within a parish. A "closed" vestry consisted of a narrow oligarchy. An "open" vestry was more democratic in its make-up.

wapentake a hundred.

watch the group of men patrolling the streets of a community at night time looking for wrongdoers.

Watch Committee a committee set up in boroughs under the Municipal Corporations Act (1835) with responsibility for managing the police.

Bibliography

Medieval

Attenborough, F. J. (ed.). *The laws of the earliest English kings* (Cambridge, 1922).

Bolland, W. C. (ed.). *Select bills in Eyre,* "Selden Soc.", xxx (1914).

Clanchy, M. T. (ed.). "Highway robbery and trial by battle in the Hampshire eyre of 1249". In *Medieval legal records edited in memory of C.A.F. Meekings,* R. F. Hunnisett & J. B. Post (eds.) (H.M.S.O., London, 1978).

Gomme, G. L. (ed.). *Court Rolls of Tooting Beck Manor,* vol. 1 (London, 1909).

Gransden, A. (ed.). *The chronicle of Bury St Edmunds* (London & Edinburgh, 1964).

Gross, C. (ed.). *Select cases from the Coroners' Rolls,* "Selden Soc.", ix (1896).

Hall, G. D. G. (ed.). *Glanvill* (London, 1965).

Harding, A. *The law courts of medieval England* (London & New York, 1973) [Essay plus documents].

Harding, A. (ed.). *The roll of the Shropshire Eyre of 1256,* "Selden Soc.", xcvi (1981). Public Record Office, Just. 1/422, m.1.

Kaye, J. M. (ed.). *Placita corone,* "Selden Soc.", supplementary ser., vol. 4 (1966).

Ross, J. B. (ed.). *The murder of Charles the Good, Count of Flanders by Galbert of Bruges,* 2nd edn (London & New York, 1967).

Warren, W. L. *Henry II* (1973).

Sixteenth Century

Burne, S. A. H. (ed.). *The Staffordshire Quarter Sessions Rolls, vol. 3, 1594–1597 (Collections for a history of Staffordshire)* (1932).

Emmison, F. G. (ed.). *Elizabethan life: disorder* (Chelmsford, 1970) [extracts from Essex Quarter Sessions and Assizes].

Emmison, F. G. (ed.). *Elizabethan life: morals & the church courts* (Chelmsford, 1973) [extracts from church court records of Essex].

Emmison, F. G. (ed.). *Elizabethan life: home, work and land* (Chelmsford, 1976) [includes extracts from manor court records of Essex].

Greene, R. *A notable discovery of coosenage now daily practised by sundry lewd persons* (London, 1592).

Hale, W. (ed.). *A series of precedents and proceedings in criminal causes 1475 to 1640* (London, 1847).

Hamilton, W. D. (ed.). *Wriothesley's Chronicle*, 2 vols., "Camden Soc.", new ser., xi (1875) & xx (1877).

Harman, T. *Caveat for common cursitors* (London, 1566).

Harrison, W. *Description of England* (London, 1577; 2nd edn., 1587).

Judges, A. V. (ed.). *The Elizabethan underworld* (London, 1930) [collection of coney-catching pamphlets].

Leighton, W. A. (ed.). "Early chronicles of Shrewsbury, 1372–1603", *Trans. Shropshire Arch. & Natural Hist. Soc.*, iii (1880), 239–352.

Mander, G. P. (ed.). "The Staffordshire Quarter Sessions Rolls", *Collections for a history of Staffordshire* (1927), pp. 119–81.

Nicholas, J. G. (ed.). *The diary of Henry Machyn*, "Camden Soc.", xlii (1848).

Nicholas, J. G. (ed.). *Grey Friars Chronicle of London*, "Camden Soc.", liii (1851).

Nicholson, W. (ed.). *The remains of Edmund Grindal*, "Parker Soc." (1843).

Sneyd, C. A. (trans.). *A relation . . . of the island of England*, "Camden Soc.", xxxvii (1847).

Tawney, R. H. & E. Power (eds.). *Tudor economic documents*, iii (1924) [includes some conycatching material].

Thomas, A. H. & I. D. Thornley (eds.). *The great chronicle of London* (London, 1938).

Seventeenth Century

Cockburn, J. S. (ed.). *Somerset Assize Orders, 1640–1659*, "Somerset Rec. Soc.", lxxi (1971).

Cunnington, B. H. (ed.). *Some annals of the Borough of Devizes* (Devizes, 1925).

Earle, J. *Microsmography* (1628).

Gretton, M. S. (ed.). *Oxfordshire Justices of the Peace in the seventeenth century*, "Oxfordshire Rec. Soc.", xvi (1934).

Kettle, A. J. (ed.). "Matthew Craddock's Book of Remembrance, 1614–15", *Collections for a history of Staffordshire*, ser. 4, xvi (1994), pp. 67–169.

Merson, A. L. (ed.). *The third book of the Remembrance of Southampton, 1514–1602*, vol. 2 (Southampton, 1955); "Southampton Rec. Soc.", vol. 3.

Raine, J. (ed.). *Depositions from the castle of York relating to offences committed in the northern counties in the seventeenth century*, "Surtees Soc.", xl (1861).

Redwood, B. C. (ed.). *Quarter sessions order book, 1642–1649* (Lewes & Chichester, 1954); "Sussex Record Society", Record Publication, no. 3.

Eighteenth Century

Cobbett, W. (ed.). *Cobbett's complete collection of state trials . . .* iii (1809).

Cook, G. T. (ed.). *The complete Newgate Calendar* (Navarre Society, London, 1926), 6 vols.

Fielding, H. *A true state of the case of Bosavern Penlez . . .* (1749).

Fielding, H. *An enquiry into the causes of the late increase of robbers, &c. with some proposals for remedying this growing evil . . .* (London, 1751).

Fielding, H. Introduction, *The journal of a voyage to Lisbon* (1755).
Howard, J. *The state of the prisons in England and Wales* . . . (Warrington, 1777).
Pelham, C. (ed.). *The chronicles of crime or the new Newgate calendar being a series of memoires and anecdotes of notorious characters* . . . *from the earliest period to 1841* . . . , 2 vols. (London, 1887).
Urban, S. (ed.). *The Gentleman's Magazine and Historical Chronicle.*

Nineteenth Century

Guide

Hawkings, D. T. *Criminal ancestors: A guide to historical criminal records in England and Wales* (Alan Sutton, Stroud, 1992) [covers period sixteenth to nineteenth century, but mainly nineteenth].

Manuscript material

Chester City Record Office, DPO/5, Police Receiving Book, Chester Police Force.
Chester County Record Office, Quarter Sessions Files: QSF153, January & July 1857; QSF159, January 1863; QSF161, January & July 1865; QSF167, January & October 1871; QSF167, 1871; QSF184, October 1888.
Cheshire County Record Office, CJP 4/1, Cheshire County Constabulary, Chief Constable's Orders 1856–72.
Cheshire County Record Office, CJP/2, Cheshire County Constabulary, Confidential Instructions 1866–75.
Huntingdon County Record Office, HCP/2/320/1, Gaol Keeper's Journal 1833–8, Huntingdon County Gaol.
Public Record Office, H/O 6/4, Judge's correspondence with the King.
Staffordshire County Record Office, D4842/15/4/32, *Articles of agreement for the Audley Association for the Prosecution of Felons, 1832.*
Staffordshire County Record Office, C/PC/1/1/1, *Report of the Chief Constable of the Constabulary Force of the County of Stafford, 1865.*

Newspapers

The Chester Chronicle, 8/2/1833 & 10/1/1840.
Gentleman's Magazine (November, 1831).
Household Words, vol. 1 (1850).
The Illustrated London News, 6/12/1862.
Macclesfield Courier, 26/12/1829.
Poor Man's Guardian, 24/9/1831.
Punch, vol. 6 (1843), p. 132 & vol. 7 (1844).
The Strand Magazine, vol. 7 (1894).

Quarterly Review, vol. 36 (1828); vol. 82 (1848); 99 (1856).
Staffordshire Advertiser, 24/12/1870.
Stockport Advertiser, 9/11/1832 & 26/10/1860.
The Times, 2/10/1888.

Parliamentary papers

Report on the nightly watch and police of the metropolis, 1812, P.P. 1812, vol. ii.
Report of the Select Committee on the state of gaols, etc., P.P. 1819, vol. vii.
Vagrancy Act, 1824 5 Geo. IV cap. 83.
Royal Commission on County Rates, P.P. 1836, vol. xxvii.
Report of the Select Committee on transportation, P.P. 1837–8, vol. xxii.
The Select Committee on a uniform system of police in England, Wales and Scotland, P.P. 1852–3, vol. xxxvi.
The Select Committee on the Public Prosecution Bill, P.P. 1854–5, vol. xii.

Books & Articles

Barnett, M. G. *Young delinquents – a study of reformatory and industrial schools* (London, 1913).

Booth, C. (ed.). *Life and labour of the people*, vol. 1 East London (London & Edinburgh, 1889).

Brougham, H. *The works of Henry, Lord Brougham – historical and political dissertations*, vol. 8 (London, 1857).

Chadwick, W. *Reminiscences of a Chief Constable* (London, 1900).

Colquhoun, P. *Treatise on the police of the metropolis* (London, 1806).

Combe, G. *System of phrenology*, 4th edn (Edinburgh, 1836).

Du Cane, E. *The punishment and prevention of crime* (London, 1885).

Ellis, H. *The criminal* (London, 1890).

Guest, A. "The State of the Law Courts", *The Strand Magazine*, vol. 11 (1891), pp. 84–92.

Holmes, H. *Known to the police* (London, 1908).

Hoyle, W. *Crime in England and Wales in the nineteenth century: an historical and critical retrospect* (London, 1875).

Laing Meason, M. "Detective Police", *The Nineteenth Century*, 13 (1883).

Mayhew, H. *London labour and the London poor*, vol. 4 (London, 1861).

Mayhew, H. & J. Binny. *The criminal prisons of London and scenes of prison life* (London, 1862).

Morrison, W. D. *Crime and its causes* (London, 1891).

Paley, W. *The works of William Paley, D.D., with additional sermons [etc.] and a corrected account of the life and writings of the author* (London, 1838).

Payne, W. *Stafford gaol and its associations* (Hanley, 1887).

Pike, L. O. *A history of crime in England*, vol. 2 (London, 1873).

Plowden, A. C. *Grain or chaff – the autobiography of a police magistrate* (London, 1903).

Reade, C. *It is never too late to mend* (London, 1853).

Reports of state trials, new series, vol. 1 (1820–23).

Spearman, E. R. "Known to the Police", *The Nineteenth Century* (September 1894).

Surr, E. "The Child Criminal", *The Nineteenth Century* (April 1881), pp. 650–52.

Thomson, W. H. *Five years penal servitude by one who has endured it* (London, 1878).

Index